S

THE WOMAN MOST LIKELY
CHERYL KERNOT

THE WOMAN MOST LIKELY
CHERYL
KERNOT

DAVID O'REILLY

Published by
Random House Australia Pty Ltd
20 Alfred Street, Milsons Point, NSW 2061
http://www.randomhouse.com.au

Sydney New York Toronto
London Auckland Johannesburg
and agencies throughout the world

First published in 1998

National Library of Australia
Cataloguing-in-Publication Data

  O'Reilly, David (David Lee).
  Cheryl Kernot : the woman most likely.

  Bibliography.
  Includes index.
  ISBN 0 09 183738 3.

  1. Kernot, Cheryl, 1947– . 2. Australian Democrats –
  Biography. 3. Australian Labor Party – Biography. 4. Women
  politicians – Australia – Biography. 5. Politicians –
  Australia – Biography. I. Title.

324.294095092

Design by Yolande Gray
Typeset by Asset Typesetting Pty Ltd, Sydney
Printed by Griffin Press Pty Ltd, Adelaide
10 9 8 7 6 5 4 3 2 1

Everyone who knows her understands that without Sue Corrigan,
this book would not have been possible. Her counsel informed every page.
I dedicate it to her. And we dedicate it to Laura, Jordy and Shaney.

ACKNOWLEDGEMENTS

Many of the ideas in this book are the product of interviews granted me by some seventy individuals over a twelve-month period. Cheryl Kernot herself generously made time for a lengthy series of interviews in Canberra, Sydney, Maitland and the Gold Coast in the early months of 1997. The great bulk of her remarks, produced here in a bid to illuminate her ideas and aspirations, come from those sessions. I am indebted to her for her cooperation.

Many of the interviews with other people were on the record but, for various reasons, some remained background briefings only. To all those who helped me in those efforts, my sincere thanks.

The direction of the book and its structure obviously had to be reconsidered in the light of Kernot's decision to leave the Australian Democrats in October, 1997. Notwithstanding the difficulties her decision posed them, it would be remiss of me not to convey my thanks to so many Democrats who helped me enormously. I would also like to express my personal gratitude to Shirley Simper for all her help. I am indebted to the Kernot and Paton families—to Gavin and Sian for their forbearance, to Zena, Merv and Gail for their warmth as well as help with the family pictures. I must also thank Jane Palfreyman, Deborah Callaghan and Roberta Ivers at Random House and Jane Arms for her guidance at the outset. But one person should not be forgotten—Jennifer Byrne who, over a drink on a rainy London evening, first breathed life into this project.

To all these people, I am singularly grateful. Finally, there are my parents whose support was there in the background all the way, as always.

David O'Reilly
West Sussex, March 1998

CONTENTS

PREFACE

As she would have cause to say later so many times, it was the hardest thing Cheryl Kernot ever did in her life. Seated alone at a desk in the Canberra Parliament House office of Gareth Evans, the Deputy Leader of the Australian Labor Party, she pondered the telephone before her. Fighting to contain the nauseous dread wracking her stomach, she knew the time had passed for any more agonising, for sentiment or nostalgia, for second thoughts. A top-secret political operation of almost military precision, two weeks in the making, was now underway in Canberra and elsewhere around Australia. At its epicentre, Kernot was now required to act, to embrace the utter brutality of politics, to step off the sidelines, remade as either a genuine Australian political leader—or as a pariah.

At precisely 11 am on Wednesday, October 15, 1997, Kernot was scheduled to pick up that phone and ring a small number of key players inside the Australian Democrats, the political 'third force' established by Don Chipp back in 1977. Over twenty years this force had become not only the most successful minor party in Australia's history, but one with a unique place in Western democracies. She was faced with explaining to the handful of people who had served her loyally for four years that not only was she about to announce her resignation as Leader of that party, and from parliament, but that she intended to join the ALP. In one blockbusting moment, she would write her name into the history books among a tiny band of politicians who had 'ratted' on their own people to join the ranks of the opposition.

Drawing strength from one last big breath, Kernot lifted the phone and began to track down the Democrats' National Secretary, Sam Hudson. Hudson had not only devoted her adult life to building the party but had recognised the precocious talent of a then forty-two-year-old former schoolteacher back in 1990 and guided her passage to the leadership of the Democrats, and thus, through their balance of power role in the Senate, to the centre of the national political stage. Kernot's words to Hudson and to Democrat Deputy Leader Meg Lees were barely comprehensible to them. Her Canberra office manager, Shirley Simper, a woman for whom Kernot had great fondness, simply gasped with shock. Later when they pondered it and thought back over recent months, the event would begin to take on more definite meaning. But in those first moments of shattering revelation, they could hear Kernot's slow explanation of her imminent action, but somehow the words would not sink in. They tried to talk her out of it. They were incredulous, suddenly detached, dreaming. Was this a joke? Was she actually seriously saying she was leaving? Why? What had brought this on? What had gone wrong?

Kernot pleaded for them to understand, sensing that the explanation was too complex for the few minutes at hand, then began to explain that she had to ring off, promising to come back to them later in the day to talk in more detail. By now, it was nearing 11.30 am, and the rumblings of the earthquake were beginning to be felt in the huge parliament building. The parliamentary press gallery had been summoned to what would be an historic press conference in a nearby committee room. All around Australia a corps of in-the-know Labor Party figures were quietly beginning to explain to their networks that the stunning defection was imminent, massaging the news, heading off criticism.

Off the phone, but still seated at the desk and shaken, Kernot was alerted to the time by one of Evans' staffers. The operation had been timed to the minute, allowing Kernot half an hour to talk to her own people. But now she had to move on to the next phase. Trying to steady herself, she reached inward for the strength to walk away from the emotion-sapping conversations to face the world with the news. A four-page statement in hand, she strode out of Evans' office with a staffer in tow, heading for her rendezvous with the media and the toughest public interrogation of her seven-year political life.

Press gallery journalists were crowded into the committee room waiting for Kernot's entrance, seated down either side of a long, central table, on chairs along the walls of the room or standing behind television cameras mounted on tripods. The mood was solemn, galvanised by word spread by

Labor's spin-doctors that a big announcement was in the offing. Settling into the hot seat at the top of the table, Kernot told the journalists she had a long statement to read and wanted to get through it before she took questions. At that moment she had no clear idea of the impact her actions would make—the scale of the shock wave it would send through the political system, the hurt, alarm and savage reprisals it would provoke and more importantly, the tidal wave of public sentiment that would arrive within a few days, redefining everything.

For the statement she began to slowly read represented a declaration of political war on the Liberal and National Party government of John Howard. More than that, it was a strike at the heart of the values that underwrote conservative politics' grip on power in 1997. It castigated the political and economic—and, in a sense, even moral—rationale for so much of the Coalition's actions in its year-and-a-half in office. It promised to breathe new life back into an Australian Labor Party struggling to redefine itself after eighteen months in Opposition since Paul Keating lost the 1996 election. But it was also a circuit-breaker for those millions of people who sensed that at a time when Australia genuinely, desperately needed a defining manifesto for the future, there was a void in national leadership.

Kernot's first words were to inform the gathering that she was resigning as Democrat Leader and from the parliament. 'I fully appreciate this decision will come as a shock to members of a party I have served for seventeen years,' she said. 'But it is a decision which, in the past eighteen months, has grown unavoidable for two reasons—one, my personal and growing sense of outrage at the damage being done to Australia by the Howard government; and two, my concern that from my position in the Senate I had a limited capacity to minimise that damage.'

In the previous eighteen months, Kernot said, she had watched as the government had stepped up the process of dismantling the State, throwing thousands of people onto the scrap heap, abolishing schemes like job training that were being used as the models for nations abroad, and manically cutting back on government programs, ranging from industry research and development to family planning and health services for the poor. She had seen a government creating a crisis of confidence in education, returning to a 'development at any cost' mentality, allowing the media into Family Law courtrooms and being blind to how its actions were deepening social insecurity. 'For eighteen months I have watched as the Howard government allowed an agent of division to vilify and scapegoat black Australians and migrants under the cloak of free speech. We have all seen this do enormous damage to Australia's standing in the rest of the world.'

She charged that the government was a new one, but one shackled by old ideas, tied to the outmoded, hardline economic mantra that had driven the now discredited government of Margaret Thatcher in Britain in the 1980s. Its political response in so many areas was the cynical, time-honoured conservative appeal to the lowest common denominator, willing to exploit, in her view, the worst in people. But, she said, over and above all that, the core crime of the Howard administration was not its incompetent ministers falling by the way, its blind eye to racism, nor its pettiness. It was simply its lack of any vision about the future direction of Australia.

Then she dropped the bombshell. She would thus be standing at the next federal election for a House of Representatives seat for the Australian Labor Party in a Liberal-held marginal seat.

In making the final decision to jump ship only in recent weeks, Kernot made clear she had agonised for the Democrats, her staff and friends she would leave behind. 'Some of those close to me know of the frustrations that have slowly overtaken me,' she said. 'Other people will wonder why I take this step, joining a mainstream party, having long been a champion of a third party alternative. The answer is that I have found it increasingly difficult to stand in the middle, trying to be endlessly fair to both sides when I have grown so alarmed by the kind of politics being played out by the Coalition.'

She had concluded that the Democrats were permanently entrenched as a third party, confined to their important 'checks and balances' role in the Senate, because of the way the electoral system operated. Because of the success of the previous four years, unless the government called an early election the Democrats were guaranteed the numbers they needed in the Senate till the year 2002. If there was a time for her to leave, it was now, with the party in the best shape in years, and with a long breathing space before the next election for a new leader to settle in. Kernot said she was ready for the inevitable attacks to come from the government, but attacks on the Democrats would backfire.

For the record, she explained that for many years approaches had been made to her by individuals on both sides of politics to consider joining Labor or the Coalition. 'In the main such approaches were off-the-cuff remarks in aeroplanes or at functions, usually half in jest, or at best semi-serious feelers. My reaction was to be flattered that various people thought enough of my contribution to entertain such ideas. When it was raised though, I said my job, first and foremost, was to restore the fortunes of the Australian Democrats.' But, as her concern grew about the direction of things after 1996, she confessed she began to think about how she could make a bigger contribution.

Kernot pointed out that ahead of its 1998 National Conference, the ALP was embarked on a major rethink of its policies. 'I believe this rethink comes at a fortuitous moment in world politics. More and more parties around the globe are grappling with the problem of forging a new path; a synthesis that gets the best for society out of free market economics and government intervention.' The Howard government was still locked into prescriptions that were a hardline, Thatcherite throwback. The world was moving on and she believed Labor was moving with it, working on a 'roadmap for the new millennium'.

'Labor is reaching a position where it will be best placed to meet the economic challenges of the future. And hand-in-hand with that, to rebuild a sense of community, make society fairer, restore tolerance—in short, advance the great founding tradition of caring egalitarianism.' Labor had a precious opportunity to keep the best of its ideological changes of the 1980s when it, too, had embraced right wing economics, but also learn from the mistakes of that period. 'A new definition of the relationship between government, the people, business and industry, the States, the regions, trade unionism and families is coming. A new politics that will offer hope to a deeply disillusioned electorate.'

Being a creature of a different political culture, there were no guarantees, she acknowledged. 'Perhaps this experiment will fail. Perhaps there will be no viable role for me within the Labor Party. Perhaps it will not be possible to reinvent government and politics the way I believe—and I think millions of Australians sense—should happen. But I have decided to make the effort and try.' Kernot said she wanted to play a role helping Labor figures like Gareth Evans and Simon Crean support the ALP Leader, Kim Beazley, in rebuilding Labor's electoral support. The alternative for her was to leave politics so she did not compromise Democrat even-handedness. 'If I am to fail, then I will leave the stage. Politics for me is not about time-serving. I want to be part of building something that works. I want to restore the things that I think Australia has lost. Simple things, like confidence and trust and public service.'

In the next phase of the operation an hour later, Kernot, Kim Beazley and Gareth Evans walked out into one of the courtyard gardens of Parliament House, media photographers flaying around them, to a 'stand-up' press conference. There, Beazley welcomed the arrival of her new ideas, her 'new blood'. It was confirmation that Labor was planning a new beginning for Australia. He said Kernot had gone about the process of moving into the party 'the right way', adding that if and when she did win her way into parliament, he would give his support to moves for the Labor caucus to elect her to the front bench. Beazley was asked about the core inconsistencies, the fact that Kernot had for so long been a critic of the ALP, particularly when it was in office.

'Cheryl had an enormous amount of fight in her as Leader of the Australian Democrats and part of that role has been critical of the ALP,' Beazley acknowledged. 'Well, that's something we can live with. That is something with which we are perfectly comfortable. It's her values, that's what counts with us. And the values that she has expounded over her lifetime in politics are values that sit well with the Labor Party.'

Despite the Labor spin, the shock of many of those looking on, even some hardened press gallery professionals, was palpable. Here was a woman who had spent seven years in politics sculpting a reputation for common sense, honesty and integrity, only to be now leaping radically into the dark. Here was a woman who had talked long and hard about the failings of mainstream politics but was now not just taking sides, but transforming herself into a search-and-destroy partisan missile. Here was a woman whose great pride had been to rebuild a political party from near ruin in 1993, only to now be walking away from it.

At first blush, Kernot seemed to be casting it all to the wind in a deadly gamble. Even taking in her graphic explanation about why she had come to this, it still seemed barely comprehensible. Some of the journalists had become friends with her in recent years but none had suspected it. Sure, they had picked up on her frustrations but this was a step too far, surely. The older ones with a grasp of history and Labor mythology were struck that here was political betrayal, a modern 'ratting' politician to stand with Billy Hughes and Joe Lyons. How could she just throw it all in, trashing her seven-year rationale for life in politics—and the famous Australian Democrat dictum 'Keep the Bastards Honest'? How could she walk away from her party because she could see it wasn't getting anywhere, joining a team she had spent years berating, transforming herself from something approaching a political 'saint' into one of the reviled 'bastards', a 'queen rat'?

And so the fusillade of abuse started, just as some of the shrewdest judges in the Labor Party had privately warned Kernot it would when the defection was first discussed. Led by the imperious sneering of Australia's top political journalist, the Nine television network's Laurie Oakes, the system turned on the turncoat. Oakes demanded to know whether Kernot thought it fair to have only managed to tell the Democrats half-an-hour earlier. How did she feel becoming a 'Demo-rat'? What about all the people in her old party who had trusted her, relied on her? What about Meg Lees who had thought she and Kernot were to front another press conference at the same hour on the subject of Greenhouse? How could Kernot live with giving them such a kick in the guts? Would this not destroy the party because she was voting with her feet, deciding, despite everything she had said for years, that the Democrats' basic rationale was impotent?

Calmly, slowly, Kernot confronted every charge. Canberra journalists knew as well as she did that had she given advance warning, or if the news had leaked, she would have been swamped, vilified, unable to present her complex explanation clearly and fully so the people could judge for themselves. No, the Democrats would not be destroyed, there would always be room for them in a system in which the electorate consciously opted to have a presence in the Senate as a counterpoint to electing a government in the lower house, the House of Representatives. The Democrats were good legislators and good people. They would find another talented leader, as they had in the past. *Their* role would remain. *She* had changed, not her old party. Kernot repeated that she had reached the stage where she could no longer go on, in all conscience, trying to play the 'fair' Democrat role, exercising the balance of power in the Senate, when she didn't believe in so much of the government's intent. To have done so would have compromised the Democrats' operation itself. And yes, she knew precisely how huge this gamble was. If she failed she would walk away altogether, but she just had to try. She looked her inquisitors in the eye and told them she had not taken this step, with its hurt for so many people, lightly. In her heart she believed it was the right course.

The initial reaction of media heavyweights was mixed, some unable to shrug off the feeling that the reviled pre-war Labor phenomenon, 'ratting', would be her undoing. Alan Ramsey's front page comment in the *Sydney Morning Herald* began: 'Oh, Cheryl Kernot, what have you done?' Admitting her course was principled, honest and courageous, Ramsey still said it could prove the worst decision she ever made. In doing it, she may have destroyed herself politically because she now had to live with the fact that she had sided with her old enemy:

> How she explains that, credibly and persistently, over the year she now sits out politics until the election comes around, in the face of what will be an enduring campaign of abuse and hostility by her opponents, will be anything but easy … Indeed, the taint will stay with her while she remains in politics. It will never be forgotten, not by her opponents or the voters. The electoral standing and immense good-will she gained by not being one of 'them' and by rebuilding the Democrats as a relevant and viable force will now always be infected to one degree or another.

Kernot's great challenge was to adjust to life in the rough-and-tumble Labor culture. She had built a reputation as a class political act. 'Now we see just how first class she is,' Ramsey said.[1]

But others, like the influential Paul Kelly writing in the *Australian* newspaper, saw the deepest significance in Kernot's appeal for the country to find its way towards a 'new' politics. Here was the core truth of the defection decision. While her critics railed about her ruthlessness, her erraticism and her overarching ambition, the true gamble within the defection was the hope—perhaps ever so faint—that in beginning this journey, Cheryl Kernot could one day reach a position of *real* power, where she could help turn the wheels of change, pushing a failed, and failing, parliamentary/political/bureaucratic/social system towards a new way of doing things. Kelly said it up front:

Cheryl Kernot should be applauded for having the courage to seek executive power. She has chosen to become a serious politician instead of wasting her career as a Senate spoiler. The decision is a bonus overall for Australian politics. This is the most important point about her move and it should not be forgotten amid the exaggerations about her betrayal of the Australian Democrats. Federal politics desperately needs an injection of new spirit and spark and Ms Kernot's double shift to Labor and the House of Representatives is a tonic which, depending upon her performance, may help revive our ailing body politic.[2]

For days after her defection, and to a lesser degree for weeks and months, Kernot would be forced to endure many complex consequences of her action—among them the deep and ruthless animus of those she had called on, adjustment stresses on herself and family, and bouts of doubt about the scale of the challenge that lay ahead. She would go from being a figure of near-universal respect to one either feted or reviled by a polarised public. A sharper, less forgiving spotlight would expose her frailties alongside her strengths. The pressures would lead her to make mistakes, irritating and confusing the perfectionist in a proud and defiant woman. She would learn how hard it is to be unorthodox, to try to break free of convention, to take on a political system with its often cheap, short-termist, tediously adversarial groundrules. But she would quickly see that to survive, she too had to change, to adapt—all the time hoping that in the end the extent of her adjustment would not undermine the thing she set out to achieve.

In the main, the Australian Democrats took the blow with dignity. Initially—devastated, mystified and then enraged—some Democrat players lunged at Kernot with a vengeance. Those who passionately believed in the need for a viable third choice in politics felt insulted and let down; those who had chosen to be in the Democrat ranks solely because of their regard for her talent were shattered; and those in the party who had long borne grudges against her thought of revenge. Some of her staff turned on her, complaining that she had not been willing to trust them. In their pain they scrawled: 'Ding dong, the witch is dead!' and other insults on the office whiteboard and muttered darkly about knowing secrets but being too loyal to speak of them.

Bill Scetrine, a one-time press secretary to former Democrat Leader Janet

Powell, went public to assert that far from being the reasonable 'sweetness and light' figure she made out, Kernot was 'unbelievably Machiavellian', a natural 'machine politician' who worked without revealing her hand. He said the Democrats who were used to doing things over 'a cosy cup of coffee' had not been able to cope with her. Janet Powell herself publicly denounced Kernot as having had a role in the coup that toppled her from the party leadership back in 1991.[3]

For his part, Prime Minister John Howard came out with all guns blazing, charging that the move confirmed his long-held belief that the Democrats were a sub-branch of the ALP, that Labor had always been able to 'whistle' Kernot up whenever it wanted, and that she was after Kim Beazley's job because of the vacuum in Labor's leadership. Kernot had relinquished any right to talk of trust. Democrats had a right to feel let down. Howard said:

> I want to remind Democrat voters that it took a Liberal figure in Don Chipp to set up the Democrats; now it has taken a Labor figure in Cheryl Kernot to tear them down.

Other government leaders like the Industrial Relations Minister, Peter Reith, raged that this was the greatest political betrayal since Billy Hughes. But sensing the greatest rhetorical danger, Howard and others like Treasurer Peter Costello chose one important front for a rapid-fire counter-attack. Beazley, Howard said, was trying to pretend there was something 'new' about Labor now.

> But it just goes to show that the opportunism and self-interest of Labor never changes. That they haven't really learned at all. Nothing has changed with Labor except the faces involved in constant betrayals of trust. It's everything we ever said about Labor, a party that lost the trust of the people because of cosy deals with special interests. Now this is the cosiest deal of them all, an elitist deal tinged with all the smugness and complacency that was the hallmark of Labor in government.[4]

Within days of the defection, however, the frontal campaign of denigration had reason to pause when a volley of public opinion polls began to cast the drama in a new light. Kernot had stepped into this cauldron with no clear idea of where it would take her. So much was left to chance. Along the way she was shattering political stereotypes at every turn. She had set her course on contesting a Liberal-held seat in Queensland—no cushy fast-track into parliament via a by-election for a safe Labor one. Soon it was clear the target was Dickson, where Labor needed a 3.3% swing. Kernot had stepped away from a job that carried a combined pay of almost $140,000 with no detailed agreement worked out about the role she would play working for Labor in the eighteen months before the election. As it turned out, within days a new dual role was being devised—helping develop ideas for the party policy platform and also campaigning in marginal seats. The job would pay around $50,000 a year. By resigning from parliament when she did, Kernot immediately sacrificed a lifetime pension worth around $40,000 a year, although her entitlements would be put back on track if she did win the House of Representatives seat and serve multiple terms there.

Despite all this, Kernot just felt it was what she had to do. It was entirely conceivable that if this experiment went wrong she would be left facing the other option with which she had wrestled for months: leaving politics altogether. Had a large majority of the people looked and seen a 'rat', ditching principle, lying, obfuscating, concocting a front for her own unbridled ambition, then she was finished, her career shattered in ignominy. But the people did not see that. Far from it.

The first of a series of opinion polls, conducted in the wake of her departure, contained devastating findings. A nationwide poll by the Quadrant organisation found that 57% of Australians approved of her move to the ALP and only 36% disagreed. Nearly four in ten Australians said they were more likely to vote Labor as a result of her move. The poll put the ALP under Kim Beazley a massive 17% ahead of the government. Some 60% of people thought Kernot could become Australia's first female Prime Minister. But, stunningly, some 63% believed she was correct in charging that the Howard government had no vision.

'In twenty-five years of polling, I cannot recall such a huge swing to a federal Opposition in such a short time,' said Quadrant pollster Ian McNair.[5] But this was not some one-off set of findings. One after another, the major opinion polls found Labor, while obviously not 17% in front, had nevertheless been rocketed back into contention at the next election; that

Kernot was embraced as a big-time national player; and that, critically, the basic premise of her gamble—the message about lack of national vision—had resonated with people. Within days, Labor Party branches all around Australia reported a surge in people coming forward to join up. When Kernot later visited the seat of Dickson accompanied by Beazley to officially join the ALP, she was welcomed like royalty, members of the public pressing forward to hug and congratulate her. Over these days, she would receive bag-loads of faxes and letters from ordinary Australians, some snarling and hostile, but a massive majority supportive and describing how they were inspired by her. In this, Kernot had been served by an immense piece of luck.

When she walked into that eventful first press conference, and then joined Beazley and Evans in another soon after, she had no idea that television and radio stations had opted to broadcast them live into the homes of Australia. She said privately later that had she known that, she may have 'choked', as they say in sporting parlance. As luck would have it, Kernot was able to speak to the people of Australia directly, essentially over the heads of the press gallery, the wider media, and the Canberra political system. And as they had been doing for four years, the people listened intently to her words.

In only four years at the top in politics Kernot had established an extraordinary place in the nation's regard, even affection. How many politicians anywhere in the late 1990s are respected? Among the attributes that had propelled her, the key two were her capacity to communicate a message, and her gift for ideas, for being able to identify what ordinary people felt was really important. That she survived the initial trauma of the defection was a tribute to this intangible capacity to connect with people. Her message appealed to a nation not just ill at ease, but growing resentful and detached; one stricken by a crisis of confidence so entrenched that it felt like it had always been there. Time would show whether Kernot could survive the long haul of her hazardous journey. The attacks on her in those first dramatic hours were nothing compared to what she would soon be enduring, for she did have vulnerabilities. To those Australians who had taken the time to listen or watch, she came over as a different politician. Beyond her messages and her capacity to project, what also stood out was her boldness, her guts. Her courage was chiselled in stone in October 1997. The concomitant danger, of course, was that often the light that shines brightly in the political constellation is the one that can so easily crash back to earth.

The central paradox was that she had carved out a position above sordid politics as a figure of reassurance, holding out the prospect of answers, of a balm for people's anxiety. But in taking the step towards becoming a mainstream player, she had to employ ruthlessness, guile, manipulation— the tools of a discredited trade. As the people got to know the real person behind the cosy image, the question was whether they would continue to trust her. But more than just the essential character of Cheryl Kernot would be tested. For her crazy/heroic attempt to move mountains potentially posed important questions about what the nation wants in its leaders.

PART ONE

1
THE NEW STAR

To begin to understand the genesis of Cheryl Kernot's dramatic transformation one must take the first of two steps back in time, to a press conference convened in Canberra some fifty months prior to her defection in October, 1997. It was the moment she first arrived as a serious politician.

In late 1993 Cheryl was stirred from sleep in the small upstairs flat she rented in Lyons, a southern suburb of the national capital, not far from the big retail and public service centre of Woden. Suddenly aware of the morning twilight, she was up and out from under the warm covers, her feet hurrying down the hallway towards the sound she now recognised as the telephone ringing in the living room. As she lifted the receiver, through bleary eyes she noticed the tableside clock: 5.30 am. That phone would continue to ring, relentlessly, for the next three hours. Every television and radio news program in Australia wanted to talk to the politician of the moment, the Leader of the Australian Democrats in the Senate.

Always cooperative with the media and happy to take calls at home, this morning Kernot was finding it hard even to get herself dressed, so often was she drawn back to the incoming calls. Each time she begged off, explaining she needed to get into her parliamentary office to catch up with events overnight and thus be better positioned to speak authoritatively. By the time her white Commonwealth car pulled up at the big glass doors on the Senate side of the national parliament, a clan of journalists and camera crews had gathered, all demanding comment from the woman who held in her hands the fate of the Keating Labor government's 1993 budget.

Inside Room 112, her modest L-shaped suite of offices bounded by two garden courtyards, Kernot's staff were already hard at work, pulling together all the available information from the wire services, the offices of the other Democrat senators and wider sources around the parliament building, carefully trying to work through the implications of the tumult breaking around them. The mood was tense, and even a trace panicky and irritated that the Leader was taking so long to get in. For that morning's national media was dominated by the stark news that the value of the Australian dollar was sliding, interest rates were on the way up and the Keating government was contemplating a double dissolution election—all because of the stand Kernot was taking over the controversial first budget of Keating's Treasurer, John Dawkins.

The implication was that Australia was headed towards a currency crisis because the new powerbrokers of global capitalism—the money markets— were concerned that Dawkins' budget was on the verge of being dumped by an intransigent Senate, the upper house of the parliament. Events overnight had conspired to transform an eight-day-old climate of general political instability into a hunt for a scapegoat, just as Keating government strategists had hoped. And that scapegoat was beginning to look disturbingly like the forty-four-year-old Democrat from Queensland.

Finally freed of the media pack which trailed off once she was striding through the long, red-carpeted hallways of the building, Kernot swept into her office, to the great relief of her agitated aides. 'Do you know, my phone hasn't stopped ringing since daybreak,' she protested before anyone could speak.

'Tell us about it,' said her Press Secretary, Geoff Dodd. 'We've been trying to get on to you, too. That is, when we've had a line out.' With that, they disappeared into the heart of the office suite, her own central room with its perpetually paper-littered desk and unpretentious appointments including a comfortable, grey leather couch. It was the morning of Wednesday, August 25, 1993—just over a week after John Dawkins had presented his first budget in the 'Reps', the House of Representatives lower house chamber of the parliament. That week had proved one of the longest of Dawkins' political life but his pain would redouble in coming months. He didn't know it at the time but this was, in fact, the beginning of the end of the budget as he had crafted it. It was also the moment heralding the arrival of a new political superstar.

The scene was first set for the showdown a fortnight earlier when the federal Opposition, led by John Hewson, signalled it would move in the Senate to block tax increases mooted for inclusion in the August 17 budget package. For years the Liberal/National Party Opposition had responded with great caution to budget measures introduced by Bob Hawke's government, basically because of the residual community sensitivity over the actions of the Coalition Opposition under Malcolm Fraser back in the historic budget crisis of 1975. Then the Opposition moved to block supply— essentially, the passage through parliament of legislation that funds the operation of government itself. It was the act which precipitated the fall of Gough Whitlam.

In the five months since the March 1993 election, the Keating government had decided to defer promised income tax cuts and increase indirect tax in direct contravention of its election campaign assurances. Incensed, John Hewson and some of his lieutenants were hardening their stance on blocking tax measures, all the time insisting this did not amount to an attempt to block supply. In the 76-seat Senate chamber, the Opposition controlled 36 seats, the government only 30, with two independent Green Senators from West Australia and one unaligned independent from Tasmania. With a relatively large bloc of seven senators, the Democrats were thus in a position to lay down the groundrules in the balance of power equation. Because laws must be passed by both Houses, any parties in the Senate with this leverage can argue with a government about the nature of the laws, and negotiate changes. The Senate numbers meant the Greens could play a role too, but it would be one initially overshadowed by the Kernot operation.

In the weeks prior to the budget, Kernot signalled she had concerns with some of the leaked hints about indirect tax hikes to come. Clearly she was going to be the key player in what some political pundits were suggesting could become the biggest Senate confrontation since the ugly months of 1975. Dawkins' budget was, in fact, the most disastrous of the Hawke/Keating period in office. Within days of its unveiling there was widespread ALP, trade union, business, financial market and broader community criticism of its core measures. They included a sharp rise in petrol prices, an across-the-board rise in wholesale sales tax, a wine tax increase, higher taxes on lump sum long service leave payments and unused holiday pay and an extension of the fringe benefits tax net. The budget delivered the first tranche of tax cuts promised by Keating in the 1993 election but postponed a second tranche until 1998, with government ministers ominously hedging when questioned about whether it would definitely be delivered even then.

Kernot immediately signalled her concern at the way some budget measures were 'regressive'—hitting the poor harder than the rich. She suggested three changes: 'quarantining' the impact of the petrol price slug on rural Australians; phasing in the controversial changes to long service leave and holiday pay entitlements; and a rethink on the wine tax. But she was concerned about changes to the Austudy scheme for students, cuts to optometry services under Medicare and lifting the pension age for women to sixty-five years. She was also angry at the small size of a tax rebate supposedly helping low income earners offset the impact of the sales tax hikes. She was careful, though, to point out that the Democrats would be convening meetings with community groups around the nation to take soundings in the weeks following the budget and would spend a good deal of time looking more closely at its figuring and the exact operation of its measures before making final decisions. It was a complex package, she said, warranting close examination, without undue haste.

By the end of the budget week, however, a back-pedalling Prime Minister was defiantly describing the budget as 'Labor to the bootstraps' and accusing John Hewson of 'Senate thuggery'. Treasurer Dawkins was declaring outright he was not in a mood to do deals and canvassing the possibility that Senate obstruction could lead to another election. They both shrugged off tough criticisms from Labor figures of the stature of ACTU President, Martin Ferguson, who said he 'could not defend the indefensible'. And they blithely ignored clear evidence that a rebellion was brewing in their own ranks. Pundits observed that Labor had been stunned by the widespread community backlash against the budget. 'The government is rattled to its bootstraps,' said one.[1]

Over the weekend following the budget, the national media was full of stories about it being 'in limbo' or 'in crisis', speculating about a backbench revolt actually forcing Keating and Dawkins to retreat. When John Hewson formally announced the Opposition would vote against *all* the major tax measures, it was clear the turmoil would come to a head when the parliament resumed in Canberra the following week.

The crisis deepened on multiple fronts for the government that next

Monday. An opinion poll commissioned by the *Australian* newspaper suggested the ALP was indeed facing a thumping voter backlash. Labor support had plummeted to its lowest level ever, at only 31%. Voter satisfaction with Prime Minister Keating was only two-thirds that of Bob Hawke when he was deposed by Keating back in December 1991. Keating trailed John Hewson by 27% to 43% in the preferred Prime Minister stakes. Some 62% of people thought the budget would be bad for the economy and only 20% said it would be good. And 74% of voters thought they would be personally worse off as a result, with only 14% thinking they would be helped by it.[2]

Kernot herself had decided to agree to an Opposition request to refer the central tax bill to a Senate committee to investigate its constitutional validity. She had received legal advice suggesting the bill was uncon-stitutional because it dealt with eleven different tax changes. Section 55 of the Constitution says taxation bills can only deal with one subject at a time but the government argued its law was altering existing taxes, not imposing any new ones. But Kernot also made it clear that government bloody-mindedness was becoming counter-productive. She warned that if ministers were not willing to be conciliatory, she could be left in the situation where she had to support the Coalition and block the entire package. Kernot warned that the Prime Minister had to stop pushing the line that he would negotiate only if he liked what he heard. 'If the government insists on the budget bill being put to the parliament as one bill and not negotiating along the way, the Democrats will find it very hard to vote for that budget package,' she said.

With Kernot's cards now firmly on the table, a rattled government containing some disgruntled strategists decided to take the gloves off. They clearly had the target in their sights—Kernot herself. Here was a woman barely five months into the job of leading a political party, a relative novice. And here she was brazenly holding a gun to the head of a ten-year-old government, one which had rewritten the political history books. A govern-ment which had redefined Labor as a party of economic literacy and management capacity. A government which had electorally legitimised Labor, essentially for the first time in the post-war period. The back-room boys wondered what it would take to make this Kernot woman buckle. Not much, they surmised. It was time to bring out the blowtorch.

It came the next day, coinciding with a slump in the value of the dollar to a record low in a volatile day of trading in financial markets. As Robert Garran, the Economics Correspondent for the *Australian* newspaper, reported, the uncertainty in the markets was fuelled by a series of confusing and conflicting statements by senior ministers and by some extraordinary comments from the Governor of the Reserve Bank, Bernie Fraser.[3] During the day one minister after another was trotted out to warn of dire consequences of the budget being impeded. Dawkins himself stayed on the front foot, repeating his determination not to bargain with Senate players.

'I am just saying it isn't a negotiating document,' he said. 'We've got many weeks for this to be played out but as far as the government is concerned it is a package and you can't see bits of it falling off without having an effect on the bottom line.'

The Health Minister, the tough NSW right wing faction boss Graham Richardson, warned there was a 'pretty good chance' of the government using Senate rejection of the budget bill to call a double dissolution election. Finance Minister Ralph Willis, Employment Minister Kim Beazley and Assistant Treasurer George Gear all warned that the consequence of the Senate blocking the tax rises and forcing the budget deficit up would be higher interest rates. And in a highly unusual intervention into the political debate, Bernie Fraser said the controversy over the budget was 'unfortunate' and that uncertainty raised by the Senate threats was 'something we could well do without'.

In the wake of all this, the stalemate saw the dollar slump to a record low before it recovered with support from the Reserve. The currency dropped to a low of US66.47 cents against the US dollar, before ending at US66.70 cents, down a cent from the previous day. In the money markets, interest rates for medium-term bank bills and long-term bonds were up. But probably the most interesting play was made later that evening by the faceless but immensely powerful apparatchiks employed by government ministers to brief journalists 'off the record' about developments and interpretation of political events. The spin-doctors basically argued that international capital markets were taking a very dim view of the Senate's antics.

All in all, the campaign had precisely the desired effect as dawn broke on that Wednesday morning. The dollar was in trouble and Kernot was to blame. That was the word. Only one Canberra journalist saw the scam for what it was and punished it. Tom Burton, writing in the *Australian Financial Review*, pointed out that on the previous Wednesday following the budget, Keating himself had been telling the parliamentary press gallery to 'take no notice' of the financial markets when they gave it an initial thumbs down. It was, he said, all part of a deliberate campaign to spook the Senate into passing the budget.

> Six days later, four of his ministers, plus their minders, were doing their level best to engineer a money market crisis … In case anyone missed the point, there was some savage media backgrounding about the imminence of a market crisis if the hindrance continued. Summary justice from the markets for refusal to pass the budget was the line everyone was meant to cop. Real cowboy stuff when the dollar had already lost a cent and the Reserve Bank was in the market trying to hold the line. Though the markets were to be ignored last week, this week the sharp fall in the dollar and rise in bond yields were said to be just a taste of what was to come. How desperate is a government for legislative support for its budget when it has to resort to the risky and irresponsible strategy of fuelling market instability to jawbone Senate support?[4]

That Wednesday morning, however, the great bulk of Australian political journalism was reading the crisis in the opposite light. In the sanctuary of her office, Kernot could sense the temperature climbing in the pressure cooker of Parliament House. And the pressure valve was her desk. Calls from offices in the press gallery two floors above the Democrat head-quarters along with those from television and radio stations in every State were inundating her phone lines, demanding to know when she was going to produce a response to the central accusation that she was threatening the stability of the currency. One after another, journalists were appearing in the outer office, inquiring about any plans for a media statement, a press con-ference or its variant, the 'doorstop', the traditional, informal press briefing convened before television cameras at any of the major entrances to the parliament building. Kernot's staff were beginning to feel they could only go on denying the media a considered response for so long.

At around 9.40 am Kernot sent word she would appear at the Senate door for a doorstop twenty minutes later. Then she turned to her staffers assembled around her desk. 'OK, what's your advice on this? How do we handle it?' The minutes began ticking by as Kernot and her team were interrupted by other pressing matters that had to be dealt with. Regular door knocks from staffers brought messages coming in from all round the country. Under intense pressure, her aides ran back over the meaning of the complex piece of politics confronting them. Remaining surprisingly cool, Kernot resolved what the line would be: she would hit back at the government. And bloody hard.

'I'm not going to be bullied by anybody,' she said.

With only a few minutes to go, those in the room realised they each had only their own roughly scratched notes. A staffer transcribed the basis of Kernot's proposed remarks into a two-page note. It contained a list of dot points, basically a series of assertions which together comprised the framework of her argument. This distillation of the half-hour discussion was quickly read to her, once, and the paper then handed to her. With that, she and her Press Secretary, Geoff Dodd, his tape recorder in hand, headed out the door and up the corridor towards the Senate side door. It was the biggest moment of her five-month-old leadership. Her poise and deter-mination betrayed nothing of her inexperience. Or her tingling nerves. She was being driven by an instinctive feeling that her course was correct. Nothing more could guide her. No corporate memory. No rule books of Democrat leadership. No staff advice on handling currency crises. Kernot was out in front, taking her party into uncharted terrain. It would not be the last time.

Just outside the Senate entrance under the stone archway facade, the waiting scrum of journalists and photographers enveloped her as she came to a standstill on the basalt forecourt. A thick semi-circle of heads, four deep around her, stretched forward, tape recorders in hand, television cameras trained on her. Quickly adjusting their focus, the cameramen called 'OK' for the 'talent' to begin her spiel. Kernot began by announcing the Democrats were concerned about the budget's annual leave, optometry, wine tax and petrol excise arrangements. But, she said, she had been saying repeatedly that her party was not about wrecking the budget. She reiterated a key assertion she had been making in recent days—that she would be working up key changes to the budget that would have the effect of helping the government cut its deficit, not blow it out. The budget was unfair to the poor and the Democrats were determined to inject fairness into it. She had been saying for weeks the country could not afford the promised tax cuts.

'I want to remind the government that this is a parliamentary democracy,' she said. 'And even the non-government parties in the Senate are democratically elected and have democratic obligations. It is irresponsible of government officials to brief journalists to the effect that the non-government parties in the Senate are responsible for market jitters.'

Kernot said she would not be intimidated by anyone and pointed out how the government a few days earlier had been insisting market reaction was meaningless. 'The government created its own problems by the strait-jacket of promising, and then legislating, unaffordable income tax cuts. The Democrats opposed the cuts as unaffordable and unfair at the time and we were right.' Dawkins had boxed himself in by insisting he would not be cutting expenditure any further, or raising taxes.

'If the markets are jittery, it's because the government has lost its credibility.'

Only a brief volley of questions from the journalists followed her initial statement, further elaboration being unnecessary. After she had reinforced a couple of her basic points, a lull descended on the questioning and one of the press gang leaders called out: 'Great, thank you!' The urgency in the group subsided, the attentive focus of the microphones and the cameras in her face now eased back. The posse began to break up, with the radio journalists, close to deadlines, heading quickly back to their studios in the building. Others, the newspaper reporters with deadlines later in the afternoon, re-cued their tape recorders to ponder her words as they began more slowly to ease away. A couple of the journalists made polite chat with Kernot as she also headed back inside.

Along the corridor, Kernot permitted herself a relieved smile at Geoff Dodd. One minute a mini-crisis, the next, all the pressure gone, instantly evaporated. But would it stay that way? Once her words were fed out across the wire services, her voice hitting radio news bulletins around the country, what would the reaction be? Would the same forces that had so carefully targeted her overnight regroup? For his part, Dodd was mightily struck by the performance he had just witnessed. On the way out Kernot had glanced only momentarily at the note in her hand. She had not looked at it for guidance once during the doorstop. She appeared not only to have the power of instant recall of the brief, but had also been near word-perfect with the text in its major points. She had stuck tightly to the agreed line of argument at a moment when it was imperative to convey a clear and careful message. And she had done it under considerable pressure. In the age of television, here surely were the hallmarks of a very media-competent politician.

If anything, the tension of the morning's media circus was to be replaced by the unease of a ghostly silence back in Kernot's office suite. Her foray had stilled what half-an-hour before had seemed a rollercoaster ride of political danger. Arriving back in the office they found the phones stilled and the odd staffer grabbing the opportunity to make coffee in the small kitchen annexe attached to Kernot's room. With the media carrying her counter-attack all round the nation, Kernot slumped into her high back leather chair wondering: what next? As the morning wore on, her staff refocused on the other demands of a busy parliamentary sitting week in Canberra but on the budget issue all was now silent. No government breast-beating, no opportunistic Opposition stunts. Around midday, Geoff Dodd knocked and stepped into Kernot's office.

'What do you hear?' she asked.

'Nothing. Dead quiet. They're obviously still digesting what you said.'

Then the phone on her desk rang.

'I have a caller for you,' Kernot's Canberra office manager, Shirley Simper, said on the line from her desk out in the front foyer. 'From the Prime Minister's office.'

With the call put through, Dodd watched as wide-eyed expectation on Kernot's face slowly gave way to the hint of a smile tugging at the corner of her mouth. After a brief exchange she hung up and glanced at her PR man, the smile released and widening. 'The Prime Minister has asked if I can drop around after question time today to have a bit of a chat about what we can do on the budget front,' she said.

The pair stared at one another for a tiny moment of disoriented silence. Then, spontaneously their heads went back, Kernot cupping her chin in an explosion of laughter—a peeling eruption of relief.

'Yes!' Dodd yelled, punching the air with his arm. The bluff was called. No-one had swallowed the line that the Senate was basically about destroying the budget. Kernot had made it clear all along the deficit reduction strategy would be supported. The silly bully-boy stuff got nowhere. Now it was time to negotiate, just like she had been saying. She had won. In one sharply crafted play she had brushed aside an inept political attack.

That afternoon she met with both Keating and Dawkins, a seventy-minute preliminary conversation which signalled publicly the retreat of the government to a position of agreed and open negotiations with, firstly, the Democrats and then later the two Green senators. Thus was set in train a tortured process of wheeling and dealing that would delay the final passage through the Senate of Dawkins' troubled budget until the end of October—but that Wednesday would ultimately prove to be more than just the point at which a revised 1993 budget process got back on the rails. It was the moment Cheryl Kernot's career as a politician took flight. A moment in which many Australians would focus for the first time on a woman of real substance—one, in fact, inherently gifted enough to be the long-awaited first female Prime Minister of Australia. Here was a woman who would eke out a prominent place in politics at an important moment in the evolution of women's rights in Australia.

The late 1980s had seemed a propitious time for the cause of women winning a bigger role in politics. Even though it had taken fifty years from Federation for the first woman to be elected to the federal parliament and almost that long again for one to be made a Cabinet minister, by the start of the 1990s a woman had been made leader of a national party, two others were State Premiers and still others were high-ranking ministers. For some years political pollsters had divined a yearning among both Australian men and women for a top-class female politician to emerge on the national stage. The people running both the major parties were keenly aware of this new mood. The ALP passed an historic reform to try to get more women access to safe seats. But just a few years later, by the mid-1990s, the landscape was looking decidedly different.

What had seemed unstoppable progress into more and more positions of power had been blunted by a series of failures. Some high-flyers who had arrived in much fanfare, even lauded as Prime Ministers-in-the-making, fell by the way—Bronwyn Bishop among the Liberals and Labor's Carmen Lawrence. Janine Haines, the second leader of the Australian Democrats and the first ever female leader of a national political party, had been cut down by a campaign of dirty tricks in South Australia when she attempted to transfer from the Senate to the House of Representatives.

As the countdown to the new millennium began in the late 1990s there was only one larger-than-life female politician in the federal arena—Cheryl Kernot. For millions of Australian women she had emerged not necessarily as heroine or role model but most definitely as a voice making sense, speaking with a directness to which they could relate. Kernot was intent on cutting her own cloth as a feminist leader—but exactly what form did this take? By no means a hardline, aggressive, 'women as victims' agitator, she was nevertheless driven by her own feminist rationale—a message that would have resonance for a sizeable number, if not a majority, of Australian women.

Back in the 1970s, as a relatively naive country girl born of Celtic stock in the NSW country town of Maitland, and by then living and working as a schoolteacher in Brisbane, Kernot was first galvanised into action—politically radicalised—while sitting all evening and on into the early hours of the next morning in the public gallery of the Queensland parliament. There she came face to face with the hard evidence of the repression of the female voice. She could not believe it. There, she saw men—and only men— talking, sometimes in quite obnoxious terms, about one of the most vital issues affecting women's lives—abortion. She was affronted by the idea that there was not a greater sharing of the political decision-making, particularly when it came to issues that so deeply affected women.

It was not just that this was the tyranny of the crass, extremist Bjelke-Petersen regime. In time, Kernot would contemplate the domination of all politics by a *male* way of thinking. She would recognise a predictable, rigid, adversarial game that males exalted in. She would wonder if part of the post-Menzian collapse of respect for politics and parliament in Australia owed itself to the fact that one way of thinking was only ever being exercised in the big decisions. Less preoccupied than hardline feminists with the 'spoils' of power—the fact that women had traditionally been dealt out of prestige and patronage—to Kernot the key issue was that Australia had always been run by people thinking in this stereotypical way. She wondered whether this had always lent itself to the best outcomes for the nation, for *all* its citizens. She wondered if there would not be a qualitatively better outcome if there was more of a female way of thinking around the Cabinet table.

Once submerged in politics, Kernot was struck by a second, almost overpowering, impression. She discovered the tyranny exercised over politicians and parliament by a great, central orthodoxy: economic fundamentalism. It, too, would offend her inherent sense of fairness. As her career developed, Kernot came to understand the great myth of Australian politics in the 1980s: the notion that there was a viable choice over the fundamental elements of economic policy between the two major political parties, the Labor Party and the Liberal/National Party Coalition. Kernot saw that in this period Labor basically embraced a core set of ideas advocated by its opponents. She grasped the scope of the strategic blunder of the Hawke/Keating years: the decision to drag the ALP so far to the right on economic policy as to embrace totally what is called 'economic rationalism', the neo-classical school of economic thinking. This philosophy of economics emerged from university faculties around the world in the late post-war period to be embraced by Western nations in the wake of the oil crisis of the 1970s, just as it was prior to the Great Depression. Faced with recession and inflation in the 1970s, governments opted for this doctrine in a bid to rekindle stability and economic growth.

Its core belief is that the role of government should be dismantled and the major decisions in a nation's economy left to market forces to resolve. This was the ideological feedstock of Thatcherism in Great Britain and Reaganism in the United States. But in the late 1980s and 1990s the orthodoxy went further, arguing that the modern industrial revolution that had spawned the new information technology, high-powered global capitalism and the attendant growth of international money markets meant there was no longer room for government. The mass movement of money and the new reign of the computer meant action by the State was enfeebling. The best thing government could do would be to get out of the way, sell off to private business its agencies like telecommunications, airlines, banks, electricity grids, water companies and coal mines, and deregulate and otherwise lift the impediments to business so firms could compete as efficiently as possible out in the new, highly competitive global village.

By hitching themselves to this school of thinking in the 1980s, Hawke and Keating subordinated the Labor Party's long-standing claim of a higher moral ground of compassionate policy-making to the need to assure the domestic and international business community that after the twenty-three-year period in the wilderness after the war and the fiascos of the Whitlam period, *their* Labor Party would be economically literate, competent and reliable.

But Cheryl Kernot challenged this orthodoxy. She probed and questioned its key assumptions. She asserted that it *was* valid for a nation to question the extent to which its real estate, businesses and environment were being sold to foreign interests; she demanded to know why it should be a given that the activities of government were wrong and should be sold off or otherwise made secondary to the interests of the private sector; she insisted that a civilised society needed a strong public sector working in the best interests of the whole nation. Time and again she was the only politician with the courage to stand up publicly and say that progressive new ways of raising tax revenue had to be embraced to maintain investment in the nation's basic infrastructure; she lambasted the predilection of the major parties to only ever see tax in one light—as something that successful politicians *never* talked about raising but, in fact, talked about reducing, usually on the eve of an election to bribe their way back into power. Kernot could never understand why so many intelligent politicians could not grasp that the community saw through this time-honoured ritual.

In the crucial years in which the real powerbrokers of the economic orthodoxy—ideologically-driven economists working in powerful roles in the public service and private sector—convinced both the major parties to privatise so much of the work of federal government agencies, Kernot's was the lone voice saying enough is enough, that there are good national interest reasons why a nation should keep, for example, its telecommunications industry in public hands. She constantly questioned the *assumed* economic benefits that would flow from privatisation of public assets. She was genuinely angered by mounting job losses. She was intellectually indignant that only one voice ever got heard in the economic debate, that one group of economists peddling one particular school of thinking dominated the corridors of power. What was wrong, she asked, with healthy debate?

Kernot was the one politician who called for caution after years in which policy-makers inside both the Labor Party and Coalition unquestioningly swallowed the new notions about globalisation and the revolution in international capitalism. She was concerned that countries' leaders were just accepting as a fait accompli the notion that governments were now bit players, that real power now resided offshore with the big companies which could pick and choose where they put their high-tech industries. The 1993 budget imbroglio deepened her suspicion of the argument that governments had to tailor their economic policies to keep the international money markets onside, for fear of 'poor' policy decisions triggering a flood of capital out of the country. Indeed, shortly after the 1993 budget showdown, Kernot received phone calls in her office from money market dealers in Sydney. They congratulated her on her stance, pointing out she had been correct, that the markets had no intention of significantly marking the currency down. They had been able to read the politics of the affair quite easily themselves.

Kernot always saw the relationship between business and government as a question of balance. She was never anti-business. Far from it. After all, for years she would be the only politician arguing strenuously *for* intervention through an active, well-funded industry policy to help provide incentives and other assistance for small and medium-sized businesses to grow domestically and, if possible, into exports. It had always been the pro-market, 'level playing field' economists on the right of the business community, and those running the powerful government agencies—Treasury, Finance and the Department of Prime Minister and Cabinet—who had argued down the case for such policies.

Kernot saw significant good coming from some of the structural reforms of the Australian economy introduced by Bob Hawke and Paul Keating in the 1980s. But she developed reservations about the extent and pace of some changes. She felt the government had gone too far, too fast, triggering a backlash of community disquiet. She felt Labor had not done enough to offset this destabilisation with assurances about its determination to defend equity and enhance social justice. And she felt that business was more sophisticated than the economic orthodoxy suggested—it could and would accept governments which wanted to win back more sovereignty. She envisaged a relationship in which government did not kowtow to business. She saw room for it acting to carve out firmer groundrules for itself—a role that included a productive partnership with industry.

An avid reader, even with the paper mountain confronting her as leader, Kernot read much socio/political analysis from Britain, Europe and the US

17

about the impact of neo-classical economic ideas. She put Paul Keating's recession the nation 'had to have' in the early 1990s in its international context. And then she saw the way the coming of the Howard Coalition government in 1996 changed nothing. Despite the recession, the dominant economic doctrine remained in the driver's seat. But, plainly, Australia's economic problems also remained. What had happened to the old idea that the return to power of conservative governments always brought renewed economic well-being? After years of market-oriented economic policies, there was an unnerving sense that massive programs of cuts to government spending, privatisation, corporate globalisation and 'downsizing'—that charming, trendy euphemism for companies sacking people—were not producing the great economic leap forward the theorists of Thatcherism postulated. Far from it. Fundamentally, Kernot worried about the way the policies of the economic right seemed to be coinciding with an erosion of the bedrock of a stable nation—its sense of community.

A babyboomer, she had fond memories of the certitude that came with living in Australia in the prosperous 1950s, the stable 1960s. She didn't look back to totally dismiss Menzian Australia as the 'Rip Van Winkle age', planting the seeds of Australia's contemporary economic problems, as Paul Keating argued so stridently. Neither did she look back on its moral rigidity as anything approaching a benchmark for society in the 21st century. But she did have a sure sense that at the end of the 1990s, Australian governments had a role in working to merge the good elements of the past with those from contemporary life. She saw a need to rebuild the sense of stability that came with traditional communities. There was too much evidence of social disintegration. Government had to build regions to take the pressure off cities and the environment. It had to encourage and develop industry, through large and small businesses. It had a responsibility to build patriotic pride. To her it was government, and not business, that had the wider interests of the country at heart; that as the instrument and essence of democracy, it was government, elected by the people, that should be the final arbiter. It was government that had the responsibility to ensure society remained fair and equitable. Government should defend the basic egalitarian ethic that had since the 19th century been one of the great civilising influences in Australia, building one of the most humane and decent societies on earth.

To her critics, particularly in the business community and the right wing business press, Kernot's messages were populist pap, economically illiterate and downright irresponsible. But over the first four years of her leadership, millions of ordinary Australians concluded they liked what they heard. Over that time, the political and bureaucratic system would get to know her too, with some of its most acute professionals impressed by her evolving skills. Members of the press gallery would develop a regard for Kernot's style and achievements. Within a few years she would establish her credentials in the public mind as a politician of integrity—perhaps her greatest achievement in an era of battered disillusionment and infectious cynicism. She would re-establish the Democrats after a period in which its powerbrokers had feared it was collapsing under the weight of incompetent leadership and voter distaste. But she took the party beyond electoral success alone. In just a few years she exorcised, possibly forever, the notion that it was nothing more than a gathering of dithering economic incompetents.

The miracle of Cheryl Kernot's rise to prominence was that after such a short period as leader of a minor party in the Senate, she had managed to generate such high regard in both the general populace and in important sections of the Australian intelligentsia. Even among her harshest critics, there was grudging respect for her political skills, her mix of toughness and sensitivity and her personal graciousness. Her admirers saw something special at work. Janine Haines, whose political demise indirectly led to the Kernot ascension, would publicly describe her as the best leader the Australian Democrats had had. Highly respected judges of politics and the national mood, such as the market rearcher Hugh Mackay and the pollster Rod Cameron, would see Kernot as one of the most impressive politicians ever produced in Australia, with the perfect mix of characteristics for the contemporary electorate. Before her controversial defection changed the equation, good judges inside both Labor *and* the Coalition looked at Cheryl Kernot and knew one thing: here was a rarity, an authentic, natural leader.

By any standards, Kernot's rise was meteoric. Only one other modern-day politician is vaguely comparable in the speed of his climb to the top. John Hewson was elected to parliament in the Sydney seat of Wentworth in 1987. He quickly became Shadow Treasurer and, amazingly, within three years was Leader of the Opposition. He was legged up into the job by a desperate Liberal Party seeking a generational leap after the decade-old war between

John Howard and Andrew Peacock had precipitated yet another election debacle, this time Peacock's narrow, second loss to Bob Hawke in 1990. Four years later, of course, the Hewson experiment was over—broken by losing the unloseable election to Keating in 1993. First elected as a senator for Queensland at the 1990 election, Kernot became leader of her party in the wake of Hewson's ignominious defeat. Though in the Senate, and not the Reps, she shared with him the promise of something very different to the ordinary run-of-the-mill politician the electorate despised.

Hewson's great gambit was to present himself as an 'anti-politician'. His pitch was that he had come in from the outside, economically educated with experience as a political apparatchik but by no means a political careerist. Beholden to no-one, Hewson argued that he would have the courage to make the big changes to Australian society that routine politicians with their factional debts, party discipline, opinion poll sensitivity and fear of startling the electoral horses could not deliver. He would make the big changes or he would get out of the business. Either way, Hewson did not care. The choice was for the people to make: meaningful change or reliance on the same old tired system. In the end, the people opted for the system but not out of love of it. At the last minute they stepped back from Hewson's untried right wing radicalism, his almost obsessive faith in markets. Although positioned well to the left of Hewson on the political spectrum, Kernot too presented herself as a kind of 'anti-politician'. But from her powerful position in the Senate the community had an opportunity to watch her in action, exercising considerable leverage. And they liked what they saw. The critical question remained however: what would happen to her appeal if ever she stepped out of the upper house and made a run for the Reps where the 'real' machinery of politics, with all its tough rules, exacting set-piece dramas and grubby compromise, is played out?

The drama of the 1993 budget fight gave Kernot her first big platform and her national status developed very quickly after it. Within eighteen months or so, private research for the two major parties was showing her to be the most popular leader in the country. With her role as a key balance of power player, her media profile never dropped away. Not only had she arrived like a shooting star but her message delivery, personal style and ideas established her credentials as a permanent fixture, someone watched in the Canberra system by everyone else. She made friends in both the ALP and the moderate wing of the Liberal party. With her out-going personality, she found herself in banter with other MPs, and even the occasional minister, about how they would love to have her in their teams.

However, behind the calm, assured public presence was a politician under a good deal of pressure in those early years as leader. Kernot had come to the job amid much back-room controversy inside the Australian Democrats. By virtue of their role in the Senate, their own constitutional framework and the nature of their constituency, the Democrats provide a significant challenge, taxing the stamina and commitment of any leader. She had to deal with enemies within, jealous of her success, resistant to her approach. Such is the challenge of leadership. But Kernot felt intensely the respon-sibility of breathing life into a party she first joined back in 1979. She felt pressures to hold onto the party's position as the major 'third force' against a rising tide of support for Green parties and candidates. She was prone to being too easily agitated by the two Greens MPs in the Senate after 1993—relatively unimpressive politicians, able, however, to exploit deep commun-ity alarm at the plight of the environment. Worryingly for Kernot, they were able to create the impression that they were the only politicians fighting the conservation cause, despite the Democrats' long-standing commitment as environmental crusaders. The Greens Kernot would show no mercy. One of her defining characteristics is the toughness with which she fights her political battles. Wronged, under attack, or perceiving something to be unfair, she proved capable of hitting back very hard indeed.

As a leader with a formidable intellect, an instinctive trust in her own judgement and an inability to suffer fools, Kernot became deeply ambitious for success. She had the capacity to generate intense loyalty from those around her—the indispensable, invisible people behind the scenes who do so much to support politicians, day in, day out. But often, super-smart, rest-lessly ambitious people who set the same high standards for others as they set themselves can take people for granted, be occasionally insensitive or ungrateful, even hurt those on whom they depend. Thus were sown the seeds of some of the personal acrimony that followed her defection. And if, coming so fast to the top, Kernot was not educated to the pressures she would begin to confront, neither was her family. She would get indignant at the intrusion of politics into her personal life, the privacy-sapping demands, the back seat that husband and daughter were forced to take, the lack of anonymity that came with overnight celebrity.

From the moment she climbed onto the stage, it is possible to see Cheryl Kernot as one of the great risk-takers of Australian politics. She would take difficult positions, even politically dangerous ones, simply because she sensed it was the right thing to do. She would take advice from those around her, her aides and confidants, but she set the bar particularly high for them. She was easily capable of rejecting their advice, heading off in another direction purely on the strength of her own instincts. But her judgement was so often vindicated, surprising those whose advice she had rejected. Her calculating capacity to sniff the political wind was all the more surprising because of her innate insecurities. Publicly she disguised well her very deep anxiety about ensuring her party did as well as possible in the 1996 election. As the personality cult of Cheryl Kernot developed she was given to irritable moments when she bemoaned the fact that she carried so much of the responsibility. Some around her advised her to relax, continue being herself in the sure knowledge that, in the absense of major catastrophes beyond her control, her polish would prevail.

In the end, her first election as leader of the Democrats was a triumph, but in its wake the next phase of Kernot's career would be beckoning, gesturing her riskily on towards as tough a choice as any politician of the modern era could expect to confront. Essentially, that choice was forced upon her by the arrival in 1996 of the first conservative government for thirteen years. John Howard and his people might have thought they were in touch with the community, but Kernot believed passionately they were not, and that genuinely radical, new ideas had to be injected into the system to restore it. For her the dilemma was how she could best get those ideas introduced. For no-one would this woman set harder tests than for herself. Certainly she would drive those around her, and to her detractors she was simply motivated by personal ambition. But to apply that word in the selfish, pejorative sense is to miss the essence of Cheryl Kernot. Even in the words of as capable a political communicator as this the notion sounds corny, but in its essence, Kernot's defining hunger is for a better country. To achieve that, she would willingly take almost any risk—casting off the organisation that succoured her; destroying long-held friendships; having no compunction about laying open to public view her private life, with some of its elements a far cry from the 'goody-two-shoes' image that had grown up around her.

But the intriguing thing is that Kernot is an optimist, a person who trusts people and believes in the ultimate victory of common sense, good will, honesty, hard work and consistency. She would have the courage to try to talk to ordinary Australians about principles. In an era when the rampant individualism of liberalism was triumphantly celebrating the defeat of collectivism, when the welfare state was being dismantled, when the ethical rationale for the public sector was being battered into submission and when the 'me-generation' babyboomer elite was moving into comfortable, self-centred middle age, Cheryl Kernot was one of the very few public figures constantly going to the barricades to press for a fairer society. She was always trying to be innovative, challenging the big orthodoxies and striving to convince vested interests that it was in their interests, as well, to look for new answers. For she argued passionately that we continue to allow unbridled individualism to dismantle the very structure of community at our peril.

2
ROOTS

Defining the influences that framed Cheryl Kernot, that gave her boldness, passion and self-belief, requires a second step backwards. It is much further back in time, to a place far removed from Canberra—to a balmy Friday night in the summer of 1938 at the St Paul's Parish Hall in Hunter Street in the northern NSW mining town of Maitland.

Mervyn Paton, an eighteen-year-old football-playing local buck with wavy, black hair and soft brown eyes, was beginning to make his way working as a clerk at Maitland City Council. At the local dance that humid evening he glanced across the hall just as a dark-haired, sixteen-year-old local girl called Zena Hunter stepped in, straight from work, in a simple black skirt and white blouse. She was a calm figure among fidgety girl-friends excitedly urging decorum on each other in nervous whispers. In the decades to come, Cheryl Kernot's gregarious father would always insist that was the instant he fell in love with the woman who would share his life, bearing him four children.

Merv Paton remembers: 'There were a few of them already dancing a jazz-waltz but us fellas were standing in the corner of the hall looking up towards the door to see what chicks came in. My mate Dickie York said: "Blimey look at her!" She was beautiful. Straight away I decided to ask her for a dance. So I did. And she said yes. And that was it. From then on, she was all I could see. All I could see.'[1]

Zena Hunter was a woman of her times. It was a simpler, cloistered time then, the pre-war years in the small country towns of the Hunter Valley, the first great heartland of Australian heavy industry. It was a time when, as the feminist writer Anne Summers described it, the experiences of women in a sexist culture were unquestioningly tied to the workload of domestic life.[2] A time when life was defined by men, on men's terms, often largely in men's interests. Zena Hunter arrived at young adulthood, however, ambivalent about her life and the assumptions about the place and role of women. Her marriage, her child-rearing and her home-making would come to obediently observe all the behavioural conventions of the time. Her family would be the centrepiece of her life and all her life she would treasure that and make no apology for it. But, in her own way, Zena would also stake out an independent tract as a woman, despite Menzian norms.

Her own childhood had been dominated by one looming shadow—the austere and reproving authority of her father. His presence subsumed Zena's mother and struck fear into her sister. At the end of her teenage years Zena would set the course for the rest of her life by confronting patriarchal repression. She took on her father when others could not. Later she demanded at least the acknowledgement of her legitimacy as an individual within her marriage. Decades before feminism changed Australia, she climbed out from under convention in a very distinctive manner. When Zena Hunter stood her ground and took on the men around her, she saw at issue not solely the repression of her gender, but the intrinsic right of human beings to be treated equally.

Though they lived but a few kilometres apart, Merv and Zena sprang from very different social backgrounds. In Maitland, heads turned at the very mention of the name James Bell Hunter. 'JB', as Zena's father was known around town, cut a dashing figure. Tallish, smartly attired and groomed, always in pressed trousers, a cigarette invariably clinging to his lips, he became something of a legend in local business, ALP politics and the greyhound racing game. In short, JB was an inveterate wheeler and dealer and a bit of a rogue to boot. He had been born in the Scottish village of Alloa, where the river Forth spears inland north-west of Edinburgh. As a seven-year-old he was brought from Victorian Britain to Australia when his Scottish parents migrated to find work in the Hunter's burgeoning mining industry.

Back in the early years of the 19th century, the Hunter Valley was first developed as a food basket for the Sydneytown colony. Colonel William Paterson reported back to Governor King about the rich country he discovered in his first official expedition there in 1801. The early explorers marvelled at massive fig trees and had to battle through luxuriant cedar stands, thick with lichens, staghorns, elkhorns and mistletoe.[3] Within weeks of King establishing a settlement at the mouth of the Hunter River, the mining of coal and felling of cedar trees was underway. Over the coming decades, gangs of convicts mined coal and lime, extracted timber and salt and began the exploitation of some 16,000 square kilometres of rich agricultural country. For years great flaxen-sheeted schooners would slowly ply their way up the Hunter River to the town of Morpeth where produce for the colonies would be loaded at the wharfside.

The next phase of the region's development came with the arrival of the steam locomotive, transforming the Newcastle coalfields into a mining powerhouse of colonial expansion. In time, the great mines would stand in the valley with the local vineyards and horse studs. The coal trade was disrupted by the First World War and although world demand for steel contracted in the 1920s, by the 1930s it was booming. Newcastle, with the BHP steelworks producing the metal far cheaper than competition in Britain, had become Australia's industrial capital. And through this great explosion of industrial life the Hunter became a magnet for migration from all over Britain, with Celtic miners drawn by the promise of a new life. In the mid-Victorian years Maitland quickly grew to be the second biggest town in NSW but was soon overtaken by Newcastle which, in 150 years, had expanded from a small prison camp into an industrial giant, exploiting its seemingly unlimited reserves of coal and seaboard location.[4]

JB Hunter's parents settled in the small town of Abermain, twenty-five kilometres north-west of Maitland where his father worked in the local mines. There JB later met and married Daisy May James. Today, little is known of Daisy's early life, although she was born in Australia and worked for a while as a nurse at Kurri Kurri Hospital before moving to Abermain. Initially, JB worked as manager of a local cooperative store in the nearby town of Weston and, active in the Shop Assistants' Union, began to form important connections in the labour movement. This was, of course, Labor heartland. In the early years JB was a settled family man but increasingly his business, and then political activity as a union man and powerbroker behind the scenes in the ALP, drew him away from home. He also became involved in the greyhound racing industry as a dog owner and bookmaker.

Zena and her older sister, Margaret ('Pebby' to the family), grew up sharing a big double bed in a roomy brick and weatherboard house in

Grafton Street, Abermain. The sisters remember it as a simple life where they made their own fun, playing marbles in the street, riding horses bareback in the paddocks, climbing trees and cooking potatoes and onions in old tins on bonfires.[5] As the girls grew, JB was doing very well financially. A canny businessman, he had a brilliant mind for figures and mathematical calculation which usually kept him ahead of other bookies in the ring on the circuit of NSW greyhound racing tracks. Ultimately, he would draw Merv and his other son-in-law, Jack, into the greyhound scene with its colourful, if somewhat dodgy, dealings and characters, years before the industry was properly regulated. Merv remembers the silver hip-flask JB carried in his back pocket on race night as he paced around the bookies' circle, doing the instant mental calculations on the odds that could mean the difference between an ordinary day and a killing. 'Whether he was working as a bookie himself or having a bet he was just brilliant on the numbers. He could outfox them.'[6]

The Hunters were regarded as one of the wealthiest families in town, living, literally, on the well-to-do side of the track on which the trains rattled through, on their way north from Sydney. Although JB was not a heavy drinker, Merv also remembers signals of recklessness: 'He had this habit of pulling out of his pocket a roll of notes that would choke a horse. He'd walk into the pub and pull it out at the bar and peel notes off. I used to say to him that one of these days he wouldn't make it back to his car.'[7]

In the post-war explosion of consumerism, the Hunter family was the first in the neighbourhood to have a refrigerator and a car. JB kept all his complex business dealings very much to himself and nobody was quite sure how much he was worth. He was, however, capable of acts of philanthropy, helping out local families who fell on particularly hard times during the Depression and supporting the young family of a mate who was tragically killed. These kindnesses he insisted be kept secret, although Zena remembers an element of local resentment of her father's entrepreneurial success. 'Some people might have thought we were a bit stuck up, I guess. We didn't have a lot of clothes but we did have some nice things.'[8]

Merv remembers JB's 'brilliant' mind: 'He could enter into a conversation with the best of them yet he was completely self-taught. He used to make it a rule to learn six new words out of the dictionary every day. If his life had taken other turns, he could have done anything.'[9]

For a while JB toyed with the idea of standing as a Labor Party candidate for parliament, particularly when he was pressured by members of the famous Evatt family living in Maitland, with whom he was familiar. But he settled for a background role, helping organise the local numbers for one political play or another, often at late night meetings in his front parlour with various trade union and party heavies. That is, when he wasn't organising the prices for the week's dog meeting around a smoke-shrouded dining table with his greyhound cronies. No-one who knew him well ever had any doubt that JB was a man of high intelligence and a natural politician, attributes members of the family, including Merv and Margaret, are sure were handed down forty years later to his grand-daughter. Says Merv: 'Cheryl is very like JB in that she's very quick, and witty at times. You ask her a question and the wheels click over instantly and she's often spot on. A lot of people from the coalfields who knew JB will tell you she's a chip off the old block.'[10]

Zena's mother, Daisy, is fondly remembered by her family as a gentle-natured, softly-spoken woman, managing a genteel household, walking the children to town on Saturday mornings for treats or to Sunday School at the local Mission Hall, organising tennis on the school ground at Abermain or picnics in the bush behind their local Presbyterian church. While Zena and Margaret could never remember JB chastising them as kids, their teenage memories are of an alarmingly bad-tempered man, reserved, undemonstrative, subject to mood swings. One night he found Margaret's knitting lying on top of his account books in the loungeroom, and in an inexplicable fit of rage, hurled hours of her handwork onto the open fire and stormed out, leaving it to burn as a horrified family looked on. JB kennelled his greyhound dogs including his favourite, the pacy bitch 'Temptress', out the back at home at Grafton Street and he lavished attention on them. He'd cook their fresh meat up in a big pot in the yard and religiously make sure they were exercised. Margaret remembers: 'It's interesting that he had photos of his dogs on the wall at home and none of his children. I sometimes think the dogs used to eat better than we did.'[11]

As was the lot of so many young women of her time, when Zena reached fifteen years of age, schooling came to an abrupt end and she went out to work as a shop assistant in the local Hustler's department store in central Maitland. There she would stay for ten years, living part of that time at home and part with an aunt who lived in Abermain. During the war JB moved his family to nearby Weston where he took over the local papershop. For many years Zena would work in the business as well as holding down her job at the haberdashery and hosiery counters at Hustler's. Still later, when she was married, she would bring her small children to Weston to help out while JB took a sulky around the backstreets making deliveries. But the relationship between father and daughter came to a head when Zena, at only twenty-two, called the old boy's bluff.

For years she had been finding it harder to cope with his gruff treatment of her mother and stern demeanour towards other people. As she entered adulthood she gradually became more and more outspoken with her father. He didn't like it. 'I told him what I thought of him, about his general lifestyle and how he talked to my mother terribly in front of people. I resented it and told him off. And then one day a traveller came into the shop at Weston and Dad was just so rude. He left him standing in the shop while he went out the back and had a shave. I upped and at 'im for that. I told him he didn't like the truth—and he didn't. I told him that wasn't how you treat people. You're kind and considerate and thoughtful. That's what you do. That's the proper way to treat people. I treat people how I find them, irrespective of what other people say about them. If they're OK to me, that's how I am to them.'[12]

In his own way JB undoubtedly loved his daughter, chiding her as a 'tomboy' with her love of the outdoors, horse riding, and athletics, where she excelled at school and in Sunday School carnivals. But as she grew, he was irritated by what he saw as her cheekiness, and when the explosion finally came this was not a man who would take upbraiding from a mere woman. Margaret remembers him as a person who was 'hard to get close to', around whom everybody else had to 'fit in': 'All his life he did exactly what he wanted to.'[13]

The upshot was that JB ordered his daughter from the family home in an almighty row, a schism that took months to make over but one that irrevocably changed the power balance in their relationship, ultimately creating a more confident young woman. Zena had made the break.

Merv Paton's father, Osborne Izat, was born in Edinburgh and emigrated from Scotland as a small boy, with his family originally settling in Sydney.

While the details are sketchy, it appears that as an adult Osborne lived for a while in the small town of Cundletown, near Taree, north of Newcastle, before meeting Elsie Shoesmith at Morpeth, the small town on the river bank near Maitland where the big schooners docked. Eventually Merv's parents settled in a tiny weatherboard house in Melbourne Street, West Maitland. There, despite their meagre finances, Osborne and Elsie set about raising eight children, including Mervyn Royden Paton, born on April 17, 1920, and his elder brother Cliff. Working on the engines for the South Maitland Railways, Osborne made a bit of a name for himself as a local rugby footballer but at the end of 1926 noticed he had developed an unusual lump in his throat. He went into Maitland Hospital for tests, after which he was sent by his doctor on the old steam train from Maitland to Sydney to see a Macquarie Street specialist. He was diagnosed with lymphatic cancer. Over the next year or so the disease was found to have spread to his stomach, and his condition began to deteriorate. He made regular train trips to Sydney for radiation treatment, collapsing during one visit on the platform at Central railway station. Osborne died in Sydney Hospital on April 13, 1927. He was only thirty-six.

Impoverished, with no breadwinner and little assistance from the State, Elsie faced herculean problems in maintaining her brood. Friends suggested she consider farming the children out until her circumstances improved. Finally, in desperation, she agreed. Within months of her husband's death, she sent two of her four daughters to her sister who lived nearby. But Merv, then only seven, and Cliffy, just over eight, went, amid a wall of tears, to live with a wealthy farming family by the name of Duck at a place called Vacy near the town of Paterson, fifteen kilometres north of Maitland.

Immediately, the kindly Duck family began tending the boys' needs— their teeth, for example, were overdue a visit to the dentist. The youngsters were warmly interwoven into their adoptive family, riding the family horse, an old gelding called 'Flipper', attending the Vacy public school, being measured up for new suits and heading off to local bush dances with the grown-ups in the farm sulky. They had to earn their keep, working around the farm, husking corn, loading it into an old dray and walking the horse into the bush to dump the husks in a hole in the ground. The boys were even promised a pony each because Flipper was old. But they desperately missed their mother, crying themselves to sleep at night. After three months they lay awake one night plotting their escape. Seventy years later, Merv's memory of the pain is still vivid: 'We were homesick. We missed Mum. We cried at night, both of us. The Duck family had their hearts in the right place but there were a couple of things we couldn't take to. They used to make us drink this bloody hot cow's milk. And Mrs Duck would give us salts for our bowels.'[14]

Whispering in the dark, the boys slowly devised an escape plan back into Maitland. Cliffy came up with the idea of using the milkman as their ticket to freedom. They knew what time Alf Watson came each day and they knew his route. Their chores included humping the big tin milk cans down to the little roadhouse outside the gate where Alf would unload fresh milk off the tail-gate of his truck each day, retrieving the empty cans for the dairy. The next day the boys timed it so that once the delivery was made, just as they waved Alf off, bold as brass they jumped aboard, clambering up to hide down low under the flat-top's canopy among the empty cans, just behind the driver's cabin. When the truck got back into East Maitland heading into the milk depot to unload, the boys picked the moment to jump out. They then walked the railway line into Maitland High Street, headed across the familiar local park and on up to home. In their mother's arms the three cried and cried. When they told her their story she reassured them they would never be forced to go away again. The next day the Ducks came in their horse and sulky but Elsie was resolute. She would keep the boys, insisting somehow they would survive.

'We all knew from then, the whole family knew, that everybody had to do their share. We had to do something. All of us went out and got work. We got some work milk carting, delivering ice before school. I used to go round on the ice truck, chopping it up for delivery. Whatever was offering, we'd do it.'[15] For sorting and delivering vegetables at the big local markets like Kennedy and Sons, the Paton boys got paid in kind, with leftover bags of produce. Down at McLaughlin's bakery they cleaned the floor and greased the tins for which they got bread which their mother cooked up into a milk pudding. As the Depression deepened, the family was, of course, not alone in its destitution. The kids from various impoverished families would meet up on the bridge near Maitland railway station and empty all their bags. If one had been paid with a bag of carrots and another beetroot or turnips, they'd swap or barter. Thus were fed families in the neighbourhood, month in month out. Merv's older sister, Rita, also remembers the tough times: 'We struggled but you know, we kids were never hungry. My mother used to say she felt like asking the baker to back his wagon into the doorway of the house and just tip it all out.'[16]

As a young teenager Merv longed to be shot of school, despite the best efforts of his teachers at St Ethel's in Maitland. Deprivation had seared him, forging ambition to find income for his family. Jobs came and went in places like the local foundry and on the buses but being short and slight, he found it hard to get the better paying jobs which required stouter types. Then a vacancy came up for a junior clerk at Maitland City Council.

Some 140 local youngsters applied but Merv spent several nights sitting at home with his mother as the other children slept, concocting as clever an application as they could pen. The fancy words must have made some kind of impact for soon word came that he should attend a job interview. As he headed off that morning in a patched, hand-me-down set of breeches, Merv was full of high hopes but returned down-hearted at what he saw as the quality of the others boys sitting in the council offices, waiting their turn for an interview. But then came a letter telling him he'd won his way into the last twenty-five applicants. And then another arrived with the seemingly miraculous news that there were three final candidates for the last round of interviews and he was one. Merv had to attend the council chambers for an interview with the Mayor of Maitland, the Town Clerk and another councillor. Elsie had found the money to get him into new clothes but when he realised the two other candidates had well-placed local family connections, the boy didn't fancy his chances.

In the big interview Merv thought he had gone well but as the weeks dragged on following it, he grew impatient. He would head down to the council office and climb up on the steel boot rail to see in to the office of the chief cashier.

'Any news today, Mr Ireland?' he'd ask.

'Oh, not you again, Merv,' would come the reply. 'It won't be long, son. You'll hear soon.'

When the boy's irrepressibility became too much for him, one day Glen Ireland, with whom Merv would later work for years, told him to wait while he disappeared off into the council building. Returning, Glen said a letter was in the mail, and not to say anything until he received it but that it probably contained some good news. The boy ran all the way home, bursting in to tell his stunned mother that he had won a job that would bring the family its first sustained income since his father died—one pound and seven shillings a week.

'And do you know,' Merv recalls, 'the first day I started work—on November 16, 1934—when it came to knock-off time at five o'clock, I walked out of the offices and Glen Ireland came out of another door and came up and shook my hand. He said: "You made it, son."'[17]

Merv Paton would work for Maitland City Council for forty-five years, shifting only once after two years from the general financial side into the management of the council's Electricity Supply Department. In brand new offices built at the top end of Maitland High Street, he witnessed over many years the program of amalgamation of the individual Hunter region county councils (Maitland, Cessnock and Singleton) into the one body. For this mega electricity supply and distribution agency, Merv would eventually become the manager of the stores and head of purchasing, overseeing a massive budget and, along the way, acquiring an encyclopaedic knowledge of the electricity industry.

Dancing with this young man that Friday evening in the Parish Hall, Zena remembers she was amused, but not instantly knocked over by his charm. But with an elegant neck and shining brown hair in a pageboy cut, her self-possession enthralled Merv. In time his persistence would pay off as she got to appreciate his conviviality, his basic good cheer. But persistent he had to be. Being so completely smitten helped overcome his basic inferiority complex about their relative social stations. Here, after all, was the daughter of JB Hunter of Abermain! And he, very much from the wrong side of the tracks, living with his mother and seven siblings in a house far too small. The night they met, Merv was actually 'going' with another girl who worked at Hustler's, but after he walked Zena home that night he resolved to break off the other friendship first thing Monday morning. But then the problem—how could he get to see his new love?

It was around twenty-five kilometres from Maitland out to Abermain but Merv was determined to get the money together for the forty-minute run by bus, if only to stand by a light pole down the street waiting to catch a glimpse of the girl. Later they would communicate by leaving notes in the grass at the base of the pole. Merv remembers he got to know all the bus drivers and conductors and it helped that he was a local rugby player. 'When I was broke sometimes we'd come to arrangements. I played football with a couple of the conductors and they'd say: "How's the pocket tonight, Merv?" and I'd say: "I'm broke, mate", and they'd give me a ticket and say hold it and give it back to me when you get off. I'd be right if the conductor came along and when I got off I'd shake hands with him and slip the ticket back into his hands. People thought about you in those days. They knew you wanted to go out to see your girl but you were broke so they looked after you.'[18]

When they began courting, Merv talked enthusiastically about his then four-year-old job at the council and the many characters who worked there. And about his dreams. He was already a popular young fellow around town. He always seemed happy and light. It was essentially his natural disposition but, particularly when he was with Zena, that's how he felt. Soon the love was reciprocated. Something of a certain emotional detachment was the inevitable bequest of Zena's background, but Merv saw early on that here was a dignified young woman with an unusually developed thoughtfulness for others, a sense of duty, a respect for convention and strong assumptions about how the affairs of the world—and a family—should be ordered. A knock-about young man, he also appreciated her easiness in male company and her capacity for blunt speaking. But Merv suffered twinges of reluctance about taking Zena home to visit his family. He felt keenly the blight of the circumstances he was working so hard to overcome. But as the relationship became more serious, Zena insisted on meeting his mother. Despite her reserve, she had a deep compassion and believed almost obsessively that everyone in life should be treated equally. This would become a basic principle in the life of the Paton family.

In her reaction as a young woman to an environment far less privileged than the one she took for granted, Merv discovered his greatest insight into his wife-to-be. In his home on that first visit, Zena was as easy, as natural, as happy as he had ever seen her. His family's circumstances made not a jot of difference to her. 'She knew our family was poor and, of course, she was JB's daughter and they had money all the way through the Depression. From the start she struck me as a clean-living girl but she was also so thoughtful. Now, my Mum and I were very close—very close—and that first time Zena came home to meet Mum I walked her back to the bus and when I came back, Mum simply said: "Merv, that is a wonderful girl."'[19]

When the war came, Merv enlisted and the romance seemed doomed to be interrupted by service abroad. The military, however, recognised that the skills Merv had acquired helping run a big operation like the county council were not to be set aside for combat duty. He was posted to bases around Australia working not with armaments and training but on the administration of the war effort. This allowed the lovers to get together when he was on leave and soon they were thinking about marriage. On leave one day, Merv summoned the courage to raise the idea with JB but he was given short shrift. During a talk in the sergeants' mess one day, Merv had first heard of the Army scheme where five shillings of the weekly pay rate was deducted and put away for the wives of serving men. He raised this with JB, pointing out that it would be a nice little nest egg for them to start building a life after the war. In typical syle, JB bluntly told Merv to forget the marriage idea.

'I'm not interested in you marrying her,' he said. 'You'll never be able to afford to keep her. Look, you could get posted away overseas tomorrow, get killed and leave her a widow. Anyway, you won't be able to afford her lifestyle.'

Diffident in the shadow of the great man he might be, but that conversation left a huge impression on the young man. 'When he said that to me, I said to myself, "I don't know so much about that." I said to myself that as long as I live one day I'll prove to him that I can do it. And when he finally did say I could marry her, I thought to myself: "Well now, my friend, I'll bloody-well show you." '[20]

Soon after the war ended, JB could resist Merv no longer. But the old man's treatment of him had not only buttressed Merv's determination to succeed financially, he would also show JB that Zena would be treated 'like a lady'. 'After we were married, you know, Zena was offered jobs but I just could not let her work. I said she will never work whilstever I'm capable of working. It was probably the wrong thing but I wanted to show JB more than anybody that after what he said, I'd prove to him that I could do it. I did what I was prepared to do.'[21]

Zena Hunter walked down the aisle of the Methodist Church in West Maitland to marry Mervyn Paton on September 14, 1946. She wore a white angel-skin lace wedding dress with a long, broad train gathered on a low waist-line. Her long tulle veil was arranged with a trail of orange blossoms onto a halo of lace and she carried camellias, sweet peas, stock and carnations. But true to form, the hand of JB was everywhere. He organised the reception where he decided it should be—at the local Hotel Denman in Abermain, run by his mates. From there the groom and his bride were taken to Maitland station for the long train trip north to Coolangatta in Queensland for their honeymoon.

A year after his return from military service and now married, Merv had settled fully back into his job at the council. Determined to make a go of life, he worked tirelessly. On weekends, he travelled with JB to the dogs, on the provincial circuit and down to Harold Park in Sydney where he would 'pencil' or 'hold the bag' while JB kept book. Even without formal training, Merv's knowledge of the electricity equipment industry developed apace. Every travelling salesman would have to seek out the Purchasing Control Officer to demonstrate this new transformer or that electricity mains unit. Scrupulous about financial management, Merv at times obsessively made it his business to know everything he could about the workmen and their needs. He was answerable to the Chief Engineer on materials and to the County Clerk direct on the finances. He loved the work and he revelled in the company of his work colleagues. By the time his career was scaling down, Merv had made it to senior manager, but he was the reliable face the local farmers sought out with their problems. Around town he was known for his happy-go-lucky demeanour, whistling everywhere he went with a familiar smile. He was affectionately known as the 'Mayor of Maitland'.

Merv remembers those as hard years … 'But I don't regret any part of it. It was a great place to work. It was like a family where everyone knew everyone—you'd have picnics together and nights out. I really enjoyed seeing the young apprentices coming through—at first so shy and frightened they could hardly talk. But they'd come out some of the best tradesmen you'd ever meet. We had really dedicated men teaching them. We had one engineer who gave up his nights if any apprentice wasn't able to keep up. Upstairs in the council chambers they'd give them night lessons to get them right. No-one ever failed.'[22]

For the first two months of marriage Merv and Zena lived at Abermain and then they took a room boarding with a widow in Maitland. Then, at work Merv learned that one of the electrical mechanics had been diagnosed with cancer, was given only six months to live and was trying to sell a house at number 15 Hunter Street, East Maitland. When Merv approached him the mechanic said the diagnosis was in error, that he was going to prove the doctor wrong, but that he had to clear up his financial affairs, just in case. He wanted one thousand pounds for the house. Merv hoped JB would come to the party, helping the couple to avoid costly bank repayments. But the old man said no, arguing he didn't believe in family members borrowing money. He suggested they try another wealthy local businessman. That businesman asked why he should bail them out when Zena's own father would not. In the end the couple borrowed the money through the Starr-Bowkett building society. With the basic wage at four pounds four shillings and eight pence, it would take them twenty-two years to repay the £880 they borrowed.

Even though it needed some work, the Hunter Street house turned out to be a very good investment and a perfect start for a young family. Merv asked an architect friend to look at the house and his report confirmed the wisdom of the buy. With its sunny verandah across the front and corrugated roof, the house was a combination of timber and brick, very much in the typical Federation style of backstreet suburbs in the booming country towns of that part of NSW. The architect found virtually the entire roof structure with its main bearers and panelled walls was made of solid tallowwood, probably milled at Wingham, near Taree.

Initially Zena had been concerned the location was a bit far out of town, but quickly she realised it was handy to local shops, for the bus and the Victoria Street train station, all within walking distance. But with a steep mortgage, it meant hard work for the young couple from the outset. The internal walls were painted with kalsomine, the light-colored wash made of whiting, glue and water. Although soon pregnant with her first child, Zena set about the back-breaking task of cutting back the timber walls for repainting and scrubbing the floorboards with sandsoap. Merv made basic furniture from cast-off wooden boxes, dropped off from the council by passing work crews. He knocked shelves into the boxes, Zena put on a coat of paint and a lace fringe decoration and a cupboard was born. Zena had no elaborate household appliances to speak of, washing for example in a big old copper with a wringer and cribbing board over the tub. Merv decided he wanted to buy her a proper washing machine so he enlisted a mate's help and together they would get up at 3.30 am and head up into the mountains at the back of Gresford on the Paterson River, twenty-five kilometres north of

Maitland where they used ferrets to catch rabbits. With a haul of thirty or forty a morning, they'd clean the rabbits, wash them, wrap them in a bedsheet and then sell them in town for sixpence each. In time, Merv was able to present his wife with a Hotpoint agitator washing machine.

The Patons would have four children—three girls, Cheryl, Gail and Jill, and a boy, Craig. Over the years, Merv worked incalculable overtime at the Council. The job was such a seamless part of his life, he would often be woken at night by crews calling him in to open the stores for linesmen working to fix some electrical emergency. But to make ends meet Merv also got a second full-time job, initially just two nights a week but very soon each evening and weekends too, as the manager of the Princess movie theatre in East Maitland. It would, of course, be a bonus for the young Paton family—free tickets to the movies on weekends—but it drew Merv even further away from his family in the early years. As their four children grew, the domestic burden fell, typically, on the house-bound female, Zena.

3

ZENA AND MERV

Cheryl Paton was born on a frightfully hot December 5, 1948, in Maitland Hospital, not far from where the Hunter River courses in a looping arc through the northern precincts of the town. Within a day or so, ecstatically happy, Zena and Merv sat gazing upon the new baby out in the cool of the wide maternity ward verandah with its view of north Maitland and the Belmore Bridge across to the town of Lorn on the northern bank of the river. A joyous Merv had rung JB with the news.

'I've got a daughter!' he yelled. 'She weighs five pounds, two ounces!'

'God,' said JB, 'I've killed and skinned bigger bloody rabbits than that!'

Though her personality would be a far cry from her grandfather's sometimes brutish insensitivity, through the baby's veins coursed the same instinctively political bloodline. To that would be added key ingredients from her parents: from Zena, a firm sense of the importance of fairness in matters human; from her father, loquaciousness, a sureness of intellectual footing and a sense that one could prosper through gregarious rapport with people.

From the first the young Cheryl evinced a vigorous intelligence. At home in Hunter Street while she did housework or made baby clothes, Zena would put her out in the sun on the front verandah, in a bouncer strung from the roof or on a rug in her playpen where she could watch the comings and goings around the neighbourhood. Zena knitted her a jumper from various bits and pieces of wool left over from other garments, all coming together in layered multi-colours. By eighteen months of age, sitting on her mother's lap on the lounge, Cheryl would run her finger up each of the layers of her jumper, naming each colour as she went. At two she could engage adults in surprisingly sophisticated conversation. No babytalk, as Zena recalls.

'Cheryl was clever. She could put words together very well, like her father. Merv will say it in a hundred words, I'll say it in ten.'[1]

As a toddler, Merv says, Cheryl was unusually attentive. 'When Zena and I were talking to each other, Cheryl would be focused on us. She may not be understanding what we were saying but she was watching all the time. Later she would be endlessly asking questions. "What's this, Dad? What's that for, Dad?" She'd never stop.'[2]

Ever blunt, with an inclination to self-deprecation wrought by overbearing paternalism, Zena acknowledges her relationship with her father spawned her own determination to create a home full of love. Yet freed of one master, she was confronted with the sheer grind of marriage, mortgage, one child, then two, and yet more during tough, hard-working years. She set high standards and, as was the lot of women in the early 1950s, had precious little material help. Toil became the new master. As a baby, Cheryl was brought into a home where the furniture included adapted fruit crates. The thrill of fatherhood deepened Merv's passion for success, steeling his willingness to work beyond just a desire to prove his father-in-law wrong. By the time the Patons' second child—a daughter, Gail—was born, almost two years to the day after Cheryl, life had settled into a pattern. Merv became established at work and in the Maitland community, and Zena managed the children, saving the pennies to buy material for clothes, shoes for the kids, small luxuries, paint or curtains for the house. From the start, though, Zena was never a woman who just went along with the life she was handed. She had staked out her ground even before her marriage. In a rehearsal of the wedding ceremony, long before it became fashionable to object, she baulked at the wording of the vows in the service which talked of her 'obeying' him. 'I want that part cut out,' she said abruptly. 'Cut out that obey part, I want none of that in it. Why can't we use a word like "cherish" instead?'

Once married Zena was inclined to make clear just how big a part of their family life depended on her efforts, in partnership with Merv. 'In those days it used to annoy me when people would say to me: "Oh, Zena, Merv works so hard!" And I used to say: "I work damn hard too!" '[3]

It was a sentiment that rang loud in the ears of the young Cheryl. Memories of her mother's struggle would influence her all her life—as a woman, mother and then as career politician. She would often ponder the workload of women of this generation, how it affected their lives and minds. And how the expectations and assumptions of the next generation—the babyboomers—were so utterly different. 'My mother had a strong sense of self and the expectation of some kind of justice and equal treatment in relationships. It really wasn't any kind of big feminist thing. In those days it was simply a person saying: "I'm a person of worth and I'm doing all this and this is valuable. And therefore it is not going to be undervalued. I am making a contribution." '[4]

15 Hunter Street offered a joyful homelife for the young country kids in the 1950s. It was a safe time when they could play together around the house, in the backyard, or with other children in the street or nearby paddocks. The house was plain and big but typical of the country towns of the mining region, with a high pitched iron roof, a verandah across the front supported by brick columns and inside, a hallway right up the middle. The kids' bedroom was at the front, its timber-framed window a vantage point on the world outside. With three beds and two wardrobes, it was a bit of a squash in the girls' room, easier to jump over the beds than squeeze around, but it was a place of great fun.

Gail remembers the games she and Cheryl would play in that room with their little sister Jill, taking turns to write letters on paper stretched out on each other's backs. Cheryl's bed was near the light switch and there were tussles over its management: 'All the time Cheryl would be reading at night and we would whinge and whinge. She wanted to learn about everything in the world and we wanted to sleep. Cheryl wanted to control that light switch … and she did. It's an example of that trait coming out, her determination. If she wanted to read, she would read, and if Jill and I didn't want the light on but wanted to go to sleep we'd have to call for Mum. She was just the big sister.'[5] Eventually that problem was solved when Merv and Zena had an extra room built on the back of the house, providing that little bit of extra space for play and reading.

In his spare moments, Merv set about planting a concrete-edged garden along the fence in the backyard just beyond the long clothes line with its long forked wooden stake that lifted the washing high and up into the face of the summer breezes. He provided vegetables for the table and bought newborn chicks that grew into nice, plump chickens and turkeys at Christmas and Easter. A big mulberry tree grew in the garden but the kids had to walk in through the chook yard, carefully avoiding the moody rooster, to climb up onto it to pick their fruit treats every afternoon. Zena would drag the kids in to clean their purple-stained fingers, faces and clothes. Merv taught the girls great games, like tying a long piece of string to an old handbag of their mum's. They would head down the road to a nearby paddock and lay down in the long grass with the string extending unseen, through the brush, to the bag lying in the middle of the road. A car would pull up and a neighbour climb out, only to have the bag plucked away out of reach by two young girls who were then up and running, laughing at their boldness, all the way home.

It was a luxury-free life but there was always plenty of good food, like hot home-made apple pies in the oven when the girls came in from school at East Maitland Primary, fifteen minutes away by bus. These were the days when the man in the grocery shop down the road would deliver, when the baker dropped off bread and the milkman ran up with tinkling bottles and a 'cheerio' to a young Cheryl playing on the front verandah. Gail remembers: 'We didn't have a lot of money and we didn't know we didn't have a lot of money. Maybe we also didn't look like we had a lot of money but we felt good about ourselves. We had other things that money couldn't buy. You made your fun, you didn't need to buy it and fun came from home.'[6]

In an interview in 1997, Cheryl remembers coming in from school in the afternoon, the big, hot, square loaves of white bread, sawn up by Mum and layered with vegemite. 'Or she would have made cookies or rock cakes or coconut biscuits and that was a time all the girls would gather round and talk about what we had done at school that day.'

Zena was a firm mother, with very strict ideas about the management of the home and the behaviour of children. Early on, she and Merv decided he could not do the day-to-day disciplining for fear he'd use too heavy a hand. In truth, he was a soft-touch for his adored girls. They charmed him and quickly learned that if they waited, then went back to ask again, he'd give way. House-bound with the great bulk of the child care, Zena became the disciplinarian and on occasions brought a big, wooden kitchen spoon into play. Sometimes, only stern measures would get the message home. One day when the girls were in their early teens and ignored her instructions to keep their room tidy, they came along Hunter Street from school to spy a little pile of their clothes, books and other possessions tipped out onto the front path, not far from where the boys from the school across the way lined up for their afternoon buses. The girls ducked back around the corner and waited there until the boys' buses had pulled away. Their protests rang long into the afternoon—particularly about the bras in the pile—but for months after the room was kept neat and tidy.

Zena was also reluctant in her attitude to drinking and not a lot of alcohol was ever consumed at home, Merv basically reserving the odd tipple for the company of his mates. A stickler for cleanliness, Zena insisted that fun and relaxation came after the chores. The girls were taught the importance of presentation with clean shoes and immaculate, starched tunics for school. The house was always orderly and Zena managed the budget diligently. In a bathroom cupboard she kept her savings jars, one labelled for the electricity bill, another for rates, one for bus fares and yet another, with a few shillings going in when possible, for the end-of-year holiday. In all those years, Cheryl never recalls going without the essentials.

The auditors of the Council books, a firm called Short and Ryvy, had a high regard for Merv's work and integrity. One of the partners of the firm happened to own a number of local picture theatres in the Hunter and mentioned one day he was looking for someone to manage one down in Melbourne Street, East Maitland—the Princess. It was early 1954 and Zena was now pregnant with Jill. Merv got the job. Within no time he had the Princess ticking over but it became demanding, working there six nights a week and on Saturdays. But he was also needed in the early years to help JB at the dogs and after Zena's folks moved over to the Weston papershop, he often found he was called into action there, too.

Cheryl's childhood was one cushioned by an extended family where there were responsibilities as well as rights. Everyone pitched in. The girls never knew Merv's parents, his mother having died just before Cheryl was born, but they were close to their paternal grandmother, and, as the edge of their grandfather's venality was frayed by advancing age, JB developed a particular softspot for Gail, his 'blossom'. As he grew older, Cheryl remembers her grandfather as an impressively competent and intelligent man, but with an encroaching, barking cough, the legacy of years of smoking. As he got older the cough would irritate the household, cutting through the still of the night. In later life, JB was often ill and Merv had to step in. He remembers days when he'd start at the council at 9 am, dash home at 5 pm where Zena would have dinner waiting for him, only to have to change clothes and be in Maitland to open the Princess Theatre, finishing there at 11.30. Then he was out of bed and driving over to Weston at 3.30 am to undo the just-arrived newspapers, put them through the plastic wrapping machine JB had bought in Sydney to protect them from the elements, and then load the utility truck for a dawn delivery run.

Zena would often be at the shop too, serving with the young children playing in the flat out back. Or on some weekends she would walk Cheryl and Gail down to the Victoria Street Station and put them on the old steam train that rumbled through the green, flat countryside out to Weston. There they'd be met by their Nanna on the platform of the little country station a couple of hundred metres down a backstreet from the family papershop on the corner of the main road. The girls grew so familiar with the rail trip out to Weston they knew every stop and farm and to this day Cheryl can still hear the soothing 'clickety-clack' of the rails, lulling her as she sat with Gail, reading a book or daydreaming about the fun to come. There was the routine trip to the local fish-and-chips shop with Nanna. And before she put them back on the train home, there would be a shilling for a Violet Crumble bar. But there was also work to do behind the counter, and Cheryl loved it. She recalls: 'Serving in the shop was great and I particularly loved the lottery ticket sales. You had to order them for the customers and tear the edges apart, look up the ticket, write the person's name on it and put it in alphabetical order in this little card index. The person would come and ask if it was in and we'd have to find it. I used to think that was the high point of my intellectual existence.'

Not long after JB moved to Weston, Cheryl—probably eight or nine years of age—climbed onto a big old carved armchair in the flat at the back of the shop to peer out the window across the main road to the hotel opposite: a big, sprawling building with blue and white tiled outer walls and a huge overhanging wrought iron verandah. A drunk staggered out of the pub and, reaching for the lamppost to steady himself, vomited onto the pavement. The young girl reeled back, horror-struck. In time she would develop something of a phobia about that place over the road with its sad-looking people coming and going amid explosions of raucous argument and fighting. As an adult she would remember the graphic sense of insecurity invoked by the noise and sharp images of staggering men: 'The hotel was quite an imposing building but I used to see so many drunks, it really distressed me. I think I developed a bit of a phobia about crossing the path of drunk men. It scared me, I think. It was actually seeing people staggering, not in control. I think it affected my attitude in that it left me hardly ever indulging in anything to the point where I'm not in control. I couldn't comprehend that someone would do something to themselves that would warp their sense of reality. I wanted to know why people would do that to themselves.'

There was no such alarm across East Maitland at the Princess Theatre. There the Paton kids could even strut a bit—after all, their Dad ran the place! Merv occasionally lent a stern word if he detected any undue weight being thrown around with the other kids. Cheryl and Gail just adored the privilege of going to the pictures on Saturday afternoons, a ritual that first set in place an adult's absolute adoration of movies, particularly foreign ones. When they first saw the Disney classic *Snow White,* the girls walked home, singing 'hi-ho, hi-ho' all the way. As often as not though, the high-light of the day was not so much the movie as the ice creams served in the theatre, called 'Buffalo Snows'. Zena worked till late at night making the kids' clothes, especially party dresses, and they would go off to the pictures turned out immaculately, the best presented kids at the theatre. Gail remembers always 'feeling nice': 'We used to go and stand in front of Mum's big round mirror in her room in the new dress she was making and we'd think we were princesses. I don't know how she did it all. At the time with all her sewing we didn't take much notice. It was just part of our life. Mum would buy this beautiful material to make our party dress for the year. We used to try on these dresses and they'd have a double sash and we'd skip down the street hoping the neighbours would come out and look at us. We'd walk so proudly to church. When Cheryl was chosen to speak at church she looked wonderful.'[7]

With Merv away so much, Zena would let down her hair with the kids on Friday nights. With the work done in the house and in the schoolbooks, there would be time for music, singing, and sometimes a bit of mayhem, some horse-play. In the gentility of her own childhood Zena had learned the piano and she and Merv saved up to buy one. Of an evening she and the girls would sit around, singing. Cheryl still remembers the unifying effect it had on them all. There would be pillow fights when the rules of the game of the night collapsed, much merriment and occasionally a disaster out of the frenzy. Zena was always proud of her athletic youth. In sports, she was a natural. For years Merv dropped Cheryl and Gail off at the pool in the middle of Maitland Park later named after a great local son, Les Darcy. There, they would swim their laps and Gail, who obviously inherited her mother's athletic prowess, showed enough promise to suggest she could go a long way in the sport. At Sunday School picnics Zena would explain to Cheryl how best to hold and move her legs, which helped her win the sack-race. One evening in the backyard, the kids were showing off doing hand stands and they teased that 'old' Mum couldn't do it. Zena took the bait but as she climbed onto her hands and leaned against the wall she nudged a big panelled glass door that Merv had taken off the front of the house. It crashed to the ground, shattering. Dad was not impressed.

Two of Cheryl's clearest recollections of her childhood relate to each of her parents. One day Zena happened to be in Maitland when she noticed two aged sisters who lived a few doors away having some difficulty negotiating their shopping bags onto the bus home. That afternoon Zena walked the hundred metres or so up Hunter Street for a visit. The Marchant sisters' home on the corner of Hunter and High Streets was much larger and grander than many of the others in the East Maitland backstreets with their narrow corridors of bitumen roadway, bubbling in the summer sun and bordered on either side by baked red gravel. With its big L-shaped verandah and elaborate decorative timber facing, the Marchants' house was a Federation-style treasure with high corrugated roof. But inside was the real wonderland, a treasure trove of antiques. There was a library of bound leather books, and paintings depicting another world—England—which hung from dark-wood picture rails under high ceilings with fleur-de-lis cornices.

Cheryl and Gail were heading into their early teens and life for the family was more economically secure. Zena had acquired her driving licence and used the car every Thursday to get into town to shop and pay bills. She barely knew the Marchant sisters and was conscious of not giving offence with her approach but she sensed a real need. She politely suggested she and the girls might be of help, say, once a fortnight with their shopping needs. The old ladies were instantly grateful. Later Zena told Cheryl and Gail of their new task. Every other week they were to go up to the Marchant house straight after school, get a grocery list and bring it home for Zena to include in her own shopping. When Zena returned she would make out a full account of the Marchants' buys and then send the girls up to their house with a box of goods and their bill.

The ritual and the hour or so chatting to the old ladies and hearing snatches of the history of a one-time, well-to-do Maitland family was an exotic new experience. The dark and musty house and its fading contents had once been so grand and as the sisters fumbled with their purse for payment, Cheryl wondered about the process of growing quietly, slowly infirm. Occasionally, when the old ladies disappeared to pour the regulation glass of home-made lemonade on the hotter afternoons, Cheryl would browse the big parlour with its yellowing lamp shades, heavy velveteen curtains over high French windows, books and paintings. Sometimes Zena would send up a rice pudding and Cheryl would take it into the kitchen, glancing through to the laundry with its clothes stand festooned with big old-fashioned drawers. Then one of the sisters would lead the girls to the backyard to pick passionfruit from the garden vines for the Patons. Walking home, Cheryl and Gail would talk about it all—the two sisters' lives and their stories; their shopping choices; the way people age; of loneliness and death. They wondered if one day they would live together—old sisters, alone in a big, shambling house. They agreed they probably would not.

Cheryl remembers how over the years the two ladies became so frail, their handwriting on the grocery notes becoming more and more spidery, until at some point, she knows not when, the trips across High Street ceased. What lived on, though, were the notions that first motivated Zena, underpinning the fortnightly chore. Here were two elderly people living in some need, in a local community at a time when the simple act of spontaneously being considerate was viewed as neither a distracting imposition nor a demeaning piece of charity. But if Zena provided Cheryl with a moral underpinning, Merv gave her the bridge to the outside world.

Stark in her memory are the trips she would take with her Dad by foot down the main street of Maitland on afternoons after school, walking from the council building to the post office. First laid out by the early settlers back in 1823, the town centre reflected the wealth and drive of Maitland from its early glory years when it threatened for a while to take over from Sydney as the engine of the colony. In a time before the world became one big shopping mall, the town's grand, post-colonial buildings were hives of commerce and community life. Merv and his daughter would saunter past the old courthouse built in 1895, the ANZ building in High Street, the Church of St Mary the Virgin, begun in 1860, and St Peter's Anglican Church in William Street—all magnificent achievements in 19th century architecture and town planning. He would enchant Cheryl with stories of how the post office, with its arcade and bell-tower clock, was first opened back in 1829, receiving the mail sent, first by ship, and then overland by horse, from Newcastle. Where Zena was formal and rigorous, Merv was of more exuberant temper, a cheerful character with his perennial whistling and convivial 'G'day'. A man content with life. Cheryl adored his vitality.

Resplendent in their blazers, ties and tunics with box pleats, Cheryl and Gail would catch the train down at Victoria Street station to travel in to Maitland Girls High School, a cluster of buildings around modest gardens in the centre of town. Cheryl would leave school at 3.30 and slowly wind her way uptown to meet Merv on those days when he finished early at the council. Sometimes she would walk through the council building, the odd 'hello, Cheryl' resonating around her from Merv's workmates. There was familiarity here, warmth. A network of care and interest. There was also a sense of one's place, a belonging. If it's true she was born with politics in her, then Cheryl was introduced to the potency of it by her father's jocundity on Maitland High Street. In his own way, Merv was a politician, a trawling proselytiser of good cheer. A social being. But, given his position at the council and his reputation in the community as a source of information and problem solver, there were subtle political layers to the greetings that engaged him every few yards as he walked Cheryl and Gail down the street. The knowledge and contacts that came with his position, but his alacrity also helped make him such a popular figure.

Young Cheryl would complain that the walk would always take *forever*. They'd get down to the post office and she'd be thinking they then had to walk all the way back. People seemed to endlessly stop and mag with Merv. But the whole process had important, if subtle, effects on the girl. Unconsciously she was alive to the rhythms of the community, the power interplay between people, the political forces at work in the points being pressed in the chat. She was learning that success comes to those who are outgoing, confident, jocular and not afraid to give of themselves. When she was older and the modern world had become a very different place, she rued the death of unselfconscious, unrushed civility: 'Today, I often notice when I walk along the beach that people of my parents' generation and a bit younger engage in eye contact and say good morning to you. But it's a rarity. Most people just stick their heads under their hats and don't even look at you. Young people, in particular, seem oblivious. They don't want to engage in eye contact. There's something about our parents' generation that's special in their concern for other people, in my view. I don't know whether it's because they had a hard life with the Depression and the war and things. The people that Dad used to meet were genuinely interested. It wasn't shallow. There was an element of the ritual—"How are you?"—and all that. But beneath the ritual, I reckon there was a genuine interest. Genuine human contact. I guess the pace of life was different.'

Church also helped develop the Paton children's sense of community. Zena and Merv were never keen churchgoers themselves but from the time Cheryl was around five they ensured all the children regularly went off to Sunday School in the hall opposite St Stephen's Presbyterian Church. The girls would leave home, heading off down the road and across a small corner paddock, skipping around the puddles after spring rain. Later Cheryl and Gail went to Presbyterian Fellowship Association every Sunday night and when she was older, Cheryl taught Sunday School herself.

When church picnics came around, Cheryl and Gail wouldn't be able to sleep the night before. Zena would make shorts for them to wear, iron in creases, whiten their sandshoes and stand them on the front verandah for photographs. Then it would be off down to church for the exciting day out in Newcastle, driven there on a double-decker bus. At a church hall in town there would be dozens of kids, eating cream buns, with big enamel teapots full of cordial drinks. It was thus a long Christian upbringing but it was a moderate Presbyterianism, without hardline doctrine or wowserism. When the children were young Zena and Merv saw church helping to round out their moral framework. Says Zena: 'I was never really religious. I guess I just thought it was the proper thing to do to make sure the children were involved.'[8]

In their later years when family tragedy would descend on them, Zena and Merv would both find some relief in quiet prayer, but bringing up their young family they were often struck by the hypocrisy of the world and reacted against those who foisted particular religious views on others. According to Merv: 'I reckon if you live correctly in life and do the right thing that you are taught by your parents, you don't have to go to church. The part that made me feel the way I do is that I know an awful lot of people who go to church and they do some awful things, some terrible things. I knew a man once who was a pillar of the local church but he was a terrible man in many ways. I would say to the family that we were as Christian as many, many people who went to church.'[9]

Merv did more than just introduce Cheryl to the pulse of community and make her wary of cant. Zena put down a bedrock sense of order, discipline, management but Merv also inspired the girls' thinking in practical ways. For example, he was a real conservationist in his work at the council and it rubbed off on Cheryl. Over the years he would get into fights when he argued that equipment at work didn't need to be replaced. It could be repaired, kept in commission. A child of the Depression, he had learned the art of making do, and renewing, rather than just throwing machinery and materials on the scrap heap only to spend big money replacing them. It offended him that he saw waste, driven by book-keeping apathy. Cheryl remembers him recycling materials. Or he would work the garden conscientiously to make it serve the family, providing food for the table and, when the crops were running, abundance for the neighbours. She calls it 'stewardship'.

'I've learnt from my parents to conserve things and not just give in to disposability. I'm just not into the disposable society. I object to things that are made to be just thrown away when there are perfectly good ways they could be made to keep going for another ten years. It's perfectly clear to me that I learnt stewardship from my parents and I think it includes things like looking after your car, your computer. It's a Christian concept where you're taking care of things. You are responsible for the care of the things that come into your life. It can be the stewardship of the earth. It means respecting the natural integrity of things. To me that can mean making the computer last as long as it can. It might be more fashionable to get a new one but you should make the one you've got last as long as you can while it will do what you need.'

And then there was cricket.

Like so many Australians, Merv and his wife adored sport. As he sat listening to the Ashes Tests on the radio, cheering on Australia's unfolding 4–0 demolition of the Poms in the home series of 1958–59, Cheryl asked her

Dad about the game. Soon she was hooked on his explanation about the traditional rivalry, the story of the Ashes urn, his evocation of the champions of the sport. As an adult, Cheryl would study for a ticket as a qualified umpire but the interest was sparked all those years before, in talking to her father, about a game she felt was intellectually engaging. 'It always seemed a game with good, sensible rules. A contest. And it had skill. And Alan McGilvray was really good at describing it as we all sat around the radio.'

But Merv also loved to talk politics at home. More than that, he had a passionate weakness for a debate. About anything. Like most loquacious people, he had firm views on lots of subjects. And he would always have his say. Later, as age brought, as it tends to do, its steady conservatisation of one's views, Merv and Cheryl would have some solid old political dust-ups, particularly when she became involved in a leftist party like the Democrats. But the grounding of her love of a competitive discussion was laid at home with her father. He recalls them still at it, even as Mum and sisters Gail and Jill were heading off to bed: 'And lots of times she would roll me, you know. She would beat me. She always listened to both sides. But she had this bloody knack, even as a kid, of picking holes in the points I was making.'[10]

Merv never lacked confidence in his intellectual abilities. But Zena, like so many other women of her generation who were denied educational opportunities, badly underestimated her own intelligence. A timidity became engrained whenever she sensed unfamiliar intellectual terrain. She would withdraw, or cut off from discussion, or too easily dismiss her own views as irrelevant. Yet she was conspicuously happy with her life as a mother not only to four children but a wider community as well. When it came to the other youngsters in the neighbourhood, once again her compassionate instincts provided benefits for her children, helping socialise them and making her daughters at ease in the company of boys. For right across the road from the house in Hunter Street was Maitland Boys High School with its big component of boarders, mainly from country families around central NSW.

Some of the local day-boys from around East Maitland would leave their bikes in the Patons' timber carport at the bottom of their long steep drive in from the street front. In the afternoon when they came over to retrieve the bikes, they would slide on their Globite school bags all the way down the concrete driveway. But some of the boarding boys also took to drifting over the road to the house, particularly on Saturdays, after they had got to know

Cheryl and Gail. Zena invited them in for afternoon tea. Once one young fellow had split his trousers and she set about mending them. Soon so many boys from the boarding school were visiting, a few questions were raised by teachers. Zena talked to the boarding housemaster and it was agreed that the situation would be explained to the youngsters' parents who then happily gave permission for them to keep visiting. The Paton house became a home away from home. Zena remembers: 'They were very nice boys, we never had any trouble. I never had to shift anything around in the house, for example. I'd just tell them not to touch this or that. They were fine. We just welcomed them and we had a good time. I got on really well with the boys and they got on well with me.'[11]

Zena was never happier than when there was a tribe of kids around the place. Others might complain about the workload of school holidays but she genuinely looked forward to them. 'I loved that time. We didn't do much but it gave me a break from cleaning tunics and blazers and making sure socks were washed.'[12]

There was also a method in her madness. With young girls and a school full of young males over the way, Zena reckoned it was better to have the children around the place, welcomed and at ease, rather than off socialising where she couldn't gently keep tabs on things. All her life, Cheryl never felt anything but comfortable in the company of males. She probably had more close friendships with males than with other women, and as an adult she valued—and worked hard to preserve—contact with a handful of men with whom she had no romantic attachment but who had been friends and confidants at various stages of her life. This easiness with males was, of course, helpful in opening up to her a world of politics overwhelmingly dominated by them.

With so many boys around at Hunter Street, there were the inevitable innocent romances for her and sister Gail. 'At home it was a very healthy environment to have relationships and friends,' Cheryl remembers. 'If you developed a bit of a kid's romantic attachment, you got a chance to see the person close-up on the weekend when they came over. I had a lot of male cousins. I never felt any gender barriers. I don't know why that is. I just got on well with boys, right from primary school.' Her first 'boyfriend', at age eleven, was a lad by the name of Iven Macleod. They were respective girls' and boys' captains at primary school and would later go on to university together. Much later Cheryl and Iven would remain mates, as part of the pattern that played out so regularly in her life. But at Hunter Street, Cheryl also developed a crush on another boy boarding at the school across the way. Phil Young would essentially become her childhood sweetheart and later take an even more prominent role in her life.

Into their teenage years, the Paton girls began going off to local dances at the school hall down the road and elsewhere in Maitland. Cheryl would decide on Saturday that not only did she want to go, but she needed a new dress! Zena would set to work making a smart floral shift, edged with frills, and would still be finishing the hem as Cheryl and Gail waltzed out the door. But there were always the rules. Cheryl had to take Gail, but once they were at the dance or party the girls could head off with their own friends. In the early years, Zena insisted they be home at ten. Then it became eleven and then midnight: 'In those days it wasn't like today where the kids don't go out till midnight. I used to say to them they had to be home at twelve; that I didn't mean five past or a minute past twelve. I meant twelve because if they didn't come home then, they wouldn't be allowed out the next Saturday night. They always came home.'[13]

And, always sitting up in bed, reading with the light on, was Zena, Merv snoring at her side. The girls would come in, in a weekly ritual, to sit at the bottom of the bed, the three magging about the boys and the food and the fun. Merv would roll a pillow over his head.

'What have you got to tell all this at night for? Can't you all talk about it in the morning?'

'Oh, shoosh up Merv,' Zena would snap. 'It's not the same in the morning.'

With a doughty strength of purpose, Zena would try to inculcate into her children the need, when the occasion arose, to take firm positions, particularly when a principle was at stake. Cheryl was at times confused by the firmness of her mother's resolve. 'She would tell my sister when she got into a fight that if anybody hit her, she was to hit them back twice as hard. So the next day somebody hit my sister and she hit her back and I got called up by the headmistress. We had to go home and tell Mum that wasn't a very good philosophy. That was one area I reckon where she gave me a bum steer. I guess everyone should be ready to speak up for themselves but I'm not sure about clocking someone.'

Cheryl Paton derived a comprehensive system of formative influences from her parents and from family life. But she would also inherit a tension between some of those influences as she grew into early adulthood. It was essentially a friction between the outgoing personality that she was in part, and the withdrawn, very private person she could also be. The grinding of these psychological plates would produce some fundamental contradictions in the woman, her actions and character. For all the great benefits of her secure background, Cheryl grew up with an underlying self-doubt. It was an obscure apprehension within her, an unsettling lack of confidence. It was the quite common phenomenon of a young person's progression from childhood. With her, though, it lay disguised and unaddressed mainly because of her self-possession, poise and aptitude at school. On the outside Cheryl always seemed so competent, so in control, for one so young. But there was a ghostly turmoil within and it would be years before it was finally exorcised.

4
DRIFTWOOD

Whenshe was still at primary school, Cheryl occasionally disappeared at home, slipping away from the other kids playing in the
backyard or in the house, to be by herself. Merv would walk out
into the yard and ask Gail if she had seen her sister, and Gail, in turn, would
point to the underhouse storage area. The Hunter Street block of land fell
away slightly at the back where the house was supported by brick pillars.
The underneath section was packed with all manner of usual family belong-
ings, boxes, garden tools, toys and a couple of old armchairs. On hot days it
was cool and airy. And there, nestled into one of the chairs, a million miles
away in the distant adventureland of a book, Merv would find his Cheryl.
So often would he and Zena see her absorbed in reading that one day while
having a quiet beer with some of the locals, including Frank Bonar the
family doctor, Merv raised it.

'Cheryl's got me a bit worried, Frank,' Merv said. 'She's always got her
head stuck in a book. She doesn't seem to be playing that much. Every time
I go looking for her, she's reading books.'

The doctor asked what was wrong with that.

'Oh, I don't suppose there's anything wrong with it. It's just that I was
wondering if I should try to get her out to play more with the kiddies, get
more exercise. Is it right that a child at this age should be so book-bound?
What's the right balance?'

The doctor told Merv not to worry, that she would work it all out herself,
that there was no 'best' way and that he should not complain—most parents
had a battle royal on their hands to get children of this age to read. In fact,
from very early on, Cheryl's fascination with books and words had been a
marvel to her parents. She would come up to them and ask about words or

sentences and their meaning, their context in the story. Zena recalls: 'She may not have known what the words meant or their spelling, but she would see a big word in a book and she'd ask me is that such and such a word? And I'd say yes, and I'd know she hadn't learned it at school. So I'd ask her how she knew and she'd just say that she knew.'[1]

In kindergarten Cheryl wrote her first word at school. With a steady little hand she put pencil to paper and slowly wrote what was clearly two words: 'the smorning'. Her teacher was astonished. What was obviously first surfacing in her early years—a titanic attraction to the mysterious interplay of language, words and writing—would come to be the great strength of Cheryl's later education. But for the people managing classes full of primary school kids at East Maitland, she came over not as any kind of prodigy but as a child, overwhelmingly, of courteous manner. From the first, she adored school. Joan Stephens taught her as a six-year-old at East Maitland Infants School in 1954. She recalls a gentle child, always eager to please: 'She was a dear little girl, well mannered, always doing her best, a joy to teach. She always had a lovely little smile on her face and never got into trouble.'[2]

Cheryl was clearly bright but, as Joan Stephens recalls, she was in a class of fairly advanced youngsters at the time. She didn't stand out as the most exceptional among them but did evince the raw confidence of the older sibling. Sometimes Joan would go out dancing with Merv and Zena and so she developed an insight into the Paton family: 'Zena had a big influence on Cheryl, and Cheryl being the oldest child had leadership qualities that sometimes the younger members of families don't always have. She was very protective of the other siblings.'[3]

Young Cheryl looked a picture in the dresses her mother made. Zena would use hot curling tongs to transform her long blonde hair into shoulder-length Mary Pickford curls. As Cheryl got older her hair was swept back and tied off at the side with distinctive bows or clips but already evident was that gentle lilting posture with her head, an inclination to drop it, almost imperceptibly, to one side in a body language statement of friendliness, openness, attention-giving. That Kernot 'look' that years later would become so familiar to the wider public—the smile and the head held softly to the side—was there, already in place, in the toddler.

Cheryl was a distinctive-looking child, quite unlike her mother in appearance with her Pharaonic poise, and with only a faint echo of the cherubic charm that spoke of her father's Celtic antecedents. The set of regulation childhood album photographs so familiar to 1950s families reveal an appealing child with diminutive mouth and high sculptured forehead. But her hazel-green eyes shine as a window on a little mind already keenly sensitised to the nuances of the world around her. Joan Stephens remembers: 'It all adds up to a pretty impressive child, really. It sounds rather boring but it's hard to think of something negative about her. She was simply a joy to teach. Although she was very young, I always thought she would become a teacher. She had this naturalness about her—she was a very natural little girl. We didn't have the resources children have in schools now—we just had the class readers—but I distinctly remember her as an avid reader. In the playground she would lead the ball games and be the leader of little groups. It sounds corny to say these days but she was a child you could always rely on, very dependable.'[4]

Clare O'Shea taught Cheryl in second class and remembers her as an 'absorbed' child. While she was not the kind of youngster who instantly grabbed one's attention, Clare says when she was asked to do something or speak, Cheryl would unfailingly acquit herself. At times she seemed rather retiring but, as she grew, it was clear leadership qualities were emerging. She could be 'very positive' in her views when she did speak up, probably reflecting the stable family environment. Recalls O'Shea: 'I can still see her sitting there, very interested in everything. She was always listening carefully to what you said. At times I'd wonder if she would tell me that so-and-so was, in fact, not right. She was a real thinker, thought about everything. You always got the impression she was working things through. She asked questions and when you asked her something she would never say yes or no without giving the subject the thought it needed.'[5]

Four years later, Joan Palmer taught Cheryl and remembers a girl with very neat schoolwork who was always well organised, confident and co-operative. 'You teach thousands of kids in your career and you can't remember them all but I remember Cheryl. She was studious, eager to please and interested in everything. As a teacher she was like your ideal pupil. She would always apply herself. In their lives, people don't really change. You never know what life has in store but basically, often what you see at ten or eleven, is how people are when they grow. In Cheryl's public life now it seems to me she is basically the same person. She wasn't pushy as a child so I couldn't really describe her as being determined. She wasn't outspoken or cheeky or anything like that. There was nothing jarring about her at all. When I look back now though, in hindsight, I think I can see the leadership abilities that were there. She was always there, keen, helpful, always volunteering to be involved in things. She was good at sport, just an all-rounder really.'[6]

As early as fourth class Cheryl loved English exercises, especially the 'spelling bees' where the class was divided into two teams which set one another words to spell. Cheryl would 'wipe them out', she recalls, but she did have some help. 'I used to always win because Mum told me to ask them how to spell "phlegm". That always got them. Initially, no-one knew how to spell it but then they got used to it. They knew I'd ask that one so I got more—a repertoire of hard words, like oxygen and hymn.' As her reputation grew as a very good student, Merv could see Cheryl's progress breeding ambition for more success: 'She began to like to be best, to be first. I can remember one of the teachers telling me how bright she was. She was always first or second. She strived to be first and as she got older she studied. Boy, she studied!'[7]

At Maitland Girls High School she became involved in the debating teams and from the start excelled in the competitive challenge, the cut and thrust. The teachers found she had an extraordinary way with words, a mature capacity to be ostensibly analysing both sides of an argument, but in fact drawing out important conclusions from both sides of the ledger to support her central claims. Merv reckons her skill basically made the school a force in regional debating competitions: 'We went to some of the debates and she was brilliant. She spoke without having to use too many notes. And she didn't "um" and "ah" like so many politicians do. She doesn't do that as a politician herself but she was always like that—she was concise and didn't rave.'[8]

Merv had a sense that Cheryl could ultimately be a politician. In that, he saw one particular personal trait that would stand her in good stead—she seemed to have sensational hearing! He recalls: 'In lots of ways Cheryl is just like her grandfather, JB. He could be talking to you like I am now and somebody over there would say something, or something would come on the wireless, and he'd interrupt what he was saying to you and say across the room "Oh, I remember that", and then resume his conversation with you.

Cheryl can hear me talking to people while she's doing work or listening to the damn TV on the other side of the room. Just like that. She can take in both conversations simultaneously and follow them both. Zena has said to me many, many times her father was just like that.'[9]

Clem Ellis taught Cheryl science as a fifteen-year-old at Maitland Girls High and remembers her as an 'absolutely outstanding' student and the top debater in the senior school. He remembers her veering away from science and maths to more favoured subjects like English, history and economics. 'She really could handle herself on her feet, talking to any group. I suspect she was helped in this by her father at home where they talked a lot about politics. But she was an exceptional girl as a student, remarkably talented. You could detect this inclination towards commonsense, rationalist views of the world—a practical approach to life. Today I see it in her public life. That's Cheryl all right. She is as she was.'[10]

As would befit Zena Hunter's daughter, practicality was firmly rooted in a sense of social justice. When she was young this sense of fair play was occasionally buffeted by the outside world. Cheryl remembers sitting in class in the very early days when some of the kids were really mucking up. The teacher walked out of the classroom briefly and the class erupted in conversation. Sitting quietly, Cheryl was asked a question by another student.

'Yes,' she answered.

The teacher walked in and demanded that every child who had spoken while she was out stand up. Cheryl stood. The result was that everybody got a smack on the hand with a ruler. Cheryl can today still remember smarting over that and thinking how unjust it was.

'I can see myself standing up and admitting I spoke but I can also remember really wanting the opportunity to tell her the circumstances. But she just smacked us with the ruler. It was the first thing I ever got into trouble about at school.'

But if Cheryl loved her school days, by the end of the 1950s her weekends were a time of unremitting joy, and something approaching an idyllic picture of childhood in Menzian Australia. In the mid-1950s Merv and Zena decided to start taking the children for brief summer holidays in rented units at Nelson Bay on the southern arm of Port Stephens on the central coast of NSW. By 1958, Merv's second job at the Princess meant they had saved enough money to buy a block of land on one of the most magnificent parts of the NSW coastline, just two-and-a-half hours drive north of Sydney and a quick forty-five minutes east of the Hunter. The partly-drowned estuary of the Karuah and Myall rivers, Port Stephens was discovered and named by James Cook in May 1770. The entrance to the harbour is flanked by two headlands, Yacaaba to the north and Tomaree to the south, with a vast 'harbour' extending twenty-five kilometres inland and divided into two near-equal parts by a long promontory—Soldiers Point—which partitions the waterway from the south. Until the Second World War, fishing—particularly of sharks and lobsters—oyster farming, mixed agricultural farming, dairying, forestry and oyster shell dredging for cement production were the main industries sustaining the Port region. After the war, tourism increasingly became the engine of progress.

When Merv walked onto the block of land for sale on a rising hill of bushland at the southern end of a beach called Fingal Bay, he knew he had found a piece of paradise. Laid out before him was a crescent of bleached beachfront snugly cut into the south side of the southern headland of the huge Port Stephens waterway. Using his old Holden ute Merv subcontracted some locals to help clear the block, then set about the year-long job of constructing a roomy fibro bungalow atop iron columns, with a flat, galvanised roof. It was a huge task and as usual Zena did her bit, even helping lay the concrete slab floor downstairs, wielding the barrow with aplomb. The house was accessed from the roadway on the upland side via a timber staircase with steel rails. The view to the north-east was a visual feast of beach, bush and headland majesty. The virgin bushland overlooked the entire reach of Fingal Bay which stretches in an arc for a couple of kilometres to where its northern arm tapers into a long sandbank leading across to a big island, the Tomaree National Park. As he worked to finish the weekender, Merv would often stop and watch in awe as the oncoming tide slowly cascaded across the long 'spit' from both sides, gradually covering the sandbank in emerald water and cutting off pedestrian access to Tomaree Island. Even in the colder months when the wind would come around, gathering as a heavy southerly and driving a churning shore-break far along the beach, the place was captivating.

From 1959 onwards the Patons began spending most weekends and all their summer breaks at 'the Bay'. Soon the children got to know other kids from among the twenty-odd other families—many local fishing people—and Cheryl, Gail, Jill and little Craig would spend long, lazy days gouging sand castles at the water's edge and splashing through the crystal waves. It was a carefree, blissful time. Merv worked every weekend, developing the building from just a shell, installing the kitchen, bathroom, panelling the bedrooms. He imported ute-loads of top soil to add richness to the sandy ground. Every few months he would quietly drive into the backbush off the beachfront, where he had found a rich natural spring, to cut small pieces of lush native buffalo grass which he brought back and laid like a steadily expanding green carpet around the house. Over the years Zena took to the garden with a passion and by the time she and Merv retired there in the early 1980s, having sold Hunter Street, the surrounds were a rich tapestry of colour and greenery—Cocos and Alexander palms, bottlebrush, hibiscus, roses, lavender, daisies, ferns, camellias and azaleas.

For years, Friday evenings in Hunter Street were a ballet of disordered excitement as, done with school and work for the weekend, everyone pitched in to pack the family's 1957 blue FC Holden for the run to the Bay. One Friday Merv was rushing around the house trying to get packed to get away on time but he still had some ground in the garden to turn so it could lay fallow in their absence. He grabbed a mattock for the task. With the patch turned, he saw a gardening fork in the grass and picked it up to toss into the garden area. Unfortunately, as it left his hand, his grip slipped and the effect was to drive the implement down towards his bare feet. When he looked down the fork had pierced his instep, pinning his foot to the ground. It was a bizarre moment. Merv felt no pain, lifting his foot and with a jerk pulling the fork blades from the ground. Balancing on one leg, he saw it protruded from the sole of his foot. He instinctively called for Zena although he knew that in matters not involving her children, she was queasy at the sight of blood. Next thing, Cheryl bounded down the back stairs into the yard from the house above. She grabbed her father to steady him. At first the tool would not budge when he tried to draw it out. Then he remembered about bayonets: 'A bayonet has got the slit running down it, so when you put it in, you have to twist it to let the air get in to pull it out. Well, this day I couldn't move the fork. I put my other foot across the foot and then got Cheryl to put her foot down hard on top of mine. I just went whoosh, and pulled it out, and, as I did, the blood just went everywhere.'[11]

After injections and treating the wound, the doctor recommended the Patons put off the trip for the night but laden with pain killers Merv promised the disappointed children they would make an early start the next morning. When he opened his eyes, of course, he was incapable of getting up, let alone driving for an hour. Not only was the trip to the Bay off, but Merv was house-bound for a month recuperating. But life at the Bay had a huge influence on the Paton children. Gail remembers arriving on Friday nights, her Mum toasting a loaf for bread and jam snacks. 'We really made a wonderful time with next to nothing. It was simple. At the beach we were left to ourselves, we had freedom, our friends. We would buy schoolgirl magazines from the small bookshop at the Bay and read them lazing around in our double bunks over the weekend.'[12]

At the Bay, Merv pottered in the garden growing luscious vegetables, adjusting the tat-tat-tat of the bore water sprinkler or heading off down early in the morning to fish off the rocks. Years later, living in retirement at the Bay, he would often say that when his time came he hoped he would be at the beach fishing and just topple quietly into the water. No fuss. Go off fishing and never come back. That was the way to cast off this mortal coil! To a chorus of protesting jibes from a vaguely disconcerted family, he'd joke that at least that way they'd all be freed the expense of those 'robbing bastards' in the funeral industry.

Cheryl looks back on her entire childhood as a time of great happiness but she was particularly content at the Bay. The place made a huge impact on her, cementing a deep love of the sea and creating a place at the beachfront, to which all her life she would need to retreat—her inviolable space where she could contemplate, plan, resolve dilemmas, refire her batteries. The Bay also gave her a great consciousness of the fragility of the Australian environment and a grasp of the tension between economic development and conservation. Merv and Zena would pack a hamper, walk the children down the backstreet to the southern end of the beach and then head off all the way round to the Spit, crossing it to Tomaree Island for a picnic and a day of swimming and exploring rock pools. Cheryl recalls: 'I think that's where I got such a clear sense of space, freedom and appreciation of the quality of the environment. We basically had the run of the beach to ourselves all our childhood. I was so lucky. I remember what I loved to do was run really fast in the shallow water and then fall down in all the holes. We'd laugh ourselves silly, spending all day just floating in crystal-clear water. I used to have this cork board and Gail and I would turn it on its side and lie in the water and talk. Or I'd lie on the beach and think and read for hours.'

Through these years if there was one single principle that underlined the way Zena brought up her brood it was the key notion that they should all be seen to be treated equally, that no-one would be singled out for special attention. She would often articulate the principle—telling her family she and Merv had no favourites, that they loved them all equally. 'When school reports came home Zena and I made a point of never saying one was better than the other. We'd always say that was good with this one and this good with the other. The same if we didn't have much money. Zena would never spend one penny more on one than the other. She always worked it out like that.'[13]

The approach made a lot of sense because, as is often the case in families with one gifted or outstanding child, the other siblings can easily come to feel resentful, left out, inadequate. At home there were the normal rivalries, with the other kids sometimes accusing Cheryl of being bossy, determined to get her own way, to call the shots. Her sister Gail freely admits that for some years in high school she felt the pressure of comparison, but the two were close as children and grew to be even more so as adults. Zena and Merv worked hard to make their family as inclusive as possible. Ironically, this effort may not have had quite the anticipated effect with one family member—Cheryl herself.

To an outside observer at the time, Cheryl Paton came over as an outstanding young person, assured, articulate, able. But her intellectual development was running well ahead of her emotional development. Her childhood was so academically oriented and her raw intelligence propelled her along so effortlessly, at the time it was easy to assume she was coping. She coped with the workload but underneath, the doubts and insecurities of adolescence were mounting. She appeared not to need any extra attention when, in fact, her emotional moorings were not as secure as they seemed. Home gave Cheryl security and self-confidence in childhood—the building blocks that would underpin her long-term emotional stability. But as an adolescent she was troubled, like many youngsters, wrestling with self-doubt. From early in her education, she had a sense that she was on her own, that school was the task she had to master, her role. She remembers going off to school on her very first day in the bus with a neighbour and three other children, but without Mum, who stayed home to mind Gail. In those days there were not the kid gloves with child management that today are the norm—there were simply expectations. Cheryl remembers: 'I think about it now and I wasn't frightened going off like that at five years of age. I just tended to do things and people expected you to do it.'

While she was a healthy child, with both Gail and little Jill, Zena faced a series of health problems later on, for example, one particularly alarming bout of appendicitis. As these crises came and went, it was a relief that young Cheryl always seemed so self-possessed. At times her parents stepped in to help her when it was obvious she was emotionally troubled. Cheryl was, for example, broken-hearted when the school headmistress decided that although she was school captain, she couldn't carry the banner at an athletics carnival. It seemed a taller girl was required, but Cheryl was distressed because she had originally been selected. Zena responded by suggesting she go to the school to get an explanation. However, aware how hard it would be for her mother to get away from home, Cheryl said it wasn't necessary. With a busy, often absent father and her mother battling to keep the home functioning, living in an environment where no-one was built up higher than anyone else, Cheryl just assumed it was for her to resolve emotional questions.

Problems began to surface in her last two years of high school although no-one particularly saw the need to intercede with anything like vocational guidance for such a good student. In 1963 Cheryl had won a scholarship which helped her family financially and reinforced the assumption that all was well. She got straight As in the old Intermediate exam and continued to win school prizes including the school's Ethel M. Cramp Memorial Prize for Scholarship, Citizenship and Sport. But as she pressed on towards her Leaving Certificate, she began having trouble with maths, physics and chemistry, even though she was coming either first or near the top of the class in her other subjects, particularly history. In 1964, her teachers started to notice she was becoming anxious before exams. She appeared to do well in the trial but when she finally sat the final exams, it all went wrong.

When the results came through showing she had only managed four B's no-one at her school could believe it. Merv and Zena wracked their brains trying to think what could have gone wrong. Some of the teachers wondered if she might have been having too much of a social life. After talking it through with her parents, Cheryl decided to repeat the year but because the education system was being restructured, she had to travel by train every day with one other girl into Newcastle Girls High School, the only local school where the previous year's school curriculum was still in place. Someone also suggested that as she sat studying Cheryl may also have been neglecting her diet. So when she finally re-sat her exams she was bolstered by Zena's egg-nogs and a tight watch on her eating. Today Cheryl can still remember being able to focus so much better the second time sitting the exams. The result was five As with First Class Honours in History, the fourth-best result in that subject in NSW. She matriculated to Sydney University.

The day Cheryl headed off from Maitland down to Sydney to begin her tertiary studies, the whole family drove her to the railway station for a tearful departure. The eighteen-year-old sat up on the train with a sense of exhilaration, watching as the suburbs of Sydney gradually enveloped the train. At university she quickly made new friends but there were also people studying there she knew from Maitland, including her first boyfriend, Iven Macleod, and her current one, Phil Young. But, from the start, life in a shared terrace house in Glebe Point Road not far from the university did not settle into as happy a pattern as Cheryl had hoped.

She had won a Commonwealth scholarship, without which she would not have been able to further her education, and she was originally intent on a career as a social worker, with the back-up option being teaching. To keep herself she found two part-time jobs—waitressing in a local restaurant and serving in a cake shop. It became a bit of a standing joke with the other girls sharing the terrace that when the phone rang at 8 am every day, it should be left for Cheryl—it was her Dad calling to check all was well. But within a few months the country girl was finding Sydney University quite a troubling environment, with its overpowering sense of people everywhere, jostling her among hundreds of other students, most of whom seemed to her uneasy eye able to cope far better with the instant transformation from school, with its regulation and supervision, to a new world of self-responsibility. The crowds unnerved her—arriving late for lectures in the Wallace Theatre and being forced to find a seat on a step, queueing for what seemed forever for books in the library, stepping out through the big glass library front doors after a couple of hours' work into an ocean of people coming and going. Here was a young woman intimidated by the scale of things, the pace of life there. Looking back, Cheryl remembers feeling like a country bumpkin at Sydney University.

'I was really quite shy there. I lacked that confidence in myself as a city person, so if people go looking for my name among the big activists at Sydney University at the time, they won't find it. I was like a fish out of water.' Kernot made the effort but it just didn't work. She went off to find the women's cricket team but got the time wrong and no-one showed up at the ground, leaving her so embarrassed at the silly mistake that she would not go back. She went along and watched the student union debates but was too intimidated to step forward when the debating society asked the audience for volunteers. 'I met friends who seemed to me to be so worldly. But I felt incredibly unsophisticated and insecure, lacking in confidence. I had an organised social life but I didn't go out partying much. I just didn't feel comfortable. I wasn't desperately unhappy, I just didn't feel right.'

After two years, this sense that she just didn't fit in had not lifted so she decided to head back to her home ground and check out the courses available at Newcastle University. There she felt instantly more relaxed in the smaller, more intimate bushland campus and immediately made plans to switch. Maybe here she would have more space to sort out her bearings than the pace of life in Sydney allowed. Even though her friends in Sydney at the time could see no problem, she returned to the Hunter to live.

With the adolescent and teenage Cheryl Paton, the surface always seemed a settled calm. She was fun to be with, enjoyed parties and her relationship with Phil Young seemed strong, but she rejected parts of the youth culture, for example drug-taking. Here would surface the little girl's horror at the sight of a drunk's staggering vulnerability. She would not try drugs because she saw it as a step towards losing her grip. 'I sat in a group of people in Sydney where they passed a marijuana joint around and I was the only one who didn't take it. I just passed it on, said no. I've always liked to relax with a drink, sometimes I really enjoy it. But I've just never wanted to distort reality too much, to lose control. I'm happy to cope with reality.'

Once she had looked at the courses available at Newcastle she realised just how intellectually unhappy she had been with some of those she had taken at Sydney. Again, she felt as if she had been left to work it all out by herself at the outset in Sydney and had made some bad choices. But she chose her courses well at Newcastle—linguistics, Medieval English and Anglo-Saxon literature courses and one particularly stimulating one called Classical Civilisation. Again, once her direction was adjusted there was no holding Cheryl Paton. She got high distinction grades in nearly everything she touched.

With Phil continuing his studies in Sydney, the pair were together most weekends. Cheryl was playing with the idea of becoming a social worker but that idea died one afternoon when she and Phil went to observe a court case in East Maitland, as part of one of his prac courses. She recounts: 'It was so sad. First of all in the courthouse you would hear them being brought to the dock up from what must have been cells below. This kid was about fifteen. He was on disability pension. He had asthma or something and his mother was on an invalid pension. She was a battered wife with a few kids. I really remember all this because it affected me. His friends had asked him to stand guard at a big store while they broke in at the back and stole some record albums. He just stood guard but the court threw the book at him. The defence counsel gave all this information about how after his father had left, his mother had to keep the boy home from school to help. In court he looked so ashamed and vulnerable, like a victim. But they gave him a big sentence and I just cried in the court. I just thought how unfair the world was. But later I thought you can't be a social worker and be breaking down and crying. You're supposed to be able to show people a way through their problems. I guess I learned more about life later but at that time I realised I was temperamentally unsuited to social work.'

The period of study at Newcastle had an important stabilising influence, stimulating again Cheryl's love of learning, steering her intellectual development back on track. But matters of the heart would be problematic for some time to come. Living in Hunter Street as a child, particularly with the boarding boys visiting, Cheryl had one or two semi-serious boyfriends, but the one that lasted was Phil Young. When they headed off to Sydney to study, there was an expectation among their friends and families back in Maitland that the pair were more than just going steady. Many of Cheryl's friends at home were either getting married or preparing to do so. No-one really thought about the idea, questioned the behaviour—it was what young people did in a country town. Because Cheryl and Phil seemed so easy together, it was assumed they too were destined to tie the knot. But today Cheryl remembers herself as a 'very unaware' young person, compared to those in the 1990s: 'For example, when I went to high school, the school captain of the time came up to me in the playground and pulled the belt of my tunic in. She said: "My dear, don't you know you've got a waist?" I was walking around in a straight box-pleat tunic and literally unaware of anything remotely like body image. But in doing that to me, she made me start thinking for the first time about what I looked like.'

By the time she was finishing her undergraduate degree at Newcastle, Phil had begun to talk about the prospect of marriage. He was an attractive man and Cheryl felt she loved him. But she always had this sense of being pressured by the expectations of others. Never more so than when she contemplated Phil's offer did she feel a familiar, unsettling foreboding. One weekend she was at Fingal Bay with her parents and though there was a nip in the afternoon autumn air, Cheryl was feeling uneasy and decided to head off for a walk alone along the beach. Down there, the southerly had come up and the beachfront was a crashing cauldron of grey foam and salty spray. As the tide began to recede, matted kelp and long, stringy laces of seaweed lay deposited on the sand. As she walked, Cheryl noticed that sticky fingers of seaweed had wrapped themselves around a big piece of driftwood floating in the shallows. An old fence post or the splinter of a broken boat, she knew not, but just for that moment she felt just like that chunk of wood—drifting.

Despite the mythology of it being the time when all sorts of social liberation was taking off after the upheaval of the 1960s, for lots of young people the early 1970s were still a time when they made big decisions in their lives without consciously thinking a great deal about the implications. They were just carried along by events. It was a time when women were still not actively encouraged to think that life's agenda was in their making, that they too had options. Cheryl felt it was just expected that she would get married. She didn't talk about her innermost anxieties to anyone. It wasn't so much a question of being unsure whether she had any right to articulate her feelings to Phil or her family, she just had no assumptions that it could be done. There was no question—as perhaps to a greater degree there would be years later—of a couple overtly clarifying their individual expectations of a marriage partnership. There was no plan in Cheryl's mind, no particular focus given to big questions like children, home-making, how two careers would be reconciled. She had not consciously registered the thought that here was a case of the time-honoured female dilemma—satisfying others' expectations and subsuming their own deepest feelings as a matter of duty in the process. It would be many years before Cheryl Paton developed a framework in her mind of what *she* wanted from a relationship and how her life would be constructed around it. And when she didn't raise any apprehension with anyone, once again, externally, there appeared to be no problems. There was no signal that could alert family or friends that all was not well.

Cheryl agreed to marriage basically because she wanted to make Phil happy. She believed him when he said he needed her. She refused overtures by a professor at Newcastle University to do a higher degree there because marriage would require a shift to Sydney. But so disturbed was she that she asked for the ceremony originally set down for December, 1971, in Sydney to be postponed at the last minute. Only once did Cheryl ask Zena and Merv what they thought and, without any overt evidence of the confusion within their daughter, understandably they said the decision was hers to make. To her parents, she seemed just to be seeking their thoughts, not sending an SOS. No-one around her knew to take the step in close enough to be able to inquire about her innermost thoughts. But in the end, Cheryl herself baulked at sitting down and talking to her fiancé about what it all meant, and her fears. The decision to marry was one she chose to make by herself. But it would prove to be an unhappy step, taken for a mixture of the wrong reasons, and for too few reasons. Years later, Cheryl would look back with great sadness at the flawed beginnings of something that would inevitably fail, and wonder why it was she did not speak up.

5

A SAFE HARBOUR

In March 1972, Cheryl and Phil Young were married at his grandmother's home in Maitland. They moved into a house in the Sydney suburb of Wahroonga while Phil continued his studies and Cheryl, having graduated from Newcastle University and opted for a teaching career, won a position at Santa Sabina College at Strathfield. It was not the first, or last, time she would teach in a private school. On a Commonwealth scholarship she had done what was essentially teacher training at St Mary's Convent school in Maitland in 1970–71 and would spend her entire career, prior to moving into politics, in non-State schools. In this, there was no particular intent and, in fact, in later years Kernot would become a firm advocate of the State school system. She never had any particular philosophical attraction to denominational schools, but having been given the opportunity to do prac teaching in Maitland, contacts in the private system led her on to other employment opportunities through her twenties.

From the first moment she stood before a class, even back in the East Maitland Presbyterian Sunday School, Cheryl loved the experience of teaching. It felt natural and she enjoyed the intellectual challenge in finding ways to draw out the children in her care. And right from the start, she made a big impact on the people she taught. Beth Gilligan was a student at St Mary's in Maitland, a thirteen-year-old in 1970 when Cheryl taught her history and debating. Gilligan particularly remembers the debating sessions: 'Cheryl loved the quality of argument—you could almost say debating was a sort of intellectual bloodsport. It always had a real edge to it. She had a great wit and could be quite scathing in debate. She came across as a gentle person, but strong. In a staff/student debate, I remember her going quite red in the face and having a real edge to her argument. She became very involved in it. She never came across as a competitive person normally, but then you could see that debate and intellectual argument was really her field.'[1]

In the classroom Cheryl was totally in command, able to adjust her pitch to the needs of the different students. She could be compassionate to those who needed it but quite tough on those she felt had to be nudged along. Gilligan remembers she seemed to have a tremendous belief in herself and an ability to make clear the groundrules on which she would extend trust to her students: 'There was a maturity and mutual trust in her relationship with students. We knew a lot about her personally but she expected people to trust her, too. If she revealed something about her personal life she didn't expect us to gossip about it or use it against her. Yet she also managed to retain the student/teacher relationship very well. There was mutuality of trust. She was always a teacher who to us had a public and a private life.'[2]

Margaret O'Shea, whose mother, Clare, had taught Cheryl in primary school, was a fellow student and would drive Cheryl into Newcastle each day where they both attended university. Their families both had places at the Bay and then they taught together at St Mary's. Cheryl, Margaret says, was a brilliant teacher. 'She had a fantastic capacity as a debating coach with her students and could get them to love English and history. She was not only also interested in the curriculum but she took a personal interest in them. It was always very evident how much capacity she had to perceive needs generally, and in each individual. She had a love of learning but had interests not just confined to the schoolroom. She was articulate and very perceptive with a fine critical mind and a wonderful sense of humour. She could articulate her thoughts very clearly. She was also a very compassionate person.'[3]

Margaret sees the strong family background serving Cheryl, but did she come over as an ambitious person at that time in her life? 'I wouldn't say she was ambitious because it didn't manifest in the way that ambition often does. She seemed to be ambitious, not for herself but because she believed she could do things, and she saw ways of translating her ability into doing something for others. Leadership is not about power. It's about authority and responsibility. It's about using your talents to do things not just for your self-satisfaction but for others. When she first went into politics, I joked with her that it wouldn't be long before she was a leader. But she said no, straight away. There is just something instinctive in her, I don't know. She is able, but she makes people trust her once they see her in operation. When you look back, most of her life her leadership capacities have been apparent but underlying it, there's a kind of humility. It's a humility that says that I have these talents but I will use them to empower other people. When I knew her and worked closely with her, relaxed and had fun with her, I always thought there was an underlying humility in her. And I would think it's still there. But at the same time, I think that if you found you were not on her wavelength, you would find her a very determined person.'[4]

But Beth Gilligan offers much more than an insight into Cheryl as a teacher, for there are in her recollections more signals of the contrast between the outward competence and the struggle of a temperament finding its way towards self-awareness. Gilligan remembers detecting a tension between the conservative and the libertarian in Cheryl's personality. To her colleagues and students she was a fascinating mix, impressively diligent and principled yet also coming over as an attractive teacher wearing flattering clothes. Gilligan remembers overhearing students in one of her classes one day wondering if Kernot was wearing a tartan scarf across her neck to hide a love bite they assumed had been the result of a weekend with her boyfriend in Sydney. Kernot clearly remembers the scarf covering a nasty cyst she was having treated on her neck. She never saw herself as sexy, insisting for example, she never had a love bite in her life. But Beth Gilligan says people saw a young woman trying to find herself. 'She was quite conservative but she also seemed to have a risque side. She seemed then to be a highly sexual person, which is ironic today, given the image she has as a politician as a mumsy sort of person. Journalists often seem to use that description of her as a politician but she was a young person inventing and reinventing herself.'[5]

The house Cheryl and Phil rented in Wahroonga was a small, sunny place with a big attic/bedroom upstairs. It had originally been the coach-house of a grand old stone building nearby. Their friends at the time remember them as an outwardly idyllic pairing. She worked hard, balancing her professional life with setting up and managing the house, putting up Finnish Marimekko curtains with their stark, bold patterns, cooking and house-keeping. Phil studied long hours. But in the back of Cheryl's mind, marriage had done nothing to still a subterranean, nagging unease. Years later she would look back and conclude that for reasons she could never quite explain, it was a time of pronounced insecurity: 'I just think at that time I was very young emotionally. Professionally I was very mature but emotionally I was quite young, drifting. Drifting, all through my twenties.'

In 1973 Cheryl moved on to teach at another school in Sydney, St Leo's Boys Catholic College in Wahroonga, near where she and her husband lived. There she met a man who would become, in time, perhaps her closest friend, a former Christian Brother and teacher called Tony Walters. A red-haired, shortish, good-natured man, Walters was not only a fellow English teacher. He became something of a soul-traveller, a mate with whom Cheryl empathised. They hit it off instantly, two minds enthralled with ideas and the horizon of learning. An interesting feature of Cheryl's adult life would be the number of strong, non-romantic relationships she established over many years with males—a throwback to a robust paternal relationship. Early pictures of Merv and Cheryl show them on the sand at the beach, she smiling and cuddled down between his legs, elbows on his knees; he, soaking up the precious years of fatherhood. Hunter Street was a relatively inhibition-free place, with no overt nudity but no sanction on sexual discussion, either. Direct and to the point, Zena always had an affinity with males and encouraged her daughters' socialisation. All her life Cheryl never felt awkward, left out or threatened in the company of men.

Perhaps it was Tony Walters' instinct for social justice imbued by his Catholic upbringing that struck such a chord with her. At lunchtime at St Leo's and in the staff room, they'd talk about education, social issues and, eventually, politics. As they talked, they traced their origins and realised at one point that, as children, they had both shared long sunny days on Fingal Beach where, coincidentally, both families had holidayed. All those years playing as kids perhaps within metres of one another, only for their paths to cross twenty years later. It was a close intellectual partnership that would soon lead into big-time politics.

Merv Paton was probably the first person to see that his daughter had the raw talent of a natural politician within her. He remembers her taking note of things in the political arena a lot earlier than one would expect of a youngster. When she returned from a school excursion to Canberra where she met the then Menzies government Minister for External Affairs, Paul Hasluck, she mentioned she would like to study political science. But it was actually a practising politician who next sensed the potential—and then made an extraordinary offer to the then fifteen-year-old schoolgirl. His name was Milton Morris, the long-time State MP for the Maitland district and a minister in the Liberal governments of Bob Askin and Tom Lewis.

Morris was basically a 'left wing' Liberal, with his own firm views about social justice derived from experience of a Depression in which his family had suffered deeply. With a father, uncles and ten brothers and cousins who worked on the NSW railways, Morris' one great ambition was to become Minister for Transport, a position he held for ten years in the 1960s and 1970s. When he spoke of his job as an MP, working the electorate, it was with genuine enthusiasm. He loved the region and was always far more comfortable there than in the hurly-burly of Macquarie Street in Sydney.

For twenty-five years Morris attended every speech day in every school in his electorate and in 1964 he was at Maitland Girls High when Cheryl Paton stood up to address a special assembly. By now Cheryl had had quite a bit of experience in public speaking. She had begun to win prizes, and would take out Youth of the Year in 1965. At that assembly though, she spoke about race, a passionate polemic about its insidious danger that set the room alight. Morris sat forward in his chair, his gaze intent upon her. When it was over, he sought her out during morning tea. He recalls: 'I guess I went to hundreds of speech days over the years but at morning tea that day I had to go over to her and tell her I thought it was a fantastic speech. I said to her then that she was obviously so good that maybe she should think about following me as the member for Maitland. She said thank you very much and was very polite. In all those events she was the only young person I saw in the schools who struck me as a natural for politics. In the speech she had confidence. It may be an old-fashioned term these days but to me she also came over as a real lady. She wasn't boisterous or pushing her views. She just seemed a refined, decent young woman with a great turn of phrase and confidence.'[6]

Kernot remembers the encounter well: 'Milton said it was a great speech and that I should think about going into politics. I remember looking at him and saying that I didn't know anything about politics or parties. He said you can always learn, that's easy. And then he said if I was really interested I might even take the seat after him at some time in the future. I asked him, is that how it happens? And he'll tell you that to this day he gets berated by the Liberal Party for not closing the deal.'

In Sydney in the early 1970s, Cheryl had no intense political awareness. She had supported the coming of the Whitlam revolution and could easily see the nonsense of the 'yellow peril' anti-communist scare campaigns of the 1960s. Unlike many other babyboomers however, she was not radicalised by Vietnam. Her political awakening would not come till the late 1970s in Queensland. She was, certainly, personally opposed to the war in Indo-China, participating in the famous street marches, but as a believer rather than organiser up front with the megaphones. 'I did feel passionate about the war, I thought what they were doing was disgusting. You could see the propaganda and you could see it was great that it all disintegrated around them.' But in later years she would take issue with the stark denunciation of the years of the Menzies government that Paul Keating so vociferously tried to entrench in the nation's political psyche. Keating talked angrily of the 'Rip Van Winkle' post-war years when the Liberal and National Party hegemony 'sold out' Australia. But Cheryl was always inclined towards a more generous judgement of the past, grasping, for example, that it was a Menzian system scholarship that helped her get an education that would otherwise have been denied her.

At university she did essays on the ALP and the Democratic Labor Party and occasionally would think about the parties on offer in Canberra, but it was unfocused thought, one step removed, a distraction from her continuing education and married life. 'Nothing I read at the time was jumping off the page at me about politics, really. I was naive about it but I do think the main reason I wasn't more politically active was because I was distracted trying to sort out my emotional life. I was very naive about everything, really. It took me a long time to sort out my emotional side. Nobody really talked to me about it. You were just left to find your way, and for me that took a long time.'

By 1973, the same doubts about marriage that had first caused her to postpone her wedding in late 1971 were building in Cheryl's mind. She was becoming preoccupied with the thought that it was a mistake, that her initial apprehensions about her own readiness for such a step had been well founded. Perhaps it was simply a case of two young people settling down too early. And a case of her struggling to find a direction in her life as she grew away from her small-town background. There were the routine tensions that come with the territory in marriage. Not much overt disputation, just a surrender to the rituals. But from Cheryl's point of view, the partnership lacked communication on a fundamental level. Slowly, the realisation came that it had no anchorage for her. By 1974 the unease was more apparent, and she was haunted by the fear that something important was missing, that she was failing. Cheryl retreated into her work at St Leo's College.

The school was basically laid out in two big two-storey buildings, sitting on the edge of a big, amphitheatre sporting field. Everywhere she taught, Cheryl developed a reputation as a teacher who would throw herself into just about every school activity imaginable, donating hours of her own time to sports, following every game of the cricket and football teams, and, as was the case at St Leo's, setting up a debating society from scratch. Old colleagues at the various schools are unanimous in their praise of how giving she was of her time and energy. But by early 1975 her marriage was under the duress that would lead to a formal divorce the following year. Cheryl began to contemplate separation. Then, at Easter 1975, she and Phil did split up, her father Merv coming down to help her move out and into a flat. The rest of the year brought months of draining distraction as Cheryl and Phil came to terms with the realisation that the marriage was over and they would go their separate ways. Whenever the possibility of getting back together was raised, she knew in her heart it wouldn't work. It was a traumatic time, but lightened for her by the sympathetic support of a few valued friends, including Tony Walters, and by the onset of a close friendship with one of her former students. This was the episode that would be used, more than two decades later, by conservative politicians to try to traduce her reputation.

Tony Sinclair had been one of Cheryl's English students in 1974 and then his work had impressed her as thorough and thoughtful. During 1975, however, the pair were coming into contact in various non-classroom school activities, through her involvement with the football and cricket teams, and also in debating. Kernot helped coach cricket sides at school and was in the process of acquiring her umpire's ticket. Sober, athletic and mature for his age, in his last year Sinclair was school captain and a top sportsman, leading the first cricket XI. At practice and on sporting days, he and Cheryl sat around and talked—about all sorts of things, life generally, not just school matters. He was quite forthright in his views and impressed Cheryl with his compassion and sophistication. Right from the start a rapport was there, a symmetry of thinking. A true friendship was born. Later it would veer into love, before settling on the bedrock of a lifelong affection that could easily withstand the buffeting of those who would seek to poison it.

By the time the football season was giving way to cricket, the chemistry between the pair was surfacing. They both felt it and individually wrestled with its implications. Cheryl resolved to put the attraction to one side, disturbed that it should have come at a time of emotional vulnerability in her life. For a long time she fended it off but as they talked on sports days, occasionally around the school, and on the telephone, Tony impressed her more and more as optimistic and intelligent. The fact is that after a long period of emotional doubt, the lightness in the friendship and their shared sense of fun were a tonic for Cheryl. Despite the age gap, she felt a warmth and bond in talking to Tony that she had found in no-one else in her life to that point. She had discovered a person with whom she could communicate.

When they finally began to articulate what they felt in late 1975, they both instinctively understood the importance of him not being distracted from the upcoming end-of-year exams. Cheryl knew her feelings were beginning to run deep but she stressed she would not be a party to anything that risked the school's reputation. The key factor in her life, the troubling counterpoint to the easiness with the young man, was the continuing anguish over her broken marriage. It had started to become too much, leading her to think about leaving Sydney. When she told Tony Sinclair she was contemplating a move, he was disheartened.

At about this time Tony Walters, her St Leo's colleague and friend, mentioned he was planning to move to Brisbane where his family was based, and Cheryl raised the prospect of going with him. Then, as luck would have it, in October she noticed a newspaper advertisement for a teaching job at one of Brisbane's top private schools, the Church of England Grammar School at Oaklands Parade, East Brisbane. Cheryl wrote off, went to Brisbane for an interview and virtually straight after it, in November, learned she had won the job, to start in the 1976 school year.

Torn by guilt over her failed marriage and the hurt to her husband, confused about the direction of her friendship with Tony Sinclair and desperate that nothing escalate that could damage St Leo's, Cheryl just wanted to get away to a place where she could think things through. At Christmas 1975 she packed up her Sydney flat and headed north to spend the holidays with her family in East Maitland and at Fingal Bay, prior to going on to Brisbane. With Tony Sinclair's schooling over, the pair talked by phone during the holidays—about options for his further education and about her hopes for the new job. Maybe they would never see one another again. Maybe he could talk to his parents about moving to Queensland himself. For her part, Cheryl just knew she needed a fresh start.

Situated on twenty-five hectares on the bank of the Norman Creek on the southern side of the Brisbane River, Anglican Grammar, or simply 'Churchie' as it's colloquially known, accommodates 1600-odd day-boys and boarders from Years Five to Twelve. Cheryl was thrilled at the prospect of teaching English there. When the time came for parting from Zena and Merv, her loyal mate Tony Walters came to Maitland to help her load up her VW and then share the drive to Brisbane. There she found a small flat to rent. But after the break over that Christmas/New Year, Cheryl and Tony Sinclair realised they missed one another. Tony decided he wanted to be with her. And then came his piece of luck: he had applied to universities all around Australia and in January was notified of acceptance into Griffith University in Brisbane, of all places. He immediately accepted the offer and began preparing to go north himself. There he and Cheryl caught up, sitting and talking for hours. Thus, their serious relationship began.

They would live together in Queensland for five years, with Tony later beginning his career in the television industry, and Cheryl established in her new school. Both their families were aware of their cohabitation, and while some relatives were initially uneasy about the large age gap, the apprehension soon faded. When word filtered back to St Leo's, one of the teachers, while in Brisbane on business, rang Cheryl and dropped around for a visit. He stayed overnight but left the following day having concluded that, despite the sensitivities, the relationship had a firm base. Cheryl and Tony were obviously in love, seemed settled and completely happy.

In those days, Churchie was an extraordinary environment, a place where more formative changes would envelop Cheryl. In a long period of twelve years teaching there, she would ultimately resolve her emotional turmoil, initially in her settled years with Tony Sinclair, and then later with the man who would be her second husband. Away from Sydney, life in the sun began a stabilising process. Cheryl and Tony quickly made new friends. Cheryl began to feel more emotionally secure in Queensland, and started taking in more of the world, thinking harder about public issues, formulating a clearer picture of political things. And a sixty-five-year-old male bastion of very conservative views was a fascinating place for all this to coalesce. In the end, her maturing was aided immensely by three factors—the presence of her confidant Tony Walters as a teacher there, too; the inspired leadership of the eccentric but beloved headmaster, Bill Hayward; and, to a lesser degree, the radical school chaplain, Clarry White.

A product of the Adelaide liberal establishment, Bill Hayward believed passionately in open and innovative learning. A distinguished-looking man, he encouraged free speech, political dialogue, activist teachers and would just as happily go out and watch one of the younger teams of Churchie players in less glamorous sports than turn out for the more prestigious First XV. He gave a lead by employing at times eccentric methods, even strategically shocking his audience, grabbing their attention to get his message over. Teachers at the school remember him conducting job interviews laid out on the floor of his on-campus home because of his bad back, only to doze off and be nudged awake by a gentle prod from his wife's foot. Once, when there were protests at some of the over-willing barracking at a school football game, Hayward drew up to the lectern before a hushed school at the next assembly and uttered words that went into the annals of Churchie legend: 'Your mother sucks cocks!' As the assembled students, teachers and administrative staff gasped as one, with impeccable timing, the Head went on to calmly point out this was hardly the kind of language he expected his pupils to be screaming at their adversaries on the rugby pitch. When the art teachers requested they begin using nude models, Hayward happily concurred. He was often invoking the school's motto: 'On Eagles' Wings'. Needless to say Cheryl and Tony Walters came to adore him and the resultant educational freedom. Hayward was at once trying to hold together the traditions of Churchie, for so many years an old-school-tie institution with its rowing and rugby, while also making it a challenging, relevant place to work in the modern world. The mood of the place fitted Cheryl and Tony Walters perfectly.

She remembers Hayward as an 'amazing' principal. 'With the other teachers there at the time we had a great deal to thank Bill for with his liberal, tolerant, inclusive views of life in this kind of school. It was nothing like a stereotypical GPS school. Imaginations, freedoms—everything was nurtured and encouraged, otherwise I couldn't have stayed there. It was a real hotbed of liberal, in the best sense of the word, freedoms.' At Churchie, Cheryl blossomed into an innovative teacher. Two 'factions' of teachers existed there—a longer-lived, male group and a more recently arrived, younger and decidedly more contemporary group, mainly teaching humanities. At times there were disputes which Hayward had to settle. Clarry White, the chaplain, for example, was decidedly radical, a tall fellow with a bushy beard, given to climbing into the pulpit and demanding the overthrow of the Bjelke-Petersen government. The more conservative teachers protested vigorously at this politicisation, but to no avail.

With her radical inclinations given freedom, Cheryl too found herself in the odd stoush. Served by a gathering emotional security, the climate at Churchie made Cheryl a far more direct person. She began to speak up more assertively at staff meetings, often putting a counterview to some of the older male teachers and winning the quiet support of younger staffers. Sitting in the sunshine in Queensland with Tony Walters years later, she would ruminate on those years, pointing out that she was far less 'direct' at St Leo's. 'I was puzzled at Leo's. I didn't know how I fitted in. My private life was a mess,' she said.

Walters protested that it had not seemed so at the time, that she had always seemed confident, vivacious.

'Mmm ... I was conscientious,' she said quietly.

At Churchie she became more than just conscientious. Fellow teachers remember some of her classes as 'managed free-for-alls'. She was seen to be challenging the prevailing ethos all the time. Close friends remember her as a person who never seemed overwhelmed by authority: 'She is never fazed by people having a title, Prime Minister or school principal. She just talked to them as if they were Joe Bloggs. It's a great quality to be able to stand with your own dignity and just engage somebody and not feel intimidated. Yet at the same time, it wasn't a carping, radical or loud feminist approach. She just went about her business with the assumption that she had equality.'[7]

Kernot's approach could easily ruffle feathers, though. For example, she decided she wanted to set one of her senior classes the Ken Kesey novel about psychiatric mistreatment, *One Flew Over The Cuckoo's Nest*, which had been adapted into a controversial Milos Forman movie, starring Jack Nicholson, in 1975. To get a finer understanding of how shock therapy worked, Cheryl made plans to take her class to visit Wolston Park, the biggest mental health institution in Queensland near Gailes in outer Brisbane. 'I always took the view that a lot of the students at Churchie were going to be doctors and dentists and lawyers. I made it my business to challenge them on social issues because they would just go off and do a specialised course and not think more widely. So I set them novels like *Cuckoo's Nest*, novels with a message.'

She filled out the appropriate forms and posted notification on the notice boards, in keeping with protocol. Cheryl remembers what would be seen today as an innovative piece of teaching scandalising some of the more conservative teachers. But her major problem was that the date was belatedly found to clash with a test being given in another class. Waiting in the bus for the last of the boys to join it from their previous class, Cheryl realised something had gone wrong. She trooped over to the science block to be told the other teacher had locked the door. She knocked but he ignored her. She then went to the deputy headmaster and, after a discussion, it was suggested that the other teacher should allow the boys to leave on the excursion. Cheryl smiled triumphantly as the youngsters ran across the school grounds to the bus, not unlike the inmates of Kesey's institution, set free at last.

As the bus drew up outside the hospital, Cheryl urged the students to respect the privacy of the people they would meet. She explained she had no idea what they were about to see, that it was new to her, too, but that she trusted the people who had organised the trip. She said the organisers knew the class was studying the book and warned against any misbehaviour that may been seen as exploiting the situation.

Years later she recalled that she need not have worried about the class: 'They were fantastic. But it was a shock. What a shock! We had all lived such protected lives. They didn't let us go anywhere that might have been dangerous but all the wards were locked wards. Every time we went through one section to another it was keys on chains unlocking, then locking doors. The kids all came away with this sense of lost freedom. We had only been there a little while when this old man dropped his pyjamas and urinated on the floor. But the really powerful thing for the kids as we went through the wards was the alcohol brain-damaged people. That lingered long in our memories. All those men and women sitting there! Young and old, it was just terrible. We had so much to talk about later. And then we had this talk in the lecture theatre, and some of the staff came in to discuss alternative therapies with us. All the staff said that shock therapy was good but a lot of the kids were undecided. Anyway, it was powerful learning and all those kids did well in English. Most of them had come from normal, sheltered homes. Most of them had never had any contact with Aborigines, disabled people, the sort of things that challenge the security of their world view. But with so many of them bound for cosy careers, I thought it was good to come at it from that perspective.'

With her lifelong fascination with film, at Churchie Cheryl turned her attention to integrating film and television into schooling, and helped write a syllabus outline that was later implemented as secondary school policy in Queensland. Her debating sessions were always engaging, sometimes hilarious. One day the Churchie team got the upper hand from the outset debating a visiting girls school team on the subject: 'Every man considers himself a James Bond.' The boys walked onstage and presented the girls with a red rose each. Yet Cheryl could reach out to her students individually when the situation warranted. One problem child was relentlessly being sent to after-school-hours detention for bad behaviour. She could see the boy had a body image problem and that he was the second of two children of a university lecturer, his brother being a particularly high achiever academically. So Cheryl organised for him to have an alternative to the usual detention. She supervised him taking a job helping tend the garden of a frail local widow, for which he was paid. Suddenly, he was not at detention anymore and his family were delighted when his grades started to improve.

Stuart Page is today a musician and teacher but for a while he was also one of Cheryl's English students. Page remembers her as an inspirational teacher—provocative, but always positive. He says that she was ahead of her time in using other arts forms—film and music and recordings—to enhance the lessons: 'In an all-male school where there were a lot of boys from wealthy families and hard-working middle-class families, she challenged the patriarchal view, but in a good way. Sometimes she had to take on the sexist comments that boys of that age can make. But she never denigrated anybody or their view. In her teaching she never retreated into anger. She would always get her point across in a logical and calm way. That didn't mean she wasn't passionate on occasions but she seemed to back it up with sense.

Even then she was a charismatic person. And strong. But she didn't lead by bullying. She did it partly by inspiring but also by speaking to sensible arguments. That's how she won people over. It was not an autocratic style at all.'[8]

At the end of Year Nine, Page remembers, the class was upset they would lose her as their teacher. And in the very last lesson she produced separately penned notes for every one of the thirty members of the class. Each note to each student contained a three or four-sentence summation of what she saw as the key attributes of each individual. No criticism. All positive, encouraging remarks. 'That sort of thing certainly reinforced in all of us the feeling that she was a terrific person, as well as teacher. But it also made us feel as if we had had some sort of impact on her rather than it just being one way.'[9]

Page remembers that early the following year, as the students were returning to school after the Christmas break, he and a couple of his mates bumped into Cheryl in the school corridor as she was showing two new teachers around. Kernot introduced the teachers and made, yet again, positive references to each of the youngsters. 'She said to the teachers: "This is so and so—remember I told you he was good at such and such." It felt as if she was even looking after us after we had left her class.'[10]

Chris Latham became one of Australia's finest string musicians, playing violin with the Australian Chamber Orchestra touring Europe, Asia and the USA. He is also a published writer and poet. Back in 1978 he was a student at Churchie taught English and encouraged into debating by his Maitland-born teacher. His class had the thrill of learning to make their own five-minute animated film, based around the frame-by-frame movements of a set of clay figures they laboured to build carefully for hours, even at home on weekends. They used video cameras to create television commercial mock-ups. To Latham and his classmates Cheryl was simply inspirational. He remembers that when he went into the debating class with her, he and two of the others began to write poetry: 'And I think it was because she was nurturing us. Classes with a lot of teachers were boring but not with her. It was the highlight of the day. Every one of us was kind of in awe of her. She read us the quartets of T.S. Eliot. I always remember it was like being hit by a thunderbolt at around three o'clock on Friday afternoon. She stimulated us in all kinds of ways. I used to read voraciously when I was around her, but the interesting thing is that after I left school, I didn't read so much. For example, looking back I have absolutely no idea why I got into debating.

She just inspired me to do it. She also had good taste in what she showed to us. The stuff she made us read was really good.'[11]

Latham remembers one disturbed boy in the class who actually broke back in, out of hours, and smashed some of the clay figures. 'When he was found out, she got him to talk to the class about why he did it. She was obviously trying to help him express the problems he had. But it had an important effect on us. After he had basically explained it as best he could, she then turned and asked us if it was OK with us, whether we wanted any more explanation. I was sitting there and I suddenly realised she was handing us the responsibility—it was up to me to think about whether I forgave him or not. She was showing that she thought our opinion was worthwhile having and hearing. And at that school that was very important because there was always a sense there that you got your work done but nobody really bothered with what you may have thought. She respected us a lot more than anybody ever had.'[12]

The upshot was that Cheryl became the first female ever appointed a housemaster at Churchie—the role given to outstanding teachers to oversee the pastoral care of the day-boys, divided up into the school's twelve houses. It was quite a compliment. She poured much care into her charges—and got much back. In fact, it was one of her debaters, Geoffrey Rees, who went to some trouble to try to convince her to become active in the then embryonic political party called the Australian Democrats, formed in Queensland in June, 1977. Rees, a brilliant student from a supportive middle-class family, mentioned to her one day that his mother had joined a new party. He said that given what he understood of Cheryl's social views, it may be something she should look into. At the time she was doing a post-graduate diploma and her initial response was that with her classes plus the added reponsibility of supervising the debating, she had no time for political activism. But the lad persisted and one day brought in some Democrat literature and also a contact number for the local party office in East Brisbane. Cheryl took the paperwork home and briefly glanced at it that night. About a fortnight later she found herself at home with a bit of time on her hands and picked it up again. She read about the proposed structure of the party and its dream of a participatory ethos. Such ideas had appeal, but at the time she thought little more of it.

Cheryl had always been agitated by the political climate in Queensland

under the Bjelke-Petersen National Party regime which basically dis-
couraged political debate in the schools. She had heard claims that when
elections came up the administration made sure State schoolteachers who
stood as candidates didn't get their jobs back. She was also affronted to be
told that the government had ruled that only sitting members could go into
the schools in their areas, not candidates from other parties. Then one day
she took an excursion of students to visit the Queensland parliament
building and sit in the public gallery watching the giants of State politics in
action. She was astonished by the crass behaviour of the MPs. She realised
how much a contrast it was to see the real thing, against the pictures
transmitted by the media. She noticed that many of the MPs sat there,
slumped in their leather chairs, reading newspapers, barely listening to the
debate. When it wasn't disorderly, it just seemed so rude and disrespectful.
She was taken aback to see big Russ Hinze shamble in casting coarse insults
across the chamber. And then she realised she had brought young children
to see this!

It was the time when the Queensland street marches were on and the
police were cracking down on freedom of assembly. Gradually, as she
watched and began to analyse political debates unfolding in Brisbane and
Canberra, the scales were falling from her eyes. She was being drawn ever
closer into politics. Every night she would see Bjelke-Petersen, Hinze or
Vince Lester speaking on television, and with every prevarication, every
piece of transparent, cynical manipulation, her anger would mount. She
learned more about the Queensland electoral gerrymander, the terrible treatment of Aborigines and the betrayal of the environment. Infuriated, one evening she stood in her loungeroom and yelled at the evening news on television:
'You don't speak for me! You're not speaking for me, you bunch of inartic-
ulate, narrow, fundamentalist National Party wankers!' But the crunch arrived when the Queensland parliament moved to legislate against abortion.

By 1979 Cheryl found herself marching again, this time on the streets of
Brisbane as opposition to the Bjelke-Petersen-isation of Queensland. And as
she walked through the centre of the city, a former Churchie pupil, recognis-
ing her just ahead in the throng, pushed forward to say hello.

'See, even people who come through Churchie demonstrate, too,' said the
young man, by then studying first year law at Queensland University. As
they walked along chatting briefly about university and the demo, the

student had one foot on the gutter and one on the street. Suddenly a policeman emerged from nowhere, confronting him and ordering him to move over and back into the crowd. The student protested that he wasn't doing anything, just talking to his old teacher but the policeman insisted he move on.

'Where? There's nowhere to go,' he protested, amid the crowd.

With that, the policeman lunged forward, grabbed him, arrested him and dragged him away to a paddywagon. Cheryl stood horrified as the young man was bundled, protesting, away through the crowd. 'But the really eye-opening part of that experience was that I took the trouble to get to the court when his court case came up. And I saw this policeman get in the witness box, turn over these notebook pages and say things that were supposed to have happened that were all fabricated. I had seen exactly what happened. He said he had been belligerent and accosted the police and resisted arrest. I wanted to scream out that it was all lies. Anyway, they found him guilty.' Cheryl suddenly heard the echoing protests about the way the Queensland police state operated and she realised it was actually real. She had seen it in action. But very soon afterwards would come the second incident that completed her political transformation.

Within weeks the anti-abortion legislation that had started as a bill sponsored by a Liberal MP had been taken over and made into a private members bill by the Nationals. At that time Cheryl and Tony were living in the inner-city Brisbane suburb of Paddington and they had received a 'welcome to the electorate' letter from their local State MP who suggested that if there was anything he could do, they should get in touch. Cheryl found herself caught in a crushing anti-abortion rally in front of the Queensland legislature when she had a masterstroke. She shoved her way through the crowd until she found a public phone and rang the MP, taking him up on his offer. Back at the police-lined and locked gates, the MP met her and escorted her into the building. Seated in the public gallery, Cheryl then watched from 5 pm to 2 am the next day as the abortion debate reached its climax.

In the gallery along from her Cheryl saw seated some women from the Queensland Right to Life movement—but then realised to her horror how few other women there were seated in the chamber before her. 'I watched Joh and others amble in and out, putting in an appearance and going. And do you know, not one woman spoke. Not one woman spoke about abortion! I looked and I listened. And one particular MP, a Labor man, said something along these lines: "Well, I don't know what all the fuss is about. Really, what have you got? You've just got this little spider-like thing in there and you get this thing, like a vacuum cleaner, and you suck it out. What's the big deal?" And a lot of the women in the gallery went "hiss". And then it hit me. These men were playing a part in passing a law that affects every woman. And this man knows nothing—he has no sensitivity, no respect, yet he's doing the voting on it. And all the rest of them were the same. They knew nothing about it. Some of them tried valiantly to portray how women might feel about having an abortion. But nobody tried to link it to other big issues like sex education at school. The debate was so narrow! It was an appalling standard. I thought: "My God, why didn't I realise before what having no women in parliament meant?" All these men were passing all these laws and no women were even having a say. It was an epiphany. There and then I said to myself I can do better than that. Women have to be heard!' The next morning Cheryl went through her papers, pulled out the phone number Geoffrey Rees had given her and rang the local branch of the Australian Democrats. Soon she would be learning the ropes of local party politics in Brisbane but the development unsettled Tony Sinclair.

Nearly five years on, their relationship was confronting some big questions. By 1980, for the first time the age gap between them had begun to worry Cheryl. Into her thirties now, she was thinking of children. She and Tony discussed marriage but she could not escape the conclusion that he was too young to be contemplating settling down. Cheryl figured Tony had a lot more living to do, that she had been his first serious relationship. One part of her brain told her this meant nothing, another said it would sow the seeds of long-term problems. He reluctantly agreed he had not seen enough of life: he wanted to travel. She basically wanted to be more settled, to bring even greater stability to her life—it was obvious that their interests were beginning to head in different directions. She had basically decided to pursue politics but it held no interest for him and from the first it was clear that activism would be time-consuming. After much upset, they agreed to split up. Initially, Sinclair moved in with friends but in time his life would lead him back to Sydney. There, he long remained a close and loyal friend, Cheryl occasionally visiting him and his wife Cathy for dinner, and later meeting their three children. Today, he looks back on his time in Queensland with as deep an affection as does she. He reflects: 'As friends initially, and eventually as partners in the relationship, the equation was the same. We always tried to give each other the space to develop as individuals. Our age difference was always going to put natural pressures on us both, but from my point of view there was never any issue of our friendship being one-sided. I always felt in control—not only of my feelings, but more importantly, of the consequences of our friendship.'[13]

The great bounty of her years with Tony Sinclair was the emotional platform that enabled Cheryl to take a grip on her life. It had come late but self-awareness had triggered the process not just of option-taking but of consciously understanding that planning was open to her, her right. She didn't have to be bulldozed along by life, she had the power to make her own moves.

Soon after her separation from Tony, Cheryl went to a staff function at the Cricketers' Club at Churchie and got chatting to a tall, distinguished, Adelaide-born tutor employed in the boarding part of the school. Gavin Kernot soon struck Cheryl as open-minded, practical, thoughtful. Later that night, talking by phone to his family back in Adelaide, he happened to mention he had met the woman he would marry. Soon Kernot asked Cheryl out. Close friends say they saw her falling for him in a big way. And with good reason. Good-looking, carefree and good fun, he was a popular house-master to the boys boarding at Churchie, particularly for all the work he did coaching the rowing teams. He had a room at the school and at night the boys would come around to talk or play cards. With long, light brown hair, he came across as a self-possessed individual, a bit of a loner, often out in the grounds of the school after hours running his labrador, Ben. He also gave the impression of being entirely uninterested in the question of long-term commitment, which only made him more intriguing. Gavin came from a well-to-do Liberal establishment family in Adelaide. Later when he too became a player in the Australian Democrats he would be the butt of gentle jokes about his 'merino-set' background.

For two months the romance blossomed and then at Christmas they drove to Adelaide in stultifying heat to meet his parents. It was a wonderful, free-rolling trip, with music blaring in his Landcruiser as they charged across the plains of western NSW. At the end of the trip they climbed out of the truck in thirty-three degree heat. Gavin took Cheryl by the hand, walking her in through his parents' house, introducing her as he went, and proceeded straight out into the backyard where they leapt into the pool, fully clothed.

Not long after Cheryl and Gavin were visiting Merv and Zena at the Bay. The couple were in the kitchen alone where Gavin, who loves cooking, was preparing dinner. Cheryl walked through and he reached out and wrapped her in a big, comforting pair of arms. Cocooned in a bear hug, Cheryl realised she had found the person with whom she wanted to have a family. Here was a generous, demonstrative man who loved his work but was sure enough of himself that there would be no threat in a wife's career that had the potential to be all-consuming passion.

On February 23, 1981, Gavin Kernot very solemnly asked Cheryl to sit down in the living room. 'Oh-oh,' she thought. 'What's up?' Then she guessed, and began to giggle. When he finally got his proposal out, she burst out laughing and leapt up to hug him. This time Cheryl's antennae were tuned, she knew what she was looking for. But, more importantly, *she* was doing the looking. She was in control.

In April they were married in a simple ceremony in the chapel of Churchie school, with a reception in the lush grounds attended by their families, the teachers and many of their pupils. Cheryl wore a simple cream lace dress, cut from Zena's wedding gown, a white lace bodice buttoned to the neck with a ribbon of pink blossoms in her hair. In receding afternoon sunshine, under a giant fig tree in the gardens, Gavin stood happily chatting with their friends in a blue suit, a glass in one hand, his arm firmly around his new wife. Cheryl had found her safe harbour.

6
THE POLITICS OF HOPE

From the outset, Gavin Kernot was strongly supportive of his wife's ambition to become involved in politics. Over the years his generous backing would be a pillar of strength. He himself hailed from a blue ribbon Liberal Party-supporting background, his family in Adelaide counted as close friends of the one-time South Australian Premier, David Tonkin. So when Cheryl took her first steps towards joining an embryonic party called the Australian Democrats it was the beginning of an adventure for Gavin, too. In due course his own politics would shift to the left as his wife became enmeshed in Democrat affairs. He was backstop and counsel, but providing practical assistance too, and he was eventually drawn in as a local party official in Brisbane.

Basically, the excesses of the Bjelke-Petersen administration in Queensland mobilised Cheryl Kernot's ambition to enter politics and do something to change the country. Much later, just after she became leader of her party, she climbed aboard a plane bound for home after a busy week in Canberra when she noticed the wife of the former Premier, herself a senator for a time, sitting across the aisle. After the plane was in the air, Lady Florence Bjelke-Petersen leaned across to speak.

'I've been noticing some of the things you've been saying about the National Party in Queensland and Joh's style of government. I'm not sure I like too much of that,' she joked. 'But tell me, is it true Joh was basically the reason you went into politics in the first place?'

'Too right he was, Flo!' Kernot said with a keen smile. 'He was the catalyst.'

Infuriated by all she had seen in the Queensland parliament, Kernot first picked up the phone and rang the Brisbane branch of the Australian

Democrats in 1979. Soon after, she went into their offices and met a party official and local public servant called John Dickinson who would become a close friend and colleague in efforts to consolidate the party in the north. Tragically, Dickinson would die from an AIDS related illness in 1990, just a few weeks after Kernot was sworn in as a senator in the federal parliament.

At the end of the 1970s, the Australian Democrats needed all the help they could muster in turning a promising start as a new third force of Australian politics into something substantial and long-lived. It's now part of political folklore how Don Chipp, the then fifty-one-year-old MP for the Melbourne seat of Hotham, and former Navy, Tourism and Customs minister under the Holt and Gorton administrations, announced his resignation from the Liberal Party to a hushed parliament on March 27, 1977. Soon after he was titular head of a slowly coalescing new political organisation, addressing idealistic gatherings of potential supporters in town halls all around Australia. These were people either disgusted with the machinations of the then Liberal and National Party Coalition government of Malcolm Fraser, or disillusioned with the Labor Party under Gough Whitlam. Chipp was the right man in the right place at the right time—a moment when many Australians were hankering for something different, a new voice in the wake of the infamous dismissal of Whitlam.

Incredibly, less than nine months after his decision to ditch the Liberals, Chipp led this new party into the 1977 federal election, having managed to put together 185 branches around the country, Senate teams in all States and candidates for almost every House of Representatives seat. To the amazement of political commentators, the party won 9.4% of the primary vote in the Reps and 11.1% in the Senate, giving it two seats in the upper house—Chipp's own in Victoria and one in NSW, held by the novelist and former ABC journalist Colin Mason.

Twenty years later, in January 1997, the Democrats would have cause to celebrate not just their survival but their growth and development well beyond the first stuttering experiment that crystallised around Chipp. They could take pride in having not only established themselves as a legitimate presence on the national political stage but in having become the most successful 'third force' party in the history of the nation. In fact, in that twenty years the Democrats changed the face of politics to help create a system unique in the world, one that became a distinctive model of how bicameral democracies—that is, those with two representative chambers—operate. It was a model boasting probably the most powerful legislative upper house in the world, with the exception of the US Senate. This, despite the waves of predictions of their imminent demise, election after election.

Leaving aside the National Party which, as a coalition partner with the Liberals, is regarded as part of the 'two party' power structure, the Democrats have returned far more members in the Senate than any other non-mainstream political grouping. Back in 1948, the Labor Party Attorney-General Dr H.V. Evatt introduced what is called a 'proportional representation' voting system, or PR. Under this system, small parties have a greater opportunity to win seats. Looking back at the configuration of the Senate after every election since 1948 and counting each MP presence each term—in the period of its pre-eminence as an anti-ALP force from the split in 1955 to 1974, the Democratic Labor Party (DLP) (that other historic 'third force' phenomenon) managed to hold a total of sixteen Senate seats. Going back as far as 1949 there have been a total of twenty-two seats held by independent senators. Up until the 1996 election, the Green environmental movement managed to hold five Senate slots. Yet in a time span equivalent to that in which the DLP exercised influence, the Australian Democrats held Senate seats forty-eight times.[1] After twenty years the Democrats contested their eighth federal election in 1996 and, with seven senators, looked forward, if the post-1948 system was maintained, to a prosperous political future. The Democrats' success story, however, has been embroidered with a fair share of misunderstanding. Some of the misconceptions centre on the charismatic Don Chipp himself.

For a start, Chipp's background was the Melbourne working class, not some section of the Liberal Party aristocracy. Born on August 21, 1925, in Northcote, an inner suburb of Melbourne, Chipp was in fact a Labor Party supporter until the age of twenty-six, exploring all the shades of leftist views that existed under the broad labour movement umbrella.[2] He supported the Chifley government when he first became eligible to vote in 1946, then again in 1949, and then voted against the successful comeback to power of Sir Robert Menzies in 1951.[3]

After working with the State Electricity Commission, Chipp got a job for a period as an accountant with a machine tool company in Richmond before being appointed assistant State Registrar of the then Commonwealth Institute of Accountants in 1950. This was an important break because through his work with the Institute and then later as a councillor with the City of Kew, Chipp began to come into contact with powerful local businesspeople. Through those associations many of their conservative views began to rub off, helping frame his political beliefs. One businessman, Sir Maurice Nathan, a one-time progressive Lord Mayor in Melbourne, suggested to Chipp over coffee one day that he join the Liberal Party. Chipp remembers Nathan saying that there were two choices— the Liberal Party, if you believed in free enterprise, or the ALP, if you supported socialism. 'I believed in the first. It was as simple as that,' Chipp later wrote.[4]

Thus there was in Chipp a certain political schizophrenia. A friend remembers him agreeing in a private chat once that his big problem was that he was never a true Liberal.[5] That said, Chipp would probably have prospered in the Liberal Party were it not for his conflict with the conservative wing and, particularly with the formidable figure of Malcolm Fraser. Chipp became pigeonholed as the stereotypical 'small l' Liberal. As a controversial Customs minister in the Gorton and McMahon governments, he harboured enlightened views about censorship, introducing reforms that marked the beginning of the end of archaic laws restricting written material available on bookshelves. But conservatives, including the longtime Victorian Premier Henry Bolte, branded the reforms as 'giving free rein to filth'.[6] Right wing Liberals, the National Party, the churches and the conservative intelligentsia variously attacked Chipp for his liberal views on matters like multiculturalism, film censorship and his willingness to acknowledge that while the courts should be cracking down on drugs, their use and illegal importation were complex social problems, not easily solved by recourse to simplistic penal solutions.

Basically, Chipp and Malcolm Fraser could not stand each other. Chipp backed his friend Bill Snedden in leadership contests as far back as the vote in 1967 which replaced the drowned Harold Holt with John Gorton, who was then supported by Fraser. Chipp, the trendy 'progressive', and Fraser, the patrician pastoralist, harboured distinctly different world views on the Liberal Party political spectrum. Conflict was inevitable. The two were at odds over political and policy matters for years as each manoeuvred through the Liberal Party in Victoria. When Fraser successfully mounted the March 1975 challenge to Snedden's leadership, Chipp was bitterly disappointed. Then he was left out of the first Fraser ministry. No-one in the Canberra political system was really surprised when he finally climbed to his feet at 11.27 on that March morning to tell the parliament he was walking out of the Liberal Party.

He had made it quite clear he was disenchanted with what he defined as the ultra-right wing bias of the Fraser government in the two years after it won office. He was angry that Fraser could so easily break election promises and that the executive was taking so much power, making MPs, and even debate in parliament itself, irrelevant. He regretted the government's dismantling of welfare programs like the Australian Assistance Plan, its cuts to overseas aid and proposed abolition of funeral benefits for pensioners. He could not abide its failure to support small business, refusal to consult with trade unions, support for the uranium industry and the lack of an active Australian policy on human rights in places like China. He also gave the ALP a backhander for its inability to manage the economy. But then he came to the nub of it:

> I have become disenchanted with party politics as it is practiced in this country and with the pressure groups which have an undue influence on the major political parties. The National Country Party represents the interests of a small sectional group—some of the rural community—but improperly, in my view, and unduly influences national policies quite out of proportion to the small group it represents. The Labor party is dominated by vested interests and trade unions. The Liberal party, although properly concerned with the vital role of private enterprise, seems too preoccupied with the wants of what is euphemistically known as 'big business', to the sacrifice and detriment of medium and small-sized businessmen who form the backbone of our industrial and commercial sectors.[7]

Chipp wondered if the ordinary voter was not becoming sick and tired of these vested interests and yearned instead for the emergence of a 'third political force', representing middle-of-the-road policies. 'Perhaps it might be the right time to test that proposition,' he added.

Those last few words were portentous, for Chipp had been quietly playing with the idea of resignation for months—and contemplating options which included a radical alternative course of action, too. The key myth about the Democrats' founding is that somehow Chipp invented the party himself, that it was a creature of his own making. In fact, he was the public, if slightly gnarled, face that fate decreed should lead a new alliance pulled together from other pre-existing third party groups. One of the components of that alliance was the Australia Party.

The Australia Party had been formed by Sydney businessman Gordon Barton back in the late 1960s, basically as a protest lobby against Australian involvement in Vietnam. According to long-time Democrat senator and original Australia Party official, Sid Spindler, overtures were made to get Chipp to defect as far back as 1973.[8] In fact, many of the policy ideas eventually adopted and pursued by the Australian Democrats can be traced back to the platform of the Australia Party. Political historian Hiroya Sugita has shown those policies included things like advocating a bill of rights in the Constitution, the decriminalisation of abortion, homosexuality and prostitution, and opposing the military alliance with the US, the ANZUS and SEATO treaties and the operation of foreign military bases in Australia. The Australia Party also proposed strict control over foreign investment and its policies attracted many environmentalists.[9]

Although he had fended off the initial overtures, in early 1977 the Australia Party approached Chipp again. By now he was desperately disillusioned with Liberal politics and was privately contemplating other career options. According to the former businessman, leader of the Australia Party and later Democrat senator, John Siddons, Chipp first signalled to Geoffrey Loftus-Hills, the Australia Party's campaign director, over lunch one day in a restaurant in Carlton that he could be interested in joining.[10] The start of these negotiations with the Australia Party in early 1977 had an ironic twist. Back in the autumn of 1973 the Liberal Club at Sydney University staged a debate, entitled: 'How do you satisfy the political demands of a country like Australia? Do you work within the existing party system or start new ones?' The two public figures invited to take part were Gordon Barton and Don Chipp—with the latter arguing firmly in support of the former assertion.[11] Later, Barton made some public remarks about the possibility that Chipp might join Gough Whitlam in defecting to the Australia Party, and being deputy leader to him. Chipp responded by saying he had a great deal of respect for the Australia Party because it was basically made up of Liberals:

> But I firmly believe that, good-intentioned though they are, they are doing a disservice to the causes of Liberalism by fractionalising it. I'd love to see those people in the Liberal Party, reforming it from within.[12]

However, by early March, 1977, Chipp was ready to agree to attend a meeting convened at John Siddons' home at Lower Plenty, outside Melbourne. If he had any doubts, his mind was firmly made up to resign from the Liberals a few days after the lunch with Loftus-Hills on March 8, when he attended a public meeting at Sydney Town Hall organised by prominent republicans including historian Donald Horne. Although he might not be as strident a critic of the system of government as some of the other participants on the podium that evening—people like Frank Hardy, Patrick White and Faith Bandler—Chipp simply believed in freedom of expression. He thought it intellectually valid to be in the discussion. In fact, his defence of Sir John Kerr's action in sacking the Whitlam government almost sparked a riot. But the upshot was that a whispering campaign against him started within the Liberal Party after a newspaper story suggested he had snubbed the Queen, who was in Canberra the same night at an official reception. Chipp explained he had accepted the invitation to be main speaker in Sydney before he knew the royal reception was on. But the argument put forward by some Liberals—that it was somehow disloyal of him to even be seen on the stage with republicans—was the last straw. He later wrote: 'It was then, I believe, that I concluded I could not stay in such a Party any longer.'[13]

The historic meeting at Siddons' house on Saturday, March 19, would bring into the fold the final, vital element—after Chipp and the Australia Party structure—that would coalesce to form the Australian Democrats. After he had resigned from the leadership of the South Australian Liberal Party back in March, 1972, former South Australian Premier Raymond Steele Hall formed a breakaway faction called the Liberal Movement, in partnership with his former Attorney-General, Robin Millhouse. A progressive, Steele Hall had incurred the wrath of conservative elements in his party because of his democratic reform of government while Millhouse had pushed for abortion law reform.[14] At the 1974 federal election Steele Hall contested, and won, a Senate seat. In early 1976, however, he dissolved the new party and returned to the old one, basically because he welcomed reforms that had been made in the interim within the South Australian Liberal Party. But Millhouse remained on as Leader of the New Liberal Movement.

Under Steele Hall the Liberal Movement had talks with Siddons, then Australia Party National President, about bringing the two groups together under the leadership of the former Liberal Prime Minister, John Gorton. Siddons says they had many discussions with Gorton but the ex-PM finally made the fateful decision to stand for the Senate as an independent. Gorton subsequently failed to win the quota of votes required in the Senate to win a seat. Siddons believed that a great opportunity was then lost.[15] But another one opened at the seminal meeting some years later with Chipp at his home to which Robin Millhouse and other Liberal Movement figures were also invited.

Although it would take another fifty-one days for Chipp to make up his mind to lead the new grouping, Siddons summed up the result of the talks at his home that Saturday thus:

> The scenario that recommended itself was that our best interests might be served if Chipp were to become the 'white knight' of Australian politics; the St George tilting at the terrible dragon (Fraser); the righteous and socially responsible leader of a 'new' middle ground party, but a party which would now be the Australia Party beneath a fresh facade. The consequence of the gathering was that, instead of Chipp joining the Australia Party, we should start a new party that would be backed by the membership of the Australia Party and the New Liberal Movement of South Australia.[16]

Five days later, Chipp resigned, but within weeks he was on the road in a barnstorming national tour to test the desire in the community for a viable third force. On April 29, 1,000 people crammed into a hall in Perth and 500 had to be turned away as Chipp, Siddons and Millhouse talked about the need for a new way. It was resolved at that meeting to begin forming a new 'centreline' party and Chipp was impressed that this nascent movement was attracting sober people, thinkers willing to actually do something about their disenchantment, instead of just whingeing. There were few obvious 'ratbags', he observed. Then he moved on to what he knew would be an acid test meeting at Melbourne Town Hall, chaired by the former Governor of South Australia, Sir Mark Oliphant, on May 9. On a cold, miserable Melbourne night the place was overflowing, with 800-odd people forced to wait outside. When John Gorton arrived after busing it in from Canberra because of an airline strike, he got a rapturous reception. Chipp would later describe it as the most thrilling night of his life. Amid rousing applause, Siddons leaned over to him on the stage, urging him now to commit himself fully to the idea of the new party.

'They're searching for the politics of hope, Don,' Siddons said.

As his thoughts gradually fell prey to the powerful emotions swirling in the evening air around him, with speaker after speaker talking of their refusal to see ideals crushed, Chipp was handed a note by his assistant pointing out there were hundreds of people waiting outside in the rain refusing entreaties from police to disperse till he came out to address them. Chipp was hooked.

'We are going to have a goddamned third force which will shake the life out of Australian politics!' he declared.

For over two months Chipp then travelled the nation, addressing rallies in Sydney, Canberra, Adelaide, Brisbane, Hobart, Launceston, Darwin, Alice Springs and dozens of regional centres—a cavalcade of sometimes barely-organised effort produced almost miraculously by volunteers, hundreds of whom had never been involved in politics before. The effort to talk at dozens of gatherings week in, week out, meeting hundreds of people with often hazy perceptions of what a third force party could give them, pushed Chipp to the edge of complete physical breakdown. But by July the party had 7,000 members around the nation. This was a time when a big melting pot of ideas, philosophies, and personalities was churning, ultimately to produce a political structure and a set of ideological aspirations, operational guidelines and policy aims. If the three starting point elements—the former working class-born, small 'l' Liberal minister Chipp, the idealistic Australia Party and the Liberal Movement progressives—provided the ideological mix at the outset for the Democrats, other ideas were channelled into the party over those early months as its membership numbers climbed. Around

Australia the party drew disaffected members of both the Labor and Liberal parties.

But right from the start, the question hanging above the party was: Where did it fit in? What did it believe in or stand for? The precise definition of the Democrats as an ideological entity, and how it has changed over the years, has long fascinated students of the Australian political system ever since the party's founding.[17] Despite its broad roots, and even after twenty years as a viable entity, ordinary Australians today probably know very little about the nature of the party's central political ideology, expressed through its package of policy ideas. They would not understand that of the parties they vote for at election time, it is arguable the Democrats have been the most philosophically consistent, firmly pursuing the same core set of beliefs, largely unaltered for two decades. And, certainly, people know very little about the fundamentally democratic groundrules upon which the party was structured from the outset and which have continued to operate ever since. Such is the plight of a party caught in the shadows of third partydom, basically surviving on membership dues, ignored by the big money backers of business or unions, and thus cut off from advertising and promotion.

From the earliest, the Democrats have occasionally suffered the criticism that they have no policies, but this charge has always been entirely invalid. One thing Chipp's outfit had, right from the start, was policies. But the inter-related criticism is that they have never really had an ideology, either. This, too, is not entirely true—it is just harder to define this party's ideology than that of the others. Because something may be beyond a conventional framework of understanding does not necessarily mean it does not exist or is not viable.

The ideologies of the two major parties are coherent because they have long been the key players on the conventional political spectrum—the Westminster-style adversarial political system divided between the left and right. 'Socialist' on the left, 'conservative' on the right—in class terms, the great divide between labour and capital. For decades, Labor was seen as the party of the worker, the Coalition the party of business. In the 1980s the boundaries were blurred, of course, with the Hawke/Keating revolution in which the ALP shifted to the right. The impact of that shift ideologically may take many years to unravel. But the point about this long-standing left/right configuration is that it's easy to understand. It enables complex, competing social pressures to be compartmentalised, organised and dealt with in the clearing house of parliamentary politics. In short, the notion that Labor stands for the workers and the Coalition the bosses has been all that many people have needed throughout most of the 20th century as the starting point for building their political opinions.

When they were formed in the late 1970s, the Australian Democrats were part of a wider contemporary world movement towards the formation of new third parties. In Denmark, for example, in the early 1970s two parties sprang to life—the Centre Democrats, which were protesting against the leftist tendencies of the ruling Social Democratic Party, and the Progress Party which was a more anti-system protest party. In the Netherlands at the end of the 1960s, a party called the Democrats 66 came into being with the explicit aim of 'exploding' the party system. In Britain the Social Democrats were formed out of disillusion with the Labour Party, but within a decade this experiment had folded.[18]

Democrat scholar Hiroya Sugita has tried to devise a coherent explanation for the system of ideas that underpins the Australian Democrats by pulling together two strands of philosophical thinking in political science—'social liberalism', and the concept known as 'post-materialism'.[19] Social liberalism was defined by L.T. Hobhouse in the early years of the 20th century as a halfway house between belief in collectivism—socialism —on one hand, and individual effort—classical liberalism—on another. While based on the need to protect and encourage the rights of the individual, this new approach propounded equitable distribution of wealth, the creation of social services and cooperative national planning.

The concept of 'post-materialism' was developed to explain a seminal shift in the thinking of many people around the world about politics at the end of the 1970s. The rise of post-materialist values created a new political approach, rejecting the standard left-versus-right political tensions in favour of a new set of issue-based priorities. Among them are concerns for the environment, peace and disarmament, anti-uranium mining, equal opportunity and affirmative action. The rise of post-materialism coincided with the formation of the Australian Democrats.

The critical thing to ponder here is the fact that the key to success in politics has always been, and always will be, effective message delivery. Communication. Ideology is grasped when the idea(s) that underpin it are understood. But communication is best achieved if the message is kept simple. The problem for the Australian Democrats is that they have never been able to synthesise their policies into one simple, catchy idea. And/or they have never been able to communicate it to the wider electorate. Labor was always for the working man, the Coalition for business. Easy. When the Democrats were first formed, the party was said to be positioned on the conventional political spectrum somewhere between the Labor Party on the left and the Coalition on the right. But nobody was quite sure where. Labor's historic shift to the right in the 1980s left the Democrats as *the* left wing party on the spectrum. But again, it was a rather ill-defined position. Now, all that said, Don Chipp's other great achievement was that he did stumble onto an idea that would provide something close to a philosophical anchor, or at least an operational *raison d'etre*, that would stand in the place of a policy-framed ideology. And he was able to communicate it effectively. It was the key message he devised at the beginning of the 1980s about the role he and his Australian Democrats would fulfil in the Senate.

At the outset Chipp did his best to lay down his philosophical aims. Born in idealism, his party, he insisted, was unique in eschewing backing from vested interests, religious groupings or existing organisations. Unselfconsciously he asserted the three principles upon which it was founded were 'honesty, tolerance and compassion'. The party was in favour of free enterprise but not in the unrestrained, monopolistic actions of multinationals or big business. It supported the concept of trade unionism but denounced minority control by extremists of left or right. Chipp wrote:

> More importantly we believed in humanising the workforce, in encouraging worker participation and that the process of true conciliation between trade unions and government should replace the politics of confrontation. On social welfare we rejected the Liberals' law of the jungle approach which was becoming evident under Malcolm Fraser and the Big Brother concept of the Labor party. We believed in encouraging communities to assist themselves to prevent problems, rather than trying to cure them after they develop.[20]

Under Chipp's leadership the Democrats stood virtually alone in arguing some distinctive policies, many built around conserving the environment.

The Hunter family on the verandah in Grafton Street, Abermain. *Left to right*: 'Pebby' (Margaret), cousin Meryl Sawyer, Zena, Daisy and 'JB'.

Zena (*centre*) in 1939 with some mates from Hustlers.

Merv at work at Maitland City Council, 1950.

Merv and Zena.

Merv and Zena in 1952 and 1992.

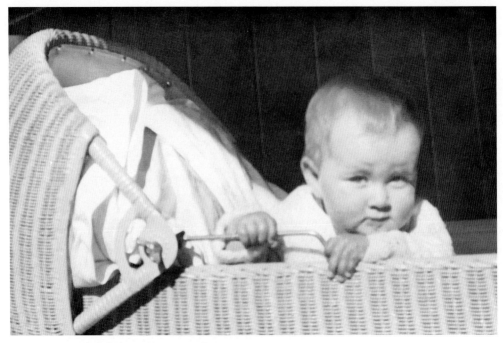

Cheryl, six months old.

Cheryl, three years old, with Gail.

At eighteen months.

Cheryl, three years old.

The Paton family on holidays in the early 1950's.

Cheryl (six) and Gail (four).

The family holiday house at Fingal Bay, 1959.

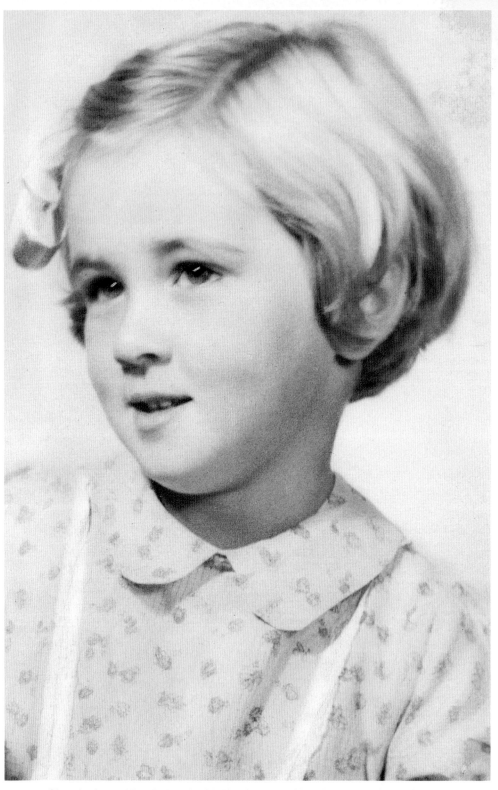

Cheryl, pictured in 1952 at the Maitland studio of local photographer Jim Lucy.

They fought to save the Franklin River in Tasmania, the Daintree Forest and other environmental treasures, playing a pioneering role in the awakening of green consciousness. Chipp pursued with a passion his call to ban nuclear armed ships and rethink the location of American military bases on Australian soil. The Democrats violently opposed uranium mining. They were at the forefront of thinking about the need for Aboriginal land rights. Democrat votes would ultimately be crucial in the passage of legislation to stamp out tax avoidance and the establishment of the National Crime Authority. But the party was also radical in its own operating rules.

The Democrats adopted the Australia Party policy of dispensing with hierarchic internal structures as far as practicable. The principle of direct democracy was embraced by rules that insisted every major decision should be taken by a ballot of all the party members, not just by MPs or delegates to a national conference corralled by a tight factional system as is the case in the Labor Party; or operating at the whim of the parliamentary leader, as is the case in the Liberal Party. That is, all policies are decided, and all the party officials, candidates and leaders are elected by the rank and file—an idea previously unheard of in Australian politics. The mechanism for such a challenging logistical operation is the party's bi-monthly *Journal* in which the policy debates are argued out before members vote by postal ballot. From fifty-six suggestions, the party membership even decided on the party's name at the outset, rejecting such colourful suggestions as the Beacon Party, the Inner Evolution Movement, the Unfettered Ideas Movement and the Civic Sanity Party. But in a climate where one of the great underlying tensions in the major parties is the constant battle to maintain discipline, in the Australian Democrats there would also be unique responsibilities imposed on the elected MPs. Chipp argued the party's parliamentary representatives would be expected to advocate the policies which the party evolved but had a clear right—even a responsibility—to vote against party policy if it conflicted with their principles or conscience.

The party pioneered the embrace of accountability in other ways, too. Long before it became politically fashionable, the Democrats agreed rules for the disclosure of political donations. It was also, without doubt, the party that most advanced the cause of women's involvement in politics. In time, the Democrats would elect the first female leader of a national political party in Australia's history, and choose women as four of its first seven leaders. It would elect the youngest ever woman to the Senate in 1991, only to then elect an even younger one in 1995.

Virtually from the moment Don Chipp embarked on his crusade, the omens were good. There seemed to be a craving for a party which peddled the sort of ideas and philosophy he espoused, an alternative to the established offerings. In July, 1977, an opinion poll by the Irving Saulwick organisation reported that 60% of voters thought a 'centre' party would be a good idea and a solid 20% said they'd vote for it. Then, in September that year, the South Australian Premier Don Dunstan called a snap poll. Robin Millhouse became the Australian Democrats' first elected MP, winning the State seat of Mitcham with 32% of the first preference votes.[21] There followed a Queensland State election where Democrat candidates won up to 20% of the vote and then, in a climate of uncertainty in Coalition ranks about the potential of the new party to draw off its support, Malcom Fraser called a federal election for the Reps and half the Senate on December 10, 1977.

His aim was to finally see off Gough Whitlam but also block the rising star, Chipp. By winning two Senate seats in NSW and Victoria, the election would prove a triumph for Chipp, even though he was initially crest-fallen that his party did not poll even better. There was also some high irony. This election marked the arrival of the Democrats, the moment when a new third force party emerged to take up the role in the Senate the DLP had played for twenty years prior to 1974. In the early 1970s the deeply conservative DLP had been among the most vociferous critics of Chipp's social reforms as a 'radical' Liberal minister. But although the Catholic-backed organisation targeted him in Hotham by standing a candidate against him, he was, of course, a lesser evil in DLP eyes than the ALP. At the 1974 election, when Billy Snedden reduced Gough Whitlam's majority from nine to five seats, the DLP failed for the first time since 1955 to return a single senator. Yet, suffering a big swing in Hotham in 1974, Chipp was only just kept in politics: saved, by 1,906 preferences grudgingly directed to him rather than to the ALP by the DLP itself.

From Chipp's arrival as a senator in 1977, electoral success and popularity for the Australian Democrats have run hand-in-hand with strong and distinctively colourful leadership. With a face that he himself described as always looking 'buggered', Chipp became an even more idiosyncratic figure on the political stage and opinion polls showed him to be more popular than the leaders of the two main parties. In the lead-up to the 1980 election his charisma and ability to attract publicity were vital ingredients because the Fraser government held thirty-five Senate seats to the ALP's twenty-six, giving it a clear legislative run in the parliament. With such a wide margin, there was no question of any third group exercising the 'balance of power'—that is, negotiating changes to legislation or parliamentary decisions and procedures in return for their support. In the campaign for the 1980 contest however, Chipp also made a seminal strategic decision—a heavy pitch for the electorate to hand the Democrats enough support in the Senate to be able to force government to keep its promises— or, as he so famously said, to 'keep the bastards honest'.[22]

This was the moment Chipp basically put in place the operational rationale that, in a sense, would stand in the stead of ideology. It was an easily communicated idea, Chipp argued it persuasively and in time, the community would come to grasp it as the basic justification for the party's existence. This slogan became the foundation stone of Democrat rhetoric for twenty years and the first of the two major factors which help explain the party's electoral success, the other being quality of leadership. But right from the outset in 1980 Malcolm Fraser's government saw danger in Chipp's play.

The Coalition hit back hard, warning that giving the Democrats power would be tantamount to giving it back to the ALP because Chipp had voted many times in the Senate since 1977 with the Opposition. Chipp argued that the bulk of these votes against the government had been on minor procedural matters—basically trying to stop the guillotining of debate. The upshot, however, was that the Democrat senators signed a statutory declaration binding them not to block supply. The 1980 election saw the percentage of the vote won by the Democrats down in both Houses: from 9.4% in 1977 to only 6.6% in the Reps and from 11.1% to 9.3% in the Senate. Yet in the Senate they increased their representation from two to five MPs. Chipp had won the balance of power, together with the Tasmanian independent and renegade former Labor man, Brian Harradine.

Back in 1978, when the Liberal Movement's Steele Hall resigned from the Senate to contest the seat of Hawker for the Liberal Party in the Reps, Adelaide schoolteacher Janine Haines was the temporary replacement, serving until 1978. Haines, originally a member of the Liberal Movement in the early 1970s, became a leading player in the Democrat structure in South Australia. At the 1980 election she was back, winning a seat in her own right. A week after Chipp originally resigned from the Liberal Party, he had received a letter from a Queensland academic with a doctorate in education called Michael Macklin, offering his services to help organise a Queensland wing for the Democrats. Macklin became one of the founders of the party in the north and was rewarded with a Senate seat in 1980, too. The other incoming senator to join Chipp and Mason was the former Australia Party boss and chief executive of Siddons Industries, John Siddons from Victoria.

Haines' arrival on the scene helps illuminate the second core explanation for the Democrats' success since 1977—its great good fortune in having produced leaders with charisma and elaborate political and communication skills. Chipp led the party to three more elections: Bob Hawke's victories over Malcolm Fraser in 1983, Andrew Peacock in 1984, and over John Howard in 1987; bringing to thirteen the total number he had contested in an amazing career since 1960. The Democrats held five Senate seats after the 1983 election, seven after the 1984 and seven after the 1987. In preparing to leave the stage, Chipp would hand over to Haines, the first ever female leader of an Australian national party. When they originally met back in the late 1970s, Haines and Chipp did not hit it off, having arguments about policy and tactics 'distinguished by raised voices and needless arguments'.[23] But after learning the ropes of parliament, Chipp argues, Haines curbed her explosive temper and developed into a talented leader. He basically groomed her as his successor as he prepared to leave in 1986. But that decision caused much dissension in the party room and brings into focus the special problems entailed in managing a party room inhabited by only a handful of people in the turbulent political atmosphere of Canberra.

As it has long operated in the capital, Chipp's party sets its MPs a Herculean task—a bold, idealistic goal which is, in the main, pursued with commitment and hard work, but which is achieved at some significant cost. Whereas a minister or shadow minister might have one or two portfolios to manage, the handful of Democrat senators are allocated multiple portfolios by their leader. Clearly, they are not charged with administering the portfolios, being across every nuance of a department's work, as is a minister. But on the other hand, winning enough seats in the upper house to hold the balance of power imposes huge responsibilities. And for years it has been a task carried out while the very legitimacy of the presence of minor parties in the Senate has been regularly in question. Basically, the Democrats thrived as a force in the Senate because of 'proportional representation' (PR). This system helps ensure that parties gain representation more closely in proportion to their share of the vote. It is much easier for members of smaller parties to win their way into the Senate than into the Reps where a different voting system operates. PR was introduced for the Senate back in 1948—prior to that time a 'first past the post' system operated which meant that all Senate seats in any State could be won by candidates of the same party.

But PR changed all that, introducing a complicated voting system in which either twelve senators in the case of a double dissolution election, or six in the case of a regular half-Senate election, are elected from each State. After preferences are distributed and a certain number of senators elected from the major parties, the system enables independent or minor party candidates who can win more than a 'quota' of votes to also be elected. This enabled the DLP to win up to five seats at any one election and, since 1977, helped the Democrats and other minor parties or independents hold up to eleven seats at any one time. And when the numbers of the major parties are so finely balanced that the balance of power is with the third parties, the seeds are sown for bitter political conflict and for the return, again and again, of controversy over the legitimacy of the Senate functioning as it does.

As events of high moment in the mid-1970s showed, and as was borne out to some degree through the 1980s and 1990s, the electoral structure and constitutional role ascribed to the Senate is a deeply contentious matter. In 1975, of course, conflict reached its zenith with the decision of the then Coalition Opposition to block supply. The trauma of that event led to the Democrats formally promising never to block supply, but under the Hawke/Keating administrations and then under the government of John Howard, enormous tensions emerged over this central issue of mandate: the right of the Senate to interfere, particularly with tax and budget legislation. At its core, the issue is whether the nation elects a government in the lower house in the expectation that it will be able to put through the parliament, unhindered, the policies it won a mandate to enact; or whether by electing third parties to the upper house, the community opts to have a 'review' process imposed on the government—a system of 'checks and balances' to ensure that no government develops unhealthy, megalomaniacal tendencies. Basically governments with majorities in the Reps resent having to negotiate or water down laws at the behest of minor parties. They argue they have the overriding mandate.

The problem is the framers of the Australian Constitution at the start of the century intended that the Senate should protect the interests of less populous States by giving them all equal representation. It was seen as a 'States' house' with power to review the activities of the Reps. When any group of senators holds the balance of power, their job is to examine and assess laws which emanate from the Reps to see if they should be passed or need modification. Every year, hundreds and hundreds of legislative changes are negotiated and the laws can be highly complex, with the power to affect the lives of every person or group in the community. Keeping watch like this, scrutinising every fine detail of every law, translates into great pressure and a huge workload. This is what is meant by being custodians of the 'balance of power'—a small group of MPs, with more limited resources than larger parties and fewer support personnel to handle the work; being called upon to be instant experts in every imaginable area; coming under pressure from the government on one side to support it, or the Opposition on the other; being lobbied forcefully by outside pressure groups; always trying to work out the most appropriate decisions not just for the Democrat party, for its leadership or membership, but in the best interests of the nation. No-one forces a Democrat to seek the job as senator, but it is, nevertheless, a demanding calling.

With Democrat senators labouring under many stresses, for many years one key question hung in the air. What was this party in the game for? After 1980 Chipp devised the 'keep the bastards honest' strategy, one that would be so compelling that sixteen years later it would be used as a specific election slogan. But a key question remained—should the Democrats aim to only hold this upper house-bound, watchdog role, or evolve into something wider? Chipp was always of the view that the party's destiny was set in 1980. While it could always stand candidates in Reps seats, Chipp counselled against the Democrats making a huge effort to break into the lower house. He said that by definition, the major parties' prime motivation was self-preservation; that they were always saying soothing things to garner votes; and that to attract multiple, often competing, special interest groups meant the result was usually compromise, constant backing away from tough decisions. He argued the two major parties were basically all about keeping as many people happy as possible. This, at a time when special interests were becoming more professional in their lobbying and use of the media and when global forces were making it more and more imperative that tough decisions be taken. Chipp argued that if a political party were to espouse the hard truths, the unpopular facts, as the Democrats sought to do, it would lose votes. It would never hope to govern in its own right.

After four years as leader, Janine Haines arrived at an altogether different conclusion. She made what was, for her, a tragic misjudgement. But it created yet another of those ironies that shroud this party—in losing Australia's first national female political leader and one widely respected, the ground would be prepared for the arrival of another female leader with even greater talent, who would go on to greater heights but who would, in her own way, also come to face perilous decisions about her future.

Haines' period as leader was not without difficulty. It was a major achievement for a woman to break through to a leadership position, even in the mid-1980s. The contest to replace Chipp was fought against John Siddons, who later made all sorts of caustic claims about Chipp, the way the party was run in the 1980s and Chipp's actions in preparing the ground for Haines. Arguing, interestingly, for the party to press on and try to break into the lower house, Siddons claimed that once Haines won the leadership, she was unhappy that he had won the deputy position and was 'uncooperative because she looked on me as a threat to her leadership'. He could not abide her 'high-handed attitude'.[24]

Like Chipp, Haines had some firm views about the need for leaders to lead, even if at times this was at the expense of the party's democratic practices or the sensitivities of her colleagues. In short, she was given to taking unilateral action in the party room and this approach did not trouble Siddons alone but drew complaints from others, including two of her successors as leader, Janet Powell and John Coulter.[25] After a big bust-up over the direction the party should take in the Senate when the Hawke government proposed an end to subsidies on imported fertiliser for farmers, Siddons had had enough. In November, 1986, he announced he was resigning from the party to sit as an independent senator. He then contested the 1987 election under a new party banner, the Unite Australia Party, but failed to win election.

Under Don Chipp's leadership, the percentage of the Senate vote won by the Democrats gradually fell until his last election in 1984, even though over that time the party's representation increased from two senators to seven in 1984. Under Haines' leadership the overall vote lifted again from 7.6% in 1984 to 8.5% in 1987, and in that election the party again finished with seven senators. It was in the lead-up to the 1990 election that Haines took the fateful decision to play for high stakes. She opted to run for the Reps seat of Kingston in the southern suburbs of Adelaide, held for Labor since the early 1970s by former diplomat Gordon Bilney. It was a big gamble. In the previous ninety years there had only been five independents elected to the lower house. Haines had brought a considerable change of emphasis in policy presentation to the party, shifting it in some way to the right on the political spectrum. The old Chipp ideas, like opposition to uranium, were still in place, but by the 1990 election Haines was hammering away on economic issues, establishing elements of the policy framework that Cheryl Kernot would later inherit. Haines took on the economic rationalist agenda about dismantling government and leaving decision-making in the economy to market forces, as embraced by both the Coalition Opposition and the ALP in the 1980s. Hers would be a comprehensive, radical policy package but Haines was constantly complaining that she couldn't get the media to pay any serious attention to her ideas. She was angered that her party was seen to be devoid of policy ideas yet journalists were almost completely preoccupied with the major parties. This was the time when the killing label, the 'fairies at the bottom of the garden', was attached to the party to devastating effect by the acid-tongued Labor Finance minister, Peter Walsh.

However, as the 1990 election approached with community-wide disquiet at the offerings of both Prime Minister Bob Hawke and Opposition Leader Andrew Peacock, opinion polls showed a wave of support for the Democrats with their 'fresh, down-to-earth, slightly risque' leader, as commentator Paul Kelly called her.[26] With only a 4.8% swing, the high-profile Haines could unseat Bilney and needed only to finish second on the first count for second preferences to push her over the line. Opinion polls were showing the Democrats running at 15% or more nationally and she was a mile ahead of Bilney and the Liberal candidate in Kingston, Judy Fuller. The party attracted a startling 47% of the two-party preferred vote in a by-election for the Victorian State seat of Thomastown. The dilemma for the Hawke government was that it had to polarise the vote at the election to reduce seepage to the Democrats but also get as many Democrat preferences as possible. So troubled was the government by the Haines threat that Peter Walsh was wheeled out to launch a blistering attack on the Democrat policy package. He claimed they were recycling 'Eva Peron prescriptions'— billions of dollars worth of unfunded promises.[27] Haines hit back, saying the minister had the figures wrong.

'This is Walshie at his best,' she said. 'When he's vitriolic, he's always entertaining.'[28]

Under more pressure, however, on the eve of the launch of the Democrat package, Haines did concede her policies could create a big budget deficit. In one interview she talked of 'never being wedded to a budget surplus', saying it was possible that her policies could create a $10 billion deficit, which was a figure she said she had 'just plucked out of the air' but was 'not particularly sizeable'.[29] Under attack on the policy front, Haines stepped up her complaint that until 1990 the media had argued the Democrats had no policies but now blindly attacked them as vague and waffly. Some over-confidence did slip into the Kingston fight, with Haines saying on election eve she had a 90% chance of winning, and predicting the Democrats could win sixteen seats, including five others in the Reps. While she was an obvious threat to the ALP, heading what seemed a surging Democrat presence, she also presented huge problems for Opposition Leader Andrew Peacock, or more particularly, the elements of his policy package like industrial relations reform, drawn from Thatcherism in Britain. All in all, both the major parties had good reason to stop Haines. And stop her they did.

Although both sides have denied it, there was some level of cooperation between the ALP and Liberal Party to form a united front. Journalist David Barnett revealed that Alexander Downer, who had been in charge of the Kingston campaign for the Liberals, rang Gordon Bilney to suggest that Peter Walsh cost the Democrat program.[30] In the closing stages of the campaign both parties hit Kingston with a massive propaganda effort, exploiting Haines' concession under persistent questioning from the media that a capital gains tax on the family home might one day be necessary. But there was also an avalanche of misleading advertisements and pamphlets implying, with deadly effect, that the Democrats would put the capital gains tax on the family home soon and would also introduce a land tax. It was suggested Haines was being deceitful in her candidacy and had a secret plan to go back to the Senate if she lost. The Coalition argued that voting Democrat was essentially voting Labor. When the vote came in Haines ran third—with 26% of the vote, behind Bilney on 37% and Fuller on 33%. She was devastated.

'We knew we were taking a risk but it looked good until the last Tuesday when the dirty tricks campaign started,' she said. Asked about her plans she said: 'I have no political future. I will not make any attempt to go back. I don't want to detract from the work of whoever our new leader is. What we learned from the campaign is that when you fight fair and nobody else does, you lose.'[31]

The post mortems were brutal, concluding she had made a strategic mistake in the choice of seat. She rejected the advice of some in this, opting for Kingston instead of less marginal seats like Mayo because she had grown up in the Kingston region, her children had gone to school there, her husband had worked there, she had shopped there. But Kingston was too marginal. For a third party like the Democrats, the better option would have been to hit a seat where there was a stronger margin for one of the main parties, then hope to win the second spot and be pushed into the lead by the preferences of the third-running, other main party.

The great irony is that while losing the leader, the 1990 election was an historic triumph for the Australian Democrats. It was the moment the party came of age, according to political commentator Paul Austin.[32] Haines achieved the best aggregate result in the party's history—better than the startling 1977 result—in fact, the best result by a third party in the history of the country. With the electorate deadlocked over whether the Hawke government should be returned or Andrew Peacock finally given his chance, the voters turned to an alternative in significant numbers. In the Reps, the Democrats polled 11.3% of the vote, up from 6% in 1987 and a low of 5% in 1983. In the Senate they polled 12.6% of the vote, up from 8.5% in 1987 and a low of 7.6% in 1984. As a result of the gains made in 1990, the party was assured of having the balance of power until at least 1996 and possibly beyond. This was because five of their senators had six-year terms. The party now had a record eight senators.

But no leader.

Weeks later, when the dust of the ensuing leadership ballot had settled, the party installed in the job Janet Powell, a forty-eight-year-old former Victorian teacher and party State President who had taken Chipp's seat when he retired in August 1986. Hers was to be a troubled and tragically brief leadership, but it also marked the start of a wider period of uncertainty for the party, a three-year disaster in which the Democrats would plummet from Haines' soaring electoral promise into a trough where senior party insiders privately harboured real fears for the party's continued existence. Out of this rubble of leadership failure, ideological conflict and personal animosity however, a woman leader would emerge from Queensland with the toughness and judgement to restore her party's fortunes. Cheryl Kernot would not only get the operation back on the rails but would remould it into something appealing to progressive-minded people, with economic credibility and renewed political legitimacy.

PART TWO

7

A NATURAL

It took her many years for Kernot to consciously make the linkage, but underlying the appeal of the new party she was joining were its fine echoes of her own religious upbringing. Even though her parents were not solid churchgoers, Cheryl and her sisters and brother were brought up Presbyterians, sections of which later broke away to help form the Uniting Church. A bit like the Democrats, this denomination had its own very distinctive character: a greater range of participatory processes, a relatively less formalised and less hierarchical power structure, the congregation empowered to elect church office holders, and a strong role for women, either directly as ordained ministers or as officials. She preferred the simplicity of the Uniting Church to the more elaborate ritual she saw in Anglican and Catholic church services.

Interestingly, a disproportionate number of people involved in the Australian Democrats came from church backgrounds under the Uniting Church umbrella. For example, John Woodley, a kindly Queensland Uniting Church preacher, joined Kernot on the Queensland Senate ticket for parliament in 1993 and won a seat. Hailing from another religious tradition altogether, the former Christian Brother Tony Walters was impressed with the Democrats' social justice doctrine, introduced to it as he was by his excited teaching colleague one Monday morning in the staff room at Churchie. In fact, Kernot and Walters were rather typical of the people attracted to the Australian Democrats.

Over the years, the party had drawn middle-class, younger, white-collar, educated, economically secure members, and as the core of its electoral support. The Democrat program had come to appeal to a particular 'thinking' leftist, perhaps reflecting the rise of 'post-materialist' concerns—the environment, the peace movement, feminism and so on. Among Democrat supporters, many are schoolteachers. Political commentator Geoffrey Barker described the party thus:

> Committed Democrats are humane, bourgeois people, generally with post-secondary qualifications. Typically they tend to be teachers, nurses, computer programmers, academics, some small business people. One senior Democrat says they are people who can afford to have a social conscience but many Democrats tend to be sqeamish about dirtying their hands in what they regard as old or business-as-usual politics.[1]

Barker added that there had always been something 'elusive, even ambiguous' about the party: 'Middle class but socially radical, critical of the dominant political culture yet pious about constitutional proprieties, the Democrats have always faced tensions between idealism and opportunism.'[2]

Cheryl Kernot and Tony Walters both came to the party as idealists. Soon after joining in 1979, both were active members of a Brisbane branch, guided by John Dickinson, who introduced them to another of the party's driving forces in Queensland, Michael Macklin, who would soon join Chipp in federal parliament as a senator. Things moved very fast for those competent people keen enough to step forward and offer their services. Twenty years later it is hard to recall that in the late 1970s this was an overnight national movement, springing up all around the country. The events of 1975 had scarred people, leaving many wondering why there could not be a better way. Neighbours were talking over backyard fences about the meeting of the interesting new political movement they had attended the night before. People were enthusing one another with the novelty of its ideas. It was a time of great anticipation. One senior Democrat official remembers: 'It *was* a very exciting change for those of us who got involved. Today it's hard to recapture the feeling of 1977 and 1978, the idea that we *were* going to change the world and that this was the party, the vehicle to do it. Thousands of people were volunteering. You'd go along to a meeting with Don [Chipp] and he'd be sitting there with his cigar like King Faruk and you'd be thinking maybe this *is* the way we can make changes.'[3]

It was a movement fired, in some areas, by enthusiasm and little else. It was no mean feat, setting up a national political party virtually overnight from scratch, built on no financial help other than whatever donations the embryonic membership could afford. Tony Walters is a walking example of the verve of the operation in those pioneering months. The first branch meeting he attended talked for hours about the avalanche of organisational jobs that had to be done. Then someone raised the issue of the upcoming federal election and the problem of finding candidates to stand in Queensland seats. Before he knew where he was, Walters was being suggested as a potential candidate for the seat of Brisbane.

'I guess I'd better join the party then,' he said.

Join he did, contesting the election in October, 1980, with Kernot as his main campaign helper. In those now faraway Joh Bjelke-Petersen days, State schoolteacher involvement in election campaigns was frowned on, basically because of the perceived leftist bias of the profession. There was no question of time off for candidates. Working in a private school, Walters and Kernot were immune from retribution but they still had to quarantine their growing political work so it did not intrude on their school responsibilities.

John Dickinson recognised early on that Kernot was exceptionally good with people, warm, outgoing, even charismatic in her own way. A natural. He began to encourage her to think about running for parliament and her chance came when Bjelke-Petersen called a State election. Kernot stood for the State seat of Ashgrove, winning 12.5% of the vote, even though the Liberals' John Greenwood retained the seat. On the hustings, the young schoolteacher was a charmer. At one point, the local Ashgrove Catholic parish organised a meet-the-candidates forum where locals could question the competing parties. It was Kernot's first exposure to sophisticated head-to-head party debating. The discussion turned inevitably to the tricky issue of abortion but she refused to fudge her opinions, making plain her strongly held pro-choice views and her anger that the debate was too often ruled by males. Her views obviously made some of those present uncomfortable. Later however, she received a note from the priest who had organised the event. He thanked her for her attendance, congratulating her for an overall impressive performance and making the point that she should not be afraid to speak up on contentious issues, irrespective of an audience's polarised views, because in the end it was important for politicians to have the courage to speak honestly. The writer of that note was Jim Soorley, who years later would become the progressive Lord Mayor of Brisbane and also one of the small coterie of confidants of the future Democrat Leader.

From her first experience of it in Ashgrove, Cheryl Kernot absolutely loved campaigning, adored the challenge of the hustings. It was all an echo of a world with which she was so familiar—those long, lazy walks through Maitland High Street with her gregarious father. But campaigning was hard work, a lot of running around, with meagre back-up and resources—the fate of third parties. Kernot and Walters used old printing equipment, primitively screening photographs to produce their electioneering literature on reams of yellow paper. Calling on a couple of their friends for extra assistance, the two did hours of letterbox drops, pressing the party's message.

Early one morning Walters picked Kernot up to go out for her first door-to-door canvassing in Ashgrove. At around 10 on a hazy, warm morning, they settled on the lay-out of streets they wanted to canvass and walked up to the first front door. A small child was sitting on the verandah, acting, they both thought, strangely. As Walters knocked on the door and said 'g'day' to the youngster, he assumed the child was just shy. When the boy's mother opened the door, Kernot was enveloped with foreboding, instantly alarmed. The child was autistic, the young mother had just been deserted by her husband, appeared to have been drinking and was clearly troubled. Invited in, the pair found a house in disarray with holes punched in walls and general squalor. They sat down with the young woman and Kernot began to make notes as the grisly story unfolded. She and Walters spent four hours in the house, it being the only piece of canvassing they managed that day. Kernot spent that late afternoon on the phone, chasing down the relevant welfare authorities, organising respite care in the first instance and trying to find a way to ensure someone could step in to help.

While she loved the campaigning, Kernot also developed a fascination with the internal machinations of politics, the way parties are structured and run. She jumped at the chance to be State policy coordinator, a role where she got to grips with the party's basic beliefs, its core messages. But then in June, 1982, her life changed direction—husband Gavin won a trip to Canada for a year-long teaching exchange. He was offered a post in an independent school in Shawnigan Lake on Vancouver Island in British Columbia where he would teach geography and social science.

Politics was slowly getting a grip on Kernot but the teaching post for Gavin was a wonderful opportunity, not to be missed. Such postings were eagerly sought after by teachers and it provided the pair with a chance to travel and see an interesting part of the world. Her political involvement, for the moment, would be put to the side.

When she and Gavin arrived at the school in Canada, they found there a vacancy for a history teacher so she was able to do some part-time work, too. But she had already organised to do a post-graduate diploma in inter-cultural studies through the Mount Lawley CAE in West Australia. This allowed her to study the culture of the indigenous peoples of North America and Canada as a counterpoint to her growing fascination with the culture of Australia's own original inhabitants. She would burrow into the work by correspondence but it, too, would be interrupted when she fell pregnant. On June 7, 1983, Kernot gave birth to a baby girl, Sian, in the small local hospital not far from the lake with its imposing pine forests and restless mountain horizon. Zena and Merv had decided to have a holiday in Canada to be with their daughter for the birth and she was glad of their company. The pregnancy proved a testing time.

Parenthood carried Cheryl Kernot to the next stage of her thinking about the role of women and mothers. Eventually, two factors would influence her to content herself with having only one child. One was the fact that she was inordinately ill during the pregnancy. This was no mere case of morning sickness. For months she was sick every day, sometimes from the moment she woke until late at night. The scope of it had a troubling resonance, for as a child Kernot had developed something of a phobia about people being physically ill. In her first weeks in pre-school she was horrified when a little boy sitting next to her suddenly threw up everywhere, including over her. But also, like many women of her generation, she was disconcerted by what she saw as the oppression of women of her mother's generation by the traditional conventions of marriage and home-building.

Zena's years of unrelenting toil to help establish her family unconsciously made an impact on the young Cheryl. She wondered whether this was all that life offered women. She was conscious, for example, of the huge difference it made to her mother's quality of life when she had access to a motor car to help with the shopping. She would say later: 'I really admire how hard women worked as homemakers in those days. We really don't have the commitment today to do it like they did. I saw what my mother went through. I don't know, though, whether I ever thought I would not do this. I think I thought I'd never have four children. But I never made a conscious decision to have one child—that was unknown to me—until I hated being so sick. I didn't have Sian till I was thirty-five, basically because I had never met a man I thought would be the father, really. I think this is relevant. It was the fact that Gavin was so good at home. I sort of knew that with him I wouldn't be condemned to the life that my mother had. The interesting thing is that he is eldest of four and his other two brothers are exactly the same, but there is nothing in their family that provides that role model. The three boys take absolutely equal share of the load and always have. They're dotty about children, have done everything but breastfeed. They've never walked away from co-responsibility for their children.'[4]

Kernot was able to get her CAE course exams finished in the weeks after Sian's birth, when an examiner came to her home. Her supervising lecturer at Mount Lawley later wrote her a note remarking on the novelty of receiving exam papers where the supervisor had annotated that the examinee had to take a break to breastfeed. But with the exams done, it was time for the newly expanded family to pack up once again, for Gavin's exchange had run its course and they readied for the return to Australia. The family was not long back unpacking in Brisbane when Kernot's journey into politics restarted. She took a phone call from the Queensland President of the Democrats, Bev Floyd, asking her to go onto the party's State Management Committee. She protested that it would be hard—she had a tiny baby to manage.

'Yes, I know,' Floyd said. 'But we'll be flexible. We'll come to you to have meetings at your house at times that suit you, when you aren't feeding. I know this is a big ask but we really don't have enough good people working on things we need to get done, and I'd just love to have your contribution again.'

Kernot said she would think about it but Floyd persisted, asking her to allow her to organise one meeting so she could see how it went. Cheryl Kernot's political career was off and running again. Soon she was Assistant Secretary of the Queensland Division as well as editor of its newsletter. But around her a major row was brewing among party officials, centring on the role of the talented but rather uncompromising Bev Floyd. Put simply,

Floyd's get-up-and-go attitude was resented by some other party people. Moves were hatched to roll her at State executive level. When that failed, a couple of officials resigned and the issue took off in the media. One male official complained publicly about the 'feminists digging potholes'.

Kernot got a phone call from senator Michael Macklin who was concerned the Floyd affair was getting out of control. He asked her if she was prepared to speak to the national media in an effort to defuse the row. Until then she had only ever done basic media work as a Queensland division official with the local papers in Queensland, had never even had a metropolitan newspaper interview. She had to ask permission from the headmaster to slip home during free periods to prepare press releases. On the day that the 'feminist potholes' remark was made on ABC radio's *AM* program, Kernot arrived home to find newspaper, television and radio journalists demanding interviews. Her line was basically that the remark said more about the person making it than the party or the row. She argued that the Democrats were an unusually democratic organisation and gave everyone a go but, like most parties, were subject to occasional fights between people. Her carefully chosen words played it all down and won the plaudits of party officials, including Don Chipp, who rang to congratulate her. The issue would have continued running were it not for the fact that later that day the nation's attention was suddenly transfixed by an attempted hijack of an airliner at Brisbane airport. The Floyd row faded from public view but Cheryl Kernot's coolness was missed by no-one in the party hierarchy.

Within a year of returning from Canada she was going from strength to strength. In 1984 she was elected State President and although she had never been particularly close to Michael Macklin, he was fair-minded enough to recognise her talent. One day he rang and asked if they could meet. It was on the eve of the 1984 double dissolution election and Macklin started by observing that Kernot had run a very good campaign back in Ashgrove.

'The problem is, though, lower house seats are basically unwinnable for us,' he said. 'I think you should start thinking about making a shift to the Senate. You obviously like politics. If you are serious about it as a Democrat the only way you're going to win your way in is through the Senate. I think you should have a go. That doesn't mean I'm endorsing you but we'd like you to consider being number four on the Senate ticket this time around.'

With Tony Walters as State Secretary, Kernot began to push for reforms of the Division's operation. They changed the structure of the various party committees to try to get more out of them and actively set out to train more activists in nuts-and-bolts tasks like producing electioneering literature and negotiating preference distribution. Kernot also developed some very firm views on the promotion of the party and its message. She argued in party forums again and again that policies had to be made cogent and the messages sharpened and presented in a sophisticated manner. In this she was influenced by an eighteen-month period in which she worked part-time—three hours a night—not in teaching, but in producing talk-back radio programs at the ABC in Brisbane. Sian was only a toddler and Gavin was working hard at Churchie but the radio work helped financially. It also gave Kernot new insights into the media and, inevitably, political message delivery. One former Queensland party official remembers: 'She looked at our documentation and argued that too much of it was too academic, obtuse or irrelevant to what people really thought in the electorate.'[5]

Another recalls how her activities and emerging attitudes were formative: 'She was always pushing for clear messages and I think her own career has built on that ever since. Her verbal skills are as good as anyone in Australian politics ... cutting to the heart of the matter, being able to explain in simple terms. She used to get annoyed when she saw the tendency of some Democrat people to be above the ordinary people, to be smug. There was a sense that our party had the right ideas but nobody ever was able to make the people understand. Within the party she was also never cynical or critical about the media. Instead she was just realistic. She just said this was how the media operated, that we needed to work within that framework. In the early days all these ideas were there. Eventually, her own academic back-ground, in teaching, her realistic ideas about the media and her personal skills came together in the way she performed as leader.'[6]

In 1986 the Democrats selected Kernot to go to the United States for a month-long study tour as part of an exchange group of up-and-coming young politicians from the various parties. It was a huge compliment that brought her into contact with a number of young people set to play big roles in politics in the 1990s—among them a newly elected Liberal Party back-bencher, Alexander Downer, and a young Victorian lawyer called Peter Costello. The trip would do nothing to endear Kernot to Downer nor to the world view of conservative politicians. And it would sow the seeds of a cautious relationship between the future Democrat Leader and Costello, the future Coalition Treasurer and Prime ministerial aspirant.

As these young political leader exchange visits go, the crop of 1986 turned out to be decidedly upwardly mobile. Downer went on to become federal Opposition Leader and Foreign Minister, and Costello Deputy Leader and Treasurer of the Liberal Party. Another Liberal delegate, Virginia Chadwick, would be a high profile minister in the NSW government. Of the ALP delegates Jenny Beacham would later become Victorian State Secretary and Sue West would graduate to the Senate. The National Party's Geoff Mort would be a top staffer working in the office of the federal leader Ian Sinclair and then later for ministers in the Fahey State government in Sydney. For Costello and Downer this was the start of the friendship that would reach a milestone in May, 1994, with the decision to form the 'youth ticket' that levered John Hewson out of the Liberal leadership. Back in 1986 the two men were energetic, youthful apostles of the dominant right wing, anti-government or 'dry' politics of the US and Britain. And travelling through the home of Reaganism, vociferously so.

The trip was characterised by them teasing or ridiculing Labor and endlessly praising the advances made by the political right. This, of course, grated with the all-female Labor delegation. Along with Downer's pranks which at times became quite aggressive baiting, the trip was weighed down by personal antagonism surfacing along party lines, with Kernot in the middle, alternately being more socially comfortable with the Labor women or trying to referee the clinches. On one occasion the tension boiled over in a minor public scene. Kernot found herself either urging both sides to desist when the pointscoring threatened to become an embarrassment, or copping her own tedious and predictable share of the flak for being a naive, woolly, economically illiterate Democrat. Her attitude to the two young Liberals had got off to a tricky start even before leaving Australia at the initial briefing in Canberra with the Foreign Affairs Department. Downer made his intention clear with his very first remarks to her. Introduced, he said: 'Oh, a Democrat! My ambition in life is to destroy you people.'

'Charming!' said Labor's Sue West, although the Liberal leader-in-waiting would be true to his word, at least in part. Four years later he would play a hand behind the scenes in the campaign that ended Janine Haines' career. Downer's antics would help sketch Kernot's enduring memory of the trip. There were a few humorous moments, however, Kernot later painting the picture of two suddenly horrified young Liberals, straight off the bus for the next American city visit, recoiling out the door of their share hotel room when they found it contained only a double bed. Kernot remembers Costello as being quieter, cautious, sitting back and taking it all in. The two men didn't take Kernot seriously, and while she knew they had no respect for her, she took no particular offence at their jibes. Sailing around San Francisco Harbour on the boat once owned by Humphrey Bogart and Lauren Bacall, Downer couldn't resist when he saw US Navy vessels in dock.

'Give Cheryl a surfboard and she can paddle over to see if there are any live sheep on board to protest about!' he laughed.

Back home, Kernot's climb continued when, in advance of the 1987 election, she was promoted to number two on the Queensland Senate ticket behind Macklin. She had caught the eye of some key party people well before she was elected Deputy National President in 1988. Probably the key official was Sam Hudson, the wonderfully voluble, long-time party National Secretary. Born to a Liberal party-supporting family in Melbourne's Albert Park, Hudson was active on the left of the Labor Party in the early 1970s, running with the ilk of the writer and academic Ian Turner, and Whitlam era figures Moss Cass and Jim Cairns, stuffing pamphlets in letterboxes as a foot soldier for MPs like the ALP's Joan Child, the first ever woman Speaker of the Reps. But in 1977 Hudson was one of those people urged by a neighbour to attend the early Democrat gatherings. Hooked on the message, she would become a player in the Victorian divisional structure and, in time, as National Secretary—the keeper of the party secrets, confidante of many, deal-doer, and strategic player of great potency. But others on the party's national executive could see, too, that Kernot was intent on a parliamentary career when she joined the national executive. One long-time executive member recalls Kernot just had 'a natural instinct' for the politics: 'Even at national executive meetings she would be angling to discuss the hot spots, the politically-edged matters, whereas that body in our party is more an administrative arm. It did discuss political things and policy type matters and obviously wider strategy, but Cheryl was always keen to be involved in the discussion of them rather than anything else. The political edge was there right from the start.'[7]

Another party insider observed that Kernot could be too pushy, ruffling feathers: 'Her whole attitude at meetings was to cut straight through and go "bang"! She wasn't into being polite, shifting round the edges or being subtle. If she had something to say, she said it. At national executive you get people coming together only two or three times a year and there are a lot of things to talk through over a couple of days so there is a lot of general discussion. Cheryl, however, was the one who would sometimes be a bit impatient, wanting to get on with it. She would very quickly see what the nub of the problem was, and how you deal with it. Bang! Straight in. Sometimes people would get a bit edgy because she wanted to do things without any niceties.'[8]

In 1988 Michael Macklin appointed Kernot to his staff. She was based in Queensland but required to travel to Canberra when parliament was in session. Opening up to her was the experience of walking into the buzzing engine-room of Australian politics, the massive building on Capital Hill. She still remembers the exhilaration the first day she drove in from Canberra airport around the edge of Lake Burley Griffin, across Kings' Avenue Bridge, up to the recently opened building with its extravagant, gleaming flagpole, its roof of turf with tourists ambling down from the lofty view of the Brindabellas. 'Right from the start I always thought that you had to go to where the decisions are made, where the people make the decisions that affect other people's lives. It was exciting because to me this was the centre of the action.'[9]

From her first weeks working in the building, Kernot sensed her future lay there. But achieving that end would not come without a struggle, for when Michael Macklin decided he had had enough of the workload, he was far from full-blooded in his support for her to succeed him heading the Senate ticket at the 1990 election. Another local party figure was in the race and Kernot and her supporters got to work to head off the threat. Basically the groundwork she had put in for years inside the party structure meant when the time came she could mobilise her support sufficient to win the vacancy.

Surprisingly, for someone rocketing irresistibly towards a political career from the bosom of a family that loved to discuss public affairs, Kernot rarely heard her parents reflecting much on their own particular electoral choices. Merv might have loved to 'gasbag' about Vietnam, abortion, the state of the economy or the merits of individual politicians, but as an adult, Kernot looked back and realised she had no clear picture of how her parents had voted over the years. She assumed they were swinging Labor voters. But as she became more entrenched in Democrat affairs, she found her folks even less forthcoming about their own views. Other members of the Paton clan were decidedly conservative and the implication was that Merv, in particular, probably had difficulty with some of the more radical positions of the Democrats, too.

When she first raised the prospect of going into parliament one day at the Bay, Merv said she had to realise it was a rough old game but if she wanted to do it badly enough, then she should give it a shot. He remembers he took the liberty then of giving her two pieces of advice: 'I said to her that it seemed to me that as a politician you must do your homework before you open your mouth. How many times do you hear politicians shoot their mouth off about something and it's just hearsay? If you're going to say something you yourself must know it's right, otherwise they'll shoot you down in flames. The other thing you have to ensure is that you keep a clean sheet. And she said: "Dad, I'm not beholden to you or anybody else. I make my mind up what I believe in." She told me, her father, she was not beholden to me or anybody! First of all, I thought that's a bit rough saying that to her father. But then I thought if she'll say that to me, if anybody tries to bribe her in any way, shape or form, they will get the same answer. So I thought that was good. I've always thought Cheryl would be straight down the centre and answer questions as she sees them.'[10]

Whatever his own political views, Merv Paton is immensely proud of his daughter and reckons she would make a great Prime Minister. He sees her personal priorities more in line with the mainstream needs of the community than many other politicians. But the key thing, in his view, is that she is a caring person with a gift for communication. The people would know that, fundamentally, she was a politician embarked on a crusade to make things fairer as well as better. But when Kernot first told her mother she had decided to enter politics, Zena was initially concerned about the pressures it could bring on her family. She worried about what it could potentially do to Kernot's marriage, and even raised the possibility that six-year-old Sian could be neglected. Zena mentioned she had just recently been reading a magazine article about the difficulties for families in politics, focusing on two political wives, Susan Peacock, the former spouse of Andrew, and Carla Zampatti, married to the Liberal Party MP and QC, John Spender.

'I'm sorry you're reticent about it, Mum, but they are hardly role models for me,' Kernot told Zena. 'I'm sorry if you disapprove but I feel it's something I just have to do.'

As a politician, Kernot would come to suffer deeply the loss of time with her family and would go to inordinate lengths to try to smooth out the disruptions. But she went into politics with her eyes fully open, knowing it would take a good deal of management to keep her family life on track. She was angry that this should be another brace of problems for women. Why should it be that a woman's career should be held back by this deep-seated worry? Why couldn't society make more allowance?

As their eldest daughter's career began to take off, Zena and Merv helped out where they could, with Zena careful to keep her reservations to herself. But she also began to see that Cheryl and Gavin were fighting hard to maintain normality as a family. Gavin adapted well to the role as part-time sole parent. Zena also began to respect her daughter's publicly emerging political philosophy. One day, just after the 1993 budget furore, the pair were on the phone, catching up. Kernot remembers: 'We were just talking and then Mum mentioned that she felt she had to say that she had been wrong all those years before when she talked about me and politics. She said she was proud of what I was doing but more proud about the way I was going about it. I said to her that that just meant the world to me. And it did. It really did.'

8

FAIRIES AND GOBLINS

With Zena, Merv and sister Gail looking down wide-eyed from the public gallery above, the fifth woman elected to the Senate from Queensland in the nine decades since Federation made her maiden speech to the chamber with its pale pink decor on August 22, 1990. The speech contained three emotional thanks—to far-sighted parents for teaching three daughters back in the 1950s that females could achieve on an equal footing with males; to husband Gavin for his generous spirit; and to daughter Sian, then only seven years old, but being forced to accept that her mother's chosen course would often mean long separations. Her family was swollen with pride but Cheryl Kernot's first appearance on the floor of the parliament could not have been more a sidelight to the frontline action of national politics at the time.

At the other side of the parliament building where the carpet and the furnishings turn to a dull shade of green signifying the domain of the lower house chamber, the subterranean pressures in one of the great struggles of modern Australian political history were gathering strength, gradually building to tear a government, and the Australian Labor Party, apart. It was two years since Bob Hawke, Paul Keating, ACTU Secretary Bill Kelty and Hawke confidant, businessman Sir Peter Abeles, met in secret at Kirribilli House in Sydney to discuss the 'deal' for the transition of the Prime Ministership from Hawke to his deputy. At his desk in the ministerial wing, just around the corner from the office he had coveted all his adult life, Treasurer Paul Keating was quietly seething. Time was wearing on, with Hawke showing no sign of moving over, so, he, Keating, could claim his inheritance. It was just weeks before Keating's fateful off-the-record address to the annual dinner of the parliamentary press gallery where his 'Placido

Domingo' remarks would signal the start of the war of attrition that, a year later, destroyed Hawke's leadership.

On her feet for the first time in the Senate at 7 pm, the unknown new MP from Queensland talked of the work of the 19th century German economic historian Max Weber who laid the foundations for the study of sociology. Weber, Kernot noted, believed that true politicians were characterised by passion, a feeling of responsibility and a sense of proportion. 'How many of us here tonight have as our motivating passion or cause the simple desire to leave the world a better place than we find it?' she asked. 'If my child and grandchildren in later years are in a better world than that in which we find ourselves today, and I have done my utmost to secure their future during my time in this chamber, then I will have realised my political passion.'[1]

Against the background of the slide of the Queensland National Party into blighted squalor and the evidence being presented before the NSW Independent Commission Against Corruption, Kernot said many people had expressed disbelief that she would want to give up teaching to become a politician. In fact, in these, her first words spoken in the parliament it's possible to detect Kernot sending an early signal about the basic concerns that would underpin her defection decision in 1997—apprehension about government short-termism and the need for a New Politics.

'An endearing quality of Australians is the way in which they call a spade a spade; many Australians tell me they find it hard to accept that their local member of parliament tells them privately that he supports their cause, but then has to vote against it because of party discipline,' she said. 'Australians are a natural part of a worldwide movement demanding participatory democracy and greater accountability. They will in the next fifty years, I believe, demand an end to rigid party-line politics. Issues and political decisions are no longer black or white—or even grey. There is an increasing need for dialogue and for a multi-partisan approach. The old rhetoric and labels of the past are unconvincing. The short term focus of successive governments has put our country in what many Australians regard as a perilous position.'[2]

She also signalled the start of what would be a career-long concern with the implications of foreign investment in Australia. As a Queenslander she had worried about what she saw of the sale of real estate in the north to offshore interests. Her suspicion had been fired when, one day in the mid-1980s in Michael Macklin's office, she noticed changes made by the government to the testing procedure that Treasury operated through a body called the Foreign Investment Review Board—the FIRB. Kernot was Queensland party State President at the time. Leafing through some books while waiting on Macklin, Kernot noticed the change in a copy of the FIRB annual report. Basically, the government had changed the 'test' for approving foreign buyouts of Australian businesses from having to prove a net economic benefit to the nation, to simply a requirement that it not be 'contrary to the national interest'. This easing of the conditions for foreign entry caught Kernot's eye, intrigued her.

In an interview in 1997 she recalled thinking the looseness of the test was 'a bit of a con', so she ordered back copies of previous years' reports. 'I found that the Liberals had previously had some really strict rules in place. But we appeared to have gone from something that seemed well structured to what Keating, as Treasurer, had put in place and I thought: "There's an agenda here." Initially it was an intuitive thing when I first saw the report but then I went out to try to put the pieces together. Then I thought: "I know what they're on about—we have got to be beggars!"'

In time, Kernot would become a fierce critic of the FIRB, something of a voice in the wilderness arguing that Australia was selling out its businesses and other assets too easily. She would come to mistrust the way the FIRB, actually just an arm of Treasury, was structured and seemed to operate as just a rubber-stamping agency. It was the first signal of her broader questioning to come of the economic orthodoxy with its vice-like grip on the system. In return, she would be castigated by that orthodoxy as xeno-phobic, jingoistic and naive, but to her this larger question of how hard Australia cut deals as an economic player, and how strong a role government played in protecting Australian interests, was a test of patriotism.

In her maiden speech in the Senate Kernot made a critical distinction, directed, though they were far away and otherwise distracted, at the Prime Minister and Treasurer. They, she said, were given to branding as racist anyone who dared to draw issue with them on foreign ownership. 'Nothing could be further from the truth,' she said. The system tried to deflect legiti-mate public concern by intentionally confusing the issues of foreign owner-ship with foreign investment. 'Of course we need foreign investment,' she said. 'We are, and continue to be, a developing country. But we do not need foreign investment at the expense of our birthright. If our country is so attractive to overseas investors—if we represent a desirable investment target in international terms—well and good. But if foreign investors want Australia, let them lease it. With majority Australian equity and the benefit of leasehold we can still enjoy title to what is ours, while the foreign investors and their Australian partners are free to enjoy the commercial success or otherwise of their ventures.'

Kernot went on to touch on her apprehension about the effects of the program of deregulatory policies that were part of the economic rationalist agenda swallowed by Hawke and Keating, including privatisation of government assets. The burden of the speech suggested it was incumbent on government to take far greater care in the big economic decisions—decisions which impacted on the people in ways that were not fully understood.

With her family, Kernot had driven into the building early that first morning as a senator, glancing up at the huge Australian flag fluttering on its stainless steel superstructure high above, and suddenly realised she would now spend the next six years of her life, and maybe more, in this place. She remembers: 'I was really, really excited. Of course, I'd worked there when I was staffer to Michael Macklin, not all that much, but enough to be familiar with the place. It wasn't a big deal about being in the building itself but I just loved the whole experience. It was wonderful.'

As fate would have it, she had been the last of the seventy-six senators elected in the complicated count process which gradually declares candidates' names one by one in the different States as they reach the required quota of votes. Being senator number seventy-six meant that on coming in, Kernot was the last on the pecking order laid down in the system for the massive bedding-in job overseen by the army of bureaucrats in the building—everything from negotiating office sizes based on seniority to selecting from the battery of paintings and furnishings for the rooms. She had to wait some little time before she was given her own office but when she and her family finally made their way there, the enormity of it was starting to dawn. When she sat down at her desk, Kernot began thinking of the future. 'It was really when the bells rang summoning the MPs into the two chambers. I felt a few tingles and then I got to walk onto the floor of the parliament to a desk that had "Senator C. Kernot" written on the glass. I just got a bit teary. I thought this is real, after all those years. After working towards it, it was real! It was terrific, a really exciting feeling. And then I thought what can I do? What will I do with this job?'

As a backbencher beginning to chart her way through national politics, Parliament House became a very conducive place for Senator Kernot. It was an atmosphere Merv Paton would have adored. It is, first and foremost, the arena where the biggest decisions are made, where the affairs of a nation are steered, where the deals are struck, the intrigues plotted, the secrets housed, sought out, sometimes uncovered. It is also an environment where Kernot's 'people skills' came into play.

Merv Paton remembers how as a young girl Cheryl seemed to have this talent for being engaged fully in a conversation yet being able to take in, with invisible antennae, much else simultaneously happening around her. In this, very good hearing was obviously an asset. But Merv detected that his daughter seemed to have this capacity to cleave her attention span into two—focusing on the conversation at hand, yet following events elsewhere without even looking around. She would beg off her own conversation for a moment to fill in a gap, or add to one going on elsewhere. This skill, exercised with wit or charm, nevertheless suggests a restless, ambitious mind, ever on the prowl for information, hankering to exercise control. As she began to settle in among the other 223 MPs and the dozens of staffers and bureaucrats in the building, Kernot quickly developed a sense of the 'pulse' of the place—an intuition about it, the people, the events unfolding. Merged with her gregariousness and innate political brain, this sense of what people were doing and thinking from how they looked, talked and carried themselves would prove a valuable asset.

Kernot began to form acquaintances with many MPs from the other parties, some ALP people from the left or centre-left factions, and some moderates inside the Liberal Party. She could enjoy a joke, gently rib or otherwise exchange pleasantries about the political process, the players, the big happenings of the day. Later, as leader, Kernot would enjoy cordial relations with most of the top players, many of whom were drawn to a woman who not only impressed with her political savvy but seemed a disarmingly 'nice' person. At key times she would generate surprising loyalty from people in other parties as secrets were traded, deals hatched. Senior members of Cabinets of both political persuasions would enjoy her company, call her round for a drink after hours, chin-wag happily on planes.

For many of them it was very much a two-way process: early on the MPs came to see that the new senator from Queensland had a sophisticated political judgement, and views worth noting. Those who got to know her well could see that in a surprisingly short period of time she was actually beginning to pick the big shifts. Soon after taking the leadership, she had an effective network of contacts and intelligence-gathering around the building. She quickly learned that the Democrat senators' roles as balance of power brokers, negotiating with government ministers and Opposition MPs alike, provided a constant flow of information about all manner of issues. She was soon an informed, well-connected political operator, with a feel for the rhythm of the game.

Kernot arrived in parliament, however, at an inauspicious time for the party. The early 1990s would see the Democrats stricken with a leadership crisis and then falling victim to problematic strategic thinking for another two years, culminating in electoral disaster. It would be a time of much turmoil inside the party room in Canberra. Located in the inner section of the southern wing of Parliament House, the Democrat HQ is a series of offices housing the leader, the party's whip (who helps organise parliamentary activities) and the all-important party room conference area. A very small space, the party room itself, R 114, is just two doors along from the leader's office, and is the engine of much of the decision-making where the senators come, often many times a day, to work through their dilemmas. Seated at a rounded, finely crafted pine table, the Democrats are surrounded by bookshelves with Hansard debates and, on another wall, a photographic record of all the MPs the party has had elected to Canberra. Beyond the main table a small teak table is surrounded by lounge chairs for staffers and other visitors occasionally permitted into the inner sanctum.

Among the many pressures Democrats contend with is the size of the caucus of MPs gathering in this small room. By virtue of the work they do—assessing the fine print of dozens of pieces of legislation—Democrat senators convene regular meetings most days and usually many times each day and on into the evening when things are busy—updating one another on unfolding events in the chamber or in the negotiations with government and Opposition senators, reporting back political intelligence, making decisions about their official policy positions, resolving arguments and alternate views. With up to eight individuals facing one another around the table in the party room, the leader perched at one end, all the ingredients are in place for tension, even fireworks. Much more so than in the major parties, these are people of independent spirit with very much an alternative view of the world, drawn to a party which promises to respect and nurture such free-mindedness. Also, they're not necessarily drawn from common ideological stock or motivated by a shared, underlying philosophy.

Here there is also not the anonymity of the much bigger ALP and Liberal party rooms where, with anything from 50 to 150 MPs in rows of seats facing the leaders' chairs, there is scope for disguising concerns, contempt or anger, hiding humiliation, relief or triumph. Here there is not the faction system of the ALP which works to smooth out the tensions, mobilise the troops, assuage frustration. With the in-built mechanism of deal-doing in the mainstream parties, one disgruntled MP's disappointment is traded off for a win later, the deal buying peace now. Like a tense family perpetually facing off with one another, the Democrats operate on a wholly different level. There is simply nowhere to hide. The senators are sworn not to cross-trade deals, their party constitution and advocacy of transparent, democratic processes making it anathema. Thus, they must deal with every case on its merits, but that requires ensuring the outcome is the right one, and sharp differences of opinion are not easily negotiated away without fights. In the end someone is left defeated, dispirited, angry. In this kind of pressured, constricting environment, very few firm relationships or genuine friendships can be forged, even though the combatants are invariably well-intentioned, committed people. Pressure on the party leader is amplified. Sitting at the head of the table with six or seven colleagues, the figurehead must also be the ameliorator, the compromise-builder, the negotiator but also, by the very nature of the process, often the autocrat who is forced to cut through time-wasting, game-playing or verbal gymnastics to impose his or her view. The group must be locked into a position that can stand up to wider scrutiny.

By and large not a great deal is ever revealed publicly about the Democrat party room pressures that occasionally boil over. Founding father and former deputy leader John Siddons, however, has provided a fascinating account of how tensions that developed between him and Don Chipp in the 1980s escalated to the point of a party room physical confrontation. Siddons, then Chipp's deputy and the party's Treasury spokesman, said that in a battle of wills with Chipp over the handling of the then government's tax plans, he had to take unusual action. Chipp, Siddons charges, was given to suddenly declaring party room meetings over when he wasn't getting his way. On this occasion, it was Siddons who jumped up, walked to the door and blocked it off with his 193 centimetre and 102 kilogram frame. From that vantage point he read out public comments his leader had made about him and threatened to take legal action![3]

Elevated to a place in that hothouse, Cheryl Kernot would come to understand the energy-sapping demands of managing a coalition of independents. The adrenalin of life in Canberra fires uncompromising ambition in MPs. It is a heady place, with even the most mediocre politician capable of developing delusions of grandeur. There is also an important tension between the culture of collective restraint and maintaining party discipline, and the need for individual MPs to be out there keeping his or her own personal profile high. The party room will quickly expose leaders who are not up to it.

One great disappointment for Kernot in arriving in Canberra was the fact that in the election where she had polled 12.5% of the vote in Queensland, Janine Haines had gone down in Kingston. Kernot had benefited enormously from the campaigning of the Democrats' distinctive, super-saleswoman with her trademark curls and round glasses. For the party at large it would mean a descent from an electoral pinnacle into a deeply troubled period in which pundits postulated the Democrats might even dissolve as a serious political force. Haines' replacement, Janet Powell, was a Democrat original, one of the foundation members from the barnstorming days of 1977, elected to the Senate in 1986 to replace Chipp himself. Quite left wing in many of her views, the former teacher was a committed social justice campaigner, stridently anti-nuclear and pro-peace. Unfortunately, Haines would prove a tough act to follow and Powell's leadership would be crushed within eighteen months in a party room coup fired by a groundswell of discontent among Democrat rank and file.

Although it would take six or seven months to flare publicly, the doubts hovering over Powell's leadership were apparent behind the scenes by 1991. In January, criticism was being aired about her strategic handling of the party's opposition to the Gulf War. Privately there were tensions with her deputy, John Coulter, a former South Australian doctor and medical researcher who had a reputation as an environmental crusader of passion to the point of obsession. Coulter believed he was not being consulted. But there were also anxieties—for a long time papered over within the party— arising from the fact that Powell had previously had a long-time romantic relationship with fellow Victorian senator, Sid Spindler. Even after the relationship was over, it was clear that politically, Powell relied heavily on Spindler. He had been a staffer to Chipp before winning the Senate seat and had considerable policy-making experience. Given he had only arrived in the place at the 1990 election, there was a danger he could be seen by some as exercising a disproportionate influence. Anxiety developed about the potential of such a relationship to cause friction in the tight-knit group of Democrat senators.

Kernot bore Powell no personal ill-will, although there was a certain degree of mutual suspicion. Perhaps Powell sensed from early on that Kernot thought she just didn't have what it took to be a national leader. Powell came over as a competent politician, with a good mind and a passion for civil libertarian principles, but she lacked charisma. Concern began to surface privately in the party about her lack of media projection. But, leaving aside the supposed image problems, Kernot and others began to ask questions behind the scenes about the way the personal relationship was affecting Powell's performance as leader and distracting the party room.

Perhaps because she raised the issue up front with her colleagues, suspicion fell on Kernot over the moves that eventually led to the unseating of Powell. The former leader's public attack on Kernot in October, 1997 reflects the residual antagonism that the development precipitating Powell's ousting emanated from Queensland. Powell's supporters argued that Kernot had her eye on the job from the start herself and was manipulating things behind the scenes. In fact, concurrent with the worries among the senators in Canberra, a mood was growing in the wider membership that Powell indeed did not have what was needed to get the messages over, and that perhaps the party should look to a replacement. It is quite clear that for some time discussions were underway between senior Democrat officials in various States, focusing on the leadership dilemma. Some people with no particular love of Powell, who could see that a problem existed, were baulking at talk of a challenge, arguing there was no obvious alternative.

Under Democrat party rules, a leadership challenge can be mounted three ways—by a party room spill, by a ruling of the national executive or by a petition signed by at least 100 rank and file members. Thus, a petition was initiated secretly by a party member in South Australia and won the support of twenty-five signatories in early 1991. When it came to the attention of senior party officials, however, they stepped in to hose the move down.[4] John Coulter reportedly advised Powell of the petition push which she then raised in the party room, defiantly insisting she was not a show-pony and pointing out she had been generating as much media coverage as Haines. Then, a party member approached Division President Tony Walters in Brisbane, urging a petition be circulated there. From his discussions with Kernot and other senators, Walters knew of the tensions in the party room but from what he saw in Canberra himself, he had his own personal reservations about Powell.

In mid-1991 a petition was circulated in Queensland, sparking much discussion in the party about leadership direction. It would all culminate at an upcoming national executive meeting in Brisbane. Party President Heather Southcott and National Secretary Sam Hudson decided a pre-conference breakfast meeting was necessary to give Powell the opportunity to confront the criticisms. Tony Walters stepped forward to put the case with a small group of powerbrokers over the breakfast table at the hotel where the executive members were staying at Brisbane's Kangaroo Point. After the tense talk, Hudson and Southcott spoke privately to Powell, telling her that she had to understand the criticism from the Queensland division was representative of wider feeling in the party. They asked her not to take any action at that three-day gathering, but to take the criticism on board and contemplate some changes to her operation. Their view was that if Powell handled the criticism calmly, making it clear she was taking steps to meet some of the concerns, she could survive. Powell ignored this advice, however, when the national executive met, raising the issue and hitting back, defiantly asserting her right to run her leadership as she saw fit. It was a tragic miscalculation. In that moment whatever support she had previously had from the Democrats' top administrative body ebbed away. The process sparked by the petition would run its course.

When news of the Queensland petition leaked out, the reasons cited had basically to do with Powell's alleged failure to consult, and her inability to generate media exposure. But increasingly it became harder to keep the lid on the wider drama. Some media journalists had known about the Powell/ Spindler relationship for some time but, to their credit, had not bothered to reflect on it. Unlike other nations, by and large Australian journalism does not peddle tabloid-style sex and scandal stories about politicians, preferring to leave their private lives private. But as the leadership battle became more bitter behind the scenes, some participants talked openly of how Spindler had become 'de facto' leader of the party. Three days after the party officially called for nominations in the required leadership ballot, with questions being raised about new allegations about overtime payments to Democrat staffers, and with Powell defiantly insisting she would recontest her position, six of the eight senators, including Kernot, reached the Rubicon. They had had enough.

A meeting was called in the party room and a no confidence motion dumped Powell from the leadership, replacing her with Coulter as interim leader until the ballot. Only Powell and Spindler opposed the move. It was an immensely traumatic time for the rebel senators, with one, John McClean, soon after suddenly resigning from the Senate in dismay. The senators were so distressed they did not want to talk to the media, to be dragged into inevitable discussion of Powell and Spindler's relationship. But in the face of a backlash suggesting Powell had been a victim of a witch-hunt over her private life, Kernot was urging her colleagues to produce a public explanation for their action. In it, the senators cited a list of concerns, including Powell's 'failure to listen to advice, stubborn determination to ignore advice on policy and strategic matters, lack of consultation with colleagues, poor sense of judgement in relation to staff administration and supervision, and failure to follow clear instructions from the national executive'. The statement included the following comments: 'Each of the six senators ... is of the view that a person's private life is exactly that and should be of no concern to her or his professional colleagues. The basis of the no confidence motion lay entirely within the area of Senator Powell's performance as parliamentary leader.' But media pundits were quick to point out that the list of Powell's supposed crimes had also included one other— 'impingements of aspects of private life on party professional judgement'. Here, personal and political pain overlapped.

Janine Haines herself had faced challenges to her leadership—from John Siddons in 1986 and David Vigor in 1987—and said, in response to the drama, that it was just something parties went through. But the Powell affair was a time of great destabilisation. A year after seeing Coulter replace her in the ballot, Powell finally decided to resign from the Democrats, launching a bitter public attack on him for being too wishy-washy as leader, failing to grasp the opportunities available to third parties and pushing the party too far to the right. She thus denied the Democrats a Victorian member but her move also split the party structure in that State. What had begun in hope and high idealism for Janet Powell ended in acrimony. Her failed attempt to stand as an independent at the 1993 election would coincide with the second Democrat disaster of the early 1990s: the nadir of John Coulter's own leadership hopes.

While all this was going on inside the Democrat cloister, the broader stage of national politics became daily more fascinating for Senator Cheryl Kernot. Initially she saw in Bob Hawke a leader of great appeal, although she was uncomfortable with all the 'ocker' baggage. She respected his basic patriotism, though, his determination, his obvious intellectual strengths. At this stage she was far less sure what she made of Paul Keating but, as time wore on, her impressions became influenced by the political thuggery she very quickly saw being played out on the Labor side as the Keating forces manoeuvred to destroy Hawke's leadership in 1990/91. Later, Kernot would develop a working relationship with Keating and then, after his retirement, get to know him far better. Beyond the 1996 election she would come across him quite a bit at official functions, while travelling and on an overseas trip. She became fascinated by a contradictory personality.

Kernot saw in Keating a man of great artistic sensitivity who could open her eyes to the most wondrous classical music, urging his portable sound system earphones, like an excited kid, on his fellow travellers on a plane trip back from China. She was impressed, too, at how he could stand and deliver a passionate exposition about Australia's foreign affairs policy to inter-national experts, a performance smacking of flair and vision. Yet in her first year or so in parliament, Kernot's stomach turned at the tactics being used by Keating's foot soldiers to blast Hawke from office. She was also struck that, from what she had been able to learn of the place and the individuals in it, many of the Labor MPs who lined up behind Hawke seemed solid and principled. She wondered if she had this right, but it seemed that some of those supporting Keating were motivated by self-interest, hatred or simply at the behest of their factional bosses. But it was the methods used that actually incensed her. And then one day she was impertinent enough to make her views known while sitting in the chamber listening to a couple of Labor MPs—Hawke supporters—talking behind her on the Senate benches, including minister Nick Bolkus. Kernot turned around and inquired how it was all going. It was by now the countdown to the second challenge, a period when Hawke's support was seeping away, to leave him finally defeated in the caucus room fifty-six votes to fifty-one on December 19, 1991.

'I've been watching it all,' Kernot told the Labor MPs, 'and I have to say I don't like what Keating's doing. I just don't like the idea that if you can demonstrate you can paralyse a whole government, then you win by default; that if you paralyse something, your opponent will just give up, roll over and say put me out of my misery. It's gutless.'

But, aside from the intrigue, for the new senator there was also work to be done. During the Powell leadership period, Kernot's portfolio responsibilities included Aboriginal Affairs, where her passion to advance the cause of indigenous people would be given free rein. When Aboriginal Affairs Minister, Robert Tickner, set up a new body—the Council for Aboriginal Reconciliation—in response to the deaths in custody scandal, Kernot was made the Democrat representative. It would prove to be an important appointment. Kernot also threw herself into work in the highly complex superannuation policy area, her first foray into a specific economic theme. Through it, she would delve back into history, learning how Labor's national welfare fund of the 1940s had been dismantled by Menzies in the mid-1950s, leaving the whole area of retirement income policy basically unattended until the 1990s. Kernot was well placed to watch the Keating superannuation reforms unfold as economists looked for ways for the nation to build its savings pool. She saw that while Australia had ignored this particular policy area for so long, other nations like Singapore had implemented innovative superannuation savings programs that funded things like national infrastructure development or even education for families. A baby-boomer herself, Kernot saw the sense in setting a national scheme in place that would help fund old age in the 21st century. These were big issues—how and by whom super funds should be run and how much needed to be drawn from the salary to fund a dignified retirement.

Supporting many of the Keating reforms, Kernot would want to take policy further—earmarking part of the hundreds of billions of dollars in super funds for a venture capital pool as start-up money for small and medium-sized businesses; allowing part of a family's super to be used to help buy housing or reduce interest payments on home loans; putting limits on the proportion of superannuation fund assets able to be invested abroad; changing the tax system to give preference to Australian investments; and establishing a special fund through the Tax Office for super for casual and part-time workers. Posing big questions about the future of the economy, this was a good training ground.

When she was made party Treasury spokesperson by Coulter, Kernot also stepped up her investigation of the vexed issue of foreign investment in Australia. During the late 1980s and 1990s she, like many Australians, had looked on with concern at the news that so many Australian companies seemed to be bought out. Brand names long associated with Australia—Billy Tea, Bundaberg Rum, Violet Crumble, Minties, IXL, Arnotts, Sidchrome, Vegemite, Presto Smallgoods, Stubbies clothing—all seemed to be falling into the hands of overseas-based companies. Under the influence of market-oriented economists, both the major parties took the view that there was nothing wrong with this, that with the shift to the global village it didn't matter who owned companies, resources and assets; that as long as companies remained based in a country they would employ locals. As well, the argument went that in a free trading environment, Australian companies were themselves investing abroad, taking over foreign firms or joint-venturing.

But Kernot's concern echoed the distinct discomfort that a lot of Australians felt as they watched the dominoes fall. People were troubled by the questions this trend begged—such as, what proportion of Australian industry and real estate was owned by foreigners? How may *new* jobs did takeovers actually create? How much of the profits of acquired firms go off-shore? Wasn't a domestically-owned company more likely to remain loyal to its base? But quite apart from the obvious questions, Kernot began to ask some technical ones. She began to see the balance swinging from Australian firms taking out foreign loans towards greater actual foreign ownership. In speeches around the country in the mid-1990s, she argued that if Australia was living beyond its means, instead of borrowing money, we had shifted to selling the silver to pay the bills. She pointed out that in the decade after the mid-1980s the total level of foreign ownership of Australian assets had increased from $36 billion to $156.8 billion. She understood foreign money had always been instrumental in building the nation but it became clear that foreign firms tend naturally to buy up the most profitable assets. Instead of paying, say, interest of 7–8% on debt, dividends of a much higher order were being paid for these top-performing assets. Kernot looked into the figures on the size of foreign investment as a proportion of gross domestic product. In 1995 she was horrified to discover that it was 36.2% compared with only 17.4% a decade earlier.

She also began to develop concerns at the wider implications of this unspoken government policy of encouraging the replacement of foreign debt with foreign equity. She saw the situation thus—when you borrow money, you make your repayments until the loan is paid off but if the borrower becomes owner, you pay profits to them forever. In the mid-1990s, Australia's trade figures began to show that profits paid overseas were one of the largest and growing components of the current account deficit. She reiterated that the Democrats were not opposed to foreign debt per se, but said it needed to be understood that although swapping debt for equity could, in the short term, make the current account look better, it was worse in the long term and would lead to higher interest rates, higher unemployment and depressed business confidence.

Kernot learnt that under the Foreign Acquisitions and Takeovers Act, the Treasurer had the sole power, and responsibility, for the approval or rejection of foreign investment proposals. There was no requirement under the legislation for reasons to be given for decisions or even for those decisions to be disclosed. Although applications could be rejected in the national interest, there was no definition of that and it was left to the Treasurer to decide. The FIRB was merely an advisory body but, in any case, it was, always a branch of the Treasurer's own department. According to the informed business journalist David Frith, in the 1970s when it was first set up, the FIRB was planned to have a public registry which would be open to scrutiny, but this idea was scrapped because of concern about keeping commercial information confidential. Said Frith: 'Instead, FIRB became a highly secretive body. It has consistently refused to discuss anything about specific foreign investment applications—everything is regarded as confidential.'[5]

With controversy about foreign control of the Australian media never far from the news, Kernot argued that countries like the USA and Canada had far tighter restrictions on the size of media holdings owned by foreigners. She regularly complained at the ease with which land was sold to overseas investors. Very soon she was calling for major reforms of the way the FIRB operated and in particular was demanding clarification of the 'test' applied to foreign applications—that is, that they not be 'contrary to the national interest'. She attempted to introduce into the Senate draft legislation that would have reformed the whole regime of foreign investment review.

On the eve of the 1993 election, she launched a foreign investment policy that had as its centrepiece a new independent statutory body called the Foreign Investment Review Commission with increased powers and responsibilities to replace the FIRB. The Commission would create a comprehensive national register of foreign investment in Australia; hold public inquiries into particular cases; follow up investment approvals to ensure conditions were being met; encourage productive foreign investment through joint ventures with Australians in areas other than real estate and primary industry; report to the parliament; and publish fully the reasons for its decisions. Kernot chose to unveil the policy on Japanese-acquired land in Queensland near Cairns that had been left undeveloped. 'This policy is not anti-foreign investment,' she said. 'Rather, it is pro-good foreign investment. The main criteria for determining investment will be that it benefits the Australian economy, as opposed to unproductive or speculative investment.'[6]

As the months ticked away towards the federal election that Prime Minister Keating would call for March 13, 1993, it was clear the Democrats were again in trouble on the leadership front. With Janet Powell having departed in fury, making all sorts of claims about how she was dumped because of her relationship with Spindler, and with the PM making a big play of his feminist credentials, the preconditions were in place for a fall in Democrat support among women. The Greens had also arrived on the scene to hive off support. The cornerstone of leader John Coulter's campaign pitch would be a 100-page *Getting To Work* manifesto but the tactical flaw in the approach would be to drape so much of the policy intent in a preoccupation with the environment. Not content to endlessly press arguments about the implications for Australia, Coulter would wax lyrical about the global crisis. Commentator Mike Seccombe would argue that in many ways Coulter was a visionary. He asked: 'Is the Australian electorate ready for this small man with a fundamentalist glint in his eye and a totally eco-centric world view?'[7]

Basically, Coulter argued that his aim was to elevate the issue of the environment to parity with economic discussions. But he just came over as obsessed with all things green. His rigid, defiant refusal to play down this central preoccupation, rather than his non-telegenic presence would ultimately prove to be his undoing. The time was just not ripe for an election campaign tilted like this. According to Democrat scholar Hiroya Sugita, it would be fought predominantly on economic issues, with the word 'environment' not raised once in the three television debates between Paul Keating and John Hewson.[8] Australians' concerns with post-materialist issues were playing a distinctly secondary role to the question of economic survival in the wake of the most severe recession since the 1930s.

Two weeks after Keating announced the election date, the Coulter campaign basically hit the rocks with the infamous decision to launch the slogan 'Don't just get Angry, get a Future' at the Melbourne Planetarium where the Democrat Leader was surrounded by eerie music, wandering witches and warlocks, and tarot card readers wearing Keating and Hewson masks. The aim, ostensibly, was to draw attention to an economic orthodoxy that had all the precision of a glorified fortune teller but all it did was expose the Democrats and Coulter to ridicule, reinforcing the 'fairies at the bottom of the garden' tag. Sugita remarks:

> From that day on, when they reported something about the Democrats, journalists could not resist mentioning witches and warlords, goblins and tarot cards. The slogan launch was not only silly but counter-productive, subliminally suggesting that the Democrats, rather than the Labor party or Coalition, decided its policies by reading tarot cards.[9]

Coulter's campaign opening was poorly scheduled, clashing with the government's arts policy unveiling and coming a day before the Liberals' launch. Although it was televised nationally, giving the party a precious opportunity to impress voters, Coulter's speech was ineptly conceived, according to Sugita:

> Instead of focusing on the Democrats' messages, Senator Coulter started his speech by drawing attention to an appeal to the governments of the world by 1,500 of the world's leading scientists, including half

the Nobel Laureates, to take immediate action to prevent further irretrievable mutilation of the earth. He spent his speech almost entirely on the state of the planet and our species.[10]

Coulter based his campaign approach around predicting a Coalition win and asserting the Democrats' intention to use the balance of power to block its alarming plans to impose a GST, pare back Medicare, and revolutionise industrial relations. This strategy was undermined in November, 1992, however, when Keating announced that if Hewson won, Labor in Opposition would not oppose the GST. Also, Coulter seemed to be projecting a message that he was at odds with virtually everything the Coalition proposed. Thus, he seemed just to be echoing the ALP stance. There was no product differentiation, so why would voters need to vote Democrat?

Coulter was dogged by ridicule and highly critical press reaction. Mike Seccombe was derisive of his blunders in the aftermath of the campaign launch. Confronted with a slump in the polls, Coulter actually began to identify the party's shortcomings, even conceding he was part of the problem. He then went on to assert there was no difference between his party and the Greens. The only difference between the two was that the Democrats were already in parliament. But Coulter thought they should merge. Seccombe observed:

> That's John Coulter for you. You might applaud his innocent honesty but is it really smart stuff for a political leader to be admitting in the middle of an election campaign?[11]

Seccombe added, as part of his analysis of the Coulter campaign, that the 'ambitious' Cheryl Kernot had managed a far more charismatic performance simply by introducing and thanking Coulter at the campaign opener. The footnote to the Seccombe story was: 'Come on down, Cheryl Kernot!' Later Coulter would continue to reject this kind of criticism of him, arguing that rather than challenging his judgement, the severity of the world environmental crisis meant that the process of Canberra journalists setting the issues agenda needed to be questioned. The journalists who criticised him were an arrogant, self-centred, self-opinionated, unelected bunch of ning-nongs by and large. They are a part of the problem with Australia. They are telling Australia about what is going on in Canberra. So they are the filter we have to somehow destroy.[12]

Perhaps this last comment is an insight into Coulter's inability to grasp the art of the possible in politics. He would go on insisting the system was wrong and its messengers had to be 'destroyed'. Whatever the heroic legitimacy of his scientific grasp of the environmental crisis, his political nous in trying to achieve his ends in Canberra was awry. Testimony to that was the 1993 election result.

The Democrats' Reps aggregate vote was down to 3.8%, the lowest the party had ever recorded, a sharp drop from the 11.3% of 1990. The Senate vote was down to 5.3% from 12.6% under Haines. The party won two seats but their total representation fell from eight to seven with the loss of a senator in NSW. The balance of power would be shared with two Green senators and Brian Harradine. Critically, the showing meant that the 'party status' would be at risk in the next poll—that is, with five short-term senators due to stand in 1996, it looked conceivable that the Democrats could lose out even further to the Greens, the outfit from which Coulter saw no need to create any product differentiation. If the Senate numbers at that next poll fell below five, then under the rules the Democrats would lose the right to be called a party, with the associated loss of vital office, research and staff resources. The election had been a catastrophe for the party and the work of sixteen years seemed one election away from obliteration.

As leader, Coulter was determined to run the show his way and differed with some very senior party officials on a number of fronts, from the choice of staff to his policy focus. Party people saw him very much as an interim leader. The air needed to be cleared after the Powell explosion and Coulter's term certainly provided that breathing space. But the election result created a new crisis and the immediate aftermath needed some deft management.

Powerbroker Sam Hudson had been watching Cheryl Kernot very closely since 1988. To anyone without a jaundiced eye, here was a leader-in-waiting but Hudson urged patience on Kernot when she first became an MP. She needed to get experience. Very quickly Kernot showed she was popular with the media and handled the spotlight well. She had previously had some political wins, having forced the government to make important changes to superannuation policy. Ultimately, Hudson would come to believe that Kernot had the best political instincts she had ever seen and an extraordinary ability to communicate in a way that ordinary people could understand. In the wake of the 1993 election, she decided Kernot's time had arrived.

When the ballot was called for the leadership positions, numbers were mobilised. Under Democrat rules, an election for the leadership is mandatory after each election and the candidates must travel around the country to the different divisions, talking to members who then vote. Hudson knew that with the disasters of recent years, a sharp vote of confidence in the incoming leader was imperative. She knew Coulter could not win, suspected that the other candidate, Sid Spindler, was not the person for the job either. While he had the intellect to lead, Spindler had always been a back-room operator, a policy specialist. But nothing was left to chance because South Australia, with its relatively large party membership, and Victoria were the States seen to have a mortgage on the leadership.

As a Queenslander, Kernot was uneasy about the lengthy, idiosyncratic ballot system. She had stood for Deputy in 1990, despite Southcott and Hudson urging her to be patient, and was dismayed when she lost out to the South Australian, Meg Lees. As well, Coulter would take rejection hard and Spindler was deeply suspicious of Kernot over the demise of Powell. If she was to win, Kernot had to have a barrier between herself and their animosity. That barrier would be a thumping vote from the rank and file.

When the membership votes were counted, some 82% of them were cast for Cheryl Kernot as the party's sixth leader.

9
GLORIOUSLY ORDINARY

The newly-elected Leader of the Australian Democrats had some quite clear ideas about how to begin the quest to save her party. She moved quickly to make changes behind the scenes but also saw the urgency in being seen publicly to be acting decisively. Kernot is a determined politician, as events in October 1997 so vividly demonstrated; setting her sights on a course of action, she can be fiercely single-minded. After arriving in parliament, she had assumed that being from a State with a smaller party presence it would be hard for her to get to the leadership. However, once she saw how the party operated she realised she could make a difference, and resolved that she wanted the job. When Sam Hudson rang in late April, 1993, to tell her the result of the ballot, initial jubilation gave way to disquiet. This was a party at the crossroads. Could she help turn it around or had the rot set in deeper than she could know? For three years Kernot would be driven by—and would hold out to those around her—the simple prospect that she just may have been elected as *the* leader who presided over the end of the great dream that underwrote the Democrats.

'I didn't come into politics to be that,' she told aides.

First up, a clarion call had to be sent to the wider community that from here on things would be different. Her leadership would put a line under past blunders.

When she stepped up to the lectern at a luncheon at the National Press Club in Canberra on May 5 for her first big set-piece speech as leader, Kernot chose a theme about 'power, passion and balance'. Thus, the new party agenda. She spoke in a forthright, no-nonsense vein, fully comprehending the need to shift the views of some influential journalists in the audience. She insisted that, after the shock of the election result and a period of introspection, the Democrats would re-emerge, disciplined and focused.

'Those who have been content to peddle the line that the Democrats are the political wing of the Nimbin Settlers Society had better reprogram their word processors,' she said. 'You won't be able to use those tired old clichés anymore. Our political opponents who, up till now, have considered us malleable and amenable—a bit too worthy, a bit too nice to really get in the way—had better brace themselves for a shock.'

Kernot promised she would turn it all around by wielding power, by working in the electorate with passion and by being balanced in the task in Canberra. In pursuit of this, there would be 'steel in the claws'. The speech set out her plans to continue the fight for indigenous Australia and also her commitment to the cause of women's rights. But she strongly reiterated her concern that the land, resources and industry should be owned and operated—as far as is possible—for the benefit of Australians. 'I refuse to sit by and watch our children become the servant class in their own land. I refuse to watch silently while Australia is sold out from under our feet by the "mates" to solve some short-term cash flow problem or worse still, some equally short-term political problem. And I confidently predict in this that I have the support of 99% of Australians.'[1]

For his part, within weeks of his amazing March 13 election victory over John Hewson, Paul Keating was laying down what he liked to call his 'big picture' policy agenda for the ALP's historic fifth consecutive term in office. It was undoubtedly an audacious picture of Australia's future but it was one ironically destined to founder on Keating's tragic flaw. For all his talk of having a greater vision for Australia than anyone else, in the end Keating never realised that arrogance and bullying politics could only be acceptable to the people for so long. His own style, and the inability of those around him to counsel greater sensitivity, inevitably meant he would be denied the political longevity he needed to breathe life into his grand scheme.

In the first half of 1993 Keating initially didn't see it but in time he would come to recognise that there was another politician in the system with vision, a genuine progressive. And one with the backbone required of any leader who wants to make a mark. Right from the outset Cheryl Kernot would be a fulcrum player as some elements of the Keating vision began to unfold. But after he had left the scene, she would still be there, on some fronts pushing the big ideas even further than Keating himself had advocated; on others defending the progressive, left-leaning agenda against political counter-attack and the tidal wave of racist antagonism whipped up by some dark forces at work in the Australian community.

Amid the post-election 'true believers' euphoria, on April 28, 1993, Keating delivered the H.V. Evatt lecture in which he argued the principal aim of his government would be to reduce unemployment. But he also dealt with two other major items: the prospects for white Australia reaching a genuine reconciliation with the Aboriginal community, and his desire for the nation to begin moving towards a republic. Within a few days Keating would use other public speeches to spell out two further agendas: a push for Australia's greater economic integration with Asia and shibboleth-smashing reforms of the labour movement, affecting trade unions and the centralised wages system. Although she was only the leader of a minor party in the 'lesser' chamber of the national parliament, Kernot was destined to have a powerful presence in the debates around such landmark themes.

Informed by what she had seen in her first term of her party's structural problems, Kernot set in train internal housekeeping changes. Despite the whopping vote of confidence in her by the membership, she re-entered Room 114, the party room, as leader with tensions abounding. John Coulter would remain disgruntled for a long time, fearing that his own great dream to make a mark on the environmental front had dissipated. It was, of course, no easy matter for him to resume a seat in the party room as a mere MP, having been responsible for the party's electoral slide. He and Kernot had sharply differing attitudes on all sorts of strategic issues and there was great tension between them. Sid Spindler was, for the moment, suspicious that Kernot was too right wing and would try to moderate some of the more radical party policies, particularly in the areas of redistributive economics.

Soon after moving into the well-appointed leader's suite Kernot sat down with Sam Hudson to map out a more effective management operation. The key thing was to reorganise the limited but vital parliamentary resources. For such a small number of MPs, the quality of their support staff was vital. Kernot identified a few staffers she wanted to move into strategic roles. She promoted former Victorian lawyer, Jacqui Flitcroft. Flitcroft was actually working on the staff of Kernot's deputy, Meg Lees, but was an excellent speech writer with a sharp political instinct, competitiveness, a belief in

THE WOMAN MOST LIKELY

egalitarianism and insights into the women's movement. Kernot promoted Geoff Dodd, a bright young South Australian party operative, to the job as her press aide. Later, when Dodd was moved into the wider job as political adviser, Kernot hired Brisbane newspaper journalist, Cheryl Thurlow, with whom she grew quite close. She also hired Queensland industrial lawyer and former State Public Services Union advocate, John Cherry, who would bring economic expertise to the big tasks ahead. Kernot worked closely with party Campaign Manager, Stephen Swift, and kept tabs on her own State division through her personal secretary, Althea Smith, and her old mate in Brisbane, Tony Walters. Keeping an ever-watchful hand on the tiller was the indefatigable Hudson, the political pro with the endearing sense of humour and the network of contacts extensive enough to smooth away nascent party problems before they evolved into full-blooded crises. All in all, Kernot and Hudson put in place a talented team for the task of ensuring that Australia continued to have a viable third political force.

Rather than keeping the bulk of the personnel servicing her office as Haines had done, or creating an unwieldy kind of democratic 'pool' of advisers as Coulter had, Kernot allocated certain staff to the other Democrat MPs. She did not want her leadership to be a one-person band and resourced the other senators so they could work more effectively. But she also moved to reverse what she saw as the well-intentioned but essentially rudderless democratisation of party processes. For example, where Coulter had given his MPs a say in how the portfolios should be divided up, she basically insisted it was her right as leader to allocate them. This caused consternation, with some suggesting it should be a matter put to a party ballot to decide. But Kernot put her foot down. Some things would be the prerogative of the leader.

She insisted that when the Melbourne-based Hudson was in Canberra, she should attend party room meetings so that the party machine was kept abreast of what went on in there. Kernot was more inclined to bring policy advisers into the party room, so opening up its options for advice. She called for the party room chair to be rotated among MPs to keep all senators involved. She wanted the message-delivery of the party made more sophisticated. She worked to get the national executive to put more effort into publications and she challenged the apprehension in the wider party about the press. Kernot wanted to develop a reputation as a politician whose word could be trusted. She told her PR people they were acting as her agents. There would be no lying, no spin-doctoring, no manipulation or stunts with the media—particularly no stunts. The Democrats were being remade into a party of substance, as well as integrity. With her background as an ABC radio producer, she would come to be a fierce defender of the national broadcaster against political attack and funding cuts. In her early days as leader, at national executive meetings she decried the instinct to blame the media.

'The answer is to come up with interesting things to say,' she argued.

But, crucially, Kernot took a strong line against outbursts of temperament among MPs. She would insist that despite the pressures they were all working under, personal slights should be seen as secondary to hard-headed decision-making. She had grown a bit obsessive about what she perceived as lack of Democrat discipline and insisted that whatever their personal views, if the party room reached majority decisions, even dissenting MPs had an obligation to fall in line. She pointed to the problems created over the years when MPs took up inconsistent positions or ran to the media with stories about party disagreements. This would become one of her core battles, trying to harness recalcitrant instincts to one consistent line. But she also wanted to bring as much intellectual rigour to the policy work as the limitation on resources and time permitted. From the start, Kernot was intent on relegitimising the party, putting it at the centre of the big debates in Australia, exorcising as fast as possible the notion of the 'fairies at the bottom of the garden'. That would be achieved through reasoned and well-thought-out decisions and then through total party unity in support of them.

For one so 'green'—having, after all, only been in parliament three years—Kernot never felt in any doubt about what needed to be done. She had an instinctive confidence in herself, a common sense. She pressured those around her to speed the reorganisation she sought. And she had no qualms about overriding the counsel being proffered if she thought it inappropriate. On one occasion she rejected advice when it was suggested by one of her aides there be an in-house assessment of her appearance—her wardrobe and grooming—to identify what may need improving or emphasised to frame her public 'image'.

It was simply a function of modern politics in the tele-visual era, she was told, that new leaders are forced to take a long, hard look at the image they are presenting. But Kernot quickly made it clear that advice about image shifts was unwelcome. She argued that she had got this far in politics looking the way she did, and she didn't see any reason to start making any radical changes for the sake of some apparatchik's idea of 'image'. Suddenly making changes would only send signals suggesting artifice, cynicism, manipulation.

'I am going to be me,' she said defiantly to her aides when the subject was gingerly raised. 'I've got this far looking like I do, dressing the way I do and I'm not going to change any of it.'

In fact, none of the people around her had any great plan to try to change anything. What was pressed on Kernot was the need to simply stop and take stock. If nothing else she would certainly be forced to expand her wardrobe, given the sharp increase in her public appearances, but its style remained unaltered. Despite her sensitivity on the matter, the fact remained that the very distinctive physical style of Cheryl Kernot was to grow as one of her great assets. She had always had her own instincts about clothing and she wasn't about to dampen them.

As a younger woman, she had made a lot of her own clothes, with a fine hand in needle-work bequeathed to her by Zena. Later, when time permitted, she would sit and relax by making a piece of casual clothing. When her career took off, she intentionally avoided the stereotypical fashion in female power dressing. Kernot says that that style of clothing never appealed to her but, also, she didn't want to be pigeonholed. 'It's an acquired image. It's not expressing yourself, necessarily. It's what somebody else has decreed makes you "powerful". I mean, that's ridiculous. It's your person, your presence, your sense of purpose that makes you powerful.'[2]

As her life became busier Kernot found an excellent seamstress in Brisbane who began to make her clothes. She went to a lot of trouble to find comfortable fabrics and she was not averse to taking a page torn from a magazine to her tailor to see if an idea could be adapted, individualised to suit her. She had always liked natural fibres and colours and would often choose bright hues—turquoise, deep blues, a rich rust—or cream. In summer she would turn to whites and linens in the Queensland heat. 'I don't think there's any neat way to describe my clothes. I just buy things that I think reflect me. I'm not trying to be anybody else. I'm not trying to be a *Vogue* cover. I'm vaguely conscious of what fashion is saying but I trust my own judgement in what I like.' She did intentionally finish off the distinctive streaked and swept-back hair with big, Romanesque brooch ear rings but she never draped herself in jewellery, wore heavy make-up, nail polish or was rigidly groomed.

'I don't think I stand out. I like to be individual, but not idiosyncratically or ostentatiously or in some way exhibitionist ... I don't look at it like that. Particularly living in Queensland, I always liked to be comfortable. I hate too much fuss about dressing. I like the casual, really. If I had my way, I'd be slipping around in linens and cottons and loose slacks and long skirts. On the other hand, I wouldn't wear a hippie skirt ... I work within expectations but still try to express my individuality.'[3]

Impatient to get on with the big tasks and irritated by the obstacles, Kernot was a walking dilemma for some of those in Democrat ranks with whom she worked. Very quickly her undeniable political skill, ability to communicate, capacity to run a policy brief and flair inside the parliament had everyone in awe. This essentially underwrote her authority. Yet, at times she could be extremely demanding of her fellow MPs, critical, even harsh, with an inclination to overreact. Sometimes she pushed staff very hard and made her complaints abundantly clear when work was not up to scratch. If there was a problem, she confronted it head on, with no pussy-footing around. The best example is clashes she began to have with Coulter over their differing views of the merits of the environmental cause and the political strategies to be utilised. Essentially, Coulter argued that without a repaired globe, eventually there would be no economy. Kernot argued that, in the real world, a party that had no credible economic policy would never be a player in the power forums that can change things, including environmental policy. In taking on her colleagues, some wished she could be more diplomatic. They said she was super-sensitive or saw motives in others' actions that may not exist. There was also the odd whinge that when she did make an error of judgement, Kernot was not inclined to own it.

On the other hand, she simply saw that time was short and the Democrat mindset badly needed changing. Floundering around with niceties or equivocation was pointless when hard decisions had to be made. She was determined to drive her party forward, firmly and quickly. She demanded problems be aired and resolved across the party room table. She was horrified at the lack of political judgement among some around her. But she also had a bloodhound's nose for the political fix, however well disguised it may have been in an individual's actions or words. To maintain cohesion and discipline, she was not afraid to flush her colleagues out in quite direct terms. She was disinclined just to brush problems under the carpet because she knew how the mainstream parties would leap onto inconsistencies or public disagreements. In all this, Kernot had the support of some of the most capable people in the Democrat structure. Some of them, even those driven hard by her, responded with great loyalty because they could see she was a professional and correct in trying to make the party itself more acute. Yet she did feel the resentment of others around her quite keenly. Says a long-time Democrat senator:

'The fact is, Cheryl only just suffered the party. She could give the impression she thought the party room was populated by people trying to get in her way. Collectively we had boundless respect for her political talents. There was no qualification on that, it was absolutely genuine. We celebrated her successes—our successes—and we all meant it. But there was not a lot of personal warmth demonstrated to the extent that I would have thought there could be. She *was* hard on people and sometimes it seemed unnecessary. Or it was without a lot of sympathy for personal situations. You'd have staff tearing their hair out at midnight working on things. Sometimes I wondered if her motive was just to keep the upper hand, to show who was boss. But, after all, this is the top level. It's the biggest political show in town and she had to keep reminding people of that. You had to admire her capacity to get things out of people.'[4]

Putting the whole show on a new viable footing and managing it would be a long, drawn-out strain, but that was a price Kernot was willing to pay. From the outset, she knew three factors worked for her: the 80%-plus leadership ballot result, the chastening realisation among Democrats at the scale of the 1993 election failure, and the fact that, in the absence of a double dissolution at the 1996 election, five of the seven senators were up for re-election. The party was facing crunch time. Invariably, Kernot got her way but the tensions in place suggested that she would maintain this iron hand over her party only as long as her political judgement was vindicated. To save her party and create a career for herself, she had many tough decisions to make and not a lot of room for misjudgement. The pressure to succeed was great from the very start.

But succeed she did, particularly in the early months, because of a number of factors. Kernot had the support of the wily Hudson in putting in place, and then managing, change. Hudson saw that Kernot potentially gave her party another chance electorally so she committed herself fully behind the scenes. Once she had designated staffers to the MPs, Kernot's own team of advisers were quickly into stride. Holding the balance of power in the Senate meant there would be frequent platforms for the Democrats to display their wares. And in the Keating agenda, Kernot would have much work to do. But she also faced on the government benches a corps of Labor politicians who had been in power for ten years. Many of the ministers were tired and burnt out. Many had made mistakes or would begin to make them. The fallout of their misjudgements would inevitably position Kernot publicly either as the compromise figure providing the way out of stalemate or, alternatively, as some kind of arbiter. Labor's disastrous 1993 budget provided the first big opportunity and it proved to be a devastating centre-stage debut.

In fact, the Dawkins budget was, for Kernot, a two-month-long triumph of deft political handiwork. The budget's contentious measures were not finally passed by the Senate until the third week in October but at virtually every turn of the negotiations that ran from mid-August, Kernot picked the mood. She saw the multiple flaws first in the budget papers; anticipated community, trade union and even ALP concerns over the basic unfairness of some of the measures; went to the barricades publicly to renounce them; came up with alternative ideas; got negotiations on track; and then, when others were seeking to ape all that, picked the moment when she divined sufficient concessions had been extracted from a reeling government; declared enough was enough and called for the budget to be agreed in the national interest.

Once she had quashed the so-called currency crisis campaign mounted against her by the government spin-doctors, Kernot convened an all-weekend meeting of her policy team in the Democrat offices in Melbourne. She knew that when parliament resumed the following week, the pressure would be on for the Democrats to explain where they stood on a number of the budget matters that were in limbo. When she started talking in more detail about what she wanted of the budget, she had to know that the numbers added up. At stake here was the rebuilding of the Democrats' reputation as numerate players. After a gruelling Sunday session around a table buried in documents in the Melbourne office of Sid Spindler, Kernot and her team had put together a package as a basis for negotiations with Prime Minister Keating and Treasurer John Dawkins.

But even as she was doing her homework, the budget was unravelling for the government. The labour movement was irate and the backbench was complaining that Keating and Dawkins had managed to make Kernot into an electoral heroine. In the lead-up to the 1993 election Keating had promised two tranches of tax cuts, to take effect in 1994 and 1996, which would cost an estimated $8 billion. But so effective had been his campaign to demonise John Hewson's big election centrepiece, the GST, that in the face of an escalating deficit, his government was left deprived of a potentially major revenue-raising source, even though in the mid-1980s Keating himself had fought for a consumption tax inside the ALP. To move to deliver the tax cuts in 1994, Keating had to get revenue from somewhere and thus was hatched the budget grab-bag of contentious measures. Treasurer Dawkins relied on a limited range of advice as he laboured for months in the bunker to pull his package together. Some ministers had no forewarning about measures that affected their portfolios, until budget eve.[5] There was simply not enough devil's advocacy brought to bear as the document was framed. And certainly, too little thought was given to the likely reaction in the Senate.

Since first elected leader, Kernot had repeatedly voiced her party's opposition to the idea of the tax cuts. In May, 1993, she even moved unsuccessfully in the parliament for a bill to overturn them because they were unaffordable in the current economic climate, and too strongly biased towards the rich. When the budget fiasco developed this would become her key starting point. She opposed the budget's sharp increase in the sales tax on wine, changes to optometry treatment under Medicare and elements of the contentious changes to tax treatment of long service leave. But, fundamentally, Kernot and her team worked the numbers until they found a way of making changes that were revenue neutral. By hammering the point, and getting it well established in the debate that she was *not* proposing anything that would blow the deficit out but was, in fact, supporting the broad thrust of the government's deficit-reduction program, Kernot was underwriting her party's claim, perhaps for the first time since 1977, as a voice of fiscal rectitude. But the other tactically important move was the way Kernot out-flanked the two Green party senators from West Australia: former consult-ant psychologist, Christabel Chamarette, and environmentalist academic, Dee Margetts.

The numbers in the Senate after the 1993 election broke down thus: ALP thirty, Liberal National parties thirty-six, Democrats seven, Greens two and Brian Harradine. Thus, the government would need the support of either the two Greens, or one of them and Harradine, as well as the Democrats to get bills passed. The Greens provided Kernot with a nagging strategic chal-lenge. As she saw it, she was fighting for the electoral future of her party and they were direct competitors for Senate seats. She was indignant that years before a green movement sprang up, the Democrats were *the* party of the environmental cause, fighting as far back as Don Chipp's day for causes like the Franklin River. Kernot would grow infuriated at the brutal tactics of some in the wider environmental movement, their attempts to play off offers of electoral support between the Democrats and Greens. Whereas she was committed to working within the system, she was angered by some of the Greens' outlandish policy demands, their seemingly anarchic tactical approach. Her position was that she was an ardent environmentalist but also a realist. Conservation of the environment was best achieved working through the system, getting to grips with issues, marshalling arguments and evidence, and winning the debates. Bullying tactics, she found, just resulted in doors being slammed in the faces of even the best intentioned people. Lacking resources and seeing issues through the one prism—environ-mentalism—meant, to her mind, there was a low ceiling on the effectiveness of the Greens in Canberra. Some of their ideas were simply off the wall and ran the risk of delegitimising the third party presence. So, rather than embrace Coulter's merger ideas, she set out on a deliberate campaign to 'product differentiate' between the Greens and her party. It would be a tricky, time-consuming process—talking often and loud about the differences in what both were advocating.

By the end of the first week in September, Kernot divined that the negotiations had reached the end of the budget concessions that could be wrung out of the government. She did not want to see the budget process discredited by incessant wrangling. So, she suggested a deadline of mid-September for it to be passed and, in the face of hostile criticism from John

Hewson, described his attempts to keep blocking it as irresponsible. With Kernot rejecting Opposition overtures to take even tougher action, negotiations between the government and the Greens continued, however, through October until, after sixty-four days of uncertainty, Chamarette and Margetts also agreed on a package of measures that compensated the unemployed and low income earners in return for support for the sales tax increases.

The upshot was that the budget had been so traumatic, that even before the process ended, Dawkins was making plans to avoid such pain the following year, 1994. He proposed a whole new set of arrangements—a budget on May 10 and a detailed process of pre-budget consultation between himself and his officers, Kernot and the Greens that would hopefully expose and settle points of disagreement in advance of the budget's actual unveiling in parliament. The aim was to speed the process so the budget was in place by June 30, 1994. Dawkins said this was not a signal that the government was ceding economic control; that many other nations had far more open processes; and that there was room to relax some of the more arcane rules of secrecy that had traditionally shrouded the whole process.

Before he could enact his changes, however, John Dawkins resigned from politics, finally fed up with its stresses, leaving the carriage of the 1994 process to his successor, Ralph Willis. Kernot had been initially suspicious of the Dawkins initiative, concerned it was merely an elaborate ploy to lock the Senate in. But she agreed to go along with it. Following the release of a fiscal framework by the government, she was invited to submit her own proposals and then go into a round of talks with Treasury and other departments before the final plan was pulled together. It was an extraordinary idea, drawing the leader of a non-government party into the process, a tribute to the impact she had made the year before. Although there would be no headline-grabbing row in 1994, this process brought big benefits to Kernot. The release of her package to the media got front page coverage, and complimentary analysis for its balance. The *Financial Review*, for example, devoted a full four pages to it—an unprecedented level of interest. But the pulling together of the document, supervised by adviser John Cherry, also allowed Kernot to crystallise many of her economic ideas. It would become a foundation document for ideas developed later, for example, in the 1996 election campaign.

The 1993 budget marked the moment Kernot came of age as a political leader. She had demonstrated that the Democrats could again be taken seriously. She had passed major tests set by the media. At one stage, at the height of the negotiations, she gave twenty-three separate media interviews in one day—a prodigious feat of stamina and message communication. She was heralded by the press gallery as a fascinating new combination: likeable but tough; idealistic but economically literate; politically canny but genuine; ambitious but compassionate; uncompromising yet reasonable. She was, according to commentator Dennis Shanaghan, a 'wheeler and dealer, yet someone who understands the art of the possible'.[6] A *Sydney Morning Herald* editorial dubbed the Dawkins fiasco the 'Kernot budget', arguing that she alone had managed to appear reasonable and in command through the whole process.[7]

Simultaneous with the budget's unravelling, Kernot was becoming caught up in other national issues with important, long-term implications. The decision of the High Court to hand down what became known as the 'Mabo decision' on June 3, 1992, vindicated her decisions on entering the parliament to take responsibility for the Aboriginal Affairs portfolio and to accept a position on the Council for Aboriginal Reconciliation. The Mabo decision basically scotched the notion of terra nullius—the long-held legal fantasy that prior to white settlement of Australia, the continent was 'empty'. The heart of the decision was that there had been prior occupation, and that those people had rights. Traditional native title existed and may continue to exist, subject to the power of the Crown to validly extinguish it. It was seen to be akin to a property right, though not of the same stature as freehold title. This historic move by the highest court in the land to at last acknowledge the basic rights of Aboriginal people would set in train years of complex and bitter debate, through governments of both political persuasions. An ardent enemy of racism, Kernot would play an integral role in the process that would see an historic native title law enacted. But she also played a part in late 1993 in the historic reforms of the industrial relations system set in train by Keating and which would later be expanded upon by the government of John Howard.

Convinced by the economic orthodoxy that in the brave new world of global capitalism, Australia would be held back if it did not deregulate its wages system while it was deregulating much else in the economy, Prime

Minister Keating and his then Industrial Relations (IR) Minister, Laurie Brereton, astounded many in the labour movement. In August, 1993, they revealed they wanted to see introduced a system of enterprise bargaining—that is, negotiations between bosses and workers at the shop floor level, without trade union involvement. It was one of the historic, some would say, most foolhardy, reform decisions of the Keating years. It put the government at loggerheads with the ACTU, with the labour movement demanding that non-unionists who wanted to have such private deals certified should have to form their own unions. With Brereton aiming to bring legislation to the parliament, Kernot and her then IR spokesperson, Senator Robert Bell, were at the heart of the talks. But the historic significance of this period was that in embracing, in part, the new right arguments about the need to reform the union system, Keating and Brereton smashed an age-old Labor canon. They opened the door to later attempts by the conservatives to further dismantle the IR system. In that effort too, Cheryl Kernot would be the pivotal player.

Ever since Don Chipp, the Democrats had been pacesetters in the evolution of radical, innovative policy ideas. Even though it was barely understood by the community, over time many of their ideas gradually became mainstream, even being adapted by the major parties. Chipp, for example, was among the first proclaiming environmental totems like the Franklin River. When no-one else said it, he called for the dismantling of the US presence in military bases in Australia. For years, Haines questioned the economic orthodoxy. Cheryl Kernot could be very populist in her policy approach, for example, taking on the banks over interest rates. From the start, she was a strong critic of the banking industry, arguing that financial deregulation by the Keating government had not seen benefits flow on to consumers. The big-business end of town had certainly been able to go on a borrowing binge, but Kernot was incensed that banks seemed to be building high profit margins into interest rates. The practices of the banks would become one of her key hobby horses and, obviously, this line would be very popular in the electorate. But Kernot would also carry on the tradition of getting out in front with bold ideas that sometime later could be aped by the mainstream parties.

Like Haines, Kernot would grow frustrated that there was little recognition that the pressure from the Democrats was shifting the other parties' views. She moved in, for example, on the issue of families and the workplace first; she called for a jobs levy, only to see the Keating government contemplate it; she called for a wholesale rethink of the tax system long before it became fashionable in the late 1990s; she urged a pause in the speed of reduction of tariff protection for industry long, long before even the Howard government was forced to embrace it. And another good example, drawn from the early months of her leadership, was her response to Paul Keating's push for the nation to become a republic.

Constrained by electoral and ALP sensitivities, Keating would probably have liked to go much further in restructuring Australia's constitutional fabric than he did with his utterances about the republic. Basically he proposed a 'minimalist position'—that is, replacing the British Crown with an Australian head of state, a president. The argument put by the republican movement in the early 1990s was that the constitution could be easily amended to accommodate that change. Strategically, this was an attempt to get to first base without startling the electoral horses. But, of course, there was a much wider and more adventurous argument which suggested Australia needed to look at the whole intricate web of its constitutional arrangements to see what changes may be needed. It may be all well and good to argue that the sense of nationhood would be enhanced by cutting the apron strings with Britain, but was it not valid to contemplate change that actually did something, that actually made the country run better? This was the position Cheryl Kernot brought to bear. And in late 1993 she fired off the first salvo by sending personal letters to both Keating and then Opposition Leader John Hewson seeking their support for an adventurous idea.

In the wake of the 1993 report of Keating's Advisory Committee on the republic, it was clear that the debate was already being hamstrung by political slanging matches. Although opinion polls were showing that more Australians were in favour of the shift than opposed, many people were put off by Keating's advocacy and there was recognition even in the republican movement that his 'imperial rhetoric' was a turn-off. The renowned author and republican leader, Tom Keneally, urged Keating to emphasise more a willingness to try to reach a consensus rather than foisting his own views on the nation.[8]

Kernot tumbled to the idea of proposing not specific change but a new framework of discussion from which some answers might eventually come.

She called for a four or five year program of discussion to be set in train, with bipartisan support, to gather concrete, practical evidence—if it existed—that either supported or scotched the need for broader constitutional change. But she suggested that the ambit of the evidence-gathering should be wide, taking in not only the possibility of a republic per se, but the question of whether the three tiers of government worked adequately; whether changes needed to be made to the operation of parliament and the voting system; the role and identity of the head of state; and whether there was a need for a bill of rights.

She said the republican debate had degenerated into a narrowly focused emotional bunfight between monarchists and republicans. The really big question was being ducked: was the constitution of the country holding it back? All sorts of claims were often made, like Australia being the most over-governed nation on earth; that federal/State relations were a nightmare; that services would be better delivered to the people under a differently organised system. Kernot suggested to Keating and Hewson that the Constitutional Centenary Foundation, an independent organisation set up in 1991 and then chaired by former Governor-General Sir Ninian Stephen, be given resources and an investigative brief to begin gathering evidence on the issues. She suggested a systemic, year-by-year investigation of specific themes to run from 1995 to 1999 to determine if the national interest would be served by making wider changes. This would then lead to a series of referenda with the public able to make its judgement on various proposals after a period of non-partisan, objective analysis of the evidence.

The minimalist position was a sham, she argued, because removing references to the Queen or her representative from the Constitution would entail changes to up to half its 128 sections. In her letter to Keating, Kernot said: 'The Constitution is an interwoven document, a complex set of ideas. The point here is that so-called limited change will set off a chain reaction of implications that roam into wider, fundamental areas. In a sense, if you remove the monarchy from the constitution, you remove the need to have the document as it is currently framed.' Why couldn't Australians simply have the confidence to set out on a process of objectively examining the options in a wide community debate, using the mass media and government information services and forums to get it all aired? In her letter to Keating, she said:

Surely the important question arising from the debate so far is not just whether Australia should maintain its links with the British monarchy but whether there is a better way of governing the country—a way which is fairer and more efficient in the delivery of services to citizens, which is perhaps less costly and less wasteful but also provides greater protection for democratic rights. Perhaps as politicians we become so much a part of the 'system' that we gradually lose the capacity and will to ask challenging questions of it. Surely though, we should not be fearful of an objective process which at least tries to ascertain some real facts about it.[9]

Kernot herself was a republican with a wider vision. She knew, of course, that most politicians being what they are, it was unlikely that there would ever be support in important sections of the polity for radical change. How could State governments be expected to cooperate in an investigation that may show that the nation of seventeen million people would be more efficiently served by eliminating them as political entities and devolving their power either to Canberra or newly empowered regional governments? But that didn't stop her from pressing on, for arguing that, at least, such things should be examined. Other politicians might, but she did not see the pursuit of these ideas as an inherent threat to her job, her hold on power, her reputation. And interestingly, when Labor was in Opposition after the 1996 election, Kim Beazley changed tack from the Keating-esque approach, proposing more conciliatory talks with the Howard government and suggesting a staged process of investigation of the issues, including a year of community consultations.

By early 1994, Kernot was declaring the demise of the 'fairies at the bottom of the garden'. And commentators were agreeing with her. In fact, she had made such an impact that she was nominated in the *Australian* newspaper's yearly selection for Australian of the Year. One newspaper felt compelled to wonder whether Kernot was Australia's best politician.[10] Television chat shows, documentary makers, radio talk-back and women's magazines were as fascinated by her as the press gallery. She was clearly having an impact in the wider community. At the beginning of 1994, the magazine *Ita* ran a cover story focusing on a politician whom journalist Dorian Wild described as unique because she was 'so normal'. Wild observed there were no padded shoulders here, no power dressing. Just normal clothes you can buy anywhere and a neat, suburban hairdo:

> And a friendly smile—mustn't forget the smile. It's the sort of smile that gives the impression that she's actually pleased to see you. And yet it's this woman, so gloriously ordinary and, when you talk to her, so totally at ease with herself, who had the Prime Minister dancing a jig to get his bills through the Senate. With Keating one of the sharpest politicians ever seen in Australia, Kernot's victory is nothing less than a championship performance. But then there's a lot that impresses about Kernot.[11]

During the 1994 summer cricket season with Australia playing New Zealand at the Gabba ground in Brisbane, radio commentator Jim Maxwell invited Kernot up into the ABC box. For half-an-hour, she chatted knowledgeably about her cricket heroes—former fast bowler Graham McKenzie on whom she had a childhood crush, Doug Walters, Allan Border, Englishman David Gower and contemporary quick Glenn McGrath, to whom, interestingly, her daughter Sian had also taken a shine. She reminisced about Walters' first Test century, didn't seem to have a lot of time for the Chappell brothers and talked about how hard it had been to give out her first batsman as an umpire. As Canberra commentator Kerry O'Brien observed, it was quite some coup to be getting her message across the cricket-loving airwaves. O'Brien observed that Kernot was striking a chord politically as a 'rare voice of commonsense'. She was stripping away much of the Democrats' 'fuzzy, sound-good policy' and confronting the economic realities of the 1990s:

> Where in the past all privatisation or all foreign ownership was bad and the solution to everything was a new ombudsman here or a new department there, Kernot's way appears to be much more intellectually honest.[12]

O'Brien observed that Kernot may just have been setting the benchmark for others to follow in Australian politics. Wearing his other hat as the then presenter of the late-night ABC current affairs program, *Lateline*, O'Brien also invited her on to try to plumb the wider question of what she was bringing to politics ideologically. Just what was this Kernot phenomenon? he wondered. When he asked her in the interview to define herself, Kernot said she was a '90s progressive', arguing that it was impossible to compartmentalise everyone into rigid left/right definitions. She and her party were much like other people—'left' on some issues, 'right' on others. But, importantly, Kernot gave an insight into her emerging thoughts about how the pace of the modern world, and particularly global shifts, were making it harder to hold to the old ideological groundrules.

'If you wanted to explore, for example, the issue of censorship … all my life I have had a very liberal view of censorship. But with the advent of deregulation, you look now at what's happening in the entertainment industry, you look at what our kids are looking at, and I start to feel a bit more conservative. I start to feel there is a need for some sort of reregulation. But, on the other hand, I still embrace passionately the views I've always had about social justice, for example, to address the disadvantages of Aboriginal people. I don't think it's easy to pigeonhole me or the Democrats. If you want to call us anything, perhaps I'll settle for 90s progressive. But the fact of the matter is I think what we do offer—which the other parties don't—is a way of identifying where change is needed and proposing some sort of sensible change that works.'

Admitting that her party had previously confronted some tough changes, including ditching economic nostrums that didn't add up, Kernot essentially provided three elements of the driving philosophy in the early months of her leadership: patriotism, a fierce belief in the role of government, and a determination to find another way of 'doing' government aside from the male-run adversarial system that had so disaffected people.

'I feel passionately about standing up for Australia and I feel passionately that there is a role for government in people's lives. And I feel that in the last decade both the government and the Opposition, in just accepting blanket solutions, have forgotten about the impact of those solutions on ordinary Australians. I also feel passionately that the style of politics in this country is holding us back, that we have two men [Keating and Hewson] who, well … I think they hate each other, and all policy is orchestrated around how they can score points off one another. In the meantime, what happens to Australia? We are not taking the steps we need to take in industry policy; we're not having a good hard look at the failure of foreign ownership policy;

171

we are not embracing the need for constitutional change; and we are in a mess on the native title Bill.'[13]

Another influential Canberra commentator, Alan Ramsey, was also impressed by Kernot through the year, but thought the interview with O'Brien was outstanding as an example of a new politician sketching new ideas. It showed, Ramsey said, that not everything had gone wrong in politics in 1993:

> In eight months as leader, Cheryl Kernot has done more to turn the Democrats' small gaggle of Senate amateurs into a disciplined, viable political force than Don Chipp and all his grimacing and posturing did in eight years. She thinks Australia might be looking for something new and different in politics. She may be kidding herself, too. For the moment it's enough to know she's part of political life. Cheryl Kernot has arrived.[14]

10

PREPARED TO OWN OUR HISTORY

In no part of her work would Cheryl Kernot cast the rule book of political caution more willingly to the wind than on the issue of the plight of Aborigines. This was more than just the political risk-taker hitting out in her own idiosyncratic direction. It was more than a case of boldly ignoring the tawdry conventional wisdom that long suggested, often in hushed tones, that there weren't any votes in Aboriginal affairs; that the issue of the funding of Aboriginal programs was a quagmire that had for years destroyed political careers; that there *was* a deep current of racism among some Australians; and that the smart politician best left the whole issue undisturbed. Here, Kernot was clearly following her heart but it was not solely an emotional response. Making a clear-headed political analysis, she divined that not only was it socially important to take a stand on black issues but that the political 'dangers' were not dangers at all—that, in fact, these seemingly intractable problems could be resolved with stamina, will and cleverness.

To Kernot this was a moral question of the highest order, one of those rare crossroads for a politician where principles intersect—things like justice, equality, tolerance. Kernot threw herself into this area of policy work because she had always had the sense that there was something wrong on a gigantic scale for Australians to put right—if only they could muster the courage and determination. It was a matter of high principle. Fundamentally, she believed the political and moral could be merged—that if leaders could find a way through the problems, the essential humanity of the majority of Australians would override the racist narrowness of a minority.

When Milton Morris walked over, cup of tea in hand, to congratulate fifteen-year-old Cheryl Paton back at Maitland Girls High that Monday morning in 1964, he had not only been struck by her poise and oratorial skills. That day, Cheryl had used a poem by Judith Wright and another by Kath Walker to reflect on white Australia's 200 years of injustice to its indigenous people. The speech had bristled with passion, the conscience-pricking sophistication of her words jolting many of the adults present in the school hall. Today Kernot barely recalls the precise argument she put forward, for she didn't keep the speech notes that so moved a canny politician like Morris to glimpse, in a moment of insight, a future national leader. In fact, peering back into the hazy days of her childhood, Kernot cannot put her finger on the source of her concern at the injustices meted out to Aboriginal people. Like most white Australian families in the 1950s, even thousands living in rural and regional Australia, the Patons never had any contact with black people. 'I had this latent thing in me,' she remembers. 'I don't know where it came from. There were never any Aboriginal people where I lived. My parents had probably never even met an Aboriginal person in their whole lives, so I often wondered where the interest and concern of a young person like me would spring from.'

When she went to Canada with Gavin in the early 1980s, Kernot chose course units in the study of indigenous peoples as part of the external degree for which she studied. Learning about the native people of Canada became the counterpoint for learning more about those of her homeland. But her active interest first came alive when she was teaching at Churchie. She read furiously about Aboriginal culture, learning from the work of people like Eric Willmot, head of the School of Education at James Cook University in North Queensland, the lawyer and academic Garth Nettheim and the author Henry Reynolds, whose books helped shape the historic revisionism about Aboriginal genocide in the late 19th century. Kernot was particularly struck to read Willmot's account, for example, of the psychological impact on Aboriginal people of enforced dispossession of their land.[1] Most white liberals had long grasped the notion that indigenous people have a special bond with the land, a relationship that ill-fitted with Anglo-Saxon traditions of private land ownership. But as she read Willmot and others she grasped that at the outset of white settlement, this had been a continent containing different nations, numbering in total some millions and that to them the land was the source of the spirits that gave rise to children. Land was the fount to which one's spirit returned in death. Leaving aside the decimation wrought by disease, social dislocation and the explicit pockets of genocidal murder in parts of colonial Australia, the mere fact of dislocation from the land—of being moved off one's spiritual base and forced to live on that of other people—meant Aborigines were made spiritual refugees, cut off from their religious as well as social and economic wellspring.

Writers like Willmot also first opened Kernot's eyes to the horror of the government policy of forced removal of Aboriginal children from their families and homes in the 1940s and 1950s. As the picture of white cruelty fell into place, she was not just moved. Responding to this ignorance, her soul was steeled. The root of it was probably her mother's uncompromising belief that a civilised society, like a loving family, treats all human beings with respect:

'I can't remember what sparked my fascination with the indigenous culture. I guess it *was* just a social justice thing. I guess I first started to pick things up from the media and reading the newspapers and then realised there was a massive injustice. I didn't know enough about it all and I wanted to learn more. I think when I studied it in my post-grad work, though, it was probably the most interesting work I had ever done. I was engrossed in the cultural dimensions of it. Like the fact that the design of white man's school-rooms offended the Aboriginal sense of space. We know the clichés about trying to educate Aborigines but I began to understand that their spatial learning is totally different from ours. For eons they have used their eyes to spot food and then the system confines them within four walls and imposes curricula with no relevance to them at all. Willmot explained to me for the first time why Aboriginal parents were so suspicious of education. It was really meaningful, learning about things like Aboriginal kinship, the *other* history of this nation. The Aborigines in chains, the massacres, the graphic pictures. I had never known that they were dragged along in chains and treated like animals. I was struck by it.'

Under headmaster Bill Hayward at Churchie, Kernot recognised the need to open the eyes of her students—many of them from privileged backgrounds—to the reality of the black world. She designed a special short course in Aboriginal studies and brought in people like the lawyer and leading civil libertarian in Queensland, Terry O'Gorman, to talk about race relations. She invited Aboriginal people in to talk to the boys about their lives. She realised that almost all the boys she taught there—including future lawyers, doctors and other professionals—had never even met an Aboriginal person, and probably never would.

Kernot remembers: 'Black people like Kath Walker talked to them about how hard it is for their kids to maintain their culture. They said things to the Churchie kids like: "You know, when our kids go to school, white kids like you come up and ask them if their shit is black." The guests would say things like that and, of course, the kids just sat there. It was the stark, evocative "This is what it really *is* like to be black" thing. In the end, we had visitors in every year to the English classes and they were brilliant.'

Then Kernot decided to invite a group of Aboriginal boys to visit the school. Through her contacts in the church, she located a group in a hostel in Brisbane's West End. With Bill Hayward in the school station wagon, Kernot in her old, yellow Datsun and the school bursar in his own car, they set off in convoy through the Brisbane inner suburbs to pick up the boys at the appointed place. When they arrived, the group was nowhere to be seen but then they spied them over the road running around in a park, kicking a football. Soon after the convoy was proceeding back through the sedate grounds of Churchie with a bunch of unruly youngsters hanging out the windows, yelling, laughing, having fun.

'When we got the two groups together at the school though, the Churchie boys were at a real loss,' Kernot recalls. 'They didn't know how to behave with indigenous people at all. We had a barbeque in a shed by the oval and a game of football and it was only then that the ice was broken. The Churchie boys were very big on football but the Aboriginal boys had a big lad called Cecil and they were brilliant. They played this wonderful game and by the end of it the Churchie kids were in awe of their natural prowess. It was wonderful. They said to them afterwards: "Shit, we've never seen anyone run like that. God, you're fast." Those kids would never otherwise have had the opportunity to meet indigenous people.'

Behind her back, Kernot was called the 'boong lover' by some students, but her efforts made a big impact on many of the youngsters at Churchie. Often some of them would stay on after a lesson, talking to their Aboriginal guests. But she learned almost as much from these school activities as the students did. She found every exercise, every visit, compelling. Critically she began to delineate cause and effect in Aboriginal behaviour—symptoms and reasons. She began to understand the complex cultural, historic and social explanations about why Aboriginal people behaved as they did. And as her understanding grew so did her impatience with white racism, with its easy clichés, its half-baked theories, its misrepresentation, its abysmal inability to grasp that one nation can be inhabited by two, or even more, diverse cultures. When she heard the old catchcries about Aboriginal people being lazy or undisciplined or backward, she forcefully begged to differ. She could only see narrow-minded bigotry, either incapable of or refusing to contemplate mitigating causes. She was increasingly irritated by people who could not see beyond their outrage about large Aboriginal families living together under one roof or their insistence that Aborigines should keep neat and tidy houses. What she saw was a kinship culture, the altogether admirable Aboriginal ethos of family structure. She got angry with right-wingers pointing self-righteously to high Aboriginal crime. When she did her research, Kernot saw instead cases of seriously dysfunctional people moulded by the mind-scarring horror of forced removal from their families as children.

Her views about Aborigines were never extremist. She had no truck with the proponents of the 'invasion guilt and blame school', endlessly hardline, angry and adversarial. 'I just don't believe there can be any progress if we can't move beyond the victim thing. I see those as very limiting views. My view is once you can understand the reality of the history, and come to terms with what it all means, then that's the way to start moving forwards. You don't stick to it in a blaming way where someone always has to be the victim and someone has to be guilty.' In short, white Australia had to go a long way towards public acknowledgement about the wrongs of the past, but once that point was reached it would be time to move on. Kernot was not won over unquestioningly to every cause mounted under the banner of Aboriginal advancement. The great social issues were never straightforward. A friend from her early days with the Democrats in Brisbane observes: 'Cheryl is passionate about the issues but she doesn't have a romanticised view of Aborigines—you know, that the whites are all wrong and that we have to do everything for the blacks. She doesn't think like that at all. She has a recognition of indigenous politics that is far more complex. For example, she is well aware that a lot of the behaviour of Aboriginal men is, by any standards, unacceptable and needs to be confronted and changed.'[2]

Kernot was drawn to people who, in looking for answers to the Aboriginal conundrum, were as resourceful as they were compassionate. One such person was the Mayor of Brisbane, Jim Soorley, and another was an Aboriginal woman elder by the name of Janey Arnold whom Kernot first met when she was planning her Aboriginal exercises at Churchie. Kernot came to see how underestimated the influence of the behind-the-scenes Aboriginal women was. With so many black men wrestling with the demons of history, hitting out in confusion and anger, Kernot noticed it was often the women battling to hold together families and communities. A tireless worker for her people, Arnold had helped create 'breakfast in the park', the program of assistance to homeless Aborigines in Brisbane. Kernot suggested Soorley take advice from Arnold about his own campaign to help the city's Aboriginal community. Instead of Aboriginal vagrants being thrown into a prison cell, Soorley had a network of carers mobilised to step in. Then, in 1991, Kernot suggested that the Mayor add Janey to the list of contenders for Brisbane's Citizen of the Year award. On Australia Day, 1992, the pair shared a wry smile across a packed Brisbane Council city hall room when a barely detectable tremor of shock went through the middle-class gathering as a shuffling old Aboriginal woman walked up to accept the honour, bestowed on her by the Brisbane community for the years of service she had given Australia.

And then came Mabo.

On June 3, 1992, the High Court handed down one of the most revolutionary legal findings in the history of the nation, named after the principal plaintiff, the, by then, deceased Eddie Mabo. In essence, by upholding the arguments brought by the Murray Islanders of the Torres Strait, the court rejected the notion of 'terra nullius'. The ruling acknowledged that Aboriginal and Torres Strait islanders had occupied the continent originally with their own customs and laws; that the common law should recognise their property rights to the land, based on native title; and that native title still existed where it had not been extinguished.[3]

In his book *The End of Certainty*, journalist Paul Kelly described the language of some of the judges in the case, including Justices Brennan, Deane and Gaudron, as 'epic'.[4] Justice Brennan argued: 'The common law of this country would perpetuate injustice if it were to continue to embrace the notion of terra nullius and to persist in characterising the indigenous inhabitants of the Australian colonies as people too low in the scale of social organisation to be acknowledged as possessing rights and interests in land.'[5]

Brennan said the law should not be 'frozen in an age of racial discrimination'. The consequences of European settlement were, according to Deane and Gaudron, a 'conflagration of oppression and conflict which was, over the following century, to spread across the continent to dispossess, degrade and devastate the Aboriginal people and leave a legacy of unutterable shame'.[6] But right from the outset, the Mabo decision became a warfront of competing ideas about the very nature of the race debate in Australia.

People like Western Mining Managing Director, Hugh Morgan, decried it as an 'exercise in the politics of guilt' and conservative lawyers talked of it creating 'a nation within a nation, complete with an Australian version of homelands'.[7] Morgan said the court decision 'put at risk the entire legal framework of property rights throughout the whole community'.[8] There were claims that the ruling meant black Australia would dispossess the mining industry and pastoralists right across the continent. Controversy was fanned by assertions that overseas companies would rethink investment in Australia and by reports that Aboriginal groups were readying to make claims like one for the entire Brisbane CBD. But Prime Minister Paul Keating was quietly making plans to make his government's response to Mabo an absolute policy priority.

In October, 1992, he announced the creation of a Mabo unit within his department and commenced a long period of consultation planned to culminate in a progress report in March, 1993, and a final report at the end of that year. Amid scare-mongering over claims by various groups over individual pieces of land, Keating addressed 2,000 people in the Sydney suburb of Redfern on a steamy day in December, 1992, unveiling what has been described as the most important statement ever by a Prime Minister on the issue of Aboriginal affairs. The occasion was the government's response to the International Year for the World's Indigenous Peoples. The PM laid the blame for the plight of Aborigines at the feet of white Australia and suggested the court decision offered the chance of a new start, a new relationship between black and white.

With the March, 1993, election out of the way, Keating turned his attention squarely to Mabo. With his commitment to seeing a Labor government responding with adequate vision to a court ruling of such magnitude, a truly historic period of political intrigue and complex negotiation was set in train—one that would only come to a close in an explosion of jubilation reverberating through the corridors of the federal parliament just after midnight some nineteen months after the High Court's original decision. The dream of land title legislation for indigenous Australians would not be achieved without the lengthiest debate ever in the national parliament, dragging on for a solid fifty hours and bringing some of Australia's best known public figures to the brink of exhaustion. In late 1993 a group of key Aboriginal, legal and political players would band together for this most arduous session of law-making, battling past one complex obstacle after another until a new edifice of Aboriginal rights was in place. At this pivotal moment, it fell to a white woman with a near-spiritual passion for Aboriginal advancement to exercise a key role holding the balance of power in parliament. In the middle of this group of players, Cheryl Kernot would prove to be a critical intermediary, using patience, stamina, policy grasp, charm and intuition to help keep the show on the road until the deal was struck. She was, in the end, only one of a team, yet what she brought was a kind of human glue holding everything together, even when tempers were fraying and the blockages seemed insurmountable. The people who worked closely with her during those days simply say that without her presence, the guiding spirit of the Mabo judgement would never have found its way into law.

In April, 1993, Paul Keating invited to Canberra key Aboriginal groups for discussion with his ministers. They wanted the Commonwealth to commit itself to affirming and protecting Aboriginal rights, establishing a tribunal to determine Aboriginal titles, not just on the basis of common law, but also on a needs basis; setting up a National Land Fund to which Aborigines who could not assert title would have access to purchase land; ensuring absolute protection of sacred sites; and entering into a process of negotiation on longer term issues. In return the Aborigines would agree to the validation of mineral titles which might otherwise be invalid due to the provisions laid down for Aboriginal protection under the Racial Discrimination Act (RDA).

This issue of the RDA would become a central plank of the complex brawl. Aboriginal groups would stand fast, defending the historic RDA legislation, introduced by the Whitlam government. In fact, the real burden of the High Court decision fell on land matters post-dating the 1975 law. In theory, governments, both State and federal, could 'extinguish' native title with impunity in cases of disputed title that arose from developments prior to 1975. But the 1975 Act made such an action a piece of unlawful racial discrimination. The answer for a lot of people bitterly opposed to Mabo was simply for government to override, or destroy, the RDA.

In June, 1993, the Keating government released a 106-page discussion paper on Mabo including thirty-three basic principles. Mining and pastoral leases granted between 1975, the year of the RDA, and June 30, 1993, would be validated by legislation and native title suspended to the extent that it was inconsistent with the rights of other title holders, like miners and pastoralists. Aborigines would have no veto over mining on these lands but native title would revive after the expiry of a lease. Tribunals would be established in each State to decide claims and the extent of inconsistency between titles and compensation where appropriate.[9] These propositions pleased no-one, with Aborigines, the mining industry, the farmers and the States all having massive reservations. Quite simply, such a revolutionary legal finding disturbed a fundamental underpinning of any society—its conventional understanding of title to land. Some powerful sectional interest groups suddenly found a question mark over the status of the land that underpinned their personal or corporate wealth, their administrative, social or political power.

Virtually straight after the court ruling, Kernot had foreseen that eventually there would have to be a legislative response through the parliament of Australia. In her position on the Reconciliation Commission she and other members were given updates by government officials on the ruling, its implications, and then on developments as they unfolded. She was thus from the outset one of the best informed people in the political system about the issues. The Keating government's first choice was to negotiate a response with the States—that is, talk through some arrangements in cooperation with the Premiers that would come together as a concerted national adjustment in the wake of Mabo. That, of course, would prove a pipe-dream, with outright hostile opposition coming in particular from West Australia early on and even some Labor States, making things difficult for Keating.

When the Council of Australian governments (COAG) met on June 8 it became clear that Victoria, Tasmania and West Australia rejected the very concept of native title and talked about the possibility of introducing their own legislation to thwart land claims. Canberra's offer of compensation for existing mining leases on Aboriginal land could not persuade the States to join a cohesive national response. In the light of this, and realising the like-lihood that the Senate would eventually have a key role, Kernot wrote to industry, pastoral, local government and tourism groups, as well as Aboriginal leaders, inviting them to a 'round-table' conference which she would chair in Canberra. It was a bold play. A relative novice in the process, she nevertheless received acceptances from some of the biggest players in Australian industry. Regretting the collapse of the COAG talks, she argued her party needed to know where many of the key players stood when the matter finally came into the Senate in the form of federal legislation. But she also argued that the row would only be resolved when the relevant participants sat down to talk. Then, on June 18, Keating confirmed the government would legislate on Mabo.

This announcement sparked months of manoeuvring by vested interests, extravagant and emotion-laden claims and threats. In the middle, the government had to wrestle with the problems of framing legislation that could navigate through all the conflicting interests. Importantly, the federal Opposition under John Hewson was by now bitterly attacking Keating's management of the issue, setting itself well outside the ambit of the negot-iations. At the end of June, Hewson officially laid down the Opposition position, which was to separate consideration of Mabo from the wider issue of Aboriginal reconciliation, to put economic development first and allow the States and Territories a free hand in formulating their own responses.

Federal Cabinet began framing its ideas for the legislation but a key sticking point would be the power it gave to the States to override decisions on land use. Canberra was suggesting it give the States power to set up their own tribunals, but only if they adopted a 'satisfactory' attitude towards the High Court decision. If they did not, the Commonwealth would set up its own tribunal in the States and retain the overriding power.[10] But then, in the face of moves by the States to frame their own laws to validate land titles since 1975, in early August Aboriginal leaders demanded Canberra draw up national legislation to override relevant State and Territory laws. They argued that Keating had caved into mining interests and failed to adequately consult black groups. The Prime Minister was wedged between the compet-ing interests of Aboriginal Australia and industry.

In September, Keating released an outline of his government's proposed legislation which he called 'a mature national response and the biggest chance the nation has ever had to correct a 200-year old problem'. It contained the following elements: all existing residential, commercial, tourism, pastoral, mining and fishing leases and interests granted by the Commonwealth would be validated and compensation would be payable to native title holders on the basis of 'just terms'; the States and Territories would be able to pass legislation validating their own grants, as long as they complied with certain conditions including the payment of compensation; pastoral leases would extinguish native title unless specific provision was made but native title would survive the granting of a mining or forestry lease; land grants made after June 30, 1993, would not extinguish native title but native title holders would not have a veto over developments on their land; a special division of the federal Court would receive, vet and decide native title claims; and a National Native Title Tribunal would arbitrate disputes over development on native title land. The States could set up their own tribunals within Commonwealth guidelines and, along with the Commonwealth, could overturn a tribunal decision in the 'State or national interest'; land subject to native title could be compulsorily acquired upon the same basis as other land; and native title could be voluntarily surrendered to the government in order, for example, to gain statutory title to the land so that part of it could be sold or leased.

In the main, there was another thunderous burst of criticism from all camps. Aboriginal groups protested that they would totally oppose any provision that allowed the RDA to be suspended in some circumstances. But they also argued there were no measures to benefit those who had already been dispossessed and had previously had their native title extinguished, that native title holders had too little control over developments on their land and that the States still had too much room to manoeuvre. As the weeks wore on, Aboriginal resistance to the legislative package hardened.

In early October, the bosses of ATSIC and a number of Aboriginal land councils had joined forces to form what was labelled the 'Coalition of Aboriginal Organisations' and a series of talks began in Canberra with Keating to try to find a way through the impasse. But when outstanding differences could not be resolved, particularly on the issue of the RDA, on October 8—later dubbed 'Black Friday'—Aboriginal Coalition members went public at a press conference, raging that they had been sold out. After a particularly tough week of negotiations, ATSIC's Lois O'Donoghue said

Keating had failed to live up to the high-sounding rhetoric of his Redfern speech. 'States' rights seem to be more important than human rights,' she said, adding that the chances of resolving the row now seemed remote.[11]

In the wake of Black Friday and despite the big question marks still hanging over government/Aboriginal Coalition talks, Kernot sensed that further upcoming rounds of negotiations would bring a breakthrough. She thought she could glimpse the ground on which the critical action in the long-running saga would eventually be fought out.

She got her staff to book a conference room in Parliament House and quietly invited the two Green senators and their advisers to come to a meeting. Working closely with the experienced Sid Spindler and her staff specialist on Aboriginal affairs, Isabelle Meyer, Kernot had framed something like 100 amendments that she wanted attached to the legislation. As it turned out, the Greens had a list of the same order. In the meeting she suggested sorting out areas of overlap and duplication. In a session that went from 2pm till 9pm with something like forty people involved, there was some coordination and clarification of the two parties' respective positions. But more importantly, in a tactical sense the meeting gave Kernot a very clear insight into the Greens' overall thinking on native title—where the sticking points would be in the future as well as hints about their negotiating methods. It was basically an elaborate piece of homework in advance of the tough test on the horizon. But the next step was to talk to the government, so Kernot suggested a meeting be convened involving everyone—ministers and advisers, Aboriginal groups, Democrats and Greens—to see how much time-saving work could be done towards solutions on various fronts in advance of the legislation arriving in the Senate.

In the interim, the Aboriginal Coalition met again with Keating in a series of rolling meetings on October 14 and 15 and out of that came an historic breakthrough built around a nineteen-point agreement, including an assurance that the RDA would not be suspended. Keating agreed to take the issue of co-existence of native title and pastoral leases to Cabinet, which a few days later endorsed the agreement with some minor amendments. The centrepiece of the historic deal was a novel approach to achieving greater Aboriginal access to land which merged the native title common law right, as handed down by the High Court, with normal commercial practices. federal Cabinet decided that existing pastoral leases owned by Aborigines or pastoral properties which might be purchased in the future—possibly through a Commonwealth land fund—could be converted to a form of land title which resembled native title. On November 16 the Native Title Bill was introduced in the Reps and with the government's majority was quickly passed, setting the scene for its tortuous journey through the Senate where it had to be passed to become law.

What could be described as the 'mainstream' body of Aboriginal opinion had basically reached a point where it was happy with the negotiated package. The Democrats would support it. But the key numbers would be those of the two Green senators who kept insisting they wanted changes. Members of the mainstream Aboriginal Coalition included the ATSIC leadership—people like Lois O'Donoghue and Mick Dodson, the Chairman of the Aboriginal Reconciliation Council Pat Dodson, the bosses of various Land Councils including Noel Pearson and Marcia Langton, and key advisers like the barrister Ron Castan and the lawyer from the South Australian Aboriginal Legal Rights Movement, Kathy Whimp. They became 'attached' to Kernot's Democrats and worked out of her office and the Democrat party room in the parliament building. As negotiations got underway, other key players like the National Farmers' Federation's Rick Farley moved in and out of this group which became known as 'the A-team'.

But a few days after the passage of the Bill through the lower house, a new factor entered the equation: the formation of a new body of Aboriginal opinion outside the 'Aboriginal Coalition'. More hardline, this second group would become known as the 'Aboriginal Alliance' and would draw its members from the NSW Land Council, various legal services and the South Australian Aboriginal Lands Trust—in the main, bodies representing people in the southern and eastern parts of Australia with particular needs because native title had long since been extinguished there by white settlement. With various environment movement players and other legal advisers, the more radical Alliance, made up of strategists like the Tasmanian lawyer Michael Mansell, helped form what became known as the 'B-team', an advisory group around the Greens.

By the time the critical week for the legislation's fate in the Senate was looming in mid-December, Cheryl Kernot was already deeply involved, plotting strategy and lubricating the wheels. Lawyer and former Attorney-General, Gareth Evans would be the government's manager and front man in the Senate chamber, arguing in defence of the legislation, nursing it through the various stages of debate, clause by clause. In the Democrat party room Ron Castan and Kathy Whimp, the lawyer/thinkers, would work at lap-top computers, drawing together drafts of clauses that would accommodate the specific negotiated needs of the various players. Isabelle Meyer, one of Kernot's staffers with the Mabo brief, her young baby lolling in a bouncer on the floor, advised Kernot on key details and kept the Democrat input going. Sid Spindler would assume a vital role on the floor of the Senate, with a direct line to Kernot. She would basically 'cruise' the building as a central negotiator, moving back and forwards between her own base, the Greens' central office upstairs and government and Opposition offices, feeling her way through the complex issues, plumbing the intent of the other players, seeking common ground and trying to identify the potholes. She would hold the threads of it all in her mind.

Basically, the 'A-team' faced a wedge of the Greens on one flank and Hewson's splenetic Opposition on the other. Although itself bitterly divided on the issue, the Coalition was trying to stick to its game-plan of opposing the legislation at every turn. Hewson would argue that the Mabo legislation was far too complex and might be unconstitutional. He said that while the Coalition recognised native title, it should be left to the States to manage, provided they did not breach the RDA. He said Mabo did not address the real problems of Aborigines—their health, education and welfare. Mabo, he said, was a 'millstone around the neck of our country's prosperity and our kids' future' and would only ensure that 'a lot of big city lawyers will be rubbing their hands together'. Opposition senators formed into four-person 'tag-teams', alternating through hours of debate, nit-picking to an inordinate degree over every fine clause in what was a complex Bill, putting Evans under huge pressure with endless questions, interjections and complaints and seeking all sorts of assurances or changes. The whole exercise was simply designed to obstruct, delay or otherwise complicate the journey of the legislation. In the end, this contributed to the debate in the Senate becoming the longest in the parliament's history—some 50 hours of talk extending from Wednesday, December 15 to Tuesday, December 21, 1993.

The critical camp in the unfolding drama would, of course, be the Greens and the 'B-team'. They insisted on working through the principles and practicalities of the Bill much more slowly than those in the Evans/Kernot team. They worked on the premise that every possible Aboriginal group that could be consulted should be consulted. They charged that the 'A-team' was not fully representative of all Aborigines. At times, they argued for arcane changes. In the face of this, some members of the 'A-team' were driven to distraction. Later Kathy Whimp would observe that the Greens' style of politics differed markedly from that of the entrenched Canberra players. Their philosophy, to Whimp, appeared to be 'transformist' instead of reformist:

> But the complex webs of influence and the competing demands of the parliamentary system make such a philosophy difficult to practise. It was necessary for the Greens to take a firm stand and they could not have done so without standing to some extent outside the arena in which compromises are struck. When the time came to make a deal, they were bereft of the backroom, hole-and-corner methods of communication so essential to reaching consensus. They found themselves operating in an information vacuum and progress made so far began to lose momentum.[12]

Reporting on the unfolding Mabo saga and the difficulties Gareth Evans encountered in dealing with Christabel Chamarette, journalist Alan Ramsey was much blunter:

> The Green senator from Western Australia is built like a mud-wrestler and behaves like one at the negotiating table. You can't even get a firm hold on her bottom line. The ground under what she wants keeps moving.[13]

Years later Gareth Evans would recall the great patience required at the time: 'The "B-team" working out of the Greens' office was vital but although they were sincere and committed, they were flaky and at times floundered. As the thing went along they were off the pace quite a bit but nevertheless the job could not be done without finding some common ground with them.'[14]

Initially, the 'A-team' had felt it was getting somewhere with the Greens but, as the talks settled into stride, they were proving very hard to read.

Then, just a week after the Bill left the Reps, the Greens dropped their first bombshell and announced substantial changes were needed before they would support the legislation. The talks began to focus on the nitty-gritty. For Kernot these were particularly testing sessions. The Greens were, in the normal course of things, the Democrats' mortal political enemies, a group Kernot saw, at times, as demanding and extremist. At one point, it fell to her to find out if the Greens would think about pulling on a guillotine motion in the Senate to speed things. After a polite negotiating session in the Greens' office the answer was a firm 'no'. The 'B-team' had control of this agenda and they would get what they could from the process, which was, of course, their democratic right. It had its ups and downs, but during the torrid, week-long Senate session, Kernot's ability to read the Greens' reactions and to manoeuvre the agenda proved critical.

The Kernot-initiated December 15 meeting involving everyone—both 'teams', Democrats, the Greens and government representatives—took place in an expansive conference room behind the PM's office. It began at 5pm and dragged on for hour after hour, with pizzas brought in to keep the combatants negotiating. So convoluted were the competing demands of the legislation's fine print that, at critical points, some of those involved wondered if an impasse would suddenly be reached where the government was forced to simply give up the effort and walk away from the attempt to legislate. It was that tortuous.

Evans, who, as Foreign Minister had only come to the issue in detail very recently, was still finding his way but there were important areas in which he was willing to give ground on behalf of the government to get a result. At one point in the talks when he was out of the room, Christabel Chamarette was evincing great frustration at the direction of things. She began to suggest that if certain elements were not fixed to her satisfaction she would call a press conference and go public with her concerns. Kernot knew things had dragged on for so long that people were close to throwing it in—and a breakdown in the talks at that point could kill Mabo. When Evans re-entered the room Kernot left and went to his staff to explain the Green threat. A note was passed in to him, alerting him to the prospect that the whole process was on the brink of collapse. When the Green senator raised her threat again, Evans was ready, demanding to know what right any individual had to be jeopardising the proceedings when so many people had been working so hard for compromise? No-one held any press conferences.

When the debate was well underway in the Senate, it also fell to Kernot at a key moment to get a message to Evans, a politician not known for an even temperament, particularly under conditions of high stress. The revered churchman and Aboriginal activist, Father Frank Brennan, another adviser to the 'A-team', told her at one point that Evans was being drawn into an Opposition trap, becoming 'bogged down with all the jurisprudence'. Kernot protested that she did not know the Foreign Minister particularly well—and after all they did hail from different parties—but it was clear someone had to make the point. When she did approach him in the chamber, Evans exploded with exasperation but, after giving it some thought, could see the point. Soon he was giving shorter answers, varying the rhythm to try to throw the tag-team off its guard, and being more selective about the points he argued.

Evans had not had a great deal to do with Cheryl Kernot before she became Leader. Having climbed through the ranks to become Foreign Minister two years before she had even entered parliament, he had a wealth of experience whereas she was very much still on the learning curve. But as the leaders of their respective parties in the Senate, they soon developed an easy working relationship, with Evans seeing early on that she was, to use his phrase, 'policy and outcome-oriented rather than game-playing oriented'. He says now he found that 'refreshing and helpful', especially when it became clear that while Paul Keating had done a huge amount to lay down the framework for Mabo, by the time the legislation came to the Senate, there were an immense number of unresolved issues to be confronted.

Evans came to share Kernot's view that with enough patience they could extract a result, despite what appeared to be a wall of paper built on foundations of intransigence and acrimony. He quickly realised how well she slotted into the role behind the scenes, identifying the issues of contention and working them through, putting out the bushfires. Evans recalls: 'It's so silly, in a way, to be making a statement of the obvious. But in situations where people get consumed by the drama of the moment, get consumed by loyalty to individuals or the cause … or confuse the individual or the group with the gut issue … it is just amazing the number of ways the human mind, coloured by emotion, can fuck up the process of producing outcomes. I always found that Cheryl—although she was very committed to the issue, the principles and the people—didn't allow herself to be diverted from the main game. And so, she was extremely helpful in clawing our way through.'[15]

At one point, the influential black leader Charles Perkins arrived in Parliament House, making it known he was deeply disenchanted with the legislation and that he would advise the Greens, through the 'B-team', to throw the Bill out. Talking to a few of the 'A-team' people, Kernot decided that Perkin's intervention could be catastrophic. In the complex web of Aboriginal politics he was a savvy player. Perkins had to be neutralised, so Kernot set off around the building. Locating him in a conference room she asked what was wrong. In a lengthy tirade, he told her he thought the legislation did nothing for Aboriginal people. He repeated his assertions that the government had been listening to the wrong camps within the Aboriginal community. And he complained bitterly that neither Keating, Treasurer John Dawkins or other senior government figures had been consulting him, making use of his vast experience. Kernot mentioned that as they were near Gareth Evans' office and he was the minister with carriage of the legislation, they should drop in and see him.

'That would be a start but I still want to talk to Keating,' Perkins insisted.

Leaving Perkins in the foyer of Evans' office, Kernot went in to see the Foreign Minister alone. She explained that she thought he had to invest time in trying to calm Perkins' concerns. Although Evans was frantically busy, he took the advice. When the Aboriginal leader was seen in, he again launched his tirade of complaint, at the end of which Evans said: 'O.K. Charlie, you've emptied your bucket of shit over my head, now what is it, specifically, that's worrying you about this legislation?' By the time the session had concluded Evans hoped he had provided Perkins with a fuller explanation of some of the specific elements of the Bill. But his anger was not yet stilled and Kernot realised she needed to go one step further.

With Perkins back in the conference room, she headed down the long corridor towards the Prime Minister's suite. While she was there, explaining the situation to one of his aides, Keating himself walked in, having just left a Cabinet meeting across the hallway. Kernot explained the importance of him also making time to hear Perkins out. After mulling it over, he agreed and a meeting was set for thirty minutes later. Seated on the lounge inside his office, the Prime Minister was at his charming best, impressing Kernot with his ability, when the occasion demanded, to listen, observe and step sensitively. He heard Perkins' complaints, gave commitments that certain matters would be considered. Evans would later observe: 'What happened with Charlie Perkins was a very, very neat exercise. But Cheryl was doing that sort of thing all the time. With her doing that and the others playing their roles, it was just a beautiful bit of teamwork. I at least had the advantage of the stuff coming in pre-packaged fashion. I was the machine dealing with it in the parliament at the end of the process but Cheryl had the stress of dealing with the endless number of interpersonal exchanges that developed.'[16]

On Monday, December 20, Kernot was becoming concerned about the direction of things. She worried that the 'tag-team' approach of the Opposition was bogging the whole process down, raising the distinct possibility that a major blow-up could see it collapse in an exhausted heap. The Opposition's rostered teams of senators, lining themselves up against Evans, were making all manner of protests about the small print of the bill. For example, Bronwyn Bishop—while snarling that Kernot was 'Senator Apologia leading the fourth faction of the Labor Party'—suggested that the filing of a flight plan by an aircraft engaged in aerial survey work for the mining industry could fall within the ambit of native title because it was somehow 'using' the land. Despite the exhausted efforts of Evans to dissuade her, Bishop kept on and on about it, demanding guarantees that this was not so. In the face of these tactics, Kernot thought again of Keating, who had largely kept his head down as the focus remained on the Senate process. She realised the Opposition had to be sent a solid message that its frustrating tactics would get it nowhere. And after all, senators on both sides were by now hanging out to get away from the place after a tough year and return to their families for Christmas.

Kernot rang Keating's office and told him it was now vital for him to buy back in, to reclaim ownership of the Mabo issue, to step back into the fight.

'The Coalition is really digging in, Paul, waiting for it all to fall apart. What you should do, I reckon, is have a press conference to make it clear the Senate will stay sitting over Christmas, if necessary, until the Bill is passed. It could be the circuit-breaker we need.' She also advised him to desist from 'bagging' the Senate, because notwithstanding his well-known contempt for the place, just at that moment, he needed it. Keating convened a press conference later that day, vowing to stare down the Opposition, saying the parliament would keep debating for as long as necessary to see the new law ratified.

In the end, the persistence of Evans, Kernot and the rest of the team paid off, when, one by one, the demands of the Greens were negotiated. After that many hours of debate, however, the 'B-team' sprang one last surprise. With all outstanding matters appearing resolved late on the night of Tuesday, December 21, Evans was on his feet rounding off, ready to call for the guillotining of the debate which, with Green and Democrat support, would have brought the session to a final vote. Suddenly Kernot got wind that the Greens had one more worry and would not suppport the guillotine motion if Evans pulled it on. She saw the prospect that at the eleventh hour—the whole thing could still fall apart, leaving the government, Evans and the 'A-team' humiliated. Kernot quickly scribbled a note and put it under Evans' nose, telling him not to close the debate, but to keep it going. Then she ran round to the outside working-lounge area adjacent to the Senate chamber asking the legislation drafting staff where the problem lay. Evans organised for another minister to keep debate going and stormed out, furious. What the hell had gone wrong now, he demanded. The 'B-team' lawyers said they were concerned there was not a provision guaranteeing protection not for native title, but for native fauna. God! Evans thought, now the Greens wanted a clause protecting furry animals! When he demanded the lawyers work out a solution, Senator Chamarette insisted there was a need for the protection of endangered animals, like the platypus. 'Stuff the platypus!' Evans yelled, before storming back into the Chamber. When the drafters had worked out a form of words, Kernot took it to Chamarette who checked it with her advisers. Finally, the 'B-team' was happy. The last hurdle had fallen by the way.

Some time later, just before midnight on December 21, word spread throughout the building that Mabo was clear. The public galleries of the Senate chamber were filled by hundreds of people, come to witness this historic vote of the upper house. There were staffers from all around the building, mixed in with participants like Noel Pearson and Lois O'Donoghue, as well as hundreds of ordinary Australians drawn to the place because of the history unfolding there. When Kernot's turn came to speak for the last time in the emotion-charged atmosphere, she first rued the lack of full consensus, complaining that the Coalition had 'dealt' itself out at every turn in the debate. But, she said, the fact remained that a majority of senators had done a 'wonderful, historic' thing for the country.

'Although delivered 205 years late, we have delivered just a modicum of justice to indigenous Australians. We have put aside the myth of terra nullius. We have said at last that we are prepared to own our history.'

The outcome of the negotiating process, she said, was a bill which finally balanced the interests of industry and Aborigines. Reserving special thanks for Ron Castan, Isabelle Meyer and Kathy Whimp, she said her vote in the parliament was her 'gift' to Aboriginal people. 'I have spent a lot of my life working for the Aboriginal cause, for the struggle, as we call it,' Kernot said. And then, turning to look up at her husband and daughter sitting with many of her Aboriginal friends, she said: 'I am very moved that I have ended up in the federal parliament playing a role and casting a vote to bring justice for Aboriginal Australians whom I honour with my vote this evening.'

When the vote was finally carried, a roar went up, the like of which the parliament building had never experienced before, or since. On the floor of the chamber—with the exception of the Opposition benches which remained glum and defiant—and in the galleries above, people cheered and embraced. Many wiped away tears. Gareth Evans punched the air, Kernot waved madly to husband Gavin and daughter Sian seated above. When she looked along to see the elation on the face of Lois O'Donoghue, it was all Kernot could do to hold back the tears herself. In early 1997, Kernot looked back at the vote as one of the highlights of her life.

'It was fantastic, so much effort went into it. There was so much passion and it was so historically important—important for the future of the country to just acknowledge all this. In an indirect way, it acknowledges prior occupation even though the Constitution doesn't and nothing else does. It says that these people have rights to the land because they were here first and have a deep connection with it. Not only that, it was saying they can prove it!'

11
THE MALE BASTION

In late 1990, around the time Cheryl Kernot was settling into her office in Canberra as a new senator, one of Australia's most astute political minds addressed a lunch-time gathering sponsored by the public relations industry on a fascinating new theme. As the Managing Director of Australian National Opinion Polls (ANOP), Rod Cameron was the pollster who, over twenty-five years, helped the ALP evolve from a federally unelectable, squabbling gang into a political machine holding, at one stage, nearly every government, State and federal, in the country. After years in the business of politics, Cameron had become an incisive judge of the temper of the electorate. His speech that chilly October afternoon was just another example of his prescience—for Cameron framed a new idea, suggesting not just that the future of politics in Australia would be 'feminine' but that the electorate was hankering for a new 'non-masculine' way of running the country. At the time, Kernot was only just beginning to find her way round the parliament building yet very soon she would be drawn towards the same type of conclusion. In his address to the National Convention of the Public Relations Institute of Australia, Cameron argued there would be three big trends in politics up to and beyond the year 2000: increasing community cynicism, the dawning realisation of the gravity of the nation's economic problems and growing divisions over social issues.

'These developments will reinvigorate the search for a new style of political, corporate and community leadership and a new order of political values in which Australians will have faith,' Cameron forecast. 'Increasing divisiveness in our society will result in a different approach to resolving complex debates. The old macho way of proving leadership credentials will decline and the community will respond to a commonsense managerial style which is in touch, honest and direct.' He called this new approach the 'feminisation of the social agenda'. It was a move away from the masculine aggression and confrontationist formula of the 'old order'. He said this feminisation meant many things—more leadership roles for women and a refocusing on issues like family, child-rearing and education. But it would also mean a change in the definition of strong leadership.

'A strong leader will not be in the mould of the brutal Robin Askin, or the aloof Malcolm Fraser, or the doctrinaire Bjelke-Petersen,' Cameron said. 'He or she will have a quiet inner strength of conviction rather than an out-wards show of bravado. Strong leaders, increasingly today, and universally in ten years' time, will be forced to show a human side. Male leaders will be less valued for their brute strength and more for intelligence, common sense, honesty and creativity—an unusual combination of virtues, more likely to be found among women than men.'

Cameron said some contemporary leaders like Bob Hawke had seen the necessity to put their aggressive behaviour to the side. But he argued that the ascension of the former psychologist Carmen Lawrence in Western Australia as the first female Premier in Australia's history would eventually be seen as 'the watershed in Australian politics that marked the start of the ascendancy of its feminisation'. With the electorate clearly searching for leaders with new values, elections at the end of the 1980s had demonstrated that women voters, for example, were 2–3% more likely to vote for female candidates. 'This trend, now it has begun to roll forcibly, is unstoppable.'

Women, Cameron argued, were more acutely aware of issues like the environment, health and education. 'The value of a country, like a family, living within its means is sure to be accepted first by women. When, out of the divisions and disillusion to come in Australia, there finally is an honest acceptance of the harsh reality of our economic condition, I expect it to be women who face up first to the decline in living standards that must follow. They will support politicians who speak honestly and frankly; politicians who forsake the double-speak about our condition that has led to the current confusion; politicians who understand the concerns and values of the women of Australia.'[1]

As the 1990s began, the future looked bright for those advocating greater involvement of women in political life. And not before time. After all, it took forty years from the moment the Franchise Act gave women the vote in 1902 for the first woman, Dame Enid Lyons, to be elected to federal parliament. Although Dame Enid held Cabinet rank in 1949, it was not until 1966 that Dame Annabelle Rankin became the first woman to run a government department when she was made Housing Minister. Not until 1976, and Margaret Guilfoyle's ascension as Social Security Minister, did any woman have Cabinet rank *and* a department to oversee. And it took until 1983 for a Labor woman, Susan Ryan, to be made a federal minister.

But by 1990 the stability of the Hawke/Keating Labor hegemony and a more confident women's movement were together spawning feminist activism on multiple fronts. Joan Child became the first woman Speaker of the Reps in 1986. Carolyn Jacobsen became the first woman to hold the position of Chair of the parliamentary Labor Party caucus, and Elaine Darling and Mary Crawford were elected Vice-Chair and Secretary respectively. On the Coalition side, two Liberal party woman senators, Margaret Reid and Susan Knowles, became Opposition Whip and Deputy Whip in 1987. And, of course, in 1986 the Democrats' Janine Haines became the first female leader of a federal party and in 1990, Janet Powell became the second. In 1990 the shifting fortunes of the ALP at State levels in both WA and Victoria saw, firstly, Carmen Lawrence become the first ever woman Premier and Joan Kirner the second, shortly after. Paul Keating's first government would boast Australia's first female Cabinet minister in the Reps, Ros Kelly. Keating would appoint the feminist writer Anne Summers to help him frame a package of women's policies. And through the early 1990s, influential ALP women politicians pressed hard to set up a quota system so that more women were given the chance in safe seats. By 1994, the Cameron vision of a female future seemed to be materialising. After her eye-catching performances in 1993, Cheryl Kernot was also a player who seemed to fit Cameron's new definition of power.

From her earliest months as a parliamentarian, Kernot was struck by the extent to which the political system was dominated by men. The whole edifice seemed constructed by males, in a male way, for the use of males. The policy agenda was entirely male-run. All the in-built assumptions were male. Just as, years before, she had seen a bunch of men brazenly laying down the groundrules for abortion in the Queensland parliament without a female voice being heard anywhere, so in Canberra she would walk through the long corridors of the building and see male ministers, departmental briefs clutched to their chests, rushing into the Cabinet room across the hall from the Prime Minister's suite, making laws affecting every woman in Australia.

On an intellectual level, she was drawn to challenge these assumptions, this central orthodoxy of power. But she would do so in a different way—and for different reasons—than a lot of active feminists. Instead of concentrating on the symbols of power—being preoccupied, for example, with things like quotas of women in certain roles as if numbers were the important factors—she set out to establish in people's minds questions about the possible *effect* of the domination of decision-making by males. Sure, she could see the argument that it was unfair, per se, that more women were not included. But the key point to her was that there was no ideas-input by women where it really mattered—around the Cabinet table. Not only did this mean the nation was being denied the intellectual skills of a sizeable number of its citizens, but a particular way of thinking about problems, a particular set of values, a particular assemblage of priorities, a particular view about policy options was just not being given expression where the decisions were being made. To some degree this was self-evident—lots of people had made the point for years that women needed to be given a bigger role. But Kernot argued that the scale of the waste of talent had not been fully grasped. She argued it was critical to rethink just how profound an attitudinal bias this may be creating in the political infrastructure. This was not just a question of numbers, the make-up of faction blocs, the convenience of having the odd token female face in some ministerial line-up. She argued that not only should male politicians share power as a matter of equity, but they should accept the theoretical possibility that more females in executive positions could lead to things being done in new ways that qualitatively improved people's lives.

Despite the strength of her views, Kernot eschewed elements of the conventional approach adopted by feminist activism. She was not comfortable being pigeonholed in the contemporary feminist order. She had her own very clear ideas about what she wanted to try to achieve in politics on behalf of other women. One thing Kernot understood was history. She had read feminist literature. Although she had never experienced it personally, she was deeply sympathetic to the argument that for so long so many women had been discriminated against. In her own personal life she had known more than enough women whose lives had never reached their potential or been fulfilled.

But Kernot would take a decidedly idiosyncratic approach. For example, in her daily work she steadfastly refused to make special concessions, to do deals, to make quiet allowance for the feminist 'cause'. She would not be anti-male. Could not be. She liked the company of men, felt comfortable with them and understood them, with all their foibles. She talked, not scornfully, but with compassion about what she saw as the preponderance of emotionally undeveloped males in Australian society. But she would never endorse the notion that because men had enjoyed superior rights for so long, now was the time to exact privileges, for women to even the balance, to set the ledger straight. She would continue to impose her intellectual discipline on feminist aspirations as surely as she brought it to bear on other areas of public policy. Zena Paton had taught her that women and men were equal—nothing more, nothing less. Women would share with men equal rights, but they would be equally responsible, as well. There should be no special pleading because, in Kernot's mind, this insinuated inferiority and incapacity. If women had to extract concessions to get what they wanted, then they were conceding the argument to those who said men were inherently more competent.

This philosophy would come into play as Ros Kelly sat nervously in Kernot's office in Canberra in early 1994, with the storm of the 'sports rorts affair' howling through Parliament House. Kelly, Paul Keating's Minister for Sport and one of his closest personal friends and factional allies, had rung Kernot and asked to see her to discuss the Democrats' pivotal position in determining the parliament's attitude to the scandal that seemed daily to ensnare Kelly more tightly.

The furore first began in late 1993 when the Commonwealth Auditor-General, John Taylor, produced a report which found an inordinate bias towards ALP-held seats in the $30-odd million of development grants allocated by Kelly's department to sports bodies around the nation. There were clear signs that officers of Kelly's department itself had concerns about how the scheme of disbursing the money was being managed. As time wore on, it would become clear the scheme was administered in an extremely cavalier fashion. Opposition Leader John Hewson claimed the 700-odd separate grants had basically been used as a cash-cow for the ALP in the lead-up to the 1993 election. When she had reservations about the way inquiries into the matter were being handled by the House of Represent-atives Environment, Recreation and Arts Committee, Kernot suggested the matter may have been serious enough to warrant a judicial investigation. Kelly made it clear she was not interested in cooperating with any inquiry but Kernot publicly urged her to reconsider appearing before the Reps com-mittee to explain the affair.

At this point came the phone call from Kelly's office seeking an appoint-ment late one evening. Kernot welcomed the minister to her office but when she sat down in the grey leather lounge chair, Kernot noticed that Kelly's hands were shaking slightly. Then forty-six, the Sydney-born Kelly had been a schoolteacher in the ACT before entering local politics, later winning a federal seat and a place in the Hawke ministry in 1987. She began by saying she simply wanted to put to Kernot her side of the 'sports rorts' story and talked briefly of the pressures she had been under, making reference to the fact that she was going home to find her children upset. Kelly mentioned that she thought that 'as a woman', they could trust one another. At this, Kernot took immediate umbrage. Kernot organised for her deputy Meg Lees, who had responsibility for the portfolio, to sit in, but having heard Kelly out, at the end of the session she made it plain to the minister that if she did not appear before the Reps' committee, the Democrats would consider the judicial inquiry.

With the pressure growing on Kelly, Prime Minister Keating was urging government MPs behind the scenes to appear to be more supportive of his minister. In the face of intense pressure, in early February, Kelly did agree to appear before the Reps' committee and her performance there would bury her political career. In over five hours of responses to more than 300 questions, mainly from Coalition members, she made some startling admis-sions, including one that would find its place in the folklore of the Labor years in power. As attention focused on whether there had been appropriate documentation kept of the grants by Kelly's office and her department, she admitted using instead a 'great, big whiteboard' in her office as her 'planning tool' for the grant allocation. Despite the disbelief of many at this, Kelly counter-attacked, rejecting Opposition claims of incompetence.

'Throughout that whole time there has been no corruption demonstrated at all, no wrong-doing, no fraud, no evidence of political bias,' Kelly told parliament.[2] It was simply a witchhunt by the Opposition, she said, without any remarkable substance. Unfortunately, Cheryl Kernot begged to differ. Acknowledging that fraud or corruption were not issues in the affair, in the light of Kelly's performance before the committee and after detailed consideration in the Democrat party room, the Democrat Leader said she believed the admissions had revealed a total disregard for accountability. Kelly had failed to reach 'even the minimum standards of ministerial accountability' the country expected. Kernot acknowledged that some people used whiteboards but she just did not see how they could be an acceptable alternative to proper documentation. Then Kernot uttered words that would reverberate around Parliament House: 'Under the doctrine of ministerial responsibility, Mrs Kelly should resign or the Prime Minister should sack her. It's up to them to take those actions.'[3] Backed by the continued threat that unless action was taken the Democrats would move for a wider inquiry, the Kernot judgement was essentially a political death sentence for Kelly. But coming so soon after the 1993 budget fiasco, it was also a signal of the political potency Cheryl Kernot was generating after only ten months in the job.

Within days, however, Kernot found herself under attack and not just from the Prime Minister and senior Labor ministers incensed at what they saw as her high-handedness. Kernot received letters from several women's lobby groups essentially asking her to go easy on Kelly because she *was* a woman. The lobbyists argued that then Opposition frontbencher Peter Costello was trying to position himself for the future leadership of the Liberal Party in his campaign to discredit Kelly, but that he would not have gone so hard had she been a male minister. Kernot reacted angrily to the pressure from the lobby groups. She had been offended by what she saw as Kelly's attempt to make a special plea to her as a woman and now she was even more outraged that women's groups should see it as their role to intimidate her into acting to 'protect' another woman. The 'sisterhood' was a powerful force in Parliament House, putting pressure on people working in different areas throughout the system to either support, or gloss over the problems of, key female politicians. In Kelly's case, for example, when the sports rorts row first surfaced, some female journalists were pressured to go easy in their criticism of her because it was argued that, as females, the journalists had to be aware of how hard it was for their gender colleagues in politics.[4]

Kernot decided to write to the lobby groups making the point that their appeals to her were inimical to the best interests of the women's movement. Speaking publicly when news of the pressure on her leaked, she argued that gender should have nothing at all to do with judgements on the issue. 'All this (pressure) does is reinforce the views of some people that some women expect other women to be given an easier go than men, while at the same time calling for gender equality in politics. The letters made me really angry because they said to me that these people think so little of my political skills that I could not spot Peter Costello's motives. Ros Kelly's sex has nothing to do with how she administered those sports grants and competence is not gender specific.'[5]

With newspaper editorials and even some Keating government MPs arguing Kelly's time was up, the pressure on the minister became intolerable. In a last ditch effort to save Kelly, early on the morning of February 28, 1994, Keating Minister Bob Collins rang Kernot asking her if she was willing to accept the demotion of Kelly to a more junior ministry. After consulting her party room, Kernot came back to say the answer was no, the Democrats had lost confidence in Kelly. Soon after, the Reps' committee report was tabled in parliament. It found that although there was no suggestion of fraud or misappropriation or corruption, Kelly's department's administration was seriously deficient and she had also been inadequate administratively. It also said there was 'at least an inference' of political bias in the distribution of the grants. An hour-and-a-half later, in light of the 'massive focus' on the row diverting national attention from other issues, Ros Kelly submitted her resignation from Cabinet to Keating.

For some time Keating would rail privately about Kernot's role in the demise of Kelly. Outside his own circle of intimates, however, his diatribe was largely ignored. It was clear the whole issue had been sparked by an independent agency, the Audit Office, and fundamentally Kelly's difficulties had been of her own making. In fact, Kernot rejected Opposition entreaties to probe 'sports rorts' further, seeking other ministerial victims. But she would not let the matter rest there entirely. She believed that if the matter was serious enough to claim a ministerial scalp of this rank then remedial action was warranted. She went public to demand from the government a range of reforms so that parts of the political process were opened up to public scrutiny, made more accountable to the parliament. This crusade for greater accountability and more transparent processes would become a Kernot passion.

The 'sports rorts' affair had a sour footnote for Labor when, without warning, Kelly resigned from the parliament in mid-1995, precipitating a by-election in her safe Canberra seat. The move was beset by bad omens for the ALP. Kelly's resignation became effective on January 30, the day John Howard returned to the leadership of the Liberal Party. The thumping 22% primary vote swing against Labor in her seat was the biggest anti-government swing in a by-election since 1939 and a clear signal that the days of Keating's government were numbered. But the demise of Australia's most senior female federal politician came at a time when other top-flight female politicians would also find their careers stalled or derailed.

In particular, Kelly's departure coincided with a by-election in the West Australian Labor seat of Fremantle vacated when John Dawkins left politics. The candidate was to be former WA Premier Carmen Lawrence, openly discussed by ALP powerbrokers as a potential successor to Keating as federal leader and certainly as Kelly's female replacement in Cabinet. After the fiascos that came to be known as WA Inc. Lawrence emerged seemingly unscathed with a personal popularity rating of some 70%, even after she had battled on with the poisoned chalice until her State government was thrown out of power. In the March 1994 Fremantle by-election Lawrence enjoyed a 2% swing, an extraordinary signal of her electoral appeal given the proclivity of voters to dump on incumbents in such contests. By the end of the following year, however, her political career was in peril, courtesy of what became known as the Easton affair.

The controversy dated from late 1992 when a petition was tabled in the WA parliament containing Family Court details involving a Penny and Brian Easton, and accusing the then WA Opposition Leader Richard Court of supplying Mr Easton with highly confidential material. The petition was later found to be misleading and four days after its tabling Penny Easton suicided. Under pressure about the political decision-making that saw the petition tabled, Lawrence, who was Premier at the time, denied knowing the details beforehand. After a controversial Royal Commission investigation, however, she was criticised over her involvement. As the row dragged on for months in the lead-up to the 1996 election, Lawrence faced the threat of perjury charges and embroiled the Keating government in debilitating controversy over taxpayer funding of her legal bills.

Less than a year after Lawrence's arrival on the scene, once the Easton affair had erupted and put her under so much pressure, she hit out with a line of argument that drew the ire of a number of female politicians, Kernot among them. Lawrence referred to the unfair baggage women are forced to carry in politics, arguing there was a 'madonna or whore' attitude to women politicians. Because she and other women were still a rarity at the top of the pecking order, they were more visible and bigger targets for attack. This line was criticised by some in the media as naive bleating, and when pressed for her reaction, Kernot felt she had to respond. Acknowledging double standards did exist, the Democrat Leader said criticism of politicians' errors was par for the course. The 'haloes and saintliness' ascribed to some women leaders were indeed the result of there being so few of them. Women had to be unusually competent to win top jobs in the first place.

'I can't agree, however, that we are subjected to excessive criticism because of our gender,' Kernot said. 'We are subject to criticism because we are perceived, rightly or wrongly, to have made public mistakes or to have misused the system. That comes with the job.' Referring to three high-profile male ALP ministers who had lost their jobs amid controversy in the years of the Hawke/Keating governments, Kernot said: 'Ros Kelly and Carmen Lawrence are no more victims than Alan Griffiths, Graham Richardson or Mick Young. It's the system that devours us—gender is only one part of it.'[6]

Kernot always understood the basic aspirations of the mainstream women's movement. Why would she not? From her childhood she has always been a female with an almost genetically-inbuilt antipathy to in-equality. Looking on, she could understand why, in November, 1994, tears and emotional embraces were the order of the day at the ALP's historic National Conference in Hobart when Labor finally endorsed a move to affirmative action quotas. After years of lobbying, the powerbrokers of the ALP agreed to introduce a quota system ensuring that by the year 2002 35% of candidates preselected in winnable seats were female. While she could understand the relief of pioneering Labor women like Susan Ryan, Joan Kirner and Carmen Lawrence, in a sense Kernot was instinctively a step ahead of their debate. She hailed from a political party with a ground-breaking record for involving women in its upper echelons. She just assumed women like herself would have prominent roles.

As feminist academic Marian Sawyer has pointed out, the Democrats established themselves as both articulating, and embodying, equal opportunity, particularly in the second of their two decades as a political party. 'Women have achieved leadership positions in the party without becoming honorary men and while retaining the respect of the organised women's movement.'[7] Sawyer makes the point that Kernot was 'somewhat less acerbic' in her presentation of gender issues than Haines. But the point here is that Kernot came to office facing an entirely different set of challenges to Haines. They operated in very different eras. Janine Haines confronted a direct gender challenge. The extent to which she personally had to win her spurs in a man's world, proving that a woman *could* be a leader, should not be underestimated. For her part, after all that had gone before her, Kernot knew that first and foremost she had to save the Democrats' reputation as economic thinkers. While she believed intrinsically in much of the feminist canon, for Kernot it would not be the starting point. She divined that by establishing her credibility and her party's presence in the big, broad national debates, she would, as an offshoot, be able to prise open the opportunity to do something about women's plight. Time and time again in the fine print Kernot would manage to include often little-noticed reforms that had a direct bearing on the lives of millions of Australian women.

As she herself conceded, more hardline elements of the Australian feminist movement were uncomfortable with her approach, that of the insider working within the system. There was unease in parts of the movement with some of her 'moderate' personal views. An avid reader, for example, Kernot found herself identifying with the revered Melbourne-born writer Helen Garner in the furore that erupted over the publication in 1995 of Garner's controversial book *The First Stone*. In it, Garner gave an account of her investigation of a case in 1992 when two female students at Melbourne University went to the police making charges against Dr Colin Shepherd, the principal executive officer of the University's prestigious residential college, Ormond College. It was a harrowing account, basically of the ostracism Garner suffered at the hands of a clique of feminists orchestrating the campaign against Shepherd. Her crimes were that, at the outset, she had expressed some support for him and then, as time went on, attempted to ask pertinent questions about whether the scale of his crimes, even if proven correct, justified the torment that battered his professional and personal life. What incensed Kernot as she read the book was Garner's portrayal of an ideologically-driven and blinkered campaign which brooked no debate and played by ruthless rules to exact vengeance.

Kernot could see that as the 1990s progressed, feminism in Australia, as elsewhere round the world, was entering difficult new terrain. Like everything else, in a time of rampant change, this ideology faced significant pressures. In the 1990s the power relationship between men and women had changed. Though a great deal still needed to be done, women had made big strides since the 1960s. There had been a righting of many imbalances. Yet Kernot could see that many of the old problems had simply been replaced with new ones for women. The progress of the past thirty years seemed only to have made the problems more complex. To her, these problems were not addressed by old-style rhetoric, anti-male antagonistic thinking. So many of women's basic problems came down to economics.

In this, Kernot had the experiences of her own background, firstly her parental family and, more recently, her own married life to draw on. From her childhood, she wrestled with the core issues about the balance in a woman's life between her own interests and those of the individuals she nurtured. Kernot saw how damn hard Zena Paton worked, penned in by economic privation. She would think: is this all there is for women? She fundamentally admired how hard women like her mother had worked as homemakers. But she knew that many contemporary women simply did not have the commitment to do it the same way that generation had. Many women today wanted another mix in their lives. Having seen what her mother went through, Kernot would look back, never sure if there actually was a moment as she grew up when she decided to opt out of that kind of life. She certainly remembered coming to the conclusion that four children was just too big a workload, although her eventual decision to only have one child owed itself to the debilitating sickness she suffered through the pregnancy. That, she most assuredly knew, she could not contemplate again. In Gavin, Kernot realised she was lucky to have found a man who loved kids, a patient, modern man who could adapt, within reason, to the demands of her career.

But all this, Kernot knew, solved nothing. All career freedom did for her, she could see, was create a raft of other, in some ways even more intimidating, problems and pressures. And, she surmised, it must be the same for lots of other contemporary women. But, like so many of them, she gritted her teeth and set about addressing the problems, and trying to make her 'new' life work. In the end, she concluded that among the issues she wanted to address in politics was the challenge of helping find some modern answers to the new dilemmas with which women wrestled.

Kernot's brand of feminism is exemplified in her response to a question about whether by being a woman, and a powerful politician, she would ultimately alarm men. Fundamentally, she said, the best indication of her overall political approach was to be found in how, as Democrat Leader, she had managed the negotiations with governments over their budgets.

'Look back at all my budget submissions. They're not women's perspectives, they are Australia's perspectives. I get criticised for not being feminist enough. I don't make the women's perspective the starting point for everything I'm doing but I do make sure that the impact of what I'm doing on women is calculated in. I've never seen women as victims. Never. And I never will. I don't think I have a persona which comes over as a strong aggressive feminist. I think it's gender-free and about leadership. It's not just about feminist values, it has other values. I *do* think the woman's way of seeing the world is very important. But I've never made it into a competition between men and women because I think that is totally counter-productive. It is not about women as victims—it's about women as partners in sharing the power for better decision-making for the common good.'[8] Thus, one hallmark of Kernotism is this desire to work within the system alongside men; asserting the right of women to have a different, valued approach to problems; using it to address the big national issues in which both men and women have a stake; but, at the same time, almost as a sub-plot, keeping a weather eye to the reforms that can further improve the lot of women. In so many specific areas of her policy work as Leader of the Democrats, this is precisely what Kernot attempted to do.

When she waded into the debate over deregulation of the wages system— the revolution driven by the new right and embraced by Keating—she was concerned about the impact on women. When she and Senator Robert Bell were first negotiating with Laurie Brereton over Labor's changes to the IR system in 1994, she demanded the new legislation include a formal mechanism to regularly measure the impact of enterprise bargaining on women because of fears that the new system would disadvantage, or even allow for the exploitation of, female workers. Such a mechanism was set up and within a year clearly showed that while women thought they were getting a better deal from the deregulated system, by and large they were winning smaller pay rises than men. Kernot had long believed that the big institutions exercising power in Australian society were not staying abreast of the changes in family structures.

In late 1994 she took the unprecedented step of applying to the Industrial Relations Commission (IRC) to intervene in a case in which the ACTU was seeking five days' paid leave for workers to be able to care for sick immediate family members. While she told the IRC three days was probably the necessary leave limit, she put a case arguing for an extension of the definition of the family to encompass 'primary caring relationships'. While she came under attack from the conservative right when it became clear this definition could include gay and lesbian couples, and from the business community over the overall cost, Kernot was adamant unconventional families should have the same rights as those with traditional structures. In fact, one of the most intriguing issues in national politics, playing on Kernot's mind from her earliest days in Canberra, was this vexed question of the relationship between families and work, and how economic change was imposing new pressures, particularly on families with children. Kernot felt the 'system' was just not making enough allowance to try to ameliorate these pressures.

She was probably the first major player to speak out publicly about this link between families and work pressures, sparking the interest of John Howard, for one, in the period when he was battling his way back to the leadership of the Liberals. Kernot saw that after two decades of declining real wages, about 60% of two-parent families with dependent children had both parents in the workplace, basically because they had to make ends meet. For women, this dramatic social change was both liberating and oppressive—liberating in that the 10% increase to 52% in the number of women in the workforce since the mid-1970s had brought greater financial well-being. But it was oppressive because women were still being forced to manage a disproportionate amount of the housework and child-rearing.

Kernot produced figures that showed that working mothers spent an average of forty-four hours a week on household work and another twenty-three in employment. She made her position clear: 'Australian women should be able to make a full contribution to the economy and society but Australian children must also be able to enjoy the right to a stable and caring family environment. A better balance must be found.'[9]

As Democrat Leader, she argued the answer lay in a combination of changes—increased support through welfare allowances like the child care payment, legislation for three months' maternity leave on 75% of salary to be paid by superannuation funds, insertion of family leave provisions in all awards and enterprise agreements but, most importantly, a concerted effort to create far more flexible working arrangements through the IRC and the award system. The latter would be achieved by establishing a 'work and family balance' principle to be accepted as a criterion in decision-making in the national wage case. The IRC would be empowered to ensure that the terms of enterprise agreements should not disadvantage workers with family responsibilities. She also called for the creation of an Office of the Work and Family Commissioner to monitor the progress of these and other measures designed to make the wages system more family-friendly.

Apart from looking closely at the impact on women of policies in areas like IR, welfare and education and training, Kernot called for a major rethink of the gender implications of retirement incomes policy. She argued not only that older women were not getting a fair deal out of superannuation now, but that this inequality could only grow as the years rolled on. As part of the regressive nature of the superannuation tax concessions introduced by Labor, the overwhelming majority of concessions went into supporting male superannuation, despite the fact that women comprised more than half the post-sixty age group. She pointed to research which showed that the majority of female employees did not have work patterns which fitted comfortably with the existing superannuation structure, which meant most women would then not be able to rely on super to support them in retirement.

Kernot led the Democrats in opposing the Labor government's move to raise the female pension age from sixty to sixty-five, not because they did not believe in the principle of parity, but because the decision was rushed, did not pay heed to history, was badly timed and would have long-term implications for the female population that had not been thought through. In a sense, here Kernot was arguing a special case for women. But her position was driven by the complex inequities at work. Making women wait longer for the pension did not acknowledge important disadvantages they had long suffered. The notion that women had now caught up to men with equal pay was nonsense—there were still big disparities in earnings. Women were continuing to work, as they had for decades, for less pay. For years they had had fewer opportunities for career advancement. Many in the pre-retirement age bracket had taken years off to have children, putting themselves at a disadvantage in earning potential and super benefits. Kernot argued that more sophisticated options like the 'stepped' pension schemes used in Europe should have been considered.

It was always a tricky balancing effort, exercising power in the big time alongside men, focusing on the key issues without alienating them, yet also managing to advance women's rights. Kernot's bottom line, though, was always clear—the agenda of national leadership had to be changed, reoriented more towards women, for two reasons, neither of which had anything to do with old-style feminist retribution. The first was that with such a deep-seated male bias in the system, issues that mattered to women were not getting onto the table for discussion. Later, when she met and had a chance to talk to Hillary Clinton during a visit to Australia by the US President, Kernot would find common ground here with what America's First Lady called 'kitchen table issues'.

'These are issues that matter to women,' Kernot would say. 'Men just don't think about some of these things and that's not a sexist comment, that's just a realistic observation of fact.' So it was, in the first instance, a simple question of equality—half the population had a right to have their concerns made more prominent. But the second, and most vital reason, was that the nation was a lesser place because of the structural absence of a female viewpoint.

Kernot believed that male politicians' preoccupation with what Paul Keating called the 'big picture' issues meant they were gradually becoming more and more remote from people's lives. Increasingly she would target the male fascination with notions like economic restructure, international trade and the jargon-laden elements of economic policy like 'micro-economic reform', arguing that while the management of a national economy was vitally important, it had to be translated into language which ordinary people could understand. It had to be made relevant to the world where people were left to struggle with new pressures, like growing joblessness, flexible working conditions, the pressures of integrating work hours and family time, care of the sick and disabled and management of retirement.

In fact, Kernot saw that globalisation had, in some ways, very particular relevance to women. While male-dominated national and international economic bureaucracies were trumpeting its benefits, more had to be done to address its devastating social and environmental consequences. There was evidence to suggest that the big losers from globalisation internationally included women and children through labour exploitation, human rights abuses and shrinking employment opportunities that came with privatis-ation. Kernot cited claims by Australian trade unions about the trend away from the factory floor work towards low paid, part-time work at home in the textile, clothing and footwear industries, with the resulting removal of sick leave, superannuation, workers' compensation rights and other protection. Unions were pointing to the rise of Asian-style sweat-shops around suburban Melbourne as the pressure grew for Australia to compete with low wage nations of South-East Asia. As well, the consequences of bungled economic management hit the poor hard, with most single parent families headed by women. Global *and* national trends made it imperative for women to be moving into positions of power in government.

Women had views worth hearing, and skills worth using. Some women were preoccupied with the bias against them in society and those who felt disadvantaged had a right to seek change. Women had important views that needed to still be heard about male/female relations. But they also had insights about how a changing world was affecting them—like the struggle to find a balance between earning enough income to survive and bringing up children; like how economic pressures were affecting men too, leaving more of them unemployed, affecting their emotional security; like how education and training programs would equip their children for the future. Women's talents went underutilised. They were good problem solvers, in Kernot's view, because they were good listeners, inclined to draw on different areas of experience in searching for answers rather than compart-mentalising their thinking, and were congenial and less confrontationist in negotiations. These characteristics had never really even been considered as a resource, let alone applied. Kernot pointed out in the mid-1990s that a surprisingly high proportion of the people running the environmental movement were female. She postulated that this was because it was a relatively 'new' profession and there were not yet traditionally entrenched males. But she also said women had a hugely underestimated role to play in the environmental debate for two distinct reasons. Firstly, they well understood the urgent need to start nurturing the environment.

In a speech to an environment conference at Murdoch University Kernot said: 'Since I was a school girl, the images drummed into my head through poems, short stories and paintings were that men did heroic and daring things in the bush while the women stood on the verandah, rocking a baby, shading their eyes and waiting for their men to come home. Of course this isn't reality because more than a third of our farmers are women. They do hard labour on farms with limited access to resources and bear the brunt of keeping the family together in a situation where they have financial, social and environmental problems.' But, apart from their nurturing, in what Kernot called their natural 'thrift' role, women also had incredible power. Invariably the person managing the family budget and making the decisions in the supermarket, it was up to women to factor in to their product choices the impact on the environment. 'At an individual level we must think about our effect on the environment when we make decisions and, believe me, we have massive power. Unfortunately, we rarely use it. Women, in particular, control most of the power in our consumerist society. They have their hands firmly on the purse strings and if they don't buy products which damage the environment, they could make an enormous difference.'[10]

Kernot saw the possibility that the remoteness from ordinary people's lives of the 'male' way of doing politics could be a contributing factor towards the growth of disillusion with government and the breakdown of trust in institutions.

'These real issues aren't on the agenda and never will be until there is someone in there in a prominent position to raise them, to refuse to accept that they're not important, to hassle about them, to get them on the agenda through a fantastic Cabinet submission. Those things don't happen because there haven't been women there who can do it. You can't talk about women really effecting change in a significant way until there is a critical mass of them where the real decisions are made. And they are not there, so all this stuff we see being presented as the big issues is really just peripheral to what ordinary people want. We haven't changed the core, and that does drive me quite a lot. Whether that's feminist or not, I just think it's about power sharing for more sensible, balanced decision-making in the country. The boys are into all the big picture stuff, but they never seem to get it balanced right with the domestic realities.'[11]

12

A TRAINED INCAPACITY TO LEARN

In her approach to an economic orthodoxy that had, since the late 1970s, established a grip on national policy-making in Canberra, Kernot inherited a strategic position first carved out by Janine Haines. She would, however, develop this role to a significant degree. Not only did she argue strenuously that there *should* be alternative ways of managing an economy, but she complained that there was something bordering on an intellectual conspiracy, involving powerful vested interests in the political, academic, media and business communities, holding onto power, resisting debate about options.

Basically, the same tough-minded school of economic thinking that underwrote Thatcherism in the UK and Reaganism in the US established a powerful, subterranean network of control over the way Australia, too, approached economic management. This way of thinking is known in the jargon as the 'neo-classical' school of economics. In essence, its proponents take the view that the working of demand and supply—market forces—should be the sole instrument of economic decision-making in society. Government, and its agencies, should exercise a minimal role, without public sector 'intervention' like the imposition of tariffs designed to protect domestic industries. Taxes should be either abolished or reduced as far as possible and many important areas of the economy deregulated or 'privatised'—given over to free enterprise to run, basically on the premise that the private sector does it better, or more efficiently, because it reflects more accurately what consumers want in the marketplace. A key part of the theory suggests that if taxes for business and the upper income brackets are kept low, this will help business expansion, generate jobs, and thus spread prosperity in a 'trickle-down' effect. This school argues for welfare to be provided on the strictest needs-based criteria. It wants trade union power and the activities of the wage fixing system pared right back, so that individual employers and employees can work out their own wage and condition deals without any third party imposing itself, interfering with the market mechanism, creating 'inefficiencies' and driving up costs. At its extreme, neo-classical theory countenances government involvement only in a few essential areas like law and order, defence and the maintenance of foreign policy. By cutting back on government spending and keeping a lid on wages, inflation would be kept low. By eliminating inefficiencies, economic agents engage in 'pure' competition. With government kept as 'small' as possible or pushed right out of the way, the individual is 'empowered' to make decisions, according to his or her desires.

The story of the contemporary rise of this school in Australia goes back to the 1960s when successive waves of economists, educated to think this way, began graduating from Australian universities. Many became adherents of the radical liberal ideas that came together as Thatcherism in the late 1970s. The most influential first stirrings on the political front came with the rise of what was called the 'dry' faction inside the Liberal Party, and within a number of important business and rural pressure groups, from 1980. This group of thinkers would win over a substantial section of the Liberal Party—the National Farmers' Federation and then the National Party itself—to a free market doctrine advocating low inflation, low protection and deregulation of the economy. This was the first great citadel to fall, for it jolted the protectionist hegemony that had long been a part of liberalism and informed thinking inside the old Country Party. In his book *The End of Certainty*, political journalist Paul Kelly argues that, along the way, anxious about the implications of the emerging dry policies, Prime Minister Malcolm Fraser had stood against them, prior to losing office in 1983. His defeat by Bob Hawke liberated—and was used to validate—the emergence of this dry 'counter-establishment'. Kelly says this group was loosely united by ideology, networks, a mutual support mechanism and a comprehensive view of the Australian 'disease'. It drew support from 'a new generation of academics, businessmen, public servants and journalists dedicated to the same philosophy'. Kelly also points out that as Fraser's Treasurer, John Howard also embraced the new order, pushing unsuccessfully for a broadly based indirect tax. Howard fought against the high level of protection afforded the car industry by his predecessor as Treasurer, Phillip Lynch. With these moves, Howard's career strategy was established. He became the 'champion of the free market lobby', according to Kelly.[1]

The second great citadel to capitulate to the free market doctrine was the ALP, for such was the apparent strength of this new set of ideas, the incoming Hawke government could not but fall under its spell in 1983. A new Labor administration was confronted by an Opposition and key special interest groups arguing the same compelling case, but to which many of its own powerful bureaucratic advisers also subscribed. Paul Keating came under the influence of members of the neo-classical school in Treasury but the orthodoxy also claimed advocates among the most powerful mandarins in the other 'central agency' departments—Prime Minister and Cabinet and Finance. Keating was quickly shifted away from some of the more 'traditional' Labor ideas that he had been publicly advocating, even weeks before the change of government. In fact, the story of his vision of the economy is the story of his induction in 1983–84 into the most powerful 'club' in Australia. This ideologically-driven clique of right wing economic thinkers had risen to influential positions in key spheres of public life; not only the civil service but also in the political parties, the finance industry, political and business journalism, some powerful companies, the lobbying industry, all sorts of political, economic and strategic think-tanks that blossomed in the 1980s and a small band of private economic consultancies in Canberra.

In embracing the fundamentals of this school of economics, Bob Hawke and Paul Keating shifted the Australian Labor Party well to the right on the political spectrum. By sending unequivocal messages to the business community that they would govern in its interests, by cracking down on welfare, but, fundamentally, by shifting away from their parties' traditionally-held expansionary economic policies, Hawke and Keating cleverly sought to disenfranchise their political opponents. Annexing the middle ground, eschewing radicalism or any hint of extremism, the Labor party appealed to the modern mass of middle-class voters, so consigning the Liberal/National Party Coalition to isolation, irrelevance and internal civil war on the far right of the spectrum. But the effect was an historic consensus throughout the 1980s and the 1990s on the foundation issues of economic management between the Labor Party and the Coalition, basically because the back-room advisers providing them with their inspiration and guidance shared the one philosophical outlook.

Keating was given to presenting himself as the great helmsman of Labor's 1980s hegemony, the visionary thinker with his hands on the levers of power. In the infamous 'Placido Domingo' speech to the annual dinner of the Parliamentary Press Club in Canberra in December, 1990, where he began his campaign to unseat Bob Hawke, he boasted that he 'walked around' with the world's financial markets 'as much in my pocket as any Finance minister has ever, anywhere in the world'.[2] In fact, there is an altogether different interpretation possible—that rather than being the great puppeteer of politics, Paul Keating was simply the puppet.

Time would show that, despite its ups and downs in Opposition under leaders Andrew Peacock, John Hewson and Alexander Downer, and despite periodic speculation that the Liberal Party would split or self-destruct, the Coalition finally prevailed against Keating's pyrotechnics when John Howard won in 1996. The Hawke/Keating strategy of shifting their party to the right was always doomed to be exposed as a catastrophic error of judgement when the electoral cycle eventually turned. In fact, there were always a number of interwoven problems with a political strategy that repositioned the ALP in the economic policy clothing of the 'new right', as it was dubbed in the 1980s. The first was that it only made sense as long as the party kept winning. Armed with its socialist inclinations, for decades the ALP had been served by the perception that it offered voters something basically more altruistic than its opponents. It may have been mismanaged at key moments, but Labor could always point to its belief in collectivism, social inclusion, the notion that government had a role looking after the poor and disadvantaged, in maintaining the great tradition of Australian egalitarianism and helping keep society cohesive. The Coalition had for decades taken up a position championing the rights of the individual, in the classic tradition of Western liberalism, above the rights of the group. By pretending to, in fact, *be* a Liberal Party in the 1980s, the ALP ran the risk of forfeiting this claim to a higher political morality. By embracing the notion that it, too, was fundamentally driven by market forces whereby the individual could flourish, the strategy also ran the risk of making the choice offered to the electorate, ever after, simply one of marketing and rhetoric;

where the test was simply which party could produce the leader who came over most appealingly on television.

The other big flaw in Labor's political strategy of the 1980s was the question of where this shift to the right would leave the party when, and if, it was concluded that the economic orthodoxy actually got it wrong, failed or had not provided all the answers. By embracing this set of economic ideas, Hawke and Keating shifted their party a long way. If it was ultimately demonstrated that the economic thesis was flawed, it was always going to be a long way to row back. That was the legacy bequeathed to Kim Beazley and his deputy Gareth Evans when they picked up the pieces after the 1996 defeat.

One Keating biographer, John Edwards, has made quite clear the revolutionary impact of Treasury thinking on Keating. Certainly at the end of the 1970s, particularly as he came into contact with many in the business community, Keating was evolving his thinking about the need for Labor to develop a rationale around the market and to ditch its more anti-business notions. For example, he was becoming convinced that Australia's long-standing system of tariff protection was proving to be simply an artificial wall behind which Australian companies were cosily featherbedded, held back from necessary exposure to the competitive forces that shape world trade. This argument, of course, would become the linchpin of the coming revolution in Labor's economic thinking—that, in an increasingly com-petitive global trading environment, Australian industry had to be thrown in at the deep end and made to compete on its own. Nonetheless, prior to the 1983 election Keating was basically 'still in the Labor mainstream of the 1970s,' Edwards says.[3] Keating had talked of the need for government to be a regulating agency, putting controls on speculative capital activity, imposing limits on debt raising by foreign companies, restricting foreign purchases of Australian assets, keeping foreign banks out and keeping controls on bank interest rates.[4] Within months of coming to office, and coming under the sway of the orthodoxy, however, such ideas were simply swept away, obliterated from the moment Treasury advised the incoming government of its blown-out budget deficit inherited from Fraser. Keating began the process that would come to dominate his yearly budget deliberations—cutting back on government to make way for his free enterprise reforms.

First edged towards market economics by his experience of the mining industry as a shadow minister and encouraged by Bob Hawke and key figures like Reserve Bank boss Bob Johnston, Keating began the historic process of deregulating the Australian economy—floating the dollar, removing exchange rate controls, opening up the system to permit the entry of foreign banks. Importantly, he also set about dismantling the regime of tariff protection for some key industries, in keeping with the core rationalist argument that manufacturing had been insulated for too long. He also began the process of privatising major government entities in a raft of industry areas that would come to include banking, telecommunications and the airlines. Then, as Prime Minister, Keating would target one of the really great Labor shibboleths, moving to deregulate the wages system and dismantle an arbitration system that had been an underpinning of egalitarian Australia since the turn of the century. That a Labor Treasurer and Prime Minister could bludgeon aside his party's basic traditions, ideology and policy platform and drag it into an unspoken consensus on the economic fundamentals with the conservative forces of Australia is not only a tribute to Keating's own determination, and, at times, brutal powers of advocacy. It is also a statement about the intellectual potency of the neo-classical ideas and the extent to which the school's laissez-faire thinkers had become systematically entrenched.

Throughout the Western world economic policies after the Second World War had been based on Keynesian principles of demand management in the domestic economy and a system of managed international currencies in the global economy. 'Keynesianism' was the doctrine of government intervention in the economy to stimulate demand propounded by John Maynard Keynes, the great early 20th century British economist who developed his policy framework to prevent a recurrence of the tragic events of the Great Depression. Russell Mathews, the Emeritus Professor at the Australian National University in Canberra, argues that despite the great success of this approach, it was discarded in the 1970s when the devaluation of the American dollar and the oil price explosion that followed the Arab oil embargo plunged the world into recession. 'Instead of strengthening the capacity of individual governments and international agencies to withstand such destabilising shocks, most countries reverted to the laissez faire approach to economic policy which had been so disastrous during the

Depression,' Mathews says.[5] Basically, thus began the tyranny of economic rationalism.

In universities around the world, new generations of aspiring economists were taught that their study essentially had a mathematics-based, quasi-scientific credo that would lead to ultimate truth—and thus, correct decision-making for businesses, for industries, for nations, and for the people who sought to run them. They were educated to understand that the economy was a system that would achieve a state of equilibrium, and full employment, if only markets were given their head to make decisions. As Australian journalist Brian Toohey puts it, according to the theory: 'Everything will operate at its full potential provided there is no friction in the system; no static blocking the "price signals"; no distortions caused by anti-competitive corporations, vote-grubbing politicians or bloody-minded unions.'[6] The orthodoxy believed it was serving the nation by insisting that reliance on markets and removal of government involvement—producing the famous 'level playing field'—was the way to make Australian businesses efficient.

At the end of the 1970s, these orthodox economists began to focus on the problem Hugh Emy identifies in his book *Remaking Australia*—that, given the changes that were increasingly affecting global commerce, Australia was not producing enough wealth to maintain the lifestyle to which its people had long been accustomed. Australia had always relied on trade, yet our main export industries—agriculture and mining—were not earning sufficient income to pay for rising imports of manufactures. Endemic inefficiencies in many industries which had traditionally been protected, and the public utilities that served them, meant there was no guarantee those industries would survive in the face of growing international competition.[7] The economists concluded Australia had to be forced to face the cold reality of global competition. But a fascinating insight into the people propounding these ideas behind the scenes in Canberra was provided by the Associate Professor of Sociology at the University of NSW, Michael Pusey.

In a seminal study in the late 1980s, involving interviews with 215 officials in the upper echelons of the Australian public service, Pusey painted a vivid portrait of the backgrounds, education and attitudes of the wave of neo-classical economists who had moved into advisory positions to ministers like Keating by the time the Labor period in office began. He found that 'a grossly disproportionate number of young men from Australia's expensive top schools' were concentrated in departments like Treasury, and that people high on the social ladder were three times more likely to hold conservative, 'new right', views. A large proportion of the officers in all departments were economists.

'Those who come from the most privileged backgrounds are likely to be the most ungenerous, individualistic, tough and anti-social,' Pusey argued. Their views about correct policy often were not so much informed by work experience, age or seniority as by 'the more persuasive and enduring formative influences' of social background, family and education. Basically, a large number of these officers wanted to see policies that encouraged more individual effort, less State provision and the dismantling of the centralised wage system. Pusey argued that the nation's top public servants were far more conservative than even they believed themselves to be. 'In their attitudes to the State and the role of governments, there is a vehement economic rationalism that is so clearly articulated and so sharply related to the central issues of economic and social policy as to cast some doubt on what is certainly the sincere claim that they can, in practice, keep their own political preferences clear of what they do at their desks,' Pusey wrote.[8] And he found an historic change in the mindset of contemporary department bosses compared with their predecessors in the post-war years.

For some twenty-five years after the Second World War, government had been served by a small group of senior 'generously-minded economists', most of whom were advocates of Keynesianism. This older generation of economists typically came from modest social backgrounds and had some historical memory of the social crises of the Great Depression, high unemployment and the war, Pusey argued.

> Whatever economics they learned at university was more often learned at night school, set within a liberal arts framework and thus within a philosophically informed view of society and the human condition. It was set, too, within a national experience in which both the State and the trade union movement, along with business interests (well before the notion of corporatism was ever invented), were long established as constituents of nationhood, national identity and economic development.

Pusey argued, however, that the economists 'of the newer kind', in contrast, had 'acquired what looks more like a trained incapacity to learn from all later experience'.

> That is the one inference to be drawn from the fact that a passage through an economics curriculum in their early twenties is the single factor that most strongly sets these young forty plus-year-old captains of a nation-building State against its historical mission.

Not only was the new generation of mandarins not influenced by the ideas of the older one but, Pusey argued, it seemed to be incapable of being influenced by any new ideas once its members reached twenty-five or thirty years of age.

> Through the new generation, national policy (and with it perhaps the fate of the nation) is held in the compass of the restrictive, technically-oriented, neoclassical economics curriculum that swept through the economics departments of Australian universities from about 1947 onwards.

At the outset of the 1990s Pusey found that the 'aggressive' economic rationalism of the central agencies of government in Canberra was 'clearly the vocabulary of a new laissez-faire minimalist State'. Asocial, with no historical memory, it was quickly burying the interventionist ideas of other government departments like Primary Industry, Trade and Industry and Technology. All departments agreed on the need for 'sound economic principles'—differences of opinion between the older and younger generations were rooted on definitional disputes about how that was defined.

> The pragmatic Keynesian liberalism of the older and mainly post-war interventionist State—a State that shared a long-established partnership with capital at the operating level of industry—was clearly losing all the arguments and battles with the conquering young rationalists from the central agencies.[9]

223

In the late 1980s there was really only one political voice in Canberra advocating a different approach—Janine Haines. Haines took issue with the notion that the public service was too large and insisted there was no reliable evidence of a necessary relationship between high levels of government spending and low levels of private sector growth. Australian business, she said, needed more government expenditure, not less. Haines attacked the notion that taxes in Australia were too high. On the tax question, she was laying a fertile field to be ploughed later by Kernot who would attack on two fronts—the rationalist argument that taxes had to be kept low, per se, as part of their minimalist government obsession; and the unspoken consensus among the major parties that tax cuts in the form of three-yearly bribes were the gold-plated means of winning office. By 1990, Haines was pointing to emerging doubts around the world about the assertion that deregulation and 'freeing up the market' would be the panacea solving all the problems of a country like Australia. She said the answer was better directed government intervention, and she derided the orthodoxy's inflexible insistence that government spending always led to a concomitant increase in the budget deficit. Haines repeatedly complained that her economic arguments were ignored, particularly by media commentators. In some of this, though, she was ahead of her time, for broader doubts about the orthodoxy only began to emerge after she was defeated at the 1990 election. That was the period in which Paul Keating's infamous recession the country 'had to have' drove Australian industry to its knees.

Keating's phenomenal effort in attuning his party to this orthodoxy was aided mightily by the fact that people like John Howard, and later John Hewson, were firm advocates of elements of the orthodox doctrine, and also by the fact that so many commentators in the media were too. Biographer John Edwards observed that without this unanimity, many of the economic reforms of the Keating period would simply never have eventuated. The trouble was that so many of the claims of Keating, the rhetorical maestro, came unstuck with the onset of the most severe downturn since the Great Depression of the 1930s, which threw a million Australians into unemployment after wrecking businesses by the score with high interest rates.

It was not just that this was a recession both Hawke and Keating vociferously denied would happen. It was not just that it gave the final lie to Keating's proud boast that his policies had ended forever the 'boom/bust cycle'. It was that this recession had culminated years of projections and promises that somehow never seemed to come off. Keating's withering capacity with words was a double-edged sword. He could present complex economic issues in imagery that made it explicable to ordinary folk. With an extraordinary internal reservoir of self-confidence, he could charm, too, and make it all seem so groundbreaking yet so under control, with him in the driver's seat. But in striving to paint the picture he very often exaggerated, or created, expectations he simply could not meet.

The effect of the recession was to draw a line under Australia's recent economic performance, providing a reference point for an assessment of how well the nation had been travelling under the influence of the orthodoxy. It was not a comforting picture. Between 1960 and the late 1980s, Australia tumbled from fourth to sixteenth position in terms of overall productive wealth in a list of twenty-six nations.[10] Inflation came under control but unemployment would stay frustratingly up close to the 10% mark for many years, with youth unemployment in some parts of the country climbing as high as 30%, and a new deeply troubling phenomenon being created—the emergence of the long-term unemployed, particularly older men, unable to find their way back into jobs after being retrenched.

In a 1996 book called *Dialogues on Australia's Future*, a collection of views of a large number of eminent Australian economists, Fred Gruen, Emeritus Professor in Economics at the Australian National University, sculpted an assessment of Australia's economic performance which drew on six separate criteria and compared them among the seventeen nations of the OECD. Overall, Australia rated a disastrous fifteenth out of the seventeen nations. Gruen said this poor showing was the result of 'a relatively poor performance' in each of the six criteria making up the mathematical index he employed. Unlike some other nations, Australia did not make up for a bad result on one criterion with a very good one on another. It was an overall uniform 'distinctly poor' performance. On unemployment, for example, Australia rated eleventh of the seventeen nations.[11]

In *Dialogues*, Russell Mathews also compiled a comparison of economic results achieved by Australia in two periods—the twenty years prior to 1973 and the Hawke/Keating decade after 1983 when the rationalist agenda had taken root. In the former period, economic growth averaged 5% compared to 3.3% in the latter; unemployment in the 1950s and 1960s averaged 1.9%

compared to 8.6% in the 1980s; inflation averaged 2.5% compared to the later level of 5.7%; and interest rates averaged 5% compared to 11.5%.[12] Research done by academics like Anne Harding, the Director of the National Centre for Social and Economic Modelling at the University of Canberra, showed disturbing evidence of a growing income inequality gap in Australia. While the income tax and welfare payments system were made more 'progressive' during the 1980s, this was more than offset by a widening in the earnings gap between the well-off and the poor.[13] Other research suggested that with the sharp reduction in manufacturing employment flowing from the reforms of the 1980s, there had been an increase in the inequality in the regions of Australia, giving rise to concerns about the possible growth of social tension.[14] Australia, for decades the haven of a unique egalitarian tradition, was becoming a dramatically less fair society.

But ordinary Australians didn't need academic treatises to tell them things had gone badly awry. They knew, and they were complaining long and hard about it. Psychologist and social researcher Hugh Mackay, who for thirty-five years had been studying the attitudes and behaviour of the nation, produced his seminal book, *Reinventing Australia*, in 1993. In some ways, this book covered themes explored back in 1991 when the former Liberal MP David Connolly coordinated an exercise for John Hewson in which the views of thousands of Australians were condensed into a book called *Australians Speak: A Report on the Concerns, Hopes and Aspirations of the Australian People*. That report found Australians desperately worried about the loss of national unity and the growth of inequality.[15] Two years later though, Mackay's work was devastating, arguing that in the previous twenty years the traditional social, cultural, political and economic landmarks of the Australian way of life had begun to be destroyed. The story of Australia had become one of a people 'trying to cope with too much change, too quickly and on too many fronts'. Ordinary Australians in their millions felt they had lost control over their lives. Mackay wrote:

> The Australian way of life is now being challenged and redefined to such an extent that growing numbers of people feel as if their personal identities are under threat as well.[16]

Despite the role in this new age of anxiety played by the Keating recession, the orthodoxy remained in the driving seat for a couple of important reasons. Firstly, rationalists continued to hold down many of the powerful jobs in the bureaucracy. But secondly, there was the continuing, compelling resonance of the argument about Australia's need to take tough action to keep up with the rapidly changing global economy. The argument continued to be put forward that protection and other barriers to trade had to come down, that Australian firms had to become internationally competitive to survive, that wages had to be kept low to compete with nations in the race to win international business. When all the theorising was boiled down, the cornerstone of this central economic argument was the issue of 'globalisation'.

This term came to mean changes to the structure of international finance, allied to the revolution in information technology. Business was now linked worldwide by satellites, computers, modems and facsimile machines. Hand-in-hand with the explosion of high-tech manufacturing on a global scale, the very nature of work and business was radically changing. Information, whisked effortlessly and instantly across continents, was the basis of new-style corporations that owed no physical allegiance to any one region or country, with new kinds of workforces containing part-time consultants, temporary staff, employees working at home. It had become virtually impossible to control the flow of money and other information across national borders. The countries conquering the new technology and produc-ing new products would compete with, and probably overtake, long-established industrial economies. Writers like Hugh Emy also pointed out that globalisation referred to 'transnational firms relocating their operations in other countries either to exploit particular production opportunities or to gain access to new or better markets'. These systems of production increas-ingly transcended national boundaries, and were driven by the imperative to find bases where they could extract the best wages deals.[17] The countries that produced goods efficiently and competitively—crucially, with low wage rates—were the ones that would prosper. Basically, the new era of global-isation imposed new restraints on nations. Power had shifted away from national governments, to the companies that made the international decisions. And to the global money markets which made judgements about the viability not just of the commercial decisions of the companies, but about the political and economic decisions of the governments. This was the new imperative.

With Haines' departure, the Australian Democrats became badly distracted by their leadership problems, and basically 'lost' an entire electoral term in which to scrutinise the work, and results, of the orthodoxy. By the time Kernot had established her leadership presence by the mid-1990s, the legitimacy of the orthodoxy was under significant pressure. In the wake of the recession, and with a confusion of ideas permeating the Keating government after it saw off John Hewson's challenge in 1993, Keating unveiled his $6.5 billion 'Working Nation' blueprint in May, 1994, a four-year plan to provide training and job creation programs with the aim of reducing unemployment to 5% by the year 2000. Here, finally, was Labor actually using the power of government to *intervene* to fight the blight of joblessness. But, as Frank Stillwell, Associate Professor of Economics at Sydney University, has pointed out, simultaneously the other precepts of the orthodoxy remained unchallenged—a reluctance to develop a pro-active industry policy, the continued acceptance of the deregulatory agenda, the emphasis on employer wage restraint unmatched by any restrictions on non-wage incomes, cuts in upper income tax rates and the commitment to continuing tariff cuts.[18]

'Working Nation' was a step in the right economic direction for Labor, but it came far too late electorally. And, as we shall see, despite John Howard's own beginnings in the early 1980s as a champion of the free market, his government too would find itself torn between, on one hand, one of the doctrine's core demands—the dismantling of protection—and, on the other, the clear social damage that rationalism had helped create. But well before Howard won, the orthodoxy's critics basically argued that while some of the reforms of the 1980s had been needed and would help Australia become more competitive, there were myriad down sides, and that some of the reforms, or their excessive speed, had actually been quite damaging to the economy and threatened to do social damage as well.

Given the constraints imposed on her by the job as Democrat Leader, as best she could, Kernot kept abreast of economic and social policy theory as a backstop to her experience in Canberra. As with the child and her love of books, so the adult. Despite a frenetic travel schedule, loaded appointments book and merry-go-round of media engagements, whenever time and fatigue permitted, she would read. In Democrat staffers Jacqui Flitcroft and John Cherry she also had two avid consumers of cutting-edge, left-of-centre economic and political theory from Australia, and around the world. The best of the global village's political and economic thinkers were trawled for the feedstock of ideas for Kernotism. Many ideas were ignored, others seemed innovative and begged further analysis, still others instantly had resonance with what Kernot and her key policy people were thinking, or suspected intuitively. It was an auspicious time—the end of the cold war, with its premature triumphalism about the final ideological victory of capitalism. For it was also a time when Thatcherism, in its harshest manifestations, was dying a slow death.

Kernot's sense of things was summed up in the conclusions of Peter Sheehan, Director of the Centre for Strategic Economic Studies at Victoria University. Also writing in *Dialogues on Australia's Future*, Sheehan argued that the science-based 'model' of economic rationalism had, by the mid-1990s, been found to contain assumptions that were 'not at all realistic' and were too inflexible to be the sole guide to policy-making. Agreeing Australia had achieved some benefits from the orthodoxy's ideas, Sheehan said the bungling of its implementation, and the refusal to accept that those ideas could have been used hand-in-hand with others, had 'cost the nation dearly'. He homed in on one great weakness in the orthodoxy's set of arguments—its incapacity to see that an interventionary set of policies designed to *assist* companies to compete was not the same as a set of tariff barriers designed to artificially *protect* industry. Sheehan wrote:

> The demise of the neoclassical model at the theoretical level, in favor of a much more diverse set of theories and of a sophisticated set of analytical and policy tools to be used to guide judgement in the understanding of many different situations, may provide the basis for a richer and more realistic approach to policy in the future.[19]

Quite so, Kernot thought. But the key question then became, what would be the most appropriate mix of policies for the future?

13

THE KISS OF LIFE

As Kernot laboured to develop and communicate the Democrats' central ideas about the economy, she was alarmed at the extent to which these ideas about level playing fields, globalisation and technological change had battered the notion of government, discrediting it. All anyone ever heard was that government was bad—no-one ever talked of its great, historic, civilising influence. She saw what seemed a logical end-point of globalisation postulated, for example, in the work of Kenichi Ohmae, author of fifty books and the former Director of McKinsey and Company, the huge management consulting firm. Ohmae concluded that because of the new capitalism, the era of the nation state itself was drawing to an end. Nations, as we had long known them, were finished. Because economic power had shifted into the hands of globalised capitalism, government action was futile. But, more than that, if global capitalism did not like the actions of a government, it would act in retribution.

The new, 'borderless' future would be based on relationships between efficient 'regions'—that is, as long as government could be shunted out of the way, allowing the free flow of trade globally. All that mattered now was the quality of the economic investment. Money would go where the best opportunities were around the world and there was nothing governments could do about that anymore. Nation states were 'coming apart at the seams' and were 'increasingly, a nostalgic fiction' or 'dysfunctional, unnatural, even impossible, business units in a global economy'.[1] Ohmae argued that with the growth of international capital markets and their instant transmission of billions of dollars of computerised transactions around the world every day, power had shifted to multinational companies, the agents now overseeing what he called the 'California-isation of taste'. Serving the mass consumer markets, globalisation meant the world was awash with Levi jeans, Nike running shoes and Hermes scarves. But there was more:

> Today the process of convergence goes faster and deeper. It reaches well beyond taste to much more fundamental dimensions of world view, mind-set and even thought process. There are now, for example, tens of millions of teenagers around the world who, having been raised in a multimedia-rich environment, have a lot more in common with each other than they do with members of older generations in their own cultures. For these budding consumers, technology-driven convergence does not take place at the sluggish rate dictated by yesterday's media. It is instantaneous—a nanosecond migration of ideas and innovations.[2]

The strategies of modern corporations were no longer shaped in response to government policies, but rather by 'the desire—and the need—to serve attractive markets wherever they exist and to tap attractive pools of resources wherever they sit'. Ohmae argued government-provided incentives were now irrelevant and the collection of taxation, like the accumulation of facts, was problematic: 'Where—in any of these business systems—can customs officers charge duties, local government claim value-added taxes or bureaucrats compile accurate trade statistics?' Ohmae asked.[3] But then, explicitly, the big threat:

> In the face of insistent, knowledgeable demand, nation states are less and less able to dictate individual economic choices. Should they try to do so in too restrictive a fashion, electronically based flows of capital will head elsewhere, penalising their currencies and starving them of funds for investment. And individual transactions will migrate to channels that lie out of their sights as well as out of their reach.[4]

Reflexive twinges of sovereignty made desired economic success impossible, because the global economy punished 'twinging countries' by diverting investment and information elsewhere. Nation states once may have been, Ohmae said, independent, powerfully efficient engines of wealth creation but the uncomfortable truth was that, in terms of the global economy, they had become little more than 'bit actors'.

Gail, Jill and Cheryl.

Gail, Craig, Jill and Cheryl, Christmas, 1961.

Cheryl's first day at school,
five years old.

Cheryl and Gail, East Maitland Primary School.

Cheryl, aged sixteen, winner of the Lions Youth of the Year Award, 1964.

As a teacher at St Leo's College,
1975. *Fairfax Photo Library*

Cheryl and Gavin on their wedding day in April, 1981.

Cheryl, Gavin and young Sian.

West End burns, Christmas, 1991.

Sian, Zena, Merv, Cheryl and Gavin at
Merv and Zena's fiftieth wedding anniversary party.

Cheryl and Gavin, 1995.

Gough Whitlam, Cheryl and Sian at the Clinton lunch, 1995.

Moreover, as the workings of genuinely global capital markets dwarf their ability to control exchange rates or protect their currency, nation states have become inescapably vulnerable to the discipline imposed by economic choices made elsewhere by people and institutions over which they have no practical control.[5]

All in all, it's tough rhetoric and Ohmae is, by no means, the only prophet of it. The early 1990s saw the emergence of a plethora of international thinkers arguing thus. This was a view, however, that Cheryl Kernot fundamentally rejected, and not because she was a national politician and this was a thesis foreboding the end of national power. To her, this kind of theorising was the orthodoxy gone mad, pushing its ideas into dangerously overblown terrain, threatening to add new layers to people's already deep-seated apprehension. But it could also be seen as anti-democratic. It posed some disturbing long-term questions. If governments were not securely in place with enough power to make a difference, who would maintain order, confront inequality, care for the dispossessed, maintain services in society? 'Nation states' were not just amorphous masses that could be dispensed with at whim. They were structured cultures, the institutions of which had evolved historically to bring order, justice and fairness, and, in the case of democracies, to afford ordinary people the right to have a say over their lives. That right was enacted through the election of governments.

In all this, Kernot saw that despite the flaws of democracy, what was being lost sight of was that governments were the embodiment of the people. They were not to be airily dismissed by businessmen scrambling for the almighty dollar. Governments had a right to pursue the policies they believed to be in the interest of the people who elected them. Kernot argued passionately that economics had had its run—now it was time for politics to be brought centre stage. In her view there were two key, worrying effects of the domination of the economic orthodoxy: the creation of yawning new inequality gaps between people, social groups and nations; and the dismantling of communities, the end of the age-old notion that people were part of a whole. It was time for Australia to focus on this issue of the role of government, and decide what it wanted. For a decade, Kernot believed, governments had been bailing out of their responsibilities. In a speech in 1996 entitled: 'The Kiss of Life: Reviving Australian Politics', she asked:

Do we want governments to sit on their hands and leave free markets to their own devices—even if that means a slow death for rural communities and the end of the Australian family farm? Do we want governments to restrict themselves to a minimum set of core activities—even if that means the significant downgrading of public hospitals and public schools? Do we want governments to stand by and do nothing while competition takes its natural course—even if it means small businesses are swallowed up through the unconscionable conduct of big business? It's a fundamental question: do we want our governments standing on the sidelines or do we want them playing a more active and dynamic role in setting national goals? We need to develop a mature and diverse politics which enables us to go forward as a nation in the so-called new era of globalisation without relinquishing almost entirely any role for government, without abrogating our community responsibilities and without going further and further down the path of social exclusion and systematic inequality. We need to restore a sense in Australia that we are not just bits of flotsam and jetsam floating on the great big ocean of global capitalism, but that we can take political action to control our own destiny and determine what sort of a nation we want to become.

Kernot was always at pains to make clear she was not opposed, per se, to greater competition in some areas, more efficient delivery of services, privatisation or contracting out where there would be obvious benefits:

I simply say that neither competition nor privatisation are acceptable goals in themselves. Both are simply a means to an end. In my view, it is a fundamentally flawed approach to decide that competition or privatisation are good things, and then mould social and economic policy goals around those goals. Surely we should first decide what sort of social and economic benefits we want to deliver to Australians and *then* explore whether or not competition or privatisation will deliver those benefits.[6]

Competition might be a good idea when selling apples and oranges, but was it in delivering health services, aged care or decent housing for the poor?

The fact is in some of these areas we accept a social responsibility—to educate or clothe or house people—and that social responsibility overrides the dictates of the market. In those areas, competition does not necessarily offer the best approach to delivering the results we want to achieve as a community. The glaring gap in the economic orthodoxy is that it simply does not acknowledge these social goals.[7]

Kernot's starting point was that politicians had to start doing things differently, but that they had to do that *through* the existing economic system. As Leader of the Democrats, she was not arguing for some kind of throwback to the 1960s with its cosy assumptions about full employment and fixed exchange rates. It was clear to her that there had, indeed, been something in the Keating argument about Australia being a closed, protected economy for too long. In the same way that Kernot would not be a budget-destroyer but would use the balance of power in the Senate to make changes within the government's deficit reduction or wider fiscal gameplans, she knew there was no way a country could 'opt out' or hark back to some 1950s nirvana. The world *was* changing and Australia had to change too.

Her concern was with the methods used and the speed at which they had been implemented but she was smart enough to see that, for better or worse, the world had moved on. Trade barriers were being dismantled, a lot of deregulation would not be wound back. Government agencies had been sold off—they were gone. The key now was to ensure that public benefit was maximised, that the nation was made as fair as possible, that all Australians had access to necessary services, that unemployment was confronted, that government was kept accountable, that domestic businesses were helped to grow and that Australia prospered as a trading nation. In all this, Kernot argued that maintaining social cohesion should be one of the new, dual aims of economics—standing, equally, alongside the thrust for efficiency and competitiveness.

But there had to be a change from the familiar, orthodox economic mindset. For years, governments had been manically cutting spending to keep the deficit down and selling off assets on a massive scale to bolster revenues. They were terrified, for political reasons, to look at the alternative of tax increases or meaningful changes to the tax mix, and they refused to see that there had to be *more* investment in public infrastructure, not less.

Kernot keenly absorbed the writings of the influential British economist and journalist, Will Hutton, who claimed that the Thatcherite cut-back mentality with its privatisation, user-pays, competition and contracting out, had extended the reach of the market into the 'very quick of society'.[8] Public investment in Australia had fallen to a forty-year low, and it was starting to show. As she travelled around the country, Kernot saw public housing, hospitals, schools and universities, the railways, sewerage and water systems sagging because of under-investment. Australians were beginning to put two and two together—they could see that budget decisions in Canberra to cut back spending meant service closures in their local suburbs and towns. Captives of the orthodox mantra, governments had been ignoring evidence showing a direct relationship between public infrastructure spending and increased private sector productivity and investment. Kernot believed that well-targeted public investment in infrastructure could stimulate job growth.

After being told for years that cutting back expenditure, sacking people, privatising and deregulating would make life better for everyone, it just hadn't happened. Kernot pointed to the revelations of a man known in the US as the 'guru' of downsizing, Stephen S. Roach, the Chief Economist of the US investment bank Morgan Stanley. In early 1996, Roach signalled a major personal U-turn when he decided that the slash-and-burn policies that companies had been employing for years to boost productivity were not a permanent solution. Tactics of ongoing retrenchments—'downsizing' in the jargon—and real wage compression were ultimately recipes for industrial extinction, Roach said. Although it had been music to the ears of investors for years, it was a myth that companies could prosper solely by becoming leaner, more flexible and competitive. Originally, Roach admitted, he had believed that companies could make cuts to be more efficient in a first phase, and then use new technology to invest in a more competent work-force. Unfortunately, all that had happened was that labour force cuts went on and on and on. There had been no upgrading in the stock of human capital. 'If you compete by building, you have a future; if you compete by cutting, you don't,' Roach concluded.[9] Translating the Roach thesis to government, Kernot argued the answer was to stop the public service downsizing and bite the bullet on tax reform to generate the revenue to begin rebuilding the State.

She also attacked the orthodoxy's collusion with politicians to privatise government assets in order to fund budget deficits. The Democrats opposed the sale of Qantas, the Commonwealth Bank, the Australian National Line, the Commonwealth Serum Laboratories and the nation's airports, to name a few. Kernot was the leading public figure opposing moves that began during the term of the Keating period, but were realised under John Howard's government, for the sale of the nation's telecommunications carrier, Telstra. She said there was emerging worldwide evidence that many of the much-lauded benefits of privatisation were not materialising and were not in the national interest. The value of Telstra had been estimated at around $55 billion by industry economists, much more than it would ultimately realise. The Department of Finance had estimated that the cost to the taxpayer of floating the organisation on the stock exchange—fees for lawyers, accountants, stockbrokers, analysts and advertising agents—could be as high as $160 million. There was no unequivocal evidence that selling it would deliver consumer benefits. And there was no reason to think that efficiency improvements could not be implemented inside Telstra while still in public hands. While the management elite in the organisation command-ed massive salaries, Telstra's workforce would be cut by 25,500 to 53,000 before the sharemarket flotation. Kernot asserted that in fifty years' time, the process of selling off government assets like this would 'surely appear the greatest act of economic vandalism in Australian history'.

Having exorcised the ghost of Peter Walsh's 'fairies at the bottom of the garden' with the breakthrough with the 1993 budget, in subsequent years Kernot was intent on building the reputation for fiscal responsibility. She would, for example, always ensure that she was able to cost her ideas accurately and was the only politician at the 1996 election to attach costing estimates to every policy platform. Her aim was to push genuinely reformist ideas with disciplined realism, an eye to the bottom line. This would be her approach to budgets under both the Keating and Howard governments.

On tax, Kernot pressed for reforms in successive budgets to make the sys-tem fairer. Basically, she shied away from recommending specific increases in income tax, company tax or the introduction of the controversial Goods and Services Tax (GST). But she kept an open mind, arguing that all options, including the GST, had to be debated, to see how the tax system should best operate in the 21st century. By talking to tax experts, she identified specific reforms that would unbundle significant amounts of new revenue. On the corporate side, she talked of the possibility of a minimum company tax, and changes to negative gearing and the tax relief on dividends. And she saw the need to make major reforms of the tax arrangements for superannuation. She called for a major government investigation of the taxation of income flowing in and out of Australia. She had reservations about the porous nature of national tax borders in the new deregulated environment. As part of her alternative to the sale of Telstra, for example, Kernot argued that a crackdown on the tax exemption on interest paid to non-residents of the country could raise anything between $200 million and $800 million. She complained that the tax system was biased towards encouraging business to develop capital-intensive industry, when it should be providing incentives to employ people. After years of agitating for tax changes to help small business, in mid-1996 she won a breakthrough when changes were agreed to the manner in which the previous year's taxable income is used to calculate small firms' current year's provisional tax liability. Yet she continued to push for other changes including a fairer pay-as-you-go provisional tax system, reductions in fringe benefits tax compliance costs, extensions to the time for monthly payment of sales tax and a waiving of capital gains tax on the proceeds of the sale of a business if those proceeds were rolled over into another business.

Fundamentally though, Kernot's bottom line on tax was that the current system was outmoded, and needed to be entirely rethought. In this she was ahead of her time, the only senior politician in Australia not afraid to pose the big question about whether the country needed to find alternative, fairer ways of raising revenue. In 1993 Australia paid 28.8% tax as a share of GDP, the second lowest among the 24 nations of the OECD, and significantly less than the OECD average of 38.5%. Only Turkey paid less tax. Canada paid 35.6%, Germany 39%, Japan 29.9%, New Zealand 35.7%, the UK 29.7% and the US 38.5%.[10] Janine Haines had been killed off politically in 1990 over her views on tax but Kernot had managed by the latter half of the 1990s to insulate herself against such attacks. She had her reputation for fiscal responsibility going for her, also her ability to communicate fluently. But she was also advancing novel ideas.

She said the starting point should be the community deciding whether it wanted public services improved or maintained. If it did, if the slash-and-burn mentality was to end, then tax had to be the answer. But the trick was not only the mix of taxes, but how they were to be administered. Kernot believed there should be a debate over the possibility of introducing more tax 'hypothecation'—that is, the earmarking of specific tax collections for certain purposes. In Australia, an example was the Medicare levy, in Britain the licence fee levied on television sets and the National Insurance levy to cover pension and benefit payments.

Kernot concluded it was time for politicians to ditch the traditional posturing on tax—that is, avoiding like the plague any suggestion of higher tax for three years, then bribing their way back into office at election time with tax cuts. She wondered whether the time was approaching when the community could be the partner of government in a bold rethink of the whole basis of tax collection. Perhaps the act of paying tax could be transformed into something deemed to have social value. She saw good omens. There was a 1994 study by the Keating government's Economic Planning and Advisory Committee which suggested taxpayers were prepared to pay more tax to fund increased expenditure on the environment, roads, education, hospitals and retraining.[11] If tax payments were clearly linked to specific service delivery, then the community would see good coming from their sacrifice. In time, this notion about the urgency of a tax rethink would come to hold sway within the Coalition, despite John Howard's blunt assurance after the 1993 election debacle that the GST was off the agenda. But as well, by the late 1990s, Kernot's complaints about the inadequate way government was addressing the unemployment crisis would also come home to roost.

In this, Kernot was quite heavily influenced by the writings of Professor Robert Reich, an economic adviser to US President Bill Clinton and the author of the powerful book, *The Work of Nations*. In examining the impact of globalisation on employment, Reich argued that the nations which survived economically would be those that developed the skills of their workforces. This, of course, was part of the thinking behind the drive in countries like Australia, the US and Britain to re-equip their economies by pouring money into retraining. But Kernot argued that much else was needed to confront persistent unemployment.

In 1994, she had first called for the Keating government to significantly increase its investment in public infrastructure and provide a special assistance package for small business. At the time she argued these measures could be funded by a combination of a special government bond issue, a jobs levy and the targeted investment of a percentage of the monies held by superannuation funds. As unemployment continued to stay high and Keating himself was forced to introduce 'Working Nation', Kernot began to build what she would call a program of 'economic nationalism'—stepped-up government assistance for Australian companies, particularly those competing internationally. She called for the phased abolition of payroll tax over three years as part of an accord with business and the unions to create jobs. There was also the extension of existing export marketing schemes to small businesses and a major shake-up to allow the government's trade facilitation arm, Austrade, to grow into a much more aggressive agency, working with firms to find markets and opportunities overseas for Australia. Kernot proposed more research and development assistance for industry, and government guarantees for low cost finance for product development. To get superannuation funds to help create more jobs, she advocated a limit on funds allowed to be invested overseas. At least $2 billion should also be invested in small or emerging Australian businesses, and she demanded a halt to further tariff cuts as well as higher tariffs to apply to threatened industries. But her major message was that government needed to step in with a sophisticated program of interventionist planning to help various sectors of industry develop new businesses and create jobs. To the economic orthodoxy, this was the ultimate heresy.

Kernot saw a frustrating contradiction at the heart of the orthodoxy's arguments. Australia's economic future would be guaranteed, so it was argued, if protective barriers were pulled down, forcing the nation's companies and businesses to become more efficient, and enabling them to go out and compete in the wider world: yet government should be specifically prohibited from doing anything directly to assist them in that. In international forums, like the Geneva-based World Trade Organisation, politicians or public servants singing from the orthodox song-sheet happily agreed targets to reduce protection. The theories said that to survive, Australia had to look to prising open opportunities in the rapidly growing markets of the world, particularly the Asian region, and that free trade was the way to do that. Yet some of the great success stories of the so-called 'tiger economies' of the near north, as well as countries in Europe and

Scandinavia, were built on interventionist policies. Here it all came back to the orthodoxy's blind-spot—equating policies in the past that had caused problems, like excessive levels of tariff protection, with those that could help business, such as industry incentive plans. Tariff walls were only one weapon a nation could use.

Kernot demanded answers to these inconsistencies. And what about the social consequences of reducing rates of domestic protection so fast that industries collapsed, throwing thousands of people onto the scrap heap? She argued that by the mid-1990s unilateral tariff reductions had cost over 200,000 jobs and seen the proportion of imported goods sold in Australia climb from 21% in 1990 to 26% in 1995. To this question, orthodox theory said the collapse of one industry—say textiles, clothing and footwear in Melbourne—would simply mean the economy's resources would be more efficiently redirected into new industries that leapt to life, like mushrooms in a field—say, new tourist developments in Queensland. Thus, there was no reason why a newly unemployed female migrant worker in inner Melbourne could not just pack up, move to the sunny north and get a job as a waitress or hotel maid. But Kernot argued this was obviously just a piece of theoretical fiction, one that turned a blind eye to the social dislocation created by factory closures. A nation had to accept that there would be industry restructures, but how much was a cohesive society able to sustain? She also asked why it was that Australia, practising what it preached at home, was going into world forums and offering up tariff cuts as evidence of its commitment to free trade, while the countries smiling approvingly over the negotiating table had been giving their own domestic industries leg-ups through all sorts of incentive devices.

In this, one of her starting points was the pioneering work done by Democrat Senator Sid Spindler in establishing a parliamentary inquiry into tariffs and industry development in 1993. Spindler was responding to complaints by industry groups concerned that under the pressure of tariff cuts, hundreds of Australian factories had closed, with 30% of the textiles, footwear and clothing industry disappearing by the early 1990s. Kernot participated as a member of the inquiry panel, which travelled around Australia taking evidence from 100 witnesses. After eight months of investigation, the inquiry found that tariff reductions were driving unemployment up and contributing to rising crime rates, family break-ups, bankruptcies and the decimation of regional centres, thus driving the population into the cities. It found Australia to have been the only country to have hit protection for its motor car and textiles, clothing and footwear industries so hard. Tariffs used by Australia's trading partners were often substantially higher— for example, 40% on Brazil's orange juice compared to 10%, and falling, in Australia. As well, other nations made extensive use of non-tariff assistance to protect their industries including bureaucratic obstruction, surcharges, export subsidies, deliberately restrictive labelling, packaging and quality controls. At last count, the report said, twenty-nine nations used such measures against Australia and the European Union applied them to 243 Australian export items.

Agreeing that, in principle, some tariff reductions were necessary, the report argued that they had, however, been implemented too fast, too deeply and without any consideration given to measures to help society adjust to their impact. It called for a twelve-month pause while a raft of safety-net measures was put in place. There should be selective use of protection as part of an industry-by-industry strategy aimed at increasing Australia's competitive capacity, while at the same time maintaining employment and minimising social turmoil. Importantly, it called for a long-term industry development plan, incorporating a scheme for helping revive Australia's regions.

The orthodoxy always argued that because the world was moving towards free trade, with individual nations dismantling protection, Australia had to follow suit. In global free trade, with everybody playing by the same rules, lay the opportunity for smaller nations like Australia to eke out new business. But as Democrat Leader, Kernot demanded a rethink of Australia's position in the world's free trade forums, like the round of talks known as the General Agreement on Tariffs and Trade, or GATT. Bodies like this were calling the tune in Canberra. Yet, without a full explanation of the implications, politicians and bureaucrats had been going off to them for years and locking future generations into international agreements to reduce protection. In 1994, Kernot used the example of the orange juice that routinely apeared on breakfast tables across Australia. For fifty years, she said, Australia had provided a special sales tax concession for fruit juices with at least 25% local content:

It is very useful law. It provides a market for oranges which aren't up to fresh market standard. It supports our citrus industry which exports over $100 million a year in whole fruit to South East Asia. And it means there is no fruit drink product on the market which has less than 25% fruit in it—so those who can't afford squeezed daily juice are assured of getting some decent nutritional value.[12]

She then pointed out that a 'bunch of bureaucrats' had signed away Australia's right to continue this concession because it did not fulfil GATT requirements. Desperate Australian citrus growers asked for a total sales tax exemption for *fresh* orange juice, arguing this would still provide them with some effective protection from imports of concentrate coming from Brazil. Kernot and the Democrats backed this call. But the Trade Department rejected the request—because, once again, it was said to be in breach of GATT. This, despite the fact that the US, for example, actively discriminated between fresh juice and reconstituted product and imposed a 47% tariff on Brazilian imports. Kernot said the impact of all this was that Australian citrus growers would be hammered by Brazilian imports, produced cheaply by using exploited labour working on cleared rainforest. Fresh orange juice would be more expensive and there would be less of it. Low income consumers could expect to pay more for a product that was more watered-down. While America continued to support its citrus industry, Australia would not, because it was argued there would be, in the aggregate, an estimated $4 billion in benefits flowing to the broader economy by abiding by GATT rules.

When economists talk about adjustment, it tends to conjure up a picture of a few scattered people losing their jobs, but being able to find new ones in a new factory that opens right next door to their old one. But primary industries such as citrus growing are geographically concentrated. There is an entire belt of communities stretching from Echuca to Renmark which is heavily dependent on the citrus industry. If the citrus industry goes down, it will take other industries in these areas with it and it will devastate those communities. The Australian parliament put the local content rule in place fifty years ago and it has been supported by Australian governments ever since. Now, even before it has come before parliament, it has suddenly become illegal. Why? Because GATT doesn't allow it.[13]

The arrival, in 1994, of the ten-year anniversary of Paul Keating's deregulation of the economy prompted Kernot to take a long hard look at what had been achieved. She did so on a number of levels. Working with her economics adviser John Cherry, she concluded that many of the promised benefits had not materialised for ordinary Australians. All the evidence seemed to suggest that there had been high levels of competition at the top end of the finance lending market to corporate customers but that the benefits of banking deregulation, for example, had not been passed on to consumers. Money was still expensive for small business and there had been no real drop in mortgage loan interest rates. Overall, the benefits of deregulation seemed to have been skewed to the corporate world—the banking industry remained concentrated in four big organisations and the Reserve Bank had seemed disinclined to intervene to protect consumers. Thus, Kernot took on the banking industry. For years she complained loud and often that bank lending margins were too high, that exorbitant service fees were being imposed unilaterally, that the benefits of deregulation were not being passed on through home loan rates and conditions. She even tried to get the law amended to stop further takeovers by banks which already owned more than 15% of the sector and called for big business representation on the Reserve Bank to be scaled down, allowing more input from consumer, rural and small businesss organisations.

Kernot focused on how deregulation and the rise of globalisation were encouraging short-termism in the business world. She was heavily influenced in this by Will Hutton's seminal 1995 book on the decline of the British economy, *The State We're In*. Before working as a journalist, then editor of the famous *Observer* newspaper in London, Hutton was a stockbroker. On study tours of Europe, Kernot exchanged ideas with Hutton in London. One of his pet themes was inspired by his insider's view of the rise of the power of the capital markets. His thesis was that the malaise of industry in Britain, as in other industrialised nations, had been created, in part, by the short-term obsession of the markets with speculative and take-over activity. Instead of valuing a company on the basis of its long-term plans and investment decisions, the focus of the markets was always on the year-to-year bottom line. The pressure was constantly on for firms to be made ever more efficient, to cut back on investment, on research and development and on staff, to produce annual balance-sheet results that headed off takeover pressures. Hutton said in all this the real, *productive* value of firms was lost to view.

The Hutton argument had real resonance for Kernot, particularly because of her experience with superannuation policy. Super fund managers had long made no secret of their reluctance to take risks when it came to such things as venture capital or long-term investment planning because they felt ruled by the monthly publication of their performance statistics. The pressure to be seen maximising returns was constantly in the background. Kernot wondered if a more active role for government, building industry sector plans in partnership with firms, would work to refocus the attention of the markets on productive enterprise, and begin to put a floor under both business certainty and employee security.

In essence, Kernot was calling for a reweighting of the balance in decision-making away from economic theory. She had major reservations about the orthodoxy but she was not totally opposed to its prescriptions. What did concern her was the way some of its apostles claimed to speak for—to wear the mantle of—*the* business community. She was angered by what she called the 'economic cheer squad', made up mainly of a small group of conservative economic journalists who dominated commentary, particularly the newspaper political and business pages. These comment-ators were completely locked into the prevailing ideology and became shrill and abusive, Kernot said, with anyone who dared disagree with their interpretations. She pointed out that bureaucrats, journalists, the bosses of industry peak councils and think-tank executives were not necessarily representative of business as it operated out in the real world. She saw that the people who actually ran the businesses were often much more comfortable with the idea that they could be in a partnership with the State, with government making clever decisions about incentives it provided. Kernot eventually concluded that, for years, the orthodoxy had parroted a self-fulfilling prophecy: working tirelessly to frustrate, criticise and impede government intervention, it then railed about the failure of the approach when it did not produce results. The orthodoxy insisted its own approach had failed to produce the predicted results because the dismantling of government had *not gone far enough*. Kernot's reply was that an interventionist approach had not worked more broadly because there had not been a strong enough government commitment to resourcing it. If government got clever about intervention, then it would produce results the business community could live with. What was needed was a new notion—what she called the 'clever State'.

In her meetings with top business leaders, Kernot saw the need for a new compact to be spelled out. Sometimes these were quite blunt encounters. For example, at one meeting with a top banker, conversation turned to the implied threat often made to government that unless a certain policy approach was taken, business, or an individual corporation, might pull out of the country. Kernot said that kind of blackmail did not 'wash' with her. But she was taken aback when she asked the banker if, in the face of globalisation, the days when a country could expect patriotic corporate action were dead. He replied: 'Nearly.'

Kernot still believed government had to bluntly talk to business about notions of shared horizons, a common community of interest. She felt it was time for governments to more forcefully point out to companies the benefits to them of being able to invest in Australia, the quality of the country's products and workforce, the stable politics and the attractive environment as a place to work and manufacture. She said that hand-in-hand with a program of national industry development, government ministers should strike tougher bargains with overseas firms. It was time, she said, to dispense with the cringe mentality.

'I think governments have got to say to corporations that we know they can go round the world picking countries where laws are lax and tax is low and labour rates are cheap,' she said. 'But I would hope to appeal to them, and support that with interventionist policies, by saying: "I'll reward you for caring about, and investing, in Australia." Some firms do, some make that choice. But to those that threaten to go offshore, I say to them: "Go offshore! You go offshore!" I'm interested in assisting the firms that have a commitment to Australia, who want to build this country and pull its communities together. I think you can run that argument. But then you need active, funded government agencies to follow through, to work with the companies. I think there is a good campaign to be run about good corporate citizenship and the way Australian companies reflect the ethics of this country in their behaviour overseas. I mean, who wants to be associated with an Australian company that exploits child labour in Thailand? We have a right to demand some kind of decent standards. But we have got the ultimate cultural cringe in this country where we talk about world best practice and we are always quoting everybody else. It's as if no world best practice could ever originate here in Australia. We produce the best but we are incapable of seeing it.

'Why does the Clinton government come out here and look at our hospitals? Why does the Blair government come here and look at our government training programs? Why can't we say isn't that great, they think we are doing a fantastic job with our health system and *they* come all this way to look at *us*? We are good at these things. We are miles ahead of other countries in education. Gavin and I taught overseas and we couldn't believe it. We were astonished. We thought Brisbane might have been Hicksville. But we were light years ahead of the Canadians in the maturity of our curricula, the integration of our subjects and the assessment methods used—light years ahead. Why do they come here to look at our multicultural policies and immigration and refugee policies? Why, in Europe, do MPs ask me about how we manage our multicultural policy? People living here don't realise that people around the world think highly of us in some of these things. In some areas we *are* the world best practice. And then we have the head-start with the natural resources we have been given. We have also got an optimistic people, with something essentially "sunny" about us. Yet all we do is have budgets of doom and gloom, and cuts and pain and suffering. And an erosion of the public infrastructure that past generations worked so hard to build. It's time for a big rethink.'[14]

Kernot argued it was simply irresponsible of government to deregulate and then somehow just retire from the field as a policy-maker. Taken to the extreme, who would be accountable when things went wrong? It would become all too easy for everyone to pass the buck if government simply denied it had any responsibility. If not government, then which agent would work to hold society together? How would the growing inequality gap and the collapse of communities be managed?

The great summoning voice of the economic orthodoxy had been Margaret Thatcher with her famous catchcry back in 1987: 'There is no such thing as society. There are individual men and women, and there are families.'[15] The upshot of this approach with its manic emphasis on the sanctity of the individual making decisions 'unhindered' in the marketplace was that, worldwide, society had become appreciably less fair, with the most privileged profiting while those at the bottom of the pile went backwards. Kernot pointed to emerging international evidence that the biggest increases in income inequalities had occurred in countries where free market economics had been pursued most zealously.

'Not only is Australia not an exception to this trend—it is a world leader,' she said. She quoted an OECD study which showed that of fifteen developed countries studied in the mid-1980s, only the US and Ireland had more unequal distribution of income than Australia. 'This is not a case of the rich getting richer and the poor getting poorer; it's a case of the gap between the rich and poor getting bigger and bigger.'

Kernot's instinctive sense that governments should be counter-attacking with policies to rebuild community was part of a religio/philosophical tradition that had as one of its arms a doctrine formulated in the early 20th century by theological philosophers in Britain. It came to be known as 'Christian Socialism'. In modern politics the most famous Christian Socialist is Tony Blair. And interestingly, it is Blair's philosophical guru, an Australian theologian he met at Oxford University in the 1960s called Peter Thomson, who has best described the wellspring of Christian Socialism. Originally this was a 19th century movement of social reform within the Anglican Church which saw itself as having a role to play in rectifying the inequities of capitalism. A key player in the movement was the Scottish theological philosopher, John MacMurray, whose ideas became deeply influential. MacMurray's core argument was that social order should recognise community as its central aim. But Thomson explains that MacMurray wanted to get away from the rationalist philosophical notion: 'I think, therefore I am.'

> [He] argued that thinking is not what determines human existence, that we live long before we become conscious. What determines our humanity is that we belong, first to the family and then to society. Our thought is determined by our sense of belonging: I am what I am by virtue of other people. You do not achieve something as an individual but because you are rooted in a social nexus of others ... in the beginning there were friendships. We belong to each other.[16]

Cheryl Kernot argued that the true test of leadership over the next twenty years would be the ability to follow a new doctrine. 'It is one that says that if we benefit the community, we benefit the individuals in it,' she said. This was not about turning the clock back.

> This is about Australia's ability to go forward as a nation in the new era of globalisation without relinquishing almost entirely any role for government, without abrogating our community responsibilities and without going further and further down the path of social exclusion and systematic inequality.

It was time to understand the great importance of the linkages between economic achievement, social cohesion and a healthy democracy. A new role had to be defined for government.

> And it will be one built on cooperation, openness and an agreement that we are not a bunch of self-interested individuals, but a community which wants to go forward together.[17]

14
CELEBRITY AND PRESSURES

A s intoxicating and flattering are the plaudits for a popular politician, life in the spotlight has its down sides. The community demands much of its leaders and can be unforgiving when let down. Certainly, politicians voluntarily choose to pursue the acclaim, the privilege, the financial reward. But there is often a price to be paid. By the time she was Leader of her party, Kernot was forty-five, a wife and mother: no wide-eyed naif. Nevertheless, her climb had been remarkably swift, from obscurity to mixing it with Prime Ministers, laying siege to ministerial careers, constructing alternatives to the national budget. Power fitted her like a glove. She adjusted easily in the way true leaders do. A generous person, she still had an instinctive need to be the one at the centre of the action, informed, understanding what was going on, drawing together the resources and know-how around her, but providing the overview strategy and direction ... being, in the end, the one in charge. The speed of her rise suited her temperament. She was in a hurry and had no patience for obstacles.

What Kernot was not prepared for, however, was the pressure, the intrusion, the sacrifice, the loss of her own anonymity as well as the impact on the life on her family. The effect of her defection to the Labor Party was to make her an even more compelling political star, a magnet for the attention of the entire Canberra system. Even after seven years in active politics, a certain equivocation about the stresses of the job was not easy to disguise—witness her surprising outburst against what she saw as a hounding media during the ALP National Conference in January 1998. In making the Faustian pact with power she would give herself totally to the work, becoming public property, her every move in daily life shifted into an appointment book managed and controlled by other people. Sometimes she felt she had lost control of her destiny, maybe even losing sight of herself. And equally, others could see the effect this huge change in her life was having on her.

She became harder, for that is what politics does to people. As a kid Kernot always had a bit of a disposition to be 'bossy'. Being the oldest child, that was natural. Hard it may be on other siblings, but a hierarchy built around the oldest child is often part of the fabric of families. When the cloud of uncertainty of her twenties passed she settled into marriage and parenthood, and a person with some firm ideas emerged. As her political career took off, members of the Paton clan saw a decided 'toughening' of their daughter and sister. Particularly when under pressure, Cheryl could be uncompromising, demanding, and she would push those with whom she worked quite hard to achieve results. Friends saw changes too. But this was hardly surprising. A politician catapulted to the top had to learn a lot, and learn it very fast.

Kernot's former student, Beth Gilligan, would look back and see a dualism in the woman with whom she became good friends in adulthood. There was a core conservatism but there was also a spirit that seemed to hanker to break free of convention; to be someone different. Gilligan saw a person ever adapting: there was young Cheryl Paton, then the married woman, the politician and finally the leader. Gilligan recalls when, in the late 1980s, she ran into Kernot's other friend Margaret O'Shea. O'Shea explained she had bumped into the then up-and-coming Democrat politician on the beach at Fingal Bay one weekend, remarking that she found Kernot somewhat preoccupied with her own life. Soon after, Gilligan also recalls she and her partner joining Cheryl and Gavin at dinner at the O'Sheas. Says Gilligan: 'It was very clear to me that night that Cheryl *was* very wrapped up in her career and her own ideas. I, too, felt a bit disappointed, thinking "where are you going, Cheryl Kernot? You are dedicated to bringing about change but how are you going to know how to do that when you aren't listening to other people?" '

But much later Gilligan met Kernot again when she was a national figure. It was at a school reunion in Maitland and when Kernot arrived she realised the school was making a little fuss of her and wanted her to make a speech. Just prior to the speech, the two friends were chatting and Gilligan realised that this important person was decidedly uneasy about the occasion. Kernot told her she did feel a trace overwhelmed coming back among so many of the people from her past. For some people such a get-together can be a simple trip down memory lane, a few laughs, a catch-up. For others it can be a more tense or difficult occasion, a nervous reminder of what they were, or what they had become. For Kernot it *was* challenging. For that night she would have been far happier to be just a face from the past, not a celebrity, not an oddity, not a trophy. Overwhelmingly that night, though, Gilligan was struck by the difficulty a public figure faces when the whole world seemingly wants to reach out to them, touch them, use them.

Now O'Shea's remarks of years before, and Gilligan's own memory of the dinner, made sense. Perhaps a bit older herself now, Gilligan realised that at the dinner she had seen a young politician being hurtled along, forced to adjust, absorbing and processing information and ideas, devising her own view of all manner of things. But Gilligan was relieved to see that, notwithstanding Kernot's slight anxiety on the reunion night, now as a more experienced politician, she was indeed a listener, receptive to other people and their words. The night left Gilligan wondering about the pressures of public life and how people in it are able to constantly muster the energy to give of themselves when confronted with one seemingly insatiable audience after another. Surely, she thought, there are limits to how much of a private person can be sacrificed to public life.

When she first began travelling from Queensland to Canberra for sittings of the parliament, Kernot's concern was not so much with the demands on her, as those on her husband and seven-year-old daughter. At the time the family lived in a magnificent, old post-colonial timber house that Gavin restored just about singlehandedly in the Brisbane suburb of West End. Kernot became fretful as the reality of the long absences from her family set in. She found the departures particularly traumatic when the time came to head into Brisbane airport for the flight south. Ahead of her would usually lie a full week in Canberra and lonely nights in her tiny flat before a return home the following weekend, or occasionally the weekend after that. She would stay on in Brisbane as late as possible so she could enjoy Sunday night with Gavin and Sian with their ritual evening together in front of TV with toasted sandwiches. Kernot recalls: 'It would be lovely and cosy with them in winter, but I tell you, the hardest thing I ever did was get up at 5am on Monday morning and leave a sleeping child to go into the pitch black for a plane to Canberra.'

Sitting on that plane, Kernot would hear all the voices in her mind, those worrying about Gavin and Sian left behind, those arguing that a woman had a right to a career, those wondering about where the priorities should lie in this, those urging her on because of the important goals like women's advancement, indigenous people's rights, a healthier economic debate, a better future for the nation. In the early months, Sian would complain that she didn't like it when Mummy went away and asked her if she really *had* to go. Kernot was torn. Some days she was actually mildly nauseated by the physical separation. But she made sure she sat down with the child, talking to her about it all as best she could. It was a tough time.

In the end, Cheryl and Gavin agreed that this problem of separation had to be addressed. One day he mentioned Sian was inclined to ask myriad questions about where her mother was, what precisely she was doing during the absences. At the end of 1990 they decided the whole family should move to Canberra for a short period. Gavin was on long service leave from teaching in Brisbane and they heard that an opening for some relief work had come up at Canberra Grammar School. Settled in a school in the suburb of Forrest near the parliament building, Sian began to discover Canberra, too. The move was a masterstroke because over a period of a few months it filled in all the missing pieces in the little girl's mind, particularly when she would come up to her mother's office, meet her staff, begin to understand about the work. Later, they would try to put money aside to fly Sian down to stay in Canberra when schooling permitted. Kernot explains: 'We weren't long back from Canberra living in Brisbane again when Sian came to me one day when I was packing to go off to parliament. She said "Mummy, I don't want you to go down to Canberra today but I suppose if you don't, all the people who voted for you wouldn't do it again and would be really upset, wouldn't they?" I felt this surge of immense gratitude to this young child for understanding. And ever since she has been the same. She has been intellectually and emotionally able to analyse the consequences of things. Gavin has been generous about it and so has she. They have been incredibly emotionally generous with me.'

The other technique the Kernots used was to include Sian as much as possible in the social activities that went with the job as Queensland senator. From her earliest years, Sian developed an extraordinary interest in Asian cultures and Kernot soon realised the girl had a fascination with China.

Later she would make Vietnamese friends at school, have pen pals in Asia and begin the study of Asian languages. Mother and daughter would sit together and watch SBS television. Kernot would take her daughter along when invited to things like the New Year's celebration with the Chinese community in Brisbane.

The Kernots were also lucky to have an especially understanding school, West End Infants and Primary. When Sian went to Canberra to be with her Mum, her teacher faxed homework down. Although Kernot was anxious about the amount of disruption, the school kept a close eye on the child, reassuring her parents about her progress. She recalls: 'Sian never once received any kind of abuse from the kids at school, you know, about her Mum being a politician. I'm immensely grateful to the school in the way they handled it. They had children there of other people in public life so their approach was well worked out. You worry that the children might be having a hard time over the contribution their parents are trying to make … I'm very conscious I owe those teachers a great debt. It's been so important having that supportive environment.'

Despite the support, at times Kernot still found great difficulty dealing with the day-to-day, personal elements of the constantly recurring separations. Gavin and Sian established their own routine, working in together at home. With Kernot off the scene so much, her husband and daughter naturally grew together, developed their own understanding. And then, suddenly, a wrung-out mother would arrive with her own ideas about running the home, organising the family. It created tensions. And, for Kernot, anxieties. At times she felt herself the outsider and, as a mother, this only exacerbated the inner uncertainty about her choices in life. She was ambivalent. On one hand she could not deny a loyal and supportive husband the affection of his daughter and, of course, his support was enabling Kernot to get on with her important work. Yet in her heart there was still this nagging dualism about it all, this deep questioning about the sacrifice she was making in her relationships, particularly with Sian. She said publicly that she had seen the development of a very private communication between her husband and daughter.

I understand that and know it's inevitable but I do get a teeny bit envious. I'll phone them up of an evening and they'll say they're working on their homework or going out somewhere—normal things. And I miss that.[1]

And then in those first few years there was the dilemma of how to deal with the ever-present pressure of the work. Kernot would arrive home and the work would follow, invading her sanctuary. Journalists would call any time of the day or night, her staff would ring or drop around paperwork, sometimes she would wake to find film crews appearing out of the blue for interviews, photographers demanding shots of her and, on occasions, the family too. As the leader of a minor party, with few resources and little money, Kernot was always dependent on the free-to-air news media to get her message across. With no budgets for advertising, it all came down to her capacity to sell the message at every opportunity. The fact that she and her party needed the coverage just exacerbated the media intrusion into family life. Says Kernot: 'The problem is you're always saying "wait a minute" to your family. They need you when they need you but it seems that 90% of the time when they need you coincidentally someone wants to talk to you on the phone or there's a vital current affairs program on TV with something you absolutely need to hear so you're informed next time they shove a microphone under your nose. So your family feel as if they always come second.' Sometimes Gavin would just wish it all away. Sian would long for her mother's return, the serenity of their family undisturbed. Both would react crankily when urged to clean up for a sudden interview or a meeting with Democrat officials at short notice. All in all the family set up its own coping mechanisms. But sometimes things could get a bit anxious.

Like the day early on when Kernot was in Canberra and her husband was suddenly brought down with a vicious twenty-four-hour virus. A proud man, he would not think of calling on the neighbours for help but at the time he didn't realise quite how sick he was. Sian was only seven. When he collapsed into bed Kernot rang from Canberra periodically, talking Sian through the task of preparing her own dinner and getting bathed. The child carried liquids to her sick Dad and then settled down on a mattress on the floor alongside him where she finally fell asleep. Despite a busy night in parliament, Kernot kept talking to her daughter till bedtime. When she no longer got calls from home, she assumed—and hoped—they had both gone off to sleep but then she couldn't ring again for fear of waking them. Later, she made Gavin promise that if anything similar happened again he would give neighbours or local friends a call.

The speed of Kernot's rise is only one factor that explains her ambivalence about her 'celebrity'. There is also her own fundamental personality dualism. An outgoing person, generous and caring, she is also a loner, needing time to herself with the replenishment of quiet periods. The sociable part of her loves the connection with others, like the good-natured banter she gets walking through airports, in shopping centres, in the street. This familiarity and warmth gave her an insight, for example, into the intoxication it all held for Bob Hawke. Kernot comments: 'People just talk to me. Out of the blue they will say: "Hello, Cheryl" and sometimes they catch me by surprise and I find myself desperately having to think if I actually know the person or they just think they can come up and say it. It *is* nice and it means people care—care about me.'

But the need for regular solitude became a necessary ingredient in her coping. A person who pushed herself hard and worked long hours needed to get off the tread-mill to refire the batteries. A strongly independent person with an ingrained need to exercise control over her life, it took her a long time to acclimatise to being dependent on so many other people, her staff and political helpers. Because her career moved so fast, with so much depending on her success as Democrat Leader, initially she felt the need to keep watch on everything, controlling decision-making in areas which should not have been troubling her, like minor office paperwork. Despite her outward calm, there was a surprising insecurity on that early, steep learning curve. She would delegate uneasily until she was entirely sure the person to whom she was entrusting responsibility was up to speed. The perfectionist needed to know that all was well, to be assured that no-one was going to create a mess that she'd have to step in and fix. In time, she began to understand that a good leader *is* one who delegates, who chooses good people to work for her, and lets them get on with the business. Yet the major pressure she felt was the overarching intrusion of other people into her life, the lack of privacy.

In an interview with the author in early 1997 while still Democrat Leader, Kernot recalled how she was at home in Queensland one day when she noticed an interview on television with the Prince of Wales. Turning the volume up, she sat down to listen and was fascinated when the subject turned to the loss of privacy that came with the job. 'He was very natural and he just said every minute of his life was programmed, like for eighteen months ahead. He said sometimes it really gets him down. And I thought that was exactly how I feel. The one thing, I think, that I hate about this job is the total loss of autonomy, the fact that someone has to go and get my lunch for me or pick up my dry cleaning. I hate the thought that people have to do that for me. It's unbelievable. Because with the best will in the world I can't find the time to do it. When I'm in Canberra, if I go round to get a sandwich in the canteen it's not a five-minute trip. It takes fifty minutes because everybody wants to talk. I'm also still getting used to my staff knowing what I'm doing every second of the day. Everything I do is down in my diary. Twenty people a day can come walking into my office and look at the diary and know exactly what I'm programmed to do. I don't know if I want people knowing me that well.'

In Canberra this sense of lack of control, combined with pining for her family, exacerbated the isolation of political life. It can be a damnably lonely existence as a politician. Exhausted after a heavy day in the Senate and retreating back to her small flat after hours, Kernot felt privacy but no intimacy. 'I spend the whole of the day keeping a lot of things to myself—I feel I have to keep some part of me private. But when I get to the flat and I lie on the bed, alone, I really want to reach out and have my family with me. I miss them. I really do.'[2] Back home in Queensland or at Fingal Bay after a draining week, Cheryl Kernot the vivacious public figure gives way to the other person, the solitary, seeking the solace of family, beach, silence. There she sleeps, then begins to clear her head, rerunning the tape of past days in her mind, analysing for errors, and then planning the next steps. But even there on her sandy home patch, the salty sea air in her face, there are other pressures; for political stardom created for Kernot something akin to overnight show-biz celebrity status.

She began to find that when she most needed it, it was hard to escape the public Cheryl Kernot, the instantly recognisable figure. She took to wearing sunglasses and big, floppy straw hats on the beach, pulled down over her head, looking away lest she be pulled up for a chat mid-walk. Sometimes she rues not being able to do 'normal' things. 'I can't go down to the shops with Sian. She will say "Oh, Mum, they've noticed you" or "They're coming over, Mum." So I find I'm pulling on the hat and sunglasses at times when no-one else is. Or I will forget altogether that people will actually be looking at me. I may be looking in a shop window with Sian and somebody will come up to me and say something and you immediately have to be on your guard. You can't walk around looking like a dag. You wake up in the morning and you think: "I'd better get dressed in case television comes to interview me today …" get up, wash your hair, put on make-up. You're always intellectually on alert so it becomes hard to relax. It's almost as if you have to leave the country to get time for yourself and family. I don't do that so it becomes hard to even have a holiday.'

At Fingal Bay for a few days relaxing with her parents, Kernot was asked by Sian to go along with Zena and a couple of the other Paton grandchildren to the local surf club for an evening of bingo. Kernot had just been bumming around in the sun, walking, swimming, eating well. Canberra and the telephone were, for a few hours at least, a long, long way away. OK, she agreed to go, but when the group reached the hall, it was packed, almost all the seats taken. Zena and the girls settled down on chairs but there were no more so Kernot happily sat on the floor nearby. Her mother protested, keen to find another seat.

'It's OK, Mum, truly,' Kernot said. 'I'm fine. Nobody can see me down here, which is great.' The bingo proceeded for a while and then out of the blue the caller pointed out that Cheryl Kernot was with the gathering and gave her a big welcome. Then he asked if she wouldn't mind stepping up to draw the raffle.

In all this, Kernot will say she's been able to adapt. It's a tricky situation, though, one which she has given much thought. She does not want to seem ungrateful, for overwhelmingly she is struck by the kindness of people, their decency, their good will. Only rarely in her years in parliament would public reaction to her have its hostile edge like the abusive phone calls or sour letters from racists over her advocacy of the indigenous cause. Her view of what people make of her is that she is 'probably quite normal'. And she sees it as her challenge to hang on to that:

'I guess people look at me and think I'm reasonably normal and probably trying pretty hard in what is a pretty dirty profession. In the main, I guess they're glad I'm there instead of not there. Not that they think I can change the world overnight. I guess it's probably just a comfort that I'm around. But I think it's important that they think I'm normal because I think I'm still fairly normal. And I want to stay that way, at least as much as it's possible to be in this lifestyle. I want to be able to keep understanding how people live.' She agrees there is a danger in the politician becoming egocentric. 'I guess it's inevitable because you're always reading what you did and trying to analyse what you said and how it's been reported. There is so much focus on you and what you think. But I don't think I'm as bad as some others. I never ask people to run around after me and I don't think I ever would.' Kernot saw other people she believed were carried away by the ego thing, waving newspapers around containing flattering stories about themselves. 'Look, the way things have been since 1993, if I needed it for ego reasons— and I'm not sure I ever did—I've had enough to last forever. I've had enough of people coming up to me and saying I'm doing a great job to last me forever. I'm quite uncomfortable with celebrity in the sense of people clapping when I arrive somewhere. I get quite uneasy about it.'

And if the demands of celebrity can be wearing, the other problem is that no-one, not even senior political leaders, are immune from life's exigencies—and disasters. When Kernot was first establishing her political career in Canberra and Gavin was working as a senior teacher at Churchie, they stumbled onto, and then bought their wonderful old house in Bristol Street, West End. Nearly 100 years old, the house was built virtually entirely of Queensland timber, tongue and groove, a magnificent verandahed struc-ture, high up off the ground on solid pylons, as is customary in Australia's north, nestling in the shade of a huge mango tree. The Kernots adored the house despite its slightly dilapidated state. For her it was big, sunny, informal—relaxing. For him it was a DIY man's dream challenge. But the house was destined for a tragic fate—one that, in part, helps explain Kernot's stressed reaction when confronted by the media at Brisbane airport while the 1998 ALP National Conference was underway in Hobart.

In a labour of love Gavin Kernot threw himself into renovating it, cutting back painted timberwork, clambering up on trestles for hours on end, sand-ing back the twelve-foot-high ceilings, building walls of bookshelves and removing sheets of wall panelling to discover the wonderful woodwork beneath. He adored some of the house's idiosyncrasies like the rare triangular-shaped, carved, wooden fretwork above the internal doorways designed to aid air circulation. On weekends he would tour local timber yards, antique shops and even demolition sites, buying lumber, occasionally picking up furniture pieces or interesting features to integrate into the house. He even took long service leave to work flat-out on the project for a couple of months. One day he drove past another old house being renovated nearby and noticed a magnificent, original, timber door frame. Inquiries at the house revealed an owner more than happy for the big structure to be taken away, but on getting it home, Gavin realised it was too big to fit any of the existing door frames so he stored it underneath the house.

After the trauma of the Janet Powell affair, Kernot was looking forward to an end-of-year break with Gavin and Sian as Christmas 1991 approached. She could not know that very soon her personal life would be thrown into absolute chaos. The Kernots had found themselves warmly welcomed from the start into the local community in Brisbane's West End, attending the local Uniting Church and becoming friends with the locals. Kernot had befriended a local old age pensioner whose full name was George Alwyn Hubbuck, known to the locals as 'Eric'.

Eric was fondly regarded by most people in West End. Born in Newcastle in 1926 and brought up by his grandmother after his parents separated, he joined the Citizens Military Force as a teenager and later the AIF, serving in New Guinea. Repatriated after the military realised he had lied about his age to serve, he then had some years in the merchant navy but fell ill with various ailments in his thirties and eventually became a familiar face around West End. He was a kindly old fellow with a soft spot for kids. According to Sam Stilianos, one of the other residents of the street, Eric would help out mowing lawns, gardening and walking people's dogs. 'We had every confidence in him', Stilianos later recalled. 'He had his moments. He was pig-headed and some felt he was a bit of a racist but he was a gentle man. There was no reason for us not to trust him.'[3] In late 1991 word went round the neighbourhood that Eric was ill, having fallen down a flight of stairs in a dizzy spell. One Friday night after Kernot returned from Canberra, Eric came to the house with his head bandaged. He said he had had a fall but Kernot was worried that one side of his mouth seemed to have dropped. She thought he may have had a minor stroke, so the next day she went to his flat and talked him into going to have a check-up. In the hospital, Eric gave Kernot's name as his next of kin.

Booked in for exploratory surgery, a prospect which terrified him, he asked Kernot to organise a 'good Christian funeral' if anything went wrong.

He survived that examination but the day after, the doctor rang Kernot with the news that he had a malignant brain tumour. He only had a few months to live.

Kernot recalls Eric point-blank refusing to accept the prognosis, shopping around until he got a doctor who would organise radiotherapy. After it, some in the neighbourhood thought he had picked up a little, although Kernot was vaguely aware that he was undergoing a personality change. He began to get very angry and rattle on and on about public issues, but it was not enough to provoke the neighbourhood into action. Three of the local families accepted his offer to look after their homes when they went on holidays over Christmas 1991. After a tough year the Kernot family were readying themselves for the trip down to Fingal Bay for Christmas on the beach, but before they set off, Eric came to the house. Kernot was troubled by his mood, his insistence that she tell him exactly about her movements and his demands to know when they were coming back. She was vague, suggesting they would not be away long but as he persisted in requesting a house key, she agreed to let him have access. She recalls: 'I didn't want to begrudge a dying man our verandah to sit on in the sunshine. We had everything and he was just an old pensioner. I thought, how can you not let the guy sit on your verandah when you know he's dying?'

Kernot rang Eric's specialist before they left to ask if it was all right for him to be left alone. He said the old man should be OK but suggested it would be helpful if there were neighbours around to keep an eye on him. Eric wanted to look after the Kernots' dog but because the doctor had suggested the old man could deteriorate suddenly, they decided to kennel the animal. At this news, Eric became irate and even came to the gate of the house as they were driving off on holidays to discuss it once again. Cheryl asked Gavin whether he had remembered to turn the gas off in the house. With Eric stalking away, she was filled with disquiet.

'I think something terrible is going to happen,' she said as they drove off. 'I hope he doesn't burn the house down or something.'

With the Kernots at Fingal Bay, neighbours at West End noticed the old man acting strangely. Early on Boxing Day, he seemed agitated and when approached by one neighbour, a retired nurse, he said he was feeling 'dangerous'. She rang his specialist who told her to call a local hospital and have him admitted. That evening an ambulance arrived but a seemingly relaxed and lucid Eric assured them he had merely missed some medication, but had now taken it, and was fine.

An hour later at Fingal Bay, Kernot took a phone call from her Brisbane staff informing her the Brisbane police had called to say her home had been burned to the ground. A massive blaze, lasting only ten minutes, had been stopped from igniting surrounding homes only by the speedy response of the fire brigade. Cheryl stood motionless, unable to speak. She dropped the phone to her side.

'Gavin,' she called. 'Our house has burnt down … it's all gone.'

Immediately, they began ringing around the neighbours and, among other things, making inquiries about Eric, fearing he may have been somehow caught in the blaze. 'I rang Eric's flat,' Kernot recalls, 'and a woman who lived in the same house said he was all right. She said she'd seen the fire start and that the fire brigade was there in six or seven minutes. The fire had been so intense that it had singed one of the fire trucks. My first thought was that it was accidental. Then the thought came into my head that Eric may have done it because of his illness. I knew one of the symptoms of brain tumours was irrationality or mood swings.'

On the way back to Brisbane the next day, the Kernots picked up a local newspaper. They instantly recognised the raging furnace on the front page as their former home. When they arrived at Bristol Street they gaped at the smouldering shell of charred beams and seared wrought iron where the building had stood for a century. The story of the tragedy was already being pieced together. Hubbuck had been seen slipping away from the house shortly before the fire began at around 9.30 at night. He had doused Cheryl and Gavin's bed with lawn mower fuel, thrown a match onto it and then done the same in the living room. The police found the old man sitting on a fence in a nearby street. They took him to be charged with arson and placed in the Moreton Correctional Centre Hospital. He admitted everything but when asked why he had done it, simply said he had grown concerned about the Kernots and had decided to help them out because he feared they had too much work on their hands with the renovations.

The majestic old house had burned like matchwood, the upper floor collapsing, taking much of the charred contents of the house through to the ground floor below. Above, the galvanised iron roof sheeting had melted, then buckled and bent down in a weirdly shaped canopy over the black frame with the wall panelling burned away. Silently, in deep shock, Cheryl and Gavin walked in through the gate. Stepping in through the rubble they struggled to align their memories of their most precious possessions with what lay before them. It took hours for the horror of it all to fully sink in, the two of them inching aimlessly through the rubble, stopping every few paces to pull the relic of an appliance or a memento from the mess. They struggled to reconcile the blackened objects in their hands with what they had been in their happy home. Everywhere the structure of the house was a maze of charred timber uprights. The walls were all largely gone. The keyboard of Gavin's computer had melted, left like a slab of blobby chocolate. In the kitchen there were the remains of food and utensils strewn around, signs that Eric had been preparing a meal. The kitchen had basically exploded. In cupboards some items of crockery had literally blown apart but miraculously, the Kernots found that a Royal Doulton teaset that Gavin's grandmother had given them had escaped unscathed. Sian's room was a burnt-out shell, only the metal frame of her bed remaining.

The family basically lost all their possessions although there was the odd small miracle in different corners of the site. Kernot had left her pride and joy, a family photograph album, sitting on the lounge in the living room. Some albums were lost, others were at Fingal Bay, but this one containing some 300 photos had fallen through the lounge as it disintegrated in the fire. In the rubble below, Kernot found the album, to find only that the plastic cover had basically congealed, sealing the contents. Though singed at the edges all the photos were saved. For years after when she looked at the pictures, the acrid smell would instantly evoke memories of the disaster. For some inexplicable reason, Kernot also suddenly thought about a ring with a huge aquamarine in it that she kept in a box in a bedroom dresser. The dresser—indeed, the whole bedroom—had disappeared, collapsing into charred remains on the ground floor. She set about going through the soil and soot and ash, sifting it, looking for the ring. After a little while of digging around, she decided to shift her position, moving a small way to the side, trying to gauge where the contents of the upstairs room would have landed. She pushed her small spade into the ashes and, amazingly, turned over the ring! Later she thought of her wedding dress which had been hanging in a dresser in Sian's room, the one made from lace material from Zena's own wedding gown. Digging through the ashes, Kernot found what she thought were the blackened and melted contents of the wardrobe. Turning over the ash she came upon one, pure white, small square of lace from the dress, a memento she clutched to her chest as she walked from the black skeleton of the room.

That night the Kernots were given the use of a neighbour's house directly opposite their home. The friends were more than happy to help out. Gavin and Cheryl could not sleep, particularly with a windy night building outside. Gavin decided to go over with some long ropes to tie down the bent roofline with its iron sheeting hanging dangerously over the house frame. As Kernot recalls, it was a hard night for them both: 'When they tell you by phone that your house has been burned down and there's nothing left of it, it's still very hard to picture in your mind what that means. I knew that Gavin was really upset so I decided I wouldn't be, basically. I just felt philosophical. I felt very sad when we walked into it but I just thought, well, what can you do about it? The worst part for me was when we were in the house across the road given to us by our friends. From up in their house we could look out the window and see what was left of ours. And every night the wind would get in under the roof sheeting and there was this groaning. We could hear it, it was awful. It was like a woman dying. Every night the house would start to make this noise and for me that was more traumatic than coming home to find it gone.'

Down the side of the house, Kernot had been nurturing a beautiful rose bush which produced the most magnificent white flowers. The bush was destroyed in the fire but after a couple of seasons began to grow again—this time with red roses. The Kernot family was forced to rent nearby in the Brisbane suburb of Hill End for six months, but there was never any question at that point of leaving their old place. Cheryl and Gavin bounced back immediately, although the loss changed them. For her, it brought on a major rethink about the value of material possessions. Later, she liked to think the whole experience left her with a more balanced view of what was important in life. The couple threw themselves into the task of rebuilding— a new timber house would replace the old. The old second-hand door-frame Gavin had bought locally but which was too big for the old house was one of the few items that had survived the fire unscathed. The design of the new house used as its starting point the frame as the new front door.

Over the following days, the Kernots' local Uniting Church minister kept them informed about Eric's condition in custody. Gavin had become quite angry and Kernot did not feel ready yet to visit the old man who, now, seemed more aware of the enormity of what he had done. He was grieving. Kernot basically felt she needed a few days to regather herself before she could confront him. But eventually she decided she had to go and see him, to say she forgave him. Despite what he had done she just couldn't get the thought out of her mind that he was alone and dying. On Friday evening she told the local minister she wanted to go to the hospital on the following Tuesday. Then, on the Monday, the phone rang. Eric had passed away.

To this day Kernot is haunted by the old man's death. She regrets she could not find it in herself to go to see him earlier: 'I just wanted to tell him to his face that we forgave him—because he wasn't responsible for what he had done. And because we still had everything in our lives and he had nothing.' But the extraordinary saga had yet another turn in it.

Because Eric was then a death in custody case and because he made Kernot his next of kin, she was then asked to go to the morgue to identify his body. On a hot January day, Gavin and Cheryl trooped into the city morgue and after all the paperwork was done, they were ushered into a room with a glass viewing partition. On the other side they wheeled in Eric's body and when they looked at his face, it was clear the old man had died in pain. Kernot remembers: 'It was really sad, desperately sad. It was a painful way to die. Our minister was with us and he just said a little prayer. And then I just whispered that I forgave him because I just had to say it to him. It was really hard.'

In the end neither Gavin nor Cheryl could feel any bitterness over the house. Gavin kept thinking back to the odd occasion when the old man had suddenly just shown up to help him move a few barrow-loads of soil or saw up a bit of timber. As next of kin, though, the work continued. Kernot had to oversee his estate and that meant in the first instance going into his little flat and making arrangements for the disposal of his personal effects. And it was in that dingy little house that the full magnitude of the George Hubbuck tragedy came home to her.

'Cleaning his flat out really put it all into perspective. He had nothing. But there were things we began to find out about him. He had a post office box and we managed to track down his family. He had told us so many lies. He concocted a whole fabricated life story. His place was just putrid, the bathroom, his bed. We had to throw most of the stuff in the wheelie-bin. But he had this little case with lots of things in it, all ordered. There was hair dye—he used to dye his hair. Among his papers there was a letter addressed to a Mary which said that he really loved her but didn't know how to tell her. And then I found his Bible and inside the cover there was some writing that he had rubbed out. In his own hand, you could see he had written himself: 'To Alwyn', which was his real name. And he had signed it himself, 'Love, Mother. Christmas, 1957.' After finding out all this I reckoned we were all together, we had the insurance for the house but, more importantly, we had all the things that really mattered in life.'

In the course of settling the estate, Kernot tried unsuccessfully to locate various members of his family but gradually began to learn more about the torment of this man's life. She wondered how this kind of decline could happen to a harmless old man, sixty-five years of age, left to fend for himself, living a lonely life. It all made her think about how society should be dealing with such cases, how support systems should be put in place to detect such need. Finally, the Kernots had to organise Eric's funeral. It was not something they relished. Kernot was pleased many of his neighbours, the people whose lawns he had mown and dogs he had walked, did turn out to say farewell. 'They came for us, really. There were about eighteen people in our church down on the corner in West End. It was so sad, we filled two little rows. Gosh it was sad. A life … an entire life.'

Kernot's old friend Margaret O'Shea reckons the way she handled the whole tragedy says a huge amount about her. 'It shows she can deal with things in a way that other people may not be able to do—to be reconciled with the person who burnt down a home Cheryl and Gavin had worked so hard to build. But it was not just their dream home. You must understand the loss of that home would have struck at the historian in her. She saved a lot of photos and she lost so many of them and other things that were so important to a person who treasures history. But then to be able to go and care for the person who had done it and recognise that it arose from his illness is a wonderful thing, I think.'[4]

Some of those in the political system who knew of the tragedy were quite supportive of Kernot through the following difficult months. She bumped into Queensland Liberal Senator John Herron at the airport one day and he explained he had been through a similar experience. Kernot remembers:

'John Herron was very kind and a great help, actually. He did say that you would never be the same again. You will never feel the same ever again about material possessions. He reckoned that afterwards he only ever had two pairs of shoes, one black and one brown. And he couldn't care about anything else. He told me that I'd reach into my drawers for years after and wonder where things were and argue with Gavin about it because he'd be sure it was lost in the fire and I'd be equally sure it wasn't. John said that would go on for years and years and years. And he was right.'

15
IN SEARCH OF TRUST

Soon after becoming Democrat Leader, Kernot's fascination with the issue of foreign investment would lead her into a lot more complicated terrain than just probing the activities of the Foreign Investment Review Board. After only eight months in the job she would take one of the most significant steps of her career, agreeing with the Liberal-National Party Opposition to set up a Senate inquiry into foreign ownership of the Australian media. The inquiry was to focus particularly on the relationship between then Prime Minister Paul Keating, Opposition Leader John Hewson and the Canadian media mogul Conrad Black, the background to Black's acquisition of part of the Fairfax newspaper empire and his attempts to buy more.

The decision to support the Opposition in setting up this inquiry was a defining move. It would catapult Kernot into a maelstrom of conflict with the government, the ALP and some very powerful sections of the bureaucracy. It would do nothing for her relations with some powerful people in the Australian media. Before she was done, a furious Black would hit out, describing her as the most 'banal' politician he had ever observed. Privately, she would take some pleasure that her probing gave him such obvious discomfort. It didn't worry her to take on an international media baron. She had only contempt for other politicians' proclivity to ingratiate themselves with those who control newspapers and the airwaves. She wanted out in the open what some leaders had traditionally preferred dealt with behind closed doors.

Agreeing to an inquiry was also an affront to Treasury and it sparked an important battle over the right of the parliament to be given information by senior public servants on matters involving government dealings with

269

business interests. But this argument led to another even larger battle over the rights and obligations of the executive in Canberra—that is, the power of the Prime Minister and his senior ministers to ride roughshod over the parliament. This, in turn, spiralled into a brawl about the relationship between the two houses of parliament, with Paul Keating arguing passionately that the superior powers rested in the Reps. This then steam-rolled into a row about the constitutional power of the Senate and its right to interfere with the workings of government.

But at the core of all these seminal issues was the question of account-ability, the obligations on MPs, ministers and Prime Ministers, to be answer-able to the people through parliament. In this, Kernot argued strenuously that the growth of executive power had led to an erosion in the role of the parliament. This flew in the face of a core notion about parliamentary democracy—that the executive arm was responsible to the lower house. She argued that in the absence of the Reps carrying out this function, somehow the executive had to be held in check. Her bottom line was that at a time of widespread community alienation and disaffection with politics and the parliamentary system itself, something had to be done to restore confidence. It was no coincidence that people were disenchanted at a time when the power of executive government had never been stronger. In short, the people were exasperated by politics because they could see all the decisions being made at the centre and no role for them, or their views, in helping frame outcomes.

The calling of the media inquiry had its genesis in events on April 20, 1993, when the Keating government controversially moved to allow Black, the owner of the British *Telegraph* publishing group as well as other newspapers around the world, to increase his ownership of the John Fairfax Group from 15% to 25%. The publisher of the *Sydney Morning Herald*, the *Financial Review* and the *Age* in Melbourne, among others, Fairfax Hold-ings was one of the most respected newspaper stables in the world, not-withstanding the corporate miscalculations of the early 1990s which saw control slip from the Fairfax family. Pressed by concerned members of his own caucus, Keating admitted the government had agreed to lift the Black holding because the Canadian had told him he needed it to be able to exercise proper control. Caucus sources quoted Keating as explaining to MPs, in their regular weekly briefing in Canberra, about Black's concern

over the need to change the 'culture' within the Fairfax papers—basically
the view that the journalists in the organisation were too powerful and
needed to be pulled into line.

Originally the Democrats had attacked the decision to increase the
holding as 'grossly irresponsible', arguing that there was great public
unease at the government's seeming willingness to allow more and more
media assets to be bought up by foreigners. With the ballot for the Democrat
Leadership in its final stages, Kernot, as Treasury spokesperson, had argued
the public was sick and tired of the secretive way national assets were sold
off. 'Decisions that affect the national interest such as this should be debated
and decided in the public forum of parliament, not behind the closed doors
of the Foreign Investment Review Board (FIRB). It is time for the FIRB to
be scrapped and replaced with an independent authority that could examine
such issues and take public submissions. The new authority should be
accountable to parliament, not some secretive offshoot of the Treasurer. This
latest decision shows the FIRB to be next to useless in protecting the
national interest. Once again the government has not released the advice of
the FIRB. So much for the public's right to know. What qualifications do
you need to judge what's in the national interest?'[1]

Then, towards the end of 1993, the Fairfax issue erupted when Conrad
Black released his autobiography, *A Life in Progress,* in which he claimed
that at a meeting in November, 1992, Keating had urged him to send an
application to the FIRB to raise his bid in Fairfax to 25%.[2] Keating, Black
said, indicated he would 'champion it'. Black went on to claim Keating had
told him that if Labor was re-elected at the 1993 election and the Fairfax
newspapers were 'balanced' in their coverage, Keating would 'entertain' the
application. Black said Keating had not been 'endeavouring to influence the
editorial position but was more concerned with the performance of
journalists'. In a media interview, Black said Keating had a view that Fairfax
journalists had been 'gratuitously hostile to him'. Keating had hoped that
'we would assert a discipline in favour of fairness,' Black said.[3] By now, the
Opposition was moving to have the whole issue of Keating's relationship
with Black referred to a Senate inquiry, a matter that was raised with Kernot
by the Shadow Communications Minister, Senator Richard Alston. Apart
from denying heatedly the inference that he had moved to sell off part of
Fairfax to get softer coverage of his activities, Keating created a big

diversion by claiming that Hewson had promised Black in private conversations he could have 100% of Fairfax if the Coalition won the election. Angrily denying that, Hewson threatened to sue Keating if he repeated the claim outside parliament.

Kernot was concerned at the Black revelations but also by Keating's apparent happy confirmation that he had indeed asked for a guarantee that Fairfax would be 'balanced'. Questioned by journalists during a visit to the US which was coincidental with the Black issue running at home, Keating admitted that soon after the election 'the government made good a commitment to reconsider' Black's application and then had allowed it to go to 25%. But he added there had been no further specific requests from Black and 'certainly no commitment'. During a media interview while visiting the US, Keating was pressed on this vexed question of who best judges bias.

Q. 'Mr Keating, should a commercial dealing of that sort rest on your judgement about whether a media organisation is fair to Labor?'

A. 'No, not whether it's fair to Labor, but whether reporting is fair.'

Q. 'You're the judge are you?'

A. 'Well, I'm the Prime Minister. That's how I become the judge.'[4]

Kernot reacted in one of the most hard-hitting utterances of her political career, going to the nub of the issue while other politicians pussy-footed around about its meaning. She claimed Keating obviously thought he was doing ALP factional deals, instead of determining important pieces of national policy. 'Here is a Prime Minister who secretly trades off media policy that has huge national interest implications in return for supportive media coverage, and happily hands over a slab of Australia's most prestigious media company to a foreign owner in the process. It is a leader who ignores his own Cabinet and caucus, who defines balance as denying media commentators a right to a view that runs contrary to his own political interests and then has no compunction about brazenly admitting the deal in public. And he does all this on the basis that because he is Prime Minister he can do anything he damn well likes. Well, Prime Minister, I'm one who believes your judgement is shot to pieces and there is something dangerous in unchecked power.' It was no business of a Prime Minister to be doing deals with newspaper proprietors based on his interpretation of balance. 'We all know balance is in the eye of the beholder and that Paul Keating has been unduly sensitive about media criticism,' Kernot said. The picture of two 'puffed up, arrogant men pompously assuming they could determine between them the media policy of this country is an ugly one,' she added. The two of them might not care about the proper processes—the parliament, the ministry and the right of MPs to be informed—but, said Kernot, the people of Australia certainly did.[5]

As she considered the options for an official inquiry, Kernot took her concerns to the parliament, asking the government to make available the relevant FIRB documents to determine if, as had been reported, the original Black bid for Fairfax had been rejected by the FIRB, only to be later overturned by the government. She once again demanded changes to the way foreign investment decisions were handled amid concerns voiced by others at the way the only wholly Australian-owned consortium of bidders had been treated in the purchase process for Fairfax. The Melbourne-based Australian Independent Newspaper (AIN) consortium would later claim it was discriminated against on the basis of claims made to the government by the FIRB which were erroneous, containing 'serious errors of fact'. The FIRB ruled there was no practical alternative to giving Fairfax to foreign owners, having cast doubt on the expertise of the AIN group. But AIN complained it had not had the opportunity to explain its case. With Richard Alston pushing for an inquiry decision, Kernot considered whether it should look at the original sale of the Fairfax organisation in 1991 and whether witnesses like Black and Keating himself should be called to give evidence.

The Canadian continued insisting there had been nothing unusual about his talks with Keating, that the PM had in no way compromised the integrity of his office. For his part, Keating continued to shrug off the affair in the US. 'It's an Australian sleeve issue,' he told reporters while visiting Seattle for a meeting of the Asia Pacific Economic Cooperation Forum (APEC). 'I mean, who cares about those things, they are ephemeral, day-to-day things. This (APEC) is the biggest of the big pictures. The Black business is not even a splash of paint on the picture. This is just simply dust in the cracks of history, just forget about it,' he told journalists when pressed.[6]

And then, on November 26, the saga took another turn when Black went further to claim Keating had offered conditional support, before the election, for increasing his company's stake to 35%. Black said that at a meeting in Sydney the previous November, Keating had repeated his earlier sympathy with Black's view that it was unfair that the *Telegraph* group should have so much responsibility in the running of Fairfax but be only able to exercise 15% control. 'He suggested we send in an application to be allowed to raise our percentage of ownership to 25% and promised to support it,' Black said. 'He added that, if at some point after the election, we wished to raise our percentage to 35%, if he were still there as Prime Minister, he might be disposed to support such an application. He said the chances of doing so would be improved if there was some evidence the company was making an effort to encourage professional standards as proclaimed by the Australian Journalists' Association Code of Ethics and to separate reporting from comment.'[7] Keating immediately denied the claim but to no avail.

Kernot believed the situation to be so serious that she reached agreement with the Opposition to convene a Senate inquiry into the issue of media ownership, comprising four government, four Coalition and one Democrat senators. It would probe the origin and basis of decisions to increase the foreign stake in newspapers in 1991 and 1993; whether those decisions were influenced by requirements for balanced coverage; and the role played by both Keating and Hewson. But the inquiry would also look at the procedures followed by the FIRB and the extent to which its deliberations were taken into account. Hewson agreed to attend to answer the claims made about him but when he confronted Keating in the parliament to ask if he too would appear, the PM said: 'Listen, brother, I know my place in the world. I don't slum it before Senate committees.'[8]

And so it turned out. While former ministers like John Kerin and even Bob Hawke himself fronted the inquiry, and while Conrad Black and other non-political people were there crossing swords with the Senate inquisitors in, at times, days of tense questioning, Keating and his senior ministers refused to attend. In the end, it was not the willingness of the government to agree or otherwise to the appearance of ministerial witnesses that caused the greater furore. It was its refusal to provide FIRB documentation.

For her part, Kernot was not singularly interested in pursuing the fine detail of what Keating or Hewson may have said to Black, or vice versa. She watched these issues with interest but basically left to the main parties' senators the job of interrogating witnesses about that. To her, the main game remained this key question of the role of the FIRB. To get more insights, she knew the inquiry had to be able to look to the documentation on Fairfax. She wanted to get to the bottom of what happened in the process of selection so the truth about the Fairfax deal would see the light of day. But she also wanted it as a model to help illuminate the modus operandi of this very powerful, yet very secretive, arm of government decision-making.

From the outset, however, the government, through the Treasurer Ralph Willis, point-blank refused the inquiry's requests to see the papers. This refusal led Kernot to, for once, overstep the mark and find herself under considerable pressure. But, more importantly, the stand-off between the government and the Senate pitchforked the parliamentary system into an important dispute over fundamental constitutional principles. This fight basically developed at around the same time the Ros Kelly 'sports rorts' affair was unfolding with its core sticking point about the power of the Senate to impose its views about the actions of ministers. Everyone remembered the classic fight between the Senate and the government over constitutional questions back in 1975 and those memories made many people in politics uneasy. But now the Keating administration was faced with an upper house baying for blood not only over ministerial competence but also over the Executive compounding existing concerns about secretive bureaucratic procedures by privately doing deals that impinged on important national policy. Through the media inquiry and 'sports rorts' controversies, Cheryl Kernot helped graft the issue of accountability onto the agenda of political debate in the mid-1990s.

Basically, the Senate committee, chaired by Richard Alston with Kernot as deputy chair, demanded the FIRB provide it with its advice to the government over Fairfax. But its officers were given Willis' full backing in refusing. The government argued that confidentiality was 'integral to departmental, inter-agency and inter-governmental consultations' and that the release of FIRB advice on foreign investment decisions could be 'embarrassing and damaging to its members'.[9] Willis argued there was the potential for 'stigma' being attached to Board members which could damage their reputations and commercial and business interests if their private views were released publicly. Yet the inquiry had the backing of a 1991 legal opinion from the Solicitor-General, Gavan Griffiths, QC, and advice from the influential Clerk of the Senate, Harry Evans, arguing the committee could compel anyone except members of the Reps and State parliamentarians to appear. The advice also suggested that unless legislation specifically exempted documents from disclosure to a Senate committee, they had to be produced. The Senate could cite witnesses for contempt, a charge which carried a $5,000 fine and up to six months' gaol.

In the face of government stonewalling, Kernot continued to bore in. In a media interview she agreed that the committee would be willing to test the full extent of its powers to get the information it needed. The committee would be willing, if circumstances required, to use its numbers to gaol FIRB officials for contempt 'to prove that ultimately the Executive has to be accountable to parliament'.[10] It was a dangerous admission, politically fraught, but testament to the force of her convictions. Kernot said she did not like the idea of gaoling anyone but that the matter was in the government's hands. All it had to do was hand over the documents. In an interview on the Nine television network's *Sunday* current affairs television program, she went even further, producing a provocative suggestion. 'I would definitely make this offer to the Prime Minister—that, in exchange for us (the Senate) becoming a better house of review with strengthened committees and the right to cross-examine public servants and ministers from both houses, I would give up the right to block supply.' With those few words Kernot found herself pitchforked into a national brawl, with some of her supporters wondering whether in going so far on both counts the gaol threat and the supply promise—she had handed the government a badly-needed diversionary tactic to take the heat out of the inquiry's investigations.

Instantly Keating's Attorney-General Michael Lavarch went on the attack, claiming Kernot's suggestion of gaoling FIRB officers was a 'bizarre and abhorrent suggestion', a throwback to the 'worst excesses' of medieval justice:

> The concept of politicians incarcerating anyone is repugnant to the Australian sense of fair play and decency, especially when the alleged crime is to be a public servant carrying out instructions of a minister of an elected government. Senator Kernot's soft-spoken style has now been revealed to disguise an arrogant agenda to extend her powers and those of her Liberal Senate colleagues well beyond the limits imposed by established parliamentary and legal practice. Senator Kernot has always presented herself as a reasonable person. Her actions in this case show how 'commonsense Kernot' will become 'constable Kernot'

when it suits her political interests. We do have bodies in this country which determine whether people should be sent to gaol or not. They are called courts and they operate by due process and people appearing before them have basic rights.[11]

Newspapers editorialised in a fury about Kernot's stand. The *Adelaide Advertiser* presumed she had been looking for an easy headline:

> She said it. The Democrats, the party of freedom, of smallest-'l' liberalism, would imprison someone for doing a simple, legal, proper, wholly-defensible job. It is no use the senator and any apologists saying the target is the government. The notion of sending an Australian public servant to prison for obeying the instruction of his minister spits in the face of everything the Democrats have said they stand for.[12]

In the wake of the Dawkins budget, Kernot had won a considerable degree of support, the *Advertiser* said. 'But this puts her in a new light. Gaoling a public servant is neither Australian nor democratic.' On the powers trade-off idea, Kernot was attacked by the government and castigated by some in the media for her effrontery in daring to speak for the whole Senate. She was 'giving something away she does not own to try to obtain something which the Senate probably should not possess,' one editorial writer suggested.[13]

In the face of the onslaught, Kernot remained calm. She accused Lavarch of overreacting, pointed out she had responded to a hypothetical question but refused to walk away from her insistence that if she had to be blunt to make a point about an area of national policy being subverted by an underhand government, then she would. She said the question of gaol had been overblown by a government desperate to deflect attention from the fact that it had no legal defence to prevent the release of FIRB documents which the Senate was 'quite properly' seeking. Kernot's basic arguments in all this were quite complex. She said the FIRB case was just an example of a wider malaise—the basic problem was that in recent years, the power of the Executive had been extended too far. Governments and ministers were not being scrutinised by the parliament. The FIRB showed that decisions were being taken with no accountability because in the lower house there were no mechanisms to do it, and, particularly in the Labor period in office, rigid factional arrangements and deals had muted internal criticism. Thus, it was for the Senate to step into the vacuum.

Kernot acknowledged there were two polarised and conflicting views of the responsibilities of a government in a case such as that involving the FIRB documents. But the Senate had been given advice to suggest that in a case where a government refused to hand over information, the issue could be referred to the High Court to make a decision, as the final arbiter. In fact, the Clerk of the Senate, Harry Evans, advised that the issue of the power of government to assert Crown privilege in relation to parliamentary inquiries had not been settled. 'Unless it is adjudicated by the courts, which is unlikely, it will continue to be dealt with case by case as a matter of political dispute and contest between the Senate and a government,'[14] Evans said. But there had to be a trigger for referring such an issue to the High Court in the first place, and one way would be a government appealing against a decision taken by the Senate against a public servant for contempt.

So the dilemma was this: to get the Court to make a ruling, something dramatic had to happen. Kernot was not intent on throwing some public servant into gaol—far from it. She was simply trying to point out the absurdity of a situation where the determination of a government to refuse to yield on accountability required extreme action to extract a defining judgement that unlocked the gridlock of competing interpretations of powers.

Underlying the whole debate was the festering issue of 'mandate', the argument about which chamber in the parliament, and which members of it, could claim the right to impose their views on other members, parties or institutions in the system. Thus Kernot's activism had, like a snaking river, meandered from one highly contentious area to another—beginning with the issue of foreign investment, it had quickly journeyed into a fundamental question about the accountability of government, its ministry and bureaucracy, then travelled on to the bedrock issue of mandate legitimacy within a parliamentary structure.

A core problem here for the Australian system is that the proportional representation voting system in the Senate gives minor players a big say. In balance of power circumstances they become potentially very influential indeed. A minor party player with the wit, intelligence, determination and stamina to use their leverage can impose searching questions on government. In the end, this makes the Australian Senate probably the most powerful upper house chamber in the world. Kernot's propensity to pursue matters she regarded as being of high principle guaranteed this issue of mandate was never far from the headlines.

Paul Keating made his position clear. This time it was no sweeping dismissal of the Senate as 'unrepresentative swill'; rather a measured argument. He told parliament: 'The Senate has a very clear role in the federal Constitutional arrangements, but it is not the representative chamber where the government is formed. The House of Representatives is the representative chamber. The Senate was designed to operate as a States' house. Perverting its use as a parties' house to try to change the principal financial legislation of governments is, of course, abusing the Senate's powers and I will say that till the cows come home.'[15]

But Kernot's pressure on the issue of accountability began to tell. Having been legitimised in the public mind by the 1993 budget, she had been playing a pivotal hand in the 'sports rorts' affair. Now she went public with a list of recommendations in the wake of the FIRB row. Shrugging off her miscalculation over the gaol threat, she plunged ahead with some explicit demands. She openly linked these to the threat of a Senate inquiry into the Kelly affair, with its strong inference that a blowtorch may be brought to other ministers' apportionment of various government grants. Kernot called for a stronger role for a better funded Auditor-General, either by making the national Audit office an independent statutory authority or by making it accountable to a powerful parliamentary committee rather than to the government. She called for the reconvening of a cross-party working group which had originally been created in the wake of a public controversy involving former minister Graham Richardson. It would be commissioned to develop a code of ministerial conduct. But Kernot also wanted changes made to the system by which ministers allocate discretionary grants to community bodies. Keating reacted by saying he didn't like the 'veiled threat' about the Senate inquiry and challenging the senators to declare all their assets and interests, as was required of MPs in the lower house. Kernot responded by happily adding that to her list of demanded reforms!

Within days, she received a letter from the Minister for Finance, Kim Beazley, informing her that the government would, in fact, back a Democrat motion in the Senate enacting all her proposals. It was a huge political win, if one backed by the sure knowledge that one thing the Keating government wanted to avoid was any more senatorial inquisitions of ministers. Throughout this early phase of her leadership of the Democrats, Kernot was presenting government with a perplexing spectre. On one hand, she was proving a principled and tough fighter with Labor for Aboriginal land rights, on the other she was a tormentor of wayward ministers. She initially attracted the ire of Keating, for example, in the demise of Ros Kelly. But in time, particularly as Mabo unfolded, he began to develop a sneaking regard for her political skills. From his office he watched her every move, monitoring her public utterances. Always finding defeat hard to stomach though, Keating, the street brawler, could not resist. Within a day of the Beazley letter he hit back, turning his attention to the vexed issue of the relative representation of MPs in the two houses of parliament. He raised the prospect that the government might try to change the voting system for the Senate from proportional representation to a first-past-the-post system, possibly involving a zonal system inside each State. Such a change, of course, would be fatal for minor parties who were able to win seats under PR with a small proportion of the votes. While it was not revealed at the time, Keating, in fact, had gone to the trouble of having draft legislation drawn up that would have reconstituted the Senate into twelve single-member State constituencies.[16] This whole idea, however, faced huge difficulties.

One of them was that ministers had told him bluntly the idea was too radical and he would not get it through his own Cabinet. The other was that the Senate voting system was a product of Labor reforms implemented with the agreement of the lower house in 1948. As an editorial in the *Sydney Morning Herald* pointed out, it would take legislation to change the system back. And that would again require the support of the Senate itself.

> Given the present credibility of Senator Kernot and the accusation that Mr Keating is intent on an 'imperial' Prime Ministership, it is certain that any attempt to change it will fail. Mr Keating, therefore, will have to learn to live with a difficult Senate. A little more patience, and less hot air, may make that task a lot easier.[17]

Opinion polls also suggested Keating would need to do a lot of convincing to get the community to agree to changes that undermined the independence of the Senate. The people were just not receptive to the argument that it had too much power. Kernot firmly defended the legitimacy of the Senate and its players, arguing that greater accountability would improve government, not destabilise it. She pointed out that at the 1993 election, Keating had won a famous victory which allowed him virtually to select his own Cabinet and extend his personal control over the executive. But, at the same time, the electors had delivered him a Senate where the balance of power was held by third parties. Far from being a Senate out of control since that election, it had been one doing the job it was elected to do.

When the final report of the media inquiry was released, predictably the Opposition and Democrat 'majority' damned the government's handling of the Fairfax matter, concluding Keating had attempted to 'improperly influence' the political coverage of Fairfax papers. Keating himself, overseas in Europe at the time, was asked how he would respond.

'Oh, just by giving them a big raspberry,' he said. 'Simple as that. With meaning of course, delivered with meaning.'[18]

The inquiry's Labor MPs argued in a 'minority' report that there was not 'one scintilla' of evidence that Keating had any sort of improper arrangement with Conrad Black. But the majority report also found 'fundamental flaws' in the FIRB advice to the government during the original Fairfax sale process in 1991. It called for the replacement of an advisory FIRB with an independent body called a Foreign Investment Council. It would be able to make decisions on foreign investment in 'non-sensitive' industry sectors, with the Treasurer, acting on its advice, handling more problematic industries like the media, banking and aviation. It also called for the government to clearly spell out its definition of national interest and insisted that domestic bidders' interest in buyouts be clearly considered in all cases.

In fact, in their thoughts on the FIRB, even the minority MPs conceded that the body probably should be made more accountable, which represented no small victory for Kernot. They recommended the Treasurer be required to publish reasons for decisions in foreign investment cases involving amounts over $50 million. Following revelations during the inquiry that the FIRB rarely followed up on conditions imposed on foreign buyers, the minority report also recommended these be made public and the FIRB properly monitor them. It also wanted the FIRB restructured to permit a more open and consultative process and that the body provide regular updates on levels of foreign investment. Some of these lesser steps were later adopted by the government but for the rest of its term in office, the Keating government did little to implement any of Kernot's firmer recommendations. After months of controversial publicity and debate, the dead hand of bureaucratic inertia descended once again.

Typically, Kernot refused to give up on the issue, remaining an advocate of reform for the rest of the Keating period in office, and then after the Howard government came to power in 1996. As part of her wider campaign to draw attention to the impact of privatisation policies, for example, she complained about the decision of the Victorian government to sell three power distribution companies to foreign power firms. She opposed Canberra's decision in the middle of 1995 to increase the allowable level of foreign ownership in Qantas from 35% to 49%. She criticised the sale of 49% of the Moomba gas pipeline to foreign interests and also the sale of BankWest to the Bank of Scotland. She argued that, increasingly, privatisation didn't mean just moving assets from public to private control but shifting them from Australian to foreign control.

But if her campaign to investigate the Fairfax sale had bolstered her apprehension about foreign investment, Kernot also came to believe there was an urgent need to help assuage public cynicism about the political system by enacting a package of reform to bring more honest and trans-parent government. She pointed to developments like the blanket acceptance of economic rationalist principles by the major parties, the growth of executive power and the blunting of accountability by 'modern day Napoleons' like Paul Keating and Jeff Kennett as creating, across the board in Australia, a creeping curtailment of parliamentary democracy.

> I think it is the very essence of democracy—the right, not just to choose who is going to govern you, but also to have some opportunity to scrutinise, amend and even reject the measures chosen by those who are doing the governing. Democracy is about scrutiny. It relies on accountability—and if we don't have institutions which can effectively scrutinise the actions of the executive and bring it to account, then we are setting ourselves up for—at best—sloppy government and—at

worst—corruption and cronyism. The trouble is that governments throughout Australia are using all sorts of means to dodge public and parliamentary scrutiny of their actions.[19]

In late 1995, an opinion poll published in the *Bulletin* magazine found that some 84% of electors believed that politicians lied at election times. Half agreed there was little difference between the two major parties and around 95% said MPs should stop arguing with each other and focus on running the country. Only 20% of people thought the quality of today's politicians as good as twenty years ago. And a solid 66% of respondents thought neither side of politics had the courage to take the tough decisions required for the long-term good of Australia.[20] These findings made a big impression on Kernot. Clearly, as was apparent overseas, respect in Australia for politicians was at a pretty low ebb. While the ALP had long talked about the need to introduce a 'code of conduct' for MPs without ever getting round to it, Kernot decided to set up a special community 'phone-in' line in late 1995, inviting people to call her office with suggestions about how they would like to see politics cleaned up. When she sat down and examined the data from the responses of 250 callers, she thought she detected a community deeply dissatisfied with the whole system. So she decided to build what she later called a 'Charter for Reform', a thirty-point plan to try to inject more integrity in politics.[21]

Divided into six key areas, the Charter would become a cornerstone of her attempt at the 1996 election to win back credibility for her party. She said that far too often it had appeared to the wider community that politicians were more concerned with the benefits of public power than the power of public benefit. 'Far too often, decisions are made which are secretive, which waste government money, which hover on the edge of illegality, which breach public trust.' The first set of ideas she proposed was aimed at improving the accountability of MPs and included the adoption of a Code of Conduct and the establishment of a parliamentary Commissioner for Standards to investigate any breaches of the Code and refer them to a new, powerful Ethics Committee. This Committee would include representatives from the wider community and would have powers to enforce sanctions laid down by the parliament. The Commissioner for Standards would also have responsibility for keeping a strict and detailed register of pecuniary interests of all MPs. Junior ministers, senior bureaucrats and senior advisers would be banned for a period of three months from taking jobs with any firms with which they had previously had dealings while in office, but this moratorium would stand for two years in the case of Cabinet ministers. The Speaker of the Reps and the President of the Senate would be made more independent and banned from party meetings or party activities.

Apart from further strengthening the office of the Auditor-General, Kernot also urged the creation of an independent parliamentary budget Office because of concerns at the way the Treasury had long operated. Such a new Office would publish independent pre-budget fiscal information, report on and cost major economic proposals between elections and independently evaluate formal party election pledges. Kernot also called for major improvements to budget documentation, assurances that government business enterprises and other contracted-out public services were fully accountable to the parliament, and a tougher process for scrutinising the costs and benefits of privatisation.

To keep closer watch on ministers, she proposed new requirements for them to cooperate with Senate committees, and also called for the creation of a new Commissioner for Appointments to vet all prospective appointments by ministers. As well, governments would be required to ensure that parliament was informed first before they moved to ratify major treaties or international conventions.

On the public service side, Kernot called for new protection for 'whistle-blowers' and the scrapping of the controversial performance pay system in the bureaucracy. She urged a strengthening of freedom of information laws, steps to remove blatant politicking from government-funded advertising and tough action to crack down on overtly political advertising that was shown to be misleading. As well, there would be a public register of all decisions made by federal Cabinet.

Finally, Kernot demanded reforms to try to resurrect the reputation of the parliament. She said there should be fixed terms of both houses to remove the spectre of politicians manipulating the electoral cycle. Proportional representation would be entrenched as the voting system for the Senate. And she called for the scrapping of the Senate's power to block the specific budget appropriation bills referred to as supply, arguing that, as things stood, it was not beyond the realms of possibility that at some time in the future the upper house could be inhabited by people intent on repeating the events of 1975. Kernot said:

> I don't think we should be afraid to talk about this issue in terms of morality. Twenty years on [from the 1975 crisis] I do not believe it is a moral or ethical thing to wilfully destroy a properly elected government by denying it supply, the money to conduct its daily affairs. It may be a legal action. It may be a tough political action. But I do not consider it to be a moral or principled one.[22]

She added, however, that it would be essential to embroider onto this one historic reform the clear recognition—and carefully spelled-out codification—of the Senate's powers to scrutinise new spending and taxation decisions.

PART THREE

16

TRIUMPH AND PAIN

The 1996 federal election would finally pit against one another two long-standing adversaries and politicians of genuine quality—Paul Keating and John Howard. Judgement day arrived on March 2, 1996, for a rivalry that had, over the years, veered from the friendship of intimates to the scowling hostility of sworn enemies. Both men were battle-worn and scarred from the sheer effort required to prevail for long enough to win the leadership of their respective parties. Both had dreamed long and hard of winning the Prime Ministership but for a long time Howard had been forced to confront the likelihood that the goal would elude him. First he had to endure a decade-long rivalry with Andrew Peacock and then wait while John Hewson, then Alexander Downer, failed leaving the Coalition no alternative but to turn to him once again. When Kernot's young politician tour mates of 1986, Alexander Downer and Peter Costello, formed the ticket that toppled Hewson in May 1994, Howard declared: 'I accept that I'll never be the Leader of the Liberal Party again. It's out of the question.' Before the luckless John Kerin failed as Bob Hawke's Treasurer in the wake of Keating's first party room challenge, for a while it seemed leadership may be beyond Keating, too. But having prevailed against the odds, the two best parliamentarians of their generation were in place at the helms of their respective parties in 1996 for the final showdown.

From the start of Howard's second stint as Leader, Liberal Party polling showed he could win if he avoided making the mistakes Hewson had made. He worked to convey an image of reasonableness and moderation, exorcising not only the ghost of Hewson's particularly hardline economic rationalist agenda, but also that of his own previous failed stridency on issues like immigration and trade unionism. He steered clear of articulating policy detail, Hewson's great central gamble that went so badly wrong. In retrospect, some leading Labor figures look back at a clever, if cynical, double-layered campaign that worked to kill the ALP on election day 1996, a strategy first put in place in the early months of Howard's leadership.

On a national level Howard's pitch would be as the harbinger of a new mood of security. His pledge was to remove the pall of unease that had fallen over the community in the wake of the earthquake of structural changes that gripped the 1980s and early 1990s. The Keating rollercoaster would be replaced by a concerted effort to bring stability into ordinary people's lives. Yet at the level of the marginal electorates—and especially those in rural and regional Australia far from the urban centres—another set of themes altogether was being fanned by conservative politicians. There were the perennial bread and butter issues like the inequity of the differential in petrol prices, country and city. But there were three darker, less explicit, but no less effective, themes utilised—ones that were designed to exploit rather than put a balm on 'age of uncertainty' worries. In electorate after electorate rhetoric, sometimes overtly, sometimes less so, was recycled about the supposed scandals of political correctness, of indulgent, wasteful Aboriginal affairs programs and of the long-term threat to nationhood presented by Keating's 'Asianisation' of Australia. While he preached moderation and stability nationally, John Howard's troops out in the rural backblocks were talking real dissent against the big social changes that had overtaken Australia since 1983. It would prove a defiantly effective two-layer strategy.

Quickly, Howard disowned the GST that had done so much to undermine Hewson. He was unequivocal on it, pressing the point hard, cleverly under-lining his new image as a leader of certainty and trustworthiness, intent on reassuring a nervy electorate. The contrast was always with the volcanic Keating. Once before as leader, when he based his great failed 'incentiv-ation' program on party research, Howard found himself in trouble. But in his second incarnation, he embraced the party research which suggested the aim should be to keep the focus demonstrably off his own intent, and on the record and threatening presence of Keating himself. And in this the ALP played right into the Coalition's hands by building the theme of 'leadership' for the actual election campaign in 1996. Unable to open a new strategic front, Labor fell back on reliance on Keating, hoping that, as in 1993, he would at some point be able to pin Howard down and win a second unwinnable triumph. A survey released just after the election showed that this strategy so badly backfired against Labor that it may have lost up to 2.2 percentage points of their vote.[1]

Amid mounting speculation about the timing of the coming election, in late 1995 Kernot divined two campaign challenges. First, she had to out-campaign the Greens, keeping the pressure on them by stressing at every turn 'product differentiation' between her offerings and theirs. After all, they were after Democrat-held seats in the Senate. The other problem was the danger that the 1996 contest could essentially become a re-run of 1993. Back then, with the huge debate around the GST, the campaign focused firmly around the major players. The minor parties did it tough. As the electorate faced a choice between Keating and the untried Hewson, the vote polarised, spurning third alternatives. Kernot saw the danger in 1996 that an 'It's Time' mood for change could do the same thing, leaving the minor parties struggling in its wake. She kept urging her troops on to get their messages across so well that middle Australia might turn to them as an active alternative.

When the time finally came for Keating to call the election date, Kernot's Democrats were ready, having completed much advance planning. Led by Sam Hudson, they all knew how much was at stake in this election. With five of their seven senators standing in the half-Senate leg, memories of the 1993 disaster were paramount. Hudson got the various party State divisions to agree that decision-making should emanate from campaign headquarters in Kernot's Canberra office. Kernot had a pre-planned schedule of travel for the campaign proper, an agenda for the release of policies and announce-ments, and themes for set-piece speeches. The State divisions provided their own campaigning schedules but any changes by individual senators had to be cleared with Kernot's office. Hudson worked tirelessly, smoothing out the party bumps as only she could. The Canberra office was the nerve centre with Hudson, coordinator Jacqui Flitcroft, media adviser Geoff Dodd, eco-nomist John Cherry and campaign manager Stephen Swift based there. Only Kernot and her Press Secretary, Cheryl Thurlow, were 'on the road'. Party pros rated this the sharpest campaigning team the Democrats had ever put in the field. And it showed. As it turned out, with the exception of a few minor hiccups, the campaign went like clockwork, one of those unusual moments in politics when it all falls into place much as the script had been laid down.

Kernot herself had become quite passionately driven to succeed in this election. She had the ultimate responsibility to re-establish the party. But part of her drive was also personal ambition—the need to show she could pull it off. Even on election eve, with the opinion polls having signalled some positive trends, no-one was quite sure whether the people would return to the Democrats in sufficient numbers to rule off the page of the Coulter period as an aberration. So there was a certain insecurity. Though inexperienced, Kernot had made a sensational impact with the public, and a party which had grown very quickly to depend on her built the entire effort around her. The effect of this was to magnify the pressure. She began to betray resentment that the same people she had to fight behind the scenes to get the Democrat operation transformed were so heavily dependent on her efforts for their survival. She became even more demanding that every element of the Cheryl Kernot political machine be seen to operate effectively. There was no room for faulty thinking or amateurism.

Amid growing speculation about an election date, on Saturday January 27, 1996, Kernot got wind that Keating was to announce it that weekend. The timing could not have been better. The following day she was due to do an ABC *7.30 Report* interview in Brisbane, before flying to Sydney to do the *Sunday* program with Laurie Oakes after which she would go on to Melbourne to unveil the Democrats' election slogan—'Keep The Bastards Honest'. The Democrats' decision to go with the old Chipp refrain about those 'bastards' was re-enforced by a general view that the principal players and the atmospherics of this campaign would be right for it. The phrase had, in fact, never been used as an official slogan before. Market research that Stephen Swift and Sam Hudson had commissioned in Sydney and Melbourne showed it still had resonance. Of the three advertising agencies shortlisted, two came back recommending the party use it. Keating did, in fact, make his move as Kernot had suspected. The upshot was that on the Sunday she got saturation coverage, with 'grabs' from Oakes' *Sunday* interview used on the television news. On the Monday morning, the first official day of the campaign, the launch of the slogan produced front page coverage, including huge, flattering photographs of the leader in newspapers. Right from the outset a perception was entrenched in voters' minds that Kernot and her party were on the front foot, organised, relevant. It couldn't have been a better start.

The Kernot team constructed a twenty-eight-day campaign program containing plenty of flexibility so they could switch more effort, if needed, to the two toughest states—Tasmania and West Australia. Basically, the Democrats wanted to run hard with lots of policy launches in the first and last weeks of the campaign when people were taking most notice and make sure there was, as one insider said, 'lots of colour and movement' in the quieter, middle weeks. The team managed Kernot well, keeping her out among the people at public rallies and canvassing shopping centres. She would come out of big days on the campaign trail 'buzzing', as one minder said, but the team was also very careful to keep everything positive. Said one Democrat operative: 'When she asked to see the newspaper clippings we were not averse to pulling the odd one that may be critical. If she had been hearing criticisms, she would have started to have doubts and then doubts can lead to anxieties about the direction of things, and then everybody would've been scrambling around changing things.'[2]

A highlight of the campaign for Kernot came at the official launch in a big lifesaving club in the Victorian bayside suburb of Port Melbourne on February 11, 1996. She drove home her underlying theme about the reliability of her party by stressing she had promised to take the party to the cutting edge of the national policy debate. She reminded everyone she had promised not only to act as the honest broker but to be an advocate of ordinary people—to lead a much smarter, tougher party. Time and again in the past three years, her party had been the only one standing alone on the big issues.

Kernot was given an unexpected bonus at the launch. In her own speech introducing Kernot to the audience, Janine Haines spontaneously lauded her as the best leader their party had ever produced. Haines did not have to produce such an endorsement. In fact, given the way the roll of the political dice had fallen against her, she could be forgiven for harbouring a touch of resentment. That one fatal misjudgement back in 1990, after all, had led to the period of leadership turmoil that brought Kernot to the job. It was a generous, helpful gesture on the former leader's part. In early 1997 Kernot recalled: 'It meant a great deal to me, what Janine said and did that day. I felt quite humble really. Coming from her it was praise indeed.'

For months in advance of the election, Kernot had been preparing the ground for one of her key electioneering themes—that voters should ask some big questions of the strategic claims made by the Greens. During the campaign she would take the gloves off, making it quite clear she was not going to cede one single vote of the precious support base her party had struggled to build up over twenty years to a bunch of people who now claimed status as *the* parliamentary representatives of the conservation movement. And she would not baulk at publicly taking on an environmentalist of the stature of the Tasmanian green crusader, Bob Brown. Kernot had a real problem with the Greens. She was furious that they paraded themselves as the real voice of the environment when the Democrat record was second to none.

She had real reservations about single-issue fixated MPs holding balance of power in the Senate, believing the role of parliamentarians was to deal with policies across the board. She was troubled about the capacity of independents, however well intentioned, to cope with the workload alone. She concluded that if anyone was well positioned to maintain a check on big government and give proper attention to the big issues, it was a sizeable gathering of like-minded individuals such as the Democrats. She was alarmed at the anarchist tendencies of some Greens and the suggestion that their MPs, for example, would provide no promise, as the Democrats did, never to block supply. At one point she argued that the alternative to the Democrats was these 'feral obstructionists' in the system. Her frustration through hours of negotiations with the Greens made her determined to fight hard to defend the Democrat patch. And it became a pretty nasty fight.

1995 had been a very good year for the Green movement nationwide. They polled well in the ACT election in February, in the Canberra federal by-election in March and in the Queensland State election in July. As the federal election neared, the widely respected Bob Brown came to Canberra to announce the Senate candidates for the Green movement's eastern States coalition. The hero of the Franklin River campaign had been a State MP for ten years in Tasmania and had two previous runs at federal politics—losing the Senate seat to the Democrats' Robert Bell in 1990 and then unsuccessfully contesting a Reps seat in 1993. He now lined up Bell again, but along the way made remarks that infuriated Kernot, particularly his claim that voters need not worry about differentiating between Democrat and Green, that they were basically the same, and that, anyway, in Tasmania he and Bell could both be elected.

Kernot expressly repudiated Brown, insisting the voters understood they did have to choose between the two. Her tactic was to drag Brown off his wholesome pedestal because she believed others in the wider Greens movement were quite happy to dirty their hands with cynical politics.

'Bob Brown cannot be responsible for everything the Green groups do but they have been more ruthless than us and sometimes dishonest,' Kernot said.

> I have been struggling with this contradiction in the emphasis on the pure, ethical, new-way-of-politics approach that they take and the experience of ruthless, hard-core politics played every bit as hard as the Labor party. I think Bob does have environmental credentials but they were gained as an environmental activist. He has been a State MP for ten years—that is, a politician. Bob is a politician first and an environmentalist second. I don't say that unkindly. I say that realistically.[3]

During the campaign, the Democrats reinforced their green credentials at every opportunity, producing an eighty-page booklet documenting their record and releasing three separate environmental policies. But the issue of preference distribution became the subject of tense, at times hostile, negotiations between the Democrats and Greens. Kernot complained the Greens had decided to change the long-established groundrules and act strategically in the Queensland election by directing preferences to the Coalition to teach the ALP a lesson.[4] For a while it seemed all-out war could ensue with all the parties distributing their support strategically in different seats and States but, in the end, an agreement was hatched to exchange preferences and the tensions subsided. But there was also an important green link in probably the most testing issue Kernot had to deal with during the campaign proper: the commitment by the Howard government to create a $1 billion environment fund from the proceeds of the sale of a third of Telstra. The pivotal place of this issue in the campaign, and Kernot's defiant position on it, ensured that, after the good start, she would be prominent in the big debates all the way to polling day.

Kernot announced that, just as they had with the Keating government's moves to sell off the Commonwealth Bank, the Serum Laboratories, the Australian Industry Development Corporation (AIDC) and Qantas, the Democrats would oppose the privatisation of Telstra. There was just not sufficient public benefit. Privatisation for the sake of balancing the books had to stop when both sides of politics refused to face up to the task of tax reform. Opinion polls showed that 61% of the public was opposed to the Telstra sale idea. The linkage with environmental protection was not a choice that Australians should be asked to make. 'I'm afraid that if John Howard, who was, after all, Treasurer for six years, can't come up with some ways of funding his environment program other than by flogging off Telstra, then there is something seriously wrong with Liberal Party policy,' Kernot said.[5] Then, at a campaign luncheon in Melbourne, she provided a package of six measures that she said Howard could use to fund an environment policy without selling Telstra. The package included a 10% levy on export woodchips, a crackdown on tax avoidance by non-residents and a reduction in energy-inefficient diesel subsidies paid to the mining industry.

As the campaign wore on, Howard set the scene for the big post-election issue—that of an elected government's mandate—by saying that if he beat Keating he would have the community's support for the Telstra sale. But Kernot hit back quickly. If Howard won a majority in the Senate, he may be right, she said. 'But, if as the polls suggest, he wins government but does not control the Senate, then he is wrong. If Australians elect a Senate where the majority do not want to privatise Telstra, then Telstra will not be privatised.' There were compelling reasons to keep Telstra in public hands.

'For a start, Australian-owned Telstra returns a profit of nearly $2 billion a year,' she said. 'That is $2 billion less tax revenue the government has to raise, and $2 billion to spend on Australia for Australians. Regional Australians have a lot to fear from privatisation—in particular the loss of cross-subsidies which make telecommunications affordable and accessible for country people.' She said the British experience showed privatisation and the user-pays principle almost always led to the rich paying less and the poor paying more. 'I believe it is the role of government to use its power to promote equality, not inequality.'[6]

Later, Kernot would be a strident critic of the savage job cuts inside Telstra, even as some of the organisation's bosses were taking massive remuneration packages. She plaintively argued that the people being made redundant were not just numbers—these were the real jobs of real people, with families and mortgages. Cut-backs inside the organisation did not make the carrier more attractive to international investors. During the election campaign she was defiant, spelling out clearly that potential invest-ors needed to know that, as far as she was concerned, the sale would not get through parliament. In claiming that her party would hold the balance of power and continue the fight for Telstra, Kernot would be proved correct. But her prediction that the carrier would remain in public hands would ultimately go awry.

As the campaign moved along, Kernot and her team were quietly amazed at the publicity her policy announcements generated. She got blanket media coverage for a package of job creation ideas which included the abolition of payroll tax, a new wages Accord, a three-year pause in tariff cuts, a $400 million national Community Service Program for the long-term un-employed and a $200 million 'green jobs' plan to build the skills base in the environment industry. Even though the intriguing Keating/Howard clash dominated the airwaves, the media devoted significant effort to marking her progress. Remembers one senior Democrat official: 'The Accountability Charter for Reform was a good example. We had been struggling for three years to make accountability sexy as an issue and it was hard going. So we weren't sure how it was going to be picked up in the campaign lead-up. But it got marvellous media coverage when it was released and a lot of good, positive response. It surprised us. We got a lot of third party endorsement for other policy things. For example, within hours of the housing policy going out, the industry endorsed it. The Australian Education Union gave us strong endorsement, describing Cheryl as the "people's champion". The industrial relations policy ended up being endorsed by the Womens' Electoral Lobby and the ACTU.'[7]

The only glitch in the campaign would be a protest from one electorate in Queensland, where some locals briefly grabbed media attention by refusing to have Democrat posters in their shopping centre because they objected to 'swear words' like 'bastard'. By late February opinion polls were not only suggesting Howard would win but adding that high Democrat support levels would deny the Coalition control of the Senate. Kernot's Democrats were being taken extremely seriously in a climate in which she was looked at by many people as the person who would keep the brake on the activities of an incoming Coalition administration. If the Keating government had any chance of surviving, it was probably lost in the closing days of the campaign with the blunder by Treasurer Ralph Willis in releasing documents which he originally claimed showed John Howard had a secret plan to slash funding to the States. The papers were quickly found to be forged, an elaborate hoax.

When the election results were tallied in Canberra on the night of March 2, the news was dominated by the end of an era, the exit of Labor's thirteen-year political experiment and the departure from the stage of Keating, one of the nation's toughest, most able leaders ever, yet one with a graphic, killing flaw—inordinate arrogance. Despite his extraordinarily misplaced claim to the 'true believers' mantle, the fact remains Keating did *not* win the 1993 election—a bleary-eyed John Hewson, with his unconvincing explanation in one or two key televised debates about his tax revolution, handed it to him. In 1993 the people left it to another, safer day to deal with Paul Keating and that day arrived in early March, 1996. Aptly, the exhaustive academic study of the election edited by political scientists Clive Bean, Marian Simms, Scott Bennett and John Warhurst was entitled *The Politics of Retribution*.[8] On Sunday, March 3, the sun rose on a new Prime Ministership, on a new faith vested in a short, balding man dubbed the 'comeback kid'. After all he had gone through, it seemed incredible that John Howard had finally made it. Lazarus had survived the bypass operation as Australians stepped away from the Keating rollercoaster ride. They looked around the theme park for something more reassuring, down to earth, ordinary. Someone who understood their problems and could comfort them in a time of failed dreams.

As a sub-plot to a national decision of this magnitude, the Democrats' triumph was a peripheral matter. It always takes longer for the complicated Senate voting to be finalised and it would be weeks before it became clear that Bob Brown had indeed defeated Robert Bell in Tasmania. But, based on the early figures, Kernot was jubilant. She had put the Democrats back together as a serious electoral force. The Democrats polled 6.8% in the Reps and 10.8% in the Senate nationally. It was enough to see a new Democrat senator replace one of the Greens in West Australia, offsetting the loss of Bell in the south. That left seven Democrat senators again, enough to control the balance of power, jointly with the Greens. This was precisely the outcome Kernot herself had predicted mid-campaign. She recorded the highest-ever Democrat vote in her home State of Queensland—13.2%—and the party more than doubled its vote in six Queensland Reps seats. Importantly, the result helped secure the Democrats' immediate future in that in the next half-Senate election only two of the seven members would face election. On the eve of the party's twentieth birthday, when it would become the longest-lived third force political party in the nation's history, the position of the Democrats as a viable player was secured into the first decade of the 21st century.

On the raw aggregate figures, the election result was the third most successful in the eight federal campaigns the Democrats had fought. In 1977 Don Chipp's embryonic party polled 9.4% of the primary vote in the Reps and 11.1% in the Senate. Only Janine Haines' effort in 1990 bettered that, with 11.3% in the Reps and a thumping 12.6% in the Senate. In 1996, Kernot's Democrats polled 6.8% in the Reps and 10.8% in the Senate. The point here is that particular broader circumstances of each election contribute to the relative results. Notwithstanding the aggregate votes, academic research suggests that, by 1996, Cheryl Kernot had, in fact, become the most personally popular leader the Democrats ever produced—in effect, the most favoured politician ever produced by third force politics in Australia's history.

Political scientist Clive Bean, from the School of Social Sciences at the Queensland University of Technology, traced the changing popularity of Democrat Leaders, as measured by six national surveys at various times over the past twenty years.[9] To that mix, Bean pumped in data from various national sociological surveys to find that, as a party, the Democrats are surprisingly dependent on the strength and popularity of their leaders for electoral success. But interestingly, Bean found that although Kernot's 1996 aggregate result trailed Haines in 1990 and Chipp in 1977, she was the most popular Democrat Leader ever. He also found that the party has been more popular under Kernot than at any other time. Using a complex measurement scale, Bean's work found that Chipp recorded a reading out of 10 of 5.3 in 1979 and 4.7 in 1984. Haines rated 4.5 in 1987, John Coulter rated only 3.3 in 1993. But Kernot rated 5.4 in 1996. In 1996, the Democrats rated a 5.2 under Kernot in this very broad measurement of ongoing popularity, with the party under Chipp next best on 5 back in 1979.[10]

When the official election results were in, the Democrat partying would go all night. Kernot herself did not leave the ABC television set in the Canberra tally room until after midnight. At the National Press Club down the hill from Parliament House in the suburb of Barton, the Democrats had booked a room for one hell of a celebration and Kernot headed straight for it. There politicians, staffers and journalists raged into the early hours with music, dancing and choruses of celebratory song. As the morning broke Kernot's energy was undiminished. She was tired but buzzing, still on her feet at 6am, playing pool downstairs in the Press Club with other late-stays including journalist Kerry O'Brien. When she travelled straight over to studios at Parliament House to record interviews for various current affairs programs, another legend had enveloped the smiling senator—the one about her stamina as a party-goer as well as campaigner!

In the mid-1990s the Kernots sold their rebuilt home in Brisbane's West End and moved down to a two-storey house in a beachfront location on the lower Gold Coast. The house itself was modest but its outlook, with the sea breeze buffeting the front windows, was superb. It had a big timber verandah at the front with an unimpeded view over the ocean, nestled under three huge pine trees. With the tawdry lights and hurtling traffic of the Gold Coast highway inland a kilometre or so, the house was located in one of the quieter beach areas of the coast, with its neatly suburban stretch of curbed middle-class comfort, its homes shoulder-to-shoulder with the occasional block of flats. With its straight, two-kilometre stretch of sand and the hypnotic sound of waves beating on the shore, the beachfront provided Kernot with the essential retreat for rest.

When the election night celebration finally did abate, exhausted, she came home. After a day of sleep, she walked the beach or sat and read, every now and then recalling events from the campaign trail, the highs, the tough calls, the risks, the final exhilaration, and then, the overwhelming relief. Every now and again though, walking on the beach, a cloud would overcome her, a refrain recalling the one distressing passage in an otherwise problem-free campaign. It was one of those moments when the travails of a politician's private life suddenly intrudes into her public one. It was the moment the electorate was made privy to the Paton family's tragedy, involving Kernot's forty-year-old brother, Craig.

Zena and Merv's last child and only son was born in 1957. As a little boy,

Craig was adored by his parents and spoiled by three sisters who fussed over him, probably too much as they grew, shining his shoes for school, packing his bag while he was off playing. However, from when he was a very small boy, Craig seemed to have a surprisingly volatile temper. He also struggled academically and as he went through primary school, Merv and Zena began to worry as he fell behind. They made a point of encouraging him, always remembering to find complimentary things to say about his efforts too when the girls' pleasing school reports came in.

But Craig was soon repeating at school and Cheryl would read to him or help with his spelling and tables. On top of what was clearly significant learning dysfunction, the boy's self-esteem began to suffer. He lost confidence in the whole process. Zena read numerous educational books and tracts on childhood disorders. She swotted on the subject of learning difficulties, but nothing seemed to ring true. Merv hit on the idea of trying to get Craig interested in woodwork, wondering if his future lay in a good trade. As the years went by, the parents grew more troubled, yearning for some answers to the boy's temperament outbursts and bouts of inertia. Some days it was nearly impossible to stir him from bed and on others he seemed revved up as if the cap of some adolescent volcano was about to fly off. They turned to doctors.

The local medicos scotched suggestions there was anything significantly awry with the boy. They postulated it was just the normal devilry of adolescence or, more gently, that he was the spoilt youngest sibling. When Merv raised the possibility of taking him to see a psychiatrist, one doctor said he would 'knock his block off' if he took him to 'one of those shrinks'. No, the doctors all said, it would pass, it was just part of growing up. And they concluded the answer was to bear down on the boy, discipline him, refuse to give in, punish the tantrums. So Merv argued with his son, but all it did was lead to a schism developing between them.

Finally, the doctors did begin to prescribe medication, which, in the end, included some strong drugs like lithium. Some of them were calming but that only created the ongoing problem of ensuring he was regularly taking them. The frustrating part was that his symptoms could not be linked to any specific illness, the doctors shrugging their shoulders when Merv and Zena asked the obvious questions, trying to inch their way towards a fuller understanding of what they sensed was a real physical disorder. It remained an enigmatic, worrying puzzle for years. At one stage specialists suggested there may be pressure on part of the boy's brain, maybe a tumour. So Merv loaded him off to the Nuclear Medicine section at Newcastle Hospital for a scan. It found nothing. Another dead end.

At seventeen, Craig first moved out of home but for years after would return, periodically, for short spells. Sometimes he would stay with Cheryl and Gavin. They were always supportive until he felt the need to move on. He would often ring his sister, seeking advice. With her help, he got his C-class driver's licence, which enabled him to get work driving a van for an ice cream company. For six months all was well. Things were looking up and Craig seemed the happiest of his young life. Then he was involved in a car accident—the fault of the other party—injuring his back, putting him off work and setting him back psychologically. The moods were back, the erratic behaviour. When he was fifteen, Craig had had his first, albeit minor, run-in with the law, over vandalism to a house with a group of other youths. For years, he didn't get into any further trouble, but in his twenties, warning signals developed. His family was uneasy about the group he had fallen in with. He started to experiment with drugs and began to smoke marijuana. He started drinking and it gradually became clear his occasional binge sessions badly exacerbated the underlying problem. His moods were at best more uneven, at worst turbulent, under the influence of drugs and drink. He began to have trouble in his relationships with women and then for a period went off with a group of people, flirting with a branch of Christian fundamentalism.

Then came a couple of serious incidents involving the law. In the wash-up to one incident where he was arrested for being disorderly in a disagreement with a female friend, his group of young mates was found to be in the habit of carrying knives. Later in another incident he was given a twelve-month good behaviour bond when he was arrested after a scuffle with a woman in the Sydney suburb of Artarmon. And then, at 1am on a sultry October night in 1995, with a sharp wind hammering across Fingal Bay from the Spit, Merv and Zena were suddenly woken by the telephone. It was a police officer from Burwood station in Sydney informing them that Craig had been involved in an incident where a woman and her child had been held hostage in a boarding house in the suburb of Ashfield. The woman had been stabbed, Craig had absconded and was now on the run. He was being urgently sought by police for questioning.

Panicked, Merv rang Cheryl, waking her in her Canberra flat. A week earlier, while talking on the phone, Zena had mentioned to Cheryl that she was particularly concerned about Craig. She had not seen him for some time and was worried he might have been off his medication. She just had a premonition that things were 'not right' with him. Now Merv and Zena thought he might head to Canberra to find Cheryl.

'If he shows up down there it might make it hard for you,' Zena said.

'God, don't worry about that, Mum. As long as he's all right, that's the main thing. If he does come to Canberra I'll let you know straight away but I'm not even sure if he knows where my flat is. He might ring later today, maybe. God, I hope so.'

Half-an-hour later, the Fingal Bay darkness was cut by the silver-blue beams of motor car headlamps as police vehicles pulled up, abruptly, at the front of the house. The Patons' neighbours' bungalow was empty while they were away, and Merv had the key to keep an eye on things. The police took up a suggestion Kernot had made—that her parents spend the night over there while the officers awaited Craig's arrival. At 3am the confused couple crept away from their own home by torchlight into the darkness. Sleep was never a consideration for the rest of that night. It would be just the start of many, many nights, pacing the darkness, borne down by heartbreak.

Craig Paton was on the run for three days but then, in the middle of the fourth day, the phone at the Bay rang and he talked in disoriented tones to both his parents. He wasn't making much sense when his father pressed him on what had happened. After some time he agreed to give himself up to the police but Merv would not ring off until he felt he had his son's assurance that he would meet them in Newcastle. Reunited with his tearful parents for a solemn car trip back to the coast, they headed into Nelson Bay, where they walked into the local police station, up on the hill on Church Street over-looking the azure southern bayline of Port Stephens.

They were the first steps of a horrifying journey, one made more frustrating and debilitating because there remained the wracking, unanswered questions about why. Questions that had gone round and round in their heads for years would suddenly come from the mouths of others—stern-faced police officers, lawyers, disputatious doctors and other experts, all trotting out their particular views about Craig Paton and his life, for all the world to hear. Merv and Zena had long sensed their son was suffering some kind of disorder, never mind that the so-called experts, with their medical babble, could never put a name to it. They believed there was a reason for his behaviour—it was as simple as that. But now, while he sat across the courtroom, alone, his head bowed, they would endure the legal system contemplating this idea, and then rejecting it.

The family battled to comprehend the horrifying circumstances in which Craig could detain a twenty-nine-year-old woman and her child for hours in his Ashfield boarding house flat when she had gone there to help him move. He had stabbed her and sexually assaulted her. The woman had finally escaped with her child, fleeing to a neighbouring apartment where she collapsed. Later she underwent surgery. In essence, the legal battle came down to a difference of view about whether he suffered a neurological condition or whether he had exhibited anti-social behaviour that made him a menace. Three psychiatrists who examined him after he was detained supported the former conclusion but in the end, in the court the latter view prevailed. Perhaps with a view to his previous history, when he was finally found guilty of attempted murder and attempted sexual assault, he was sentenced to twelve years in prison with a non-parole period of seven-and-a-half years, on the judgement of many astute legal experts a hefty sentence indeed.

The Paton family fully accepted that Craig had done wrong, had, in fact perpetrated a crime for which they felt regret and sympathy for the victims. They were as horrified as they were bewildered. In the end, though, their loyalty to him, their refusal to disown him was founded on the notion that there was something in all this, some factor not of his making or under his control that helped make his actions explicable.

Craig Paton was sent to gaol as a compelling debate was underway internationally about the nature of crimes of violence. In the book *A Mind To Crime*, British geneticist Anne Moir and author David Jessel theorised that many people commit crimes because their brains are malfunctioning in one or several ways—hormonally, chemically or electrically. Frequently, these malfunctions are genetically inherited, in other instances the result of brain damage in utero, from a difficult birth or through other trauma or head injury. 'Morality', they argued, can, to an extent, be a function of brain chemistry, not solely a matter of choice or free will and conscience, as had long been assumed.[11] The implications of this argument were quite staggering, suggesting the legal system should be able to find ways to ascertain if there is actually a chemical reason why someone may commit a violent crime. The book contained a fairly scathing attack on the subjective and arbitrary nature of psychiatric examinations, arguing instead that criminals should be routinely tested with sophisticated brain-scanning technology. When it was released in Britain in 1995, the book caused a storm, particularly within the authoritarian right which argued that to excuse the individual responsibility for his or her actions in this way would be to take a step towards social anarchy. But the book came out at a time when other pioneering research was underway in the US, led by experts like psychiatrist Dorothy Lewis and neurologist Jonathan Pincus, adding new layers to emerging theories about the high rate of neurological impairment among criminals. Lewis, a professor at New York's University Medical School, and Pincus, from Georgetown University in Washington, examined hundreds of violent criminals and found statistical evidence that the crime rate was demonstrably higher among neurologically impaired people.[12]

Whatever the causes or background to Craig's actions, the tragedy changed the life of the Paton family forever. In some ways, it pulled them together, in others, worked to tear them apart. Although, at that stage, no journalists had realised Craig was Cheryl Kernot's brother, Merv and Zena came under pressure from the media, which infuriated Kernot and her sisters. From the moment the press got word Craig had given himself up at Nelson Bay, a crowd of journalists and cameramen surrounded the police station, forcing the elderly couple to be secreted out. Craig would be held at Sydney's Long Bay gaol and the process of getting down to see him was exhausting for his parents, both in their mid-seventies. This was a massive culture shock for a genteel family, thrown into the world of warders and check-point body-searches, and suffering the emotional pressure of seeing an incarcerated loved-one confronting his demons.

Kernot visited Craig at Long Bay, diverting from her schedule when in, or passing through, Sydney, often visiting him for longer spells at the end of a parliamentary week, en route to Brisbane. This went on for some months and her family and political staff constantly waited for the moment the media would get wind that Craig was her brother. The visits to the gaol were a sobering experience for her. At times, individual prisoners would come over to try to speak to her, or their desperate families would wait outside the gaol until she left, approaching her with pleas for help. She would say she, too, was there visiting a relative and would not use her position to interfere. At one point, she had cause to approach a gaol officer with a request and he reacted in a manner which suggested he thought she was pulling rank, making some kind of special application for assistance. Kernot emphatically made the point that she was not requesting any special action, simply seeking information, as would any other member of a visiting family. Though the media was not, the whole prison community certainly was aware of her relationship with prisoner Paton.

'Give our regards to that bloody Paul Keating fella,' a more gregarious warder yelled as she walked through the visitor processing point at the gaol's front gate one day. And as he grew used to the life of the convicted criminal, the 'system' seized its moment to make it quite clear to Craig Paton that it knew who his sister was, too. One day Merv and Zena arrived at the gaol for their weekly meeting to find Craig's eye nearly closed, his face cut. He had clearly been bashed.

'What the hell has happened?' his father pleaded.

'Nothing,' Craig said. 'Forget it. Just leave it alone. I'm all right.' Weeks later, when it became clear Craig had taken his initiation into the system in silence, neither protesting nor using whatever 'influence' he might have in high places, he was none too subtly told that he had been 'tested' to see how he would react. And he had passed. After all he had done, Craig lived with the fear that somehow his situation could also be used against Cheryl. He felt he owed her more than that.

So much of what the Paton family and Cheryl Kernot saw and learned about gaol alarmed and troubled them. Everyone has views of the prison system. But to actually see it up close, experience it, be part of its processes, was a huge revelation. They worried endlessly about whether Craig was being given the correct medications. They wondered about the wisdom of a system that takes psychologically disturbed individuals and drives them together into corrupted, violent, and confined spaces. Cheryl Kernot, private citizen, was being forced to face a complex human and social dilemma. It left her feeling helpless and wondering at times whether she should somehow build a new career in the study and reform of prison policy when her life as a federal politician ran its course.

At the outset of the 1996 election campaign, Kernot knew that during it, Craig would be sent to a hearing. Then on the morning of February 14, she was on a flight from Canberra to Melbourne for a morning rally and taping of the Democrats' television commercials that night. While she was travelling, a TV news report broke the story that a Craig Paton had been sent for trial on serious charges and that he was the brother of the Democrat Leader. In Canberra, Kernot's office sprang into action. This just happened to be one of those very rare moments in the campaign when she did not have her Press Secretary with her. Her staffers could not get a message to her in the air so they sent through an SOS to the Commonwealth car fleet.

When Kernot landed in Melbourne and walked through the airport she was waylaid by a Commonwealth driver who handed her the urgent message. Well, the news had finally broken, she thought. What to do now? She rang Canberra on her mobile phone to take advice. Her people were of the view that she should go to ground, just putting out a brief written statement, confirming the linkage, but refusing to make any further comment. Kernot rang off, saying she would need some time to think it through. She asked the driver to take her to the hotel near Tullamarine where she was booked in for the night. As the car headed out onto the freeway, Kernot sat back, pictures of Craig as a child running through her mind, his mother and father playing with him, cajoling him, worrying about him. In her hotel room she sat on the bed and picked up the phone with a view to ringing others for advice. Replacing it, her head dropped as pictures of Craig as a very young child came into her mind. She could see him running along the beach at the Bay, joyful, innocent. She tried to push the images of childhood away, but they persisted. Soon she began to weep.

Wiping the tears away, Kernot grabbed for a piece of paper from her bag and began jotting down notes. The words were coming from the heart, steeped in her deep convictions about the basic fairness of people. She rang her staff, telling them she would not duck away, that there were things she felt she could say without doing any legal damage to the court case, things that were in the public interest because she was not just a private citizen but a politician seeking office in the middle of an election campaign. She said that the issue was not going to go away unless she took some firm action. This way, she argued, she got the opportunity to deal with it on her terms. Fundamentally though, Kernot would face the media not because of this matter's political impact but because she thought three members of her family needed her to step forward. She told her Press Secretary to book a media conference room at the airport.

Driven back there, Kernot took a big breath as she walked into a press conference at Tullamarine an hour later. She remembers being nervous about it beforehand although once the session got underway, her anxiety evaporated. Only once did she almost give in to emotion when she talked of her parents, but throughout she maintained a dignified composure. Reading from her hand-written statement, she confirmed the man in question was her brother. She said that while some things in politics were hard, they were 'not as hard as what I have to say now'. She stressed she did not want to reflect on the legal proceedings about to get underway.

'My brother has had a long history of illness and throughout that time he has been lovingly supported by my parents and my sisters. That doesn't in any way attempt to mitigate an explanation for his actions or for the distress that his actions have caused others.' Describing the situation as a private tragedy, Kernot hit out at the media's handling of it. She could not accept the media's 'disgraceful' treatment of her aged parents during Craig's court appearances. They had been confused and upset by the media siege and she appealed to journalists to 'respect the privacy and distress of my parents and sisters'. She drew attention to the timing of the media's interest, calling it 'curious'.

'The offences occurred at the end of last year ... I've been to visit my brother in prison. I have a very well-known face and it's a matter of some passing curiosity to me that today happens to be the day that somebody chooses to make the link in the middle of an election campaign.' When she had been to the prison she had handed in identifying material and worn nothing to try to conceal her identity. Yet no media attention had ensued. She had no idea who had leaked news of the proceedings but she wondered if they were trying to damage her politically. She said she understood the lives of public figures were under scrutiny.

'I can understand the public's interest in the link. But I hope people will understand that public figures have tragedies in their lives, too.' Asked directly by journalists, she denied out of hand any suggestion that the issue would do political damage. 'I think people will understand ... that they will think that sometimes other people have problems of their own.' Then she added: 'I love my brother very much. He had a very tortured life, he's relied on me a great deal and I know he'll continue to rely on me when my parents are no longer here. I accept that responsibility and I will continue to support him in whatever way I can.'

Afterwards, Kernot would often insist that she never had the slightest regret about opening up the subject during the campaign. She recalls: 'I needed to do it for my brother and my parents. I think the most important thing about doing it was my parents seeing their so-called famous daughter standing by her brother on television, saying I loved him. And saying that my parents had been wonderful parents. They needed me to do that, more than anything in the world. I know that it meant everything to them—they told me later. My judgement was I needed to do it for them rather than for me because they were stressed beyond belief by all this. I don't think any of us can imagine what it's like to be in prison. And to think you had also ruined your sister's political career was a burden Craig shouldn't have had to take on as well. That's why I wanted him to know that he was very important to me and that my family, and their pain, were very important to me.'

In the end, perhaps the most galling element for the Paton family, as they were left to contemplate their son's predicament, was the fact that on the morning of the day he committed the offence, Craig had made an unscheduled, desperate visit to the office of one doctor who had been treating him for some time. He was in a distraught state, pleading to see the MD, complaining that he was not well. The doctor's receptionist was unmoved. He could not see the doctor without an appointment.

'But I just want to talk to him,' Craig pleaded. His entreaties got him nowhere, and soon after he left. When the case came up for trial, that doctor was left to tell the court that the fact that he had been unable to see Craig that morning was something he deeply regretted. At the very last minute, when perhaps intervention could have headed off a tragic crime, the same medical profession that had in the past either suggested there was nothing inherently wrong or been unable to put a name on the disorder, was otherwise occupied.

Though he faced the prospect of a long spell in gaol, there was no reason why Craig Paton should not be given the opportunity to contribute his impressions of his sister's life and political career. In mid-1997 he was invited to commit his thoughts to paper. He wrote a letter expressing gratitude for the opportunity to say something, as other members of his family had, about Cheryl and her life. His letter read:

As you probably know I have three sisters. I love them all very much but as for Cheryl there is a special bond between us and I feel that bond cannot be broken. During my life, on many occasions, I have brought embarrassment on my family but Cheryl has always—and I mean always—been there for me. She has gone out of her way to help me and no matter whenever I knocked on her door with luggage in hand, I have always been welcomed. I have lived with her on several occasions. On one occasion she gave me her car so I could get a job and I needed the car seven days a week. She sacrificed her routine just for me. Now this part hurts so much. As you know, I am serving a long jail sentence. When Cheryl was standing for re-election someone leaked to the press that her brother was in jail for a serious offence. It was all over the papers and radio and Cheryl went through sheer torment because of me. I wanted to kill myself because of what I had done to her. The next thing I know here she is on national television telling Australia how much she loves me and supports me. I just wanted to jump through the TV and hug her. Even when she's flat out she goes out of her way to come and visit me. There are so many stories to tell but what I want to say is that Cheryl is deep in my heart and will always be. She is the most loving, caring, forgiving sister a brother could ask for. When God made her he most certainly destroyed the mould.

Yours faithfully,
Craig Paton.

17
NEW ERA, SAME OLD FIGHT

A long with millions of other Australians, Cheryl Kernot put her faith in the message of reassurance that underlay John Howard's election commitment to inject security back into the lifeblood of the nation. She had seen at close hand one government worn out. She, too, sniffed the wind of change. From what she had seen of John Howard, she was not disposed to any particular concerns about his intent—she had an open mind.

Kernot sensed that Howard was indeed a decent man, honest as well as experienced. She was somewhat disappointed that when asked about his visions for the nation, he had confined himself to talking about making Australia comfortable and relaxed. She was uneasy that in the hour of his greatest triumph, he had not been ready to respond to such an obvious question with something more uplifting. Perhaps, she thought, this was just being clever—understating it so that expectations were not high, giving him the room to deliver far more in power than he had presented at the outset. 'Image' remained a problem for Howard, but she surmised that after Keating maybe it was time for a sober, less abrasive, if duller, leader. When out selling her blueprint for accountability during the election campaign, she had made the point that the prospects of honest and open government were stronger under the Coalition than with a continuation of an exhausted Labor administration. After all, Howard specifically said as much, and there was no reason not to believe he would deliver on his pledges.

Kernot's first personal contact with Howard had occurred back in the period when he was just a team player while Hewson was leader. Walking through the sun-soaked corridors of Parliament House to an appointment on the Reps side one day, she came across him walking alone in the same direction.

'Hello,' he said breezily, smiling. They began to chat as they walked and the conversation turned to Kernot's pet theme of the moment—how families were coping with workplace upheaval.

'I've been noticing the work you've been doing on this family and work stuff and the area really interests me,' Howard said. Kernot said she had noted his recent remarks too, although she was unsure about his suggestions on family income splitting. He suggested they have a cup of tea and explore the ideas a bit further. She happily agreed. Howard made an impression on Kernot that day: She recalls: 'John was actually the first member of the Coalition who ever acknowledged to me in a non-partisan way, that I actually had an idea worth thinking about and discussing. He struck me as a person who was open to dialogue. Although he was in the wilderness at the time, and may have had time on his hands, I still respected him for that openness. I thought to myself that I always said when I came here I was going to listen. So I made an appointment the next day and went round to see him.'

Over a cup of tea in his office they talked long about the general policy area, declaring their opposition to aspects of one another's developing ideas, agreeing in other areas where there were intriguing questions that should be further developed. Kernot recalls Howard talking about how the experiences of his own family were making him appreciate that for contemporary women, the choices were tough.

In the early months of his government, Prime Minister Howard won Kernot's support on a number of important fronts—particularly his brave decision to implement tough, new gun control laws. While a bullet-proof-vested PM took to the podium to face down the gun lobby around the country, Kernot backed him up by vowing to throw everything into a cam-paign to defeat any Senate team the gun lobby might mount. But soon signals of tensions between the government and Democrats were apparent on key fronts—at budget time, on the issue of the passage of the Telstra legis-lation through the parliament and with the prospects of a tough industrial relations law.

Preparing the ground for his first budget, Howard's new Treasurer and Kernot's old sparring partner, Peter Costello, argued that the legacy of the Keating government was a deficit that would require massive spending cuts—up to $8 billion worth. At issue was whether such a huge cut could be managed over two years or compressed into one. Sitting quietly in her office

312

listening to Costello speak one night on the television news, Kernot looked at the paperwork on her desk. Economics adviser John Cherry had presented her with some possible political scenarios arising from the speculation that this would be a really tough budget. The media was already full of leaked reports designed to soften up the community for the bad news to come.

Costello was basically preparing the ground for massive cuts across the board—huge staff cuts throughout the public service, a 10% cut, worth $65 million, from the funding for the ABC, a 5% cut in spending on some education programs and an absolute revolution in the welfare area. There was talk the Commonwealth Employment Service would be merged with the Department of Social Security, that job and training programs should be privatised and that the government was contemplating much tougher rules including a 'dob-in a welfare cheat' program. Everywhere it was chop, chop, chop. The change of government was beginning to seem to Kernot to have provided the economic rationalist-dominated ministerial advisory system with new momentum for the task of further dismantling government. She warned that her party, for one, would not let the government get away with a 'slash and burn mentality' and that, as in 1993, she would 'apply the test of balance and fairness' to each specific budget bill on its merits.

Having just won a famous victory, Coalition ministers and their advisers quickly became irritated with the prospect of having to deal with Kernot, her party and the Senate. They believed that such a comprehensive win meant the people had put their faith in them to make meaningful changes—to press on far more comprehensively with the right wing economic restructure begun by Keating but blunted by vested interests like the unions, environmentalists, regulatory bureaucrats and Aborigines—and the balance of power coalition in the Senate. The familiar old refrain was more and more on ministers' lips: mandate. Their anger was mounting when, at the end of March 1996, Kernot announced the Democrats, the Australian Conservation Foundation and a group of unions would join forces to fight the Telstra sale.

This was the first time her party had been tied into such a coalition. But it was testament to the widespread concern about the fate of the nation's telecommunications carrier. Kernot put the alliance position very clearly— the funding of the government's environment policy should come from the dividends of a publicly-owned Telstra, not from its sale. 'We believe the government should dedicate no less than one-third of Telstra dividends to

313

the environment on an on-going basis,' she said. 'That would amount to substantially more than the Coalition has offered and would also ensure Telstra remains in public ownership.' But government officials were beginning to wonder if the time had not arrived for someone to deal with Kernot's tactics. Who the hell did she think she was? Who was running this country, anyway? She might have thought she could get away with this stuff when Labor was in power but this was a new government with the people's support for its policies. At very senior levels in the ministry a strategy began to emerge.

In the face of an obstructionist Senate, a government always had the option of a double dissolution election. Once the Senate repeatedly rejected legislation, it could go to the people arguing it had a mandate for its proposed law. If it won the election, it could call a joint sitting of the two chambers of parliament where the bill would go through on the combined numbers. The first part of the government strategy entailed upping the rhetorical pressure on Kernot on this theme of mandate, building a perception in the public mind of Senate obstructionism, with Kernot at its heart. The judgement was that the more she was provoked, the more fronts opened up against her, it would then only take one big tumble for what her critics saw as the illegitimacy of her position to be exposed.

Beginning in March 1996 and continuing largely unabated until June, the Howard government, led by the Prime Minister himself, subjected Kernot to a relentless barrage of criticism. In parliament, ministers were all singing from one sheet, accusing her of being in league with the ALP and insisting that in power Labor had gone soft on her to buy her support. But Kernot stood her ground. She caused further irritation by introducing into the parliament her own legislation to implement the Coalition's promised environmental package without selling Telstra, and she went on the offensive to argue that experience in Britain junked the government's claims that privatisation led to lower prices. In a controversial article written for the *Australian* newspaper, she claimed that during the first eight years after the privatisation of British Telecom, costs for businesses dropped but charges for consumers rose.[1] Domestic call rates rose 27% and installation went up by 61%, she said, quoting the British National Consumer Council. She said prices had only fallen after the British industry regulator moved in to cap further rises. The government saw an opening and counter-attacked.

314

In parliament, Howard quoted from a letter from the Managing Director of British Telecom in Australia which said her figures were 'incorrect and misleading'. The Minister for Communications, Richard Alston, said he was appalled by the inaccuracy of her claims. But there was more to come. Frank Blount, the American-born Chief Executive of Telstra, publicly urged the privatisation of his organisation. In a move interpreted as aiming to convince the Senate to give way, Blount said his Board supported government policy. In a speech to the Institute of Chartered Accountants, he pointed to five principal advantages flowing from privatisation—an increased commercial focus and more accountability, better management of investment trade-offs, the delivery of regulatory and policy transparency, easier access to capital and incentive schemes for staff. But Kernot hit back, taking on Blount's five specific points.

She said previous privatisations, including that of the Commonwealth Bank, had shown accountability diminished—not improved—and she added that a privatised entity would be much harder to regulate. She argued Telstra in government hands had already shown it could respond effectively to investment opportunities. 'Very few Australian companies would spend more than $3 billion a year in new investment, as Telstra does,' she said. There was no clear evidence that privatisation would give the organisation easier access to capital. 'This is a company owned by all Australians,' she said. 'It's doing well—it can do better—but you don't need private owner-ship to achieve that.' On the suggested incentive schemes, Kernot argued that previous privatisations suggested the benefits flowed mainly into big pay rises for senior managers.

Kernot said that no-one should be surprised that a boss in Blount's position should be mouthing supportive noises about the government's privatisation intent. 'What he should be doing is standing up for the interests of the current shareholders of Telstra—the people of Australia who own this wonderful asset which is producing a $2 billion income stream. I don't think the fact that Frank Blount is mouthing government policy is a persuasive reason for the Democrats, or anyone else in Australia, to change their opinion. Telstra is too important to Australia to give over to a small group of shareholders.'[2]

Under attack on multiple flanks, Kernot was being forced to dig in over Telstra. Not only had the government thrown a contradictory raft of statistics at her on one of her key arguing points, but the boss of the organisation—appointed by the Labor government—was now very firmly supporting Howard and Alston. And, after all, this was a privatisation move begun under Labor, Keating at one point fighting a bitter war in Cabinet to defeat the minister responsible, Kim Beazley, who was holding out against a broader sell-off. Labor in Opposition hardly had much political room to manoeuvre. It was beginning to look as though Kernot, with her Senate leverage, was destined to be at the centre of one of the great political showdowns. As she continued staking out her ground, Kernot could not know, however, that the political equation would soon be drastically altered. Within eight weeks of the confrontation with Blount, a political bombshell instantly changed the balance of power dynamic—one that would result in the government achieving its dream of the sale of the first part of the telecommunications carrier. For now though, the attacks against her were unrelenting.

Former Treasury Secretary and National Party Senator John Stone accused her of 'dissembling' her way through the debate over Blount's intervention, backed by the 'resources' of ABC television and radio journalists. Here, of course, was the classic demonology of right wing politico/economic opinion in Australia—Kernot was an undisciplined left wing politician with supposedly too much power being propped up by cronies in the ABC who subtly distort reportage of events. Stone said Kernot was not interested in benefiting the people of Australia:

> The truth is that Senator Kernot does not give a damn about such matters of public interest; she is solely concerned about the private interests of the party of political scavengers which she has the dishonour to lead.[3]

Stone said Kernot had responded to Blount's commonsense analysis of the benefits of privatisation by playing the man and not the ball—among other things, asking why Australia should listen to a Telstra boss with an American accent whose views reflected his lifetime in the US corporate world. On another front, the Liberal Party's Federal Director, Andrew Robb, suggested Kernot's position could lead to international investors 'junking' Australia. And then John Howard bought in, making his strongest yet denunciation of the Democrats, accusing them of being openly in league with the ALP for thirteen years. He challenged Kernot to prove she was other than a left wing acolyte of Labor. But then, a week later Howard did a curious thing— something that would for the moment take the heat out of the assault on Kernot. It would also prove to be a landmark in her evolving attitude to him, and his political modus operandi.

Delivering the Thomas Playford Memorial Lecture in Adelaide on July 5, 1996, Howard moved to intensify the pressure on her by saying the Democrats needed to know they were in a very risky position by opposing key elements of the government's program. In a clear reference to the possibility of a double dissolution, Howard said his government had been elected by the people to get on with its program.

'The recent actions of the Democrats would suggest that their central preoccupation is not with honesty but with blind partisanship,' Howard said. He then produced a list of 'core' promises he said would be delivered, whatever budget constraints the government faced. These included election commitments on family tax and health care, industrial relations changes, small-business reforms and measures to reduce unemployment. He would not allow the 'fiscal irresponsibility' of the Keating government to force him to dishonour these central pledges.

'The great farce of the current situation,' Howard went on, 'is that the obstructionism is coming from a minority party that parades itself as committed to keeping politicians honest. In presenting our legislation on these key issues in parliament we are being honest and keeping faith with commitments we undertook at the election. In denying the people these changes, the Democrats need to know they are playing for very high stakes indeed.' Business leaders like John Prescott from BHP publicly supported the suggestion of a double dissolution on the grounds it would at least bring some certainty to the business environment.

The Howard remarks were set against the background of some shifting thinking behind the scenes inside the government. After months of pretty pointed attacks on Kernot, some Coalition strategists had come to the view that perhaps the government should take another tack—setting up dialogue with the minor parties instead of just berating them. Kernot instantly responded to Howard's Playford lecture, pointing out the only area the Democrats had said they would unequivocally oppose was the Telstra sale. As in 1993 with Labor, she was facing down the threat of an election: 'We do not want a double dissolution because it would be costly and would dampen business confidence, but, if we have to endure one, then I am absolutely sure we would be supported by the Australian people, in fact we'd be returned with increased numbers.' But then Kernot delivered her double-whammy. She revealed that a few days *before* the Playford speech, John Howard himself had rung her suggesting they get together to discuss the Senate situation. She said she was astonished by this 'two-faced performance'—being conciliatory privately but attacking her party publicly. She said she would have given Howard more credit than to stoop to such tactics.[4]

Whatever the rough and tumble of national debates, Kernot could give as good as she got. Well used to the manoeuvrings of governments, she nevertheless had begun to feel the pressure, particularly with one minister after another belting her on multiple fronts, backed as they were by their supporters in the business community and in the financial press. She also knew she was showing that under governments of both persuasions, she could keep her party at the heart of the big debates. Despite the bare-knuckle stuff, she was surviving without too many bruises. But she did start to become angry at what she saw as disingenuousness. She believed that whatever politicians' opposing views, unless there was mutual respect, clear lines of communication and firm groundrules in their back-room personal dealings, then the political process was in real trouble. Coincidental with the government pressure on her, Kernot had begun talks with the minister for Industrial Relations, Peter Reith, about the government's planned reforms of the IR system. She was angered by Howard's claim that during those talks, the Democrats blocked legislation to dismantle the law covering unfair dismissals, which affected small business. She pointed out that the Democrats had agreed in the talks to hive that section off from the massive IR Bill being negotiated with Reith and deal with it expeditiously in the parliament. She said Howard had originally refused that offer but had been publicly encouraging small business to vent its anger against the Democrats for the hold-up.

For the first time, Kernot began to make public comments about losing faith in the new PM. She talked of how she was becoming 'unsure' about him. This was more than routine political rhetoric—behind the words the sentiment was clear. 'The Prime Minister entitles us to have different expectations because it is he who wants to talk about restoring trust. I made assumptions that in what is fair, robust political debate he would not distort the truth, for example, on the matter of unfair dismissals. He's gone out of his way to do that even though we have written to him about it … I think you can still argue robustly without attempting to mislead people deliberately.' Kernot spoke about her 'surprise and astonishment' at Howard's tactics.[5]

In an interview, the *Canberra Times'* Political Correspondent Ross Peake asked her whether she was not being naive in the debate. 'I think I have been a bit naive about it all … I thought he would resist the usual devices open to politicians because I still think you can engage in public debate with respect,' Kernot said.[6] She told Peake she was also disillusioned on another important front—that of parliamentary reform. Howard had talked up the possibility of an independent Speaker of the parliament, but no changes had been forthcoming. The government happily gagged debate after saying for years it was philosophically opposed to the practice. 'I heard them saying that for six years, and I believed them,' Kernot said. She concluded that one would have to see this, already, as amounting to a breakdown in standards, the beginning of the decline of yet another government into expediency. 'You can't restore trust and then behave exactly as the Labor Party did, or worse.'[7]

Every time the pressure came on from the government over mandate, Kernot's instinct was to hold to the line, knowing that any signal of a rethink would immediately be interpreted as the start of a retreat. The approaching 1996 budget merely served to deepen hostility developing between the Senate and the executive. A new administration with some big plans saw Kernot as the major obstruction. Increasingly, Coalition people began having private discussion about the possibility of solving the problem by changing the voting system for the upper house. One MP, the NSW Parliamentary Secretary, Tony Abbott, went as far as to suggest publicly that the government would consider the option unless the Senate passed its laws.

Abbott said three options were under consideration, involving changing the quota required to win a seat, increasing the overall size of the Senate or dividing each State into two constituencies. 'But whether any one of them might be further explored depends very much on the behaviour of the Democrats and the minor parties,' Abbott said. 'They are perfectly entitled to treat the Senate as a house of review but they are not entitled to try to frustrate the government's mandate.' Abbott said that a government determined to end minor party disruption could introduce amendments to the Electoral Act and force them through a joint sitting after a double dissolution.[8] Although John Howard distanced himself from the Abbott remarks, the problem for the government would remain a very real one. As its frustration built in late 1996 and into 1997, other prominent Liberals including Andrew Robb and Party President, Tony Staley, actively discussed with Howard options for legislating to change the system. The effect would be to sweep the third parties away. Kernot pointed out that when an exasperated Paul Keating had himself suggested changing the Senate rules, the then Shadow Treasurer, Alexander Downer, first flirted with the idea but then backed away from supporting it.

'Our inclination would be to oppose that type of measure because we would be suspicious that Mr Keating would not be using these types of changes to improve the operation of the parliament but to increase power for himself,' Downer had said in March, 1994. In 1997 the same rationale drove ALP warnings that it would not join forces with the government to vote for changes to the system.[9]

Kernot was a champion of the Senate, going as far as to argue that the Howard government's forty-five-seat majority was not an overwhelming mandate, even for the PM's election promises. 'A majority vote on the floor of the Senate on any issue has the same authority as the majority of the House of Representatives,' she said. Despite the size of his Reps win, it was no overpowering endorsement that could override the views of the Senate. Some voters who supported Howard directly in the Reps had voted Democrat in the Senate. But, overwhelmingly, Australian voters approached national elections anxious to have a 'political insurance mandate'. Kernot argued, for example, that the parties openly opposed to the sell-off of Telstra in their election campaigning—that is, the ALP, the Democrats and Greens —together got a majority of votes.[10]

With the Labor Party under Kim Beazley in a post-election depression throughout 1996, Kernot was playing a major role taking the economic argument to the government. Political and economic commentators took to referring to her as Australia's de facto Opposition Leader. But the old notion that the election of a conservative government would spark an immediate improvement in the nation's economic fortunes did not seem to be materialising. By mid-1996, with a tough budget nearing, Kernot was arguing strongly that the continuing obsession with cutting back public spending was taking the economy in precisely the wrong direction. She pointed out that after eighteen consecutive quarters of growth, unemployment was still 8.5%. She said that a further $8 billion in cuts would probably drive it up above 9%.

'The Coalition's election policy described mass unemployment as the single greatest issue facing Australian society and pledged to increase employment opportunities as rapidly as possible. I hope this is one of the core election promises that John Howard is going to keep,' she said. Kernot berated the government for the distinction drawn between 'core' policy commitments and others that may have to be rethought.[11] She went on the attack over plans to savagely cut the ABC budget when the government was leaving defence spending unscathed. In the face of the concentration of media ownership and the consequent reduction in diversity, she said there was a strong case to maintain a well-resourced national broadcaster. She also took on the government generally over privatisation, arguing that some of Labor's sell-offs had benefited the rich at the expense of ordinary tax-payers. Focusing on the sale of the Commonwealth Bank, she argued the nation had received $800 million less than the bank was worth, because of Labor's desperation to keep the financial markets receptive to future sell-offs.

But Kernot was demonised by leading economic commentators like the *Australian*'s Alan Wood who took umbrage that she presented herself as 'warm and compassionate' whereas those taking a responsible view of government expenditures were regarded as 'flint-hearted deficit cutters'.[12] The commentators argued that only a disciplined fiscal program could guarantee continued growth and job creation. In a peculiar attack on her, the *Age*'s Max Walsh addressed her contention over the Commonwealth Bank sale. Walsh said there was 'more than a grain of truth' in what she claimed. Yet, he then went on to argue that the Democrats, in fact, were the ones to blame for a nation's shift to privatisation. His rationale was that governments had no alternative but to sell off assets when they were faced with a party like the Democrats who would block their 'unpopular fiscal policy' in the Senate.[13] This was one line of argument too far for Cheryl Kernot.

Within days, she used a speech at the National Press Club in Canberra to launch one of her most pointed denunciations of those peddling hardline economic orthodoxy. When she was accused by 'cheer squad members' of causing the very privatisations to which she so vehemently objected, she said, it was time to stop and examine some facts, instead of ideological cant.

It's time to expose the biases, the laziness and the sloppy or non-existent research of the economic cheer squad in this country. I'm talking about those economic commentators who seem to think their particular brand of economic wisdom came down off the mountain with Moses and who never let the facts get in the way of a good whinge when it comes to those of us who don't toe their particular economic line. The same commentators who continue to base their assessment of the Democrats' past and future actions on the usual bundle of myths, distortions, lies and errors.

Kernot strongly attacked the argument that the Democrats were inept, inconsistent and unreliable. She quoted Janine Haines back in 1987 when she had sounded some of the early warnings about an approach that incessantly argued that taxes were always too high and that the only way to balance budgets was to slash expenditure to the bone. Haines had said then that to use those two rationales to cut health care, education, welfare and export development was a cruel hoax.

So don't try to tell me that our philosophy, our values or our messages have changed. The Democrats may have become more economically sophisticated over the years, but the fundamental core of our message remains. And that is that we believe economic policy for its own sake, or for the sake of appeasing the computer jockeys of the financial markets, is policy without purpose. We believe it is policy which will ultimately damage, rather than enhance, Australia's capacity to move forward as a cohesive and fair society.[14]

She argued her party had consistently supported three basic economic principles. It recognised the need for economic growth to build jobs without feeding into more foreign debt or higher interest rates. The current generation of Australians had to pay its own way and ensure that national savings and public sector assets were not squandered. Also, however, the benefits of economic activity had to be shared equitably with a clear recognition about the costs of that, particularly on the environment.

Kernot then laid out the record of the Coalition when it was in Opposition, blocking measures that both the ALP and the Democrats had proposed, but that the Howard government was now presenting as so critically important that the Senate rules may have to be changed to get them through. She raised real concerns at the unreliability of Treasury projections upon which the latest round of 'slash and burn' plans were based. When John Howard himself, in Opposition, had questioned elements of the budget figures being put by the Keating government, Kernot had offered the Opposition an inquiry to drag Treasury to the table and get to the truth. The Coalition had refused the offer. She said questions had to be asked about the orthodoxy's passion for cuts. The danger was that a society got to the point where the cuts 'sliced into the social fabric' and where a budget not only failed to deliver jobs, but itself became a cause of still higher unemployment.

This aggressive press club appearance was interpreted by some in the media as the first shot in the war to come with Costello over his budget. Kernot refused to specify which budget cuts the Democrats would block, although she reserved the right to oppose any measures that were unfair. But her other target was the Tony Abbott agenda.

'I am becoming increasingly disillusioned and angry about the way in which the Howard government is practising politics,' Kernot said. 'Once again, despite all that election rhetoric, the Coalition is going down the same belligerent, arrogant, cynical and dishonest path as its predecessor.' This was exactly the kind of behaviour Howard had condemned so long and hard in Keating.

> I think this government is making a very big mistake if it thinks Australians are going to sit back and let it change the rules and change the way the Senate is elected for the sole purpose of getting rid of the Democrats. They are also making a very big mistake if they think the Democrats are going to be intimidated by their attempts to hide a savage and unpopular budget behind the bluster and dishonesty of a manufactured political crisis.

The stridency of Kernot's outburst sparked a tough response from the financial media, which accused her of 'plotting a dangerous course' and 'showing disdain for the reasonable functioning of Australian democracy'. The *Financial Review* argued that while the Senate did have a role in ensuring a government did not break its promises, it should not prevent a properly elected government getting on with its 'main policy agenda'. Unfortunately, the paper added, Kernot's Democrats were coming 'very close to breaking their commitment not to block supply'.[15] Editorials in the *Australian* were even more indignant, claiming Kernot was acting 'with all the authority she can muster from her 11% of the vote'. She was trying to be a de facto Treasurer, playing a risky game, not content with the Senate's role as a house of review. 'It seems Senator Kernot wants to use the Senate to impose her economic policy on the country,' the paper said.[16]

Kernot's case in arguing the legitimacy of her mandate was bolstered, however, by the first opinion polls after the election on the issue of the Telstra sale. They showed that while there was a modest increase in community support for the idea of Telstra money funding environmental programs, voters did not believe the Senate was behaving irresponsibly by blocking the sale. Nearly 60% of voters thought the Senate had a right to block and 38% thought otherwise.[17] Kernot leapt on such findings, using them at every opportunity. Pro-Senate commentators like the former Labor Senator John Wheeldon also drew together the threads of history, constitutional reality and parliamentary convention to bolster the case. Fundamentally, Wheeldon argued, a functionable Westminster-based parliament needs a lower house operating on the basis of single-member constituencies with the preferential system of voting. This is necessary to allow governments to be formed with workable majorities in the Reps. But a PR-based Senate is essential, too, to allow up to 20% of the electorate who want to support minor partes but don't have a voice in the lower house, to have their views reflected somewhere in the system. It is also important that the upper house is able to work as a brake on executive power in the lower house. Wheeldon argued that whether one thinks Australia has a good Constitution or not, it does spell out clearly the powers of the Senate.

> ... Voters would be entitled to believe that, if senators did not use those powers fully to do what they thought was right or in trying to

implement policies on which they had been elected, they would not be carrying out the responsibility with which the electorate had entrusted them. Section 53 of the Constitution provides that so far as the making of laws is concerned, the Senate has the same powers as the House of Representatives, except that the Senate cannot introduce money bills— those which impose a tax or appropriate revenue—nor can it amend money bills, although it can do what is virtually the same thing, that is, it can return a money bill to the lower house with a request that it be amended.[18]

Wheeldon added that stable government did not require the automatic passage of legislation. The Constitution clearly laid down the alternative for an elected government—calling a double dissolution election to let the people have the final say. 'A reluctant Senate might sometimes be expensive but a working democracy, like any other institution worth preserving, does not come cheaply,' Wheeldon said.[19]

In early 1997, a fascinating element was added to the pro-Senate defence at the two-day conference staged at the Australian National University to celebrate the Democrats' twentieth anniversary. A couple of hundred of the party faithful, past and present MPs and office bearers came to participate in a novel exercise—one to which the ALP and Coalition parties would be highly unlikely to subject themselves. In celebrating their longevity, the Democrats decided to invite to the conference a host of academics and analysts to give a 'warts and all' summation of what the party had achieved and where it might go. The discussion proved willing but always engrossing. A keynote guest speaker was Professor Ken Carty, Canada's foremost scholar of political parties and Chair of Political Science at the University of British Columbia in Vancouver. A world expert on the evolution of third parties, Carty had come to Australia especially for the conference. Before he had finished his two-hour address, he had provided a telling rebuttal of the argument that the Democrats had no mandate. And he had sparked some crucial thinking in the mind of the party's leader, sitting attentively in the front row throughout the conference.

Carty explained it had long been assumed that national political systems around the world had largely been 'frozen' from the end of the First World War.

The argument was that these party systems crystallised a set of voter alignments established by the last great mobilisation wave which accompanied the emergence of modern citizenship and the adoption of a universal franchise.[20]

In fact, he said, in the 1970s, long-standing political systems in a number of countries had found themselves under challenge, because of various crises but also because of the emergence of third parties. And while the third parties that came forward were products of their own individual political environments, it was valid to draw some general conclusions between the histories of each of them.

The onset of an era of unprecedented affluence in the West after the 1939 War led to the emergence of a generation of people with 'post-materialist' values. Basically, they rejected the old materialistic, left versus right, capitalist versus labour style of politics. Instead, they focused on new issues like the environment, human rights, the feminist agenda, multiculturalism. The Democrats were part of this drift towards post-materialism. But Carty made the important point that while the mood change in individual nations may have prepared the ground, new parties only actually sprang to life in places where the electoral systems were congenial to them. Thus, new parties grew in countries like Australia, Ireland, the Netherlands and Denmark in the 1970s, because proportional representation operated there. But parties that spluttered into existence in countries like Britain, with single member electoral systems, would eventually fall by the wayside.

The relative failure of the Democrats in the Reps and success in the Senate over many years was a textbook case of the impact of electoral systems on the emergence of third parties, Carty said. In an analysis of comparative parties in four other countries, he attempted to evaluate whether these third parties had managed to change their political systems. Critically, the Australian Democrats had managed to split the national system into 'two, parallel, overlapping but distinct party systems'. The system in the Reps was bipolar competition between two majority-seeking alternatives, divided along traditional class lines. Carty said:

The Senate-based party system is different, for the Democrats' presence ensures that neither of the two major parties can expect to win a majority and so must play a different game. They must present a moderate face to Democrat voters and compromise with Democrat senators. [In the Senate there was a] permanent and legitimate role for the Democrats as a small party, dedicated to pursuing a distinctive agenda and representing minority interests. Such a party need not measure its practices or success by the standards of the large, office-seeking parties; nor is the failure to win governing power likely to count against it.[21]

Carty's essential point was that far from bemoaning the issue of government mandate, Australians should realise that the Democrats had helped create this unique, two-layered, electoral system:

That the House and Senate should have developed different party systems is not surprising. They represent different constituencies, are elected by quite different electoral regimes and have distinctive constitutional roles to play in Australian life. By transforming the Senate—but not the Reps—party system, the Australian Democrats have brought these important institutional differences to life.

If there is no other national party system that is split in this way, offering two distinct, parallel patterns of national party competition, that is because there is no other western system that combines a strong traditional parliamentary system with a powerful, autonomous second chamber, in the way Australia does.[22]

With this unique system, voters in Australia were well aware that they had two decisions to make when entering the polling booth. Carty's key point was that because voters had this clear understanding of the point of having such an upper house, Australians should stop constantly criticising the arrangement and think more deeply about what it represented. It may be still developing, as a kind of organic system with its historic consequences yet to be fully spelt out, but basically Australia had created its own unique and effective form of parliamentary democracy.

18
A SHIFTING BALANCE

The political earthquake that would shift the Senate's tectonic plates of power—certainly, at least, in the Telstra battle—suddenly rumbled through the corridors of Parliament House in the middle of August, 1996. The parties of Opposition in the Senate were delivered a body-blow with the abrupt decision of the long-time Queensland Labor Senator Mal Colston to resign from the ALP and sit as an independent. With the suppport of the Howard government, Colston was elected in a secret ballot by thirty-eight votes to thirty-four into the vacant position of Deputy President of the upper chamber, which lifted his remuneration by $16,000 to around $120,000.

The fifty-eight-year-old Colston was, as one newspaper put it, a large man with a low profile. Some in the parliament building could not remember him making a speech. Colston was a quiet presence, shuffling around the corridors, his hands invariably in his pockets below a lumpen midriff, his head bowed. Up until August 20, 1996, he had been best known for his indirect association with the 1975 supply crisis. When Premier Joh Bjelke-Petersen appointed the unknown Albert Patrick Field to the casual Labor vacancy caused by the death of Queensland Senator Bert Milliner, the seeds of the notorious dismissal of the Whitlam government were sown. Bjelke-Petersen simply ignored the convention that Premiers appoint replacements from the same political side. In appointing Field, who would support the then Coalition under Malcolm Fraser in blocking supply, the Premier rejected the Labor-nominated candidate, former schoolteacher Mal Colston. But years later Colston finally won a seat in the Senate for Labor. When it became clear in 1997 that he would ditch the party that had succoured him, enraged Labor Party officials demanded he resign, accused him of 'ratting', questioned his use of the perks of office and claimed he was betraying the 707,000 Labor-supporting Queenslanders who elected him. Colston's resignation was put down to pique that he had been passed over as Labor's nomination to the positions of either President or Deputy President of the Senate.

For Kernot, looking on, one word in Colston's brief resignation statement stood out—'mandate'. Colston said he would complete his parliamentary term as an independent. 'My voting pattern in the chamber will be influenced by long-held Labor beliefs, by an acceptance that the present government has an electoral mandate to pursue a number of issues and by what I judge to be the most appropriate course of action for the people of Queensland.'[1] The balance of power mathematics of the Senate were crucially changed. At the 1996 election, the Howard government had secured thirty-seven seats, which, with the election of the President of the Senate, brought its voting numbers on the floor of the chamber down to thirty-six. The ALP had twenty-nine seats, the Democrats held seven, the Greens two—Bob Brown from Tasmania and Dee Margetts from West Australia— while the irrepressible maverick independent, Brian Harradine, was there representing his home state of Tasmania. Prior to Colston's move, the Democrats' seven MPs were critical in situations when Harradine chose to support the government, bringing its numbers to thirty-seven, and the left-leaning Greens supported the ALP, bringing numbers there to thirty-one. But when Colston came over, with his support the government would need only Harradine or one of the Greens to win the day. The implication was that on any votes where Colston decided to support the government, Kernot's role was thwarted.

Prime Minister Howard signalled his delight that the Colston move could mean the free passage of the government's plans for Telstra. 'It is a very positive development from the government's point of view,' he said. 'I am encouraged by the fact that (Colston) has said that he believes that governments have a mandate for certain things that they talked about in the election campaign and that obviously includes Telstra and I hope he also sees it including industrial relations reforms.'[2] Although senior ministers tried to deny it, the government and Colston automatically came under sustained accusations that the Senate job was the pay-off in a cynical deal to deliver Howard his key legislation.

Like so many others, Kernot was affronted by the Colston affair. He had a legitimate right to resign from his party but, in so doing, she believed he should leave the parliament and await the next election. She saw in the sad episode a new ratchetting down of community respect for politics. But Kernot was also affronted at the thought that Howard could have been a party to the move to give Colston the job in return for his vote. Wasn't this the leader who had assailed Labor for any suggestion of tacky deal-doing?

When Colston finally did speak publicly about his move, the signs were ominous for Telstra. In response to the abuse he had received from the labour movement, he hit back, warning his former colleagues he would be more inclined to support the government in the Senate if the attacks continued: 'Put it this way', he said. 'If your dog bit you every time you came home from work at night, you wouldn't feel very kindly putting out his supper.'[3]

Asked if the sniping could soften his opposition to the government's proposed industrial relations (IR) reforms, Colston said: 'Probably not on the IR bill, but you never know on other things.' Commentators took that to mean that he would be supporting the government on Telstra. Later he appeared to try to distance himself from ALP opposition to the sale by saying that he was first elected to parliament in 1993 for a six-year term as senator when specific commitments to protect the telecommunications carrier were not an issue, not in his 'platform'. The writing, as far as Colston's intent was concerned, was on the wall.

Things were not so clear, however, when it came to the other key independent, Brian Harradine, the man who has often been called the great enigma of national politics. Born in South Australia in 1925, Harradine spent two years studying for the Catholic priesthood before becoming the most powerful trade union leader in Tasmania. He resigned from the ALP to join the Democratic Labor Party in the notorious split of the 1950s only to return to the Labor fold in 1959. Walking out again in the 1960s, Harradine nevertheless became an icon in the Apple Isle, standing as an independent and pulling together a unique platform, combining old-style labour movement beliefs and conservative social views. He effectively became unbeatable for one Tasmanian Senate seat. Harradine had always happily remained a background figure, seemingly a bit player. But his influence in the Canberra system was not to be underestimated. He insisted he didn't do deals yet when the balance of power equation shifted to his advantage, he was clearly a pivotal figure. At a press conference in early September 1996, Harradine argued the government could maintain public ownership of Telstra and still get the $8 billion it was seeking from the sale by adopting his proposal to issue redeemable preference shares in the Telstra corporation. He said such a scheme would allow the government to 'have its cake and eat it too'.[4] He was careful, however, to make it clear there was a possibility he could change his mind if the government reintroduced the Telstra sale legislation as a possible election trigger. His position was that he would say no the first time the legislation came into the Senate; that it 'may' be no if the government reintroduced the bill. But he added: 'There still is a bit of water to go under the bridge before that.' In the back-rooms of the Howard government, the tacticians were reading much into the spaces between those lines.

Apart from its longer term strategic implications, the timing of the Colston resignation was a godsend for the government. In fact, it came as part of a series of events which provided Treasurer Peter Costello with welcome diversions, permitting something of a clear run in the introduction of his first budget. The ferocity of the attacks on Kernot and the Senate over mandate made the actual debate over the budget itself something of an anti-climax. The government leaked a huge amount of the budget detail in the lead-up to the big day, Tuesday, August 20, 1996. Many of its plans, like increasing higher education charges, cutting funding for Aboriginal programs and wholesale changes to the social security system were signalled in advance.

When the Treasurer came to his feet on budget night, he read from a carefully scripted twelve-page speech which announced some seventy-odd policy proposals. But, as political commentator Geoff Kitney observed, the speech cleverly diverted attention from the fine print in which were contained in fact 400 separate decisions of the government's 'razor gang'. To find his $4.7 billion worth of spending reductions, Costello cut programs across the board, yet his top-line speech to the parliament referred to relatively few of them, concentrating on the 'good news' elements. Kitney observed that Costello got the pitch, tone and pacing just right: 'He delivered the toughest federal budget for a decade with a political spin which produced a soft landing and an unruffled electorate.'[5]

Labor was still in the doldrums after the election. Kim Beazley complained that the budget was one for the rich, the first step towards a two-tiered society but the inability of the Opposition to find a telling PR peg on which to hang its attack simply reinforced the feeling that Costello had managed to bring down a very harsh economic document, with minimal political damage. Incensed at the sleight of hand, and the ferocity of some of the hidden measures, Kernot took the attack to the government. She hit out on three grounds—that the budget represented a breach of faith with the electorate, was dismissive of the problem of unemployment, and was a further dismantling of the role of government in Australian society. She savaged its social impact but also the way it hit industry too. She complained about a $2.2 billion cut from research and development tax concessions, some $427 million cut from programs to encourage exporters, another $300 million cut from industry policy programs and $700 million cut from transport infrastructure programs. But, as angry as Kernot was over the budget, the government had taken the heat out of its final unveiling.

The budget amounted to an effort to pay for the delivery of Howard's election promises to families and small business by cuts to programs affecting the aged, sick, students and unemployed. It gave almost two million low and middle-income families tax relief from January 1997 through an income-tested tax package based on raising the tax-free threshold. There was also a new health insurance incentive scheme for families to be introduced from July, 1997. The handouts were funded by a massive assault on programs across a huge range of portfolios. People earning more than $85,000 were targeted with a 15% tax surcharge on super-annuation—a move aimed at stemming the large flow of funds into super schemes purely for tax minimisation purposes.

Costello argued that many of the measures were aimed at soaking the rich, but Kernot warned the cuts to departmental programs would hit almost everyone. There were estimates that the resultant job losses could be as high as 30,000 over the following eighteen months. She announced the Democrats would oppose the higher education fee hike, increased prescription charges, changes to Austudy and the savage cuts to ATSIC, the ABC, and funding of hospitals. She complained that far from doing anything about easing unemployment, cuts of this severity simply ran the risk of driving it up even further. In the end, Mal Colston supported the government on the budget and the Democrats could only get Harradine's support in making changes to measures worth around $300 million. But it was not just the Colston resignation on budget eve that created a diversion from the government's tough fiscal subtext.

Concurrent with the budget build-up, Kernot was also in consultations with the minister for Industrial Relations, Peter Reith, over his planned revolution of the centralised industrial relations system and the operation of trade unions in Australia. One day after the budget, a union-organised rally of some 25,000 people outside the parliament building, protesting at Reith's IR reforms, somehow escalated into a vicious riot, which brought the ACTU President Jennie George to tears and projected television pictures which could only harm the labour movement. Kernot joined John Howard in repudiating the attack on the parliament building itself. She said anxiety about the IR system changes was understandable but there was no excuse for violence and vandalism. 'It is important that people be allowed to register their protest at what they believe is wrong, but it was unfortunate that some people overstepped the boundary of proper behaviour,' she said, adding that the Democrats would do all they could in the upcoming IR negotiations to ensure the Howard government honoured its commitment to maintain a viable award wages system and keep the Industrial Relations Commission (IRC) in place.[6]

But the event in budget week with the long-term implications was the Colston defection. Among the critics arraigned against Kernot, there was a sense of quiet celebration when it became clear that the Colston shift would undermine her power. In an editorial, the *Australian Financial Review* deemed her the big loser:

> The fact is Senator Kernot overplayed her political hand. By letting the power of her position go to her head, she behaved as if it was her right to dictate to the government what its policy program should be. Instead of sticking with the previous policy of emphasising the Democrats' role in 'keeping the bastards honest'—a policy repeated during the last election campaign—Senator Kernot adopted a stance which sought to make her party all but the government's equal when it came to determining the legislative agenda.

Her 'hardline' position was wrong because she only had 10.8% of the Senate vote and no seats in the Reps. To do all but reject supply was a 'grossly inflated and extremely damaging view of the Senate's role'. In light of the Colston move, the newspaper called on her as a 'capable and impressive leader' to rethink her strategy and embrace a constructive, not destructive, future stance.[7]

Like the old refrain about reports of Mark Twain's death, such celebratory predictions of Cheryl Kernot's political demise would very quickly prove premature. Colston was in a position to deliver some key decisions to the government, as the Telstra case would show, but in other areas he would hold to his traditional Laborite stance, and there the old equation would prevail. Within a week of the budget's announcement, talks would begin in earnest between Kernot and Peter Reith on the IR changes. That process would only serve to reinforce her presence. After the Mabo saga of 1993, the birth of Reith's IR blueprint would prove to be the next chapter in the blooding of a national figure.

During 1995, as they contemplated the timing of the coming federal election and the likely arrival of a Howard government, Kernot and her economics adviser, John Cherry, began readying themselves for the inevitable struggle to come over IR. Union power had always been a totem issue for conservative politicians in the Hawke/Keating years, the mainstay of the emergence of the new right, the hardline, dry, rationalist economic agenda. Basically, the centralised system had to be broken down and workers given the 'freedom' to negotiate their own deals in the workplace without union involvement. Industry-wide pay increases were wrong, it was argued, because they didn't reflect the commercial reality of independent workplaces. A centralised wage fixing system, operated through the IRC, was the 'club' that had to be challenged, so that greater decision-making powers devolved to workplaces. And, of course, trade unions had come to exercise far too much control over government decision-making. This was the system the new right wanted to smash.

At different times in Opposition both John Howard and Peter Reith had previously had responsibility for the portfolio. When they won office, the expectations from sections of the conservative political constituency were immense. Now the Coalition finally had a chance to do what it had always sought—change the IR landscape forever. But there was a problem. The government did not control the Senate where any legislative changes had to pass. As early as May, 1996, it had been clear that Mal Colston and Brian Harradine, reflecting their 'old Labor' backgrounds, would oppose any dismantling of the IR system. From that moment, in fact, it was always inevitable that the Democrats would once again be the fulcrum players. Reith foresaw he would have a huge job to do after the election, a test of his political skills. And, right from the start, he saw his mark: 'It was always going to be Cheryl. It was always going to be her at the centre of the consultation phase in the final anaysis.'[8]

Early on, Reith saw the folly in bashing the Democrats. He would be conciliatory. Despite the inclinations of the new right, the new government was not intent on a hardline war of attrition over IR. During the election campaign, Howard had played down the prospects of confrontation with the unions as part of his reassuring pitch. Soon after the election, he decided a quick double dissolution was not on. That left only one route—to Kernot's door.

During the election campaign she had unveiled an IR policy which had as its hallmark a defence of the IRC as an independent umpire, and the appointment of a new body to ensure that the shift to enterprise bargaining did not undermine families. National wage cases would have to take full account of this work/family nexus—there should be three months' paid maternity leave and other welfare allowances would be increased. Basically, Kernot argued that if a new government pursued further deregulation, the Democrats would 'fight for fairness'. But she also made it clear that the Democrats' aim would be to negotiate a package that could go through the Senate.

Very early in the new government's term, Reith began making overtures for discussions to begin. But Kernot was embroiled in other big, running issues. She wasn't going to be rushed into the IR talks. Too much was at stake. She had a lot of homework to do but the delay also had a tactical edge. Says a former Democrat staffer: 'There was a period there when she didn't want to begin the meetings. She kept delaying. It was always part of Cheryl's tactics, to remind a government that the Senate has its status, to stand on the dignity of the Senate from time to time, not to be taken for granted, not to jump when they clicked their fingers. She would do it when she was ready and would not let herself be locked into an early position.'[9]

The Democrat team was Kernot, Cherry and the party IR spokesman, the new senator from West Australia, Andrew Murray. When the research was done, they had a clear bottom-line framework beyond which they would not go. Its elements were that the award system should be left in place, the IRC should continue with a meaningful role and that unions should basically be able to function effectively. Backed up by a team of IR specialists on his staff and from his department, Reith would bring his own set of hard-core demands to the talks, too.

The government wanted reforms to unfair dismissal laws, restoration of the secondary boycott provisions of the Trade Practices Act, a revolutionary change whereby voluntary work and condition agreements could be struck between employers and workers without union interference, an end to union monopolies, and provision for workers to band together in individual enterprises to form quasi-unions. From the union movement's perspective these demands were tough, but not as tough as Liberal policy had been in the past. Before the 1996 election Reith had tactically repositioned the Coalition, smoothing the edges of the more threatening 1993 policy manifesto as presented by John Hewson. Gone were demands for a low $3.50 per hour youth wage and the 'big bang' system forcing workers to opt out of the award system. Political commentator Michael Gordon saw Reith sublimating his commitment to economic rationalism in favour of practical politics:

> Reith, forty-five, tends to take on assignments in the same way that in his solicitor days he took to briefs: with a degree of detachment that suggests either a deeply cynical streak, a professionalism that is rare in the emotional business of politics, or an unlikely blend of both. Some people whose knowledge of Reith predates his first arrival in parliament in 1982 point to a simpler explanation. They say that the member for the Victorian electorate of Flinders is drawn to the idea of public service, a kind of noblesse oblige without too much emphasis on the noblesse.[10]

Early on, Reith was unsure what kind of operator he had on his hands with Kernot. Initially, he was coming from an orthodox political posture; talking, for example, about the Democrats running an ALP agenda. Much later, after

October, 1997, he would be one of Kernot's fiercest critics, raging about her betrayal of her old party. But, once the IR teams began to meet, he quickly realised—just as Gareth Evans had found in the Mabo saga back in 1993—that Kernot was intent on working through to a compromise, getting a result. Reith quickly saw she was savvy enough to objectively understand their respective political positions, but work towards identifying the areas where both could give enough ground.

In an interview in early 1997, Reith said: 'Before the first couple of meetings, quite frankly, I was a bit of an agnostic about how it might go. We had carefully gone over everything Cheryl had said about IR as far back as you could go. But that didn't give us much of a steer on where we might end up. The first thing was that she was prepared to sit down and talk to us. That was very important. And it was against the background where there had been a fair amount of aggressive attack on the Democrats by our side in the first few months which I was a bit concerned about. She had said generally that they would support the legislation but they wanted a sensible approach to their concerns. The second important thing, though, was that she saw the process as a genuine discussion on the merits. She was quite insistent that this not be a sort of trading-off exercise, one-thing-for-another within the package. She just saw it as give and take, as opposed to: "I want that amendment. When you've given me that one, I'll go on to the next one." She was genuinely looking for a bona fide discussion and amplification of what we were doing. That impressed me greatly because that's the way things should be done. She was very good like that.'[11]

The talks through September and October, 1996, were arduous in the detail, lasting in all an estimated fifty hours. Basically, it was all about navigating between the government's determination to achieve a more flexible labour market and the Democrats' concerns for sufficient safeguards for vulnerable workers. Kernot could point out that John Howard had said in the election campaign that no worker would be worse off. She insisted the wages system should leave room for responsible unionism.

In the wake of her defection, Peter Reith would be less inclined to be magnanimous but in 1996 he was quite impressed with Kernot's methods. For example, straight up she insisted there should be no leaking to the media. The two discovered they were on the same wave-length, with a shared, quirky sense of humour. He could see she wasn't into point scoring and handled her team well. He recalled: 'Part of her negotiating style is to let the analysis go on. She would encourage both Cherry and Murray to search out the argument, exhaust it and then she would tell you which way she would come down. So she is quite a good listener when it comes to hearing the arguments. Intellectually, I think she's pretty good, I don't think much gets past Cheryl.'[12]

Kernot was also impressed by Reith. His style was reasonable, self-effacing. He would happily admit that he didn't understand some things, instead of puffing himself up. He urged his departmental advisers to be frank, providing their personal views, as well as their 'official' impressions. She recalls: 'It's a tribute to Peter that in all those talks over all that time, he didn't come the heavy at all. He would say: "There's no way in the world we can do that or accept that." And we'd say: "OK, but we can't accept that." So we developed this technique where we would say we had better have a huddle. I'd say: "OK, it's your turn to huddle in the room and we'll step outside and leave you to it." Or they'd go out and we'd talk. In all the paperwork, there are actually amendments with "huddle numbers" written on them.'

But Reith was dogged, diligent: 'As the meetings went on, and particularly in his own office, he would sit at his desk and get out a pair of scissors with orange handles and a big scrap book and paste all the paperwork relating to the talks in it while talking to you. He had everything in it, as it happened. He finished up with two huge scrap books with fifty hours of paperwork—all the offers, how the negotiations unfolded. I had said to him that I thought it would be good to do it differently from most of politics, not to be so secretive. He came back with this idea of publishing everything that happened. It was such a refreshing approach when you look at how other things were being negotiated, like with Colston and Harradine. There was the historical evidence of how it had gone, the intellectual rationale for everything we did and decided.'

After around fifty hours of negotiations, the deal was nearing completion in late October. One Monday afternoon Kernot and Reith were working their way through clauses in his Canberra office when they had to break off to attend a black tie retirement dinner in one of the reception rooms, ironically enough, for one of the IR system's most enduring and respected figures, Bert Evans of the Metal Trades Industry Association. Soon after the speeches at the function, Reith and Kernot, resplendent respectively in black tie and evening gown, returned to the ministerial wing where they worked their way through the last of the clauses. When they returned to the function at around 11pm, the deal was essentially struck.

With around 170 amendments, Reith's Workplace Relations Bill was finally unveiled at a joint press conference with Kernot on October 27, 1996. The package provided for major changes to the way the award system operates, an end to compulsory unionism, a crackdown on secondary boycott strike action and a revamp of unfair dismissal laws. It gave the go-ahead for Australian Workplace Agreements (AWA), individual work contracts between bosses and employees operating in tandem with the award system. The wage system awards would be significantly pared back but they would be maintained and be the benchmark for the AWAs. Critically, Kernot won the right for the IRC to ensure the AWAs matched the relevant award provisions. The IRC would 'vet' the AWAs should a newly-created office of an Employment Advocate rule that they did not meet a 'no disadvantage test' in comparison to awards. While they would no longer provide the set of comprehensive regulations that had underpinned work practices for years, awards would still constitute a broader safety net than operated in other deregulated systems, such as the US and New Zealand.

The government also won restoration of the statutory prohibition on secondary boycotts but, as a result of Democrat pressure, the net would not cover environmentalists and consumers. A provision allowing for groups of workers to come together at the 'enterprise' level to form a 'union' was softened so that conventional industry unions were able to argue that such workers 'more conveniently belonged' to their traditional structures.

In short, the package allowed Reith to deliver a more flexible system, with the powers and operation of the union movement cut back, yet the Democrats had managed to leave in safeguards, including the powers of IRC. The deal gave both sides enough to be content that there had been progress. But the talks also came against the critical background threat that a double dissolution election could be called over the issue. On the way through, there was great suspicion of the Democrats' intent in sections of the trade union movement. Some union bosses just wanted the Democrats to stand with Harradine and Colston and block the lot. But Kernot had some strong union movement supporters, including the teachers' union boss,

Sharon Burrows, and the ACTU's Jennie George both of whom had developed a close working relationship with her. Kernot was, somewhat controversially, invited to George's investiture as ACTU President. Burrows had been happy to throw her weight behind the Democrats because they had by far the strongest pro-state schools policy. George and Burrows could see the core Kernot political argument—that the Democrats' job was to sit in the middle trying to improve laws, not serve unions.

But the key argument was that if the Democrats just blocked it, the government could take its legislation to a double dissolution and, if it won, call a joint sitting and push through far more draconian laws that dismantled the whole wages system. There was no getting away from it—the new law was a compromise under which life would be made very much more difficult in some ways for unions. But, in other ways, it put checks in place that prevented the arrival of what the unions saw as the worst intent of the new right agenda. Kernot remarks: 'I think you can say that after everything we had heard about the intent of the new right, that round of talks left the future of unionism secure, when the intent of the original bill had been to crush the unions. Now, I actually think that was quite an achievement when you had a non-Labor government in power.'

From Reith's point of view the double dissolution threat was also a factor. Ever the pragmatist, he argued that he got a good deal out of the Senate and that it just would not have been tenable for the government to go to the people saying it was incapable of negotiating a settlement. Members of Kernot's 'cheer squad' could not resist having a dig at her at the end of the talks. Economist Alan Wood said in the *Australian*: 'If nothing else, Peter Reith deserves a medal for being locked up for over fifty hours with Cheryl Kernot—and an Oscar for pretending to enjoy it.'[13] But Wood, like others, welcomed the package, saying the outcome was better than the government had expected, though Reith had been clever enough not to admit so publicly.

Relieved that the demanding process was over, Kernot's team was a trace uncomfortable with sexist elements of the media portrayal of the final deal. It was replete with cartoons of Kernot and Reith in bed on their honeymoon and big, front-page newspaper photographs of a smiling Kernot gazing wistfully into the eyes of an equally delighted minister as they exchanged copies of the agreed document. Reith was not all that thrilled with the impressions conveyed, either. The cosy images would have jolted a bit with both their respective political constituencies.

Although a good deal of massaging of interpretations of the deal would be necessary on both sides of the fence, it was an extraordinary political result—both Kernot and Reith walking away, perceived as winners. On the government side, it was a good start along the road to reform. Reith himself had emerged with a reinforced reputation as a 'doer'; in fact, with credentials in place as a potential future leader of the Liberal Party. Even though it took a while for a broader interpretation to sink in, eventually the ACTU would acknowledge Kernot had managed to safeguard important elements of the IR system. Fundamentally though, the deal reminded the political world that, notwithstanding the new balance of power mathematics, she was still a force to be reckoned with.

19

THE PROMISE DISSOLVES

In its first year in office, the Howard government managed to chalk up some significant political victories. With the ALP National Secretary, Gary Gray, admitting that in 1996 voters had come to believe the Keating government was made up of 'liars' whose 'record stank', the Labor Opposition was struggling in a pit of despondency, battling to come to terms with its past under Keating, never mind fashioning a relevant future. After such an electoral thrashing, Labor was struggling to find its ideological moorings again. At times, its new leader Kim Beazley seemed to some insiders unsure if his heart was in the job for the long haul. After tiring years as a senior minister, a long period in the wilderness seemed to stretch ahead, a test of his stamina and self-belief.

Peter Costello's first budget had gone through largely unscathed although he had suffered the occasional bruising, including being rebuked by Howard for excessive zeal in threatening a double dissolution election unless he got his way. Peter Reith's changes to the IR system won him political plaudits. In the wake of the Parliament House riot and the Reith legislation, the trade union movement was neutralised, unable to find the energy to provide any meaningful ideological opposition. The millions of dollars long funnelled into union coffers were cut off. Under the cosy partnerships between the ACTU, its Secretary, Bill Kelty, and Hawke and Keating, the unions out on the ground had become flabby and now were paying the price, forced to rebuild and rethink. Reith appeared to be working on the basis of evolution, not revolution. Left to Howard's second term was the prospect that the Coalition would return to the IR issue to extract more draconian changes.

Within his first year, Howard had heartening news from voter-land. When he was first informed of the positive development by phone at a Liberal Party Federal Council dinner at the Wrest Point Casino in Tasmania, he spontaneously grabbed a somewhat stunned security officer in a very atypical prime-ministerial bear hug of jubilation.[1] The news was that good. The Liberal Party's resounding triumph in the by-election for the NSW seat of Lindsay in October gave added potency to Howard's warnings about the Senate overstepping the mark. The poll had been required when the High Court, sitting as a Court of Disputed Returns, overturned the original March 2 election result in the western Sydney seat. The rematch proved an absolute disaster for the ALP. Having first lost the seat in March suffering an 11.5% swing, Labor then lost again with a further swing of around 5%. John Howard and his senior ministers argued that the result, which left the ALP NSW branch devastated, was a clear signal that the people believed the government had a mandate to push through its reforms. Howard bluntly told the minor parties to 'get out of the way' in the Senate. But while agreeing the result had demonstrated the Lindsay electorate's desire to give the elected Liberal candidate a fair go, Kernot fended off the attack by insisting it was no signal that the government deserved a blank cheque. And then, right at the end of 1996, came the government's triumph with Telstra.

For months, speculation had mounted about the position Mal Colston and Brian Harradine would take when the time came for a final decision on the sale. Telstra announced the biggest annual profit in Australian corporate history—$2.3 billion—but also confirmed it would cut in excess of 20,000 jobs over three years as corporatisation continued apace. The huge profit rekindled opposition to the proposed sell-off. Critics of the move argued from different perspectives. Respected *Age* newspaper commentator Ken Davidson, one of the few voices in business commentary regularly questioning the rationalist agenda, had long argued that the move to deregulate and privatise Australian telecommunications was a wasteful, inefficient and bungled saga, driven by ideological obsession. Other commentators posed the key question: if privatisation was the right course, then why wasn't the organisation completely sold off instead of just a third of it? The ALP/ Democrat majority report of the Senate inquiry set up to look into the sale accepted claims by Australian telecommunications suppliers that privatisation would be devastating to local firms. Kernot herself responded to the new profit figures by repeating her mantra—that the profit could fund the government's environment plan without dispensing with the country's most important commercial asset.

Throughout 1996, government ministers denied suggestions that a deal had been done with Mal Colston to give him the Senate deputy presidency in return for his support for the sale. Whatever his motivation, it became clear on December 5, 1996, that the government had not only won his support, but had brokered a deal with Harradine as well. The Tasmanian senator had been in the past a fierce opponent of some privatisations, yet, wooed by a $350 million package of commitments for the environment and for regional jobs, he gave his assent. His home state of Tasmania was a big winner, gaining an extra $100 million from the proposed billion dollar Natural Heritage Trust as well as $58 million to safeguard jobs and ensure the telecommunications system there was on a par with the mainland.

The Howard government was jubilant with a deal that capped a year of political wins. The Telstra sale was more than twice the size of the previous largest float, that of the Commonwealth Bank. Legislation underwriting the sale would be proclaimed as early as May, 1997. The Prime Minister told parliament the sale would provide 'world class communications services for regional Australia and the bush'. Kernot, however, was devastated at the deal Harradine had negotiated in such secrecy. She was violently philosophically opposed to the notion that a politician could trade off support on an important national issue for the sake of some regionally-restricted financial benefit. 'This is a kind of trade-off that puts the interests of a few Australians ahead of the interests of all Australians and if we continue to embrace that pork-barrelling approach to Senate votes, I predict that we will end up with an American-style political gridlock. We don't want that in this country. We want issues to be won and lost on the merit of ideas,' she said.[2]

In fact, Kernot took the loss of Telstra very badly. Apart from the national interest question, she had strenuously argued it could not be justified on public finance grounds because it would make the task of deficit reduction that much harder. What was the sense of selling off an asset which independent analysts suggested would enjoy profit growth of some 27% over the following three years? It was highly likely that the government would receive less from a share float than the market value of the organisation. For Kernot, Telstra was an issue that transcended politics, one that spoke to national sovereignty, even national identity. Her dream had been for a visionary government to keep the asset in public hands but make such changes to it that would not only help it compete in the brave new world of telecommunications, but become one of the leading middle range 'Telcos' operating across the globe. It seemed economic ideologues had sold out the nation. In the privacy of Kernot's Parliament House office, for a short time, objective analysis gave way to an explosion of anger. Says a staffer of those hours: 'On the morning Harradine made his move, Cheryl was angrier than I have ever seen her on a political issue. She was furious, spewing. She had been fighting the Telstra privatisation for five full years and she had finally lost it ... for a dirty, rotten piece of political pork-barrelling. She was angrier than anybody had ever seen her.'[3]

Though its successes were undeniable, the first year in office did witness the onset of problems for the Howard government, ones that would be amplified mightily in 1997. As an inexperienced team took time to get used to the demands of office, amazingly, ministers began to fall by the way in sometimes inept circumstances. Others would spend periods under a cloud and Howard would be forced to apologise to the people for the insensitivity and gaffes of some of them. The Prime Minister himself would make some significant strategic mistakes which, taken with everything else, would lead, in an amazingly short period of time, to a serious decline in his own standing. By the end of 1996, government spin-doctors were papering over the ructions, making much of the early successes. They were pointing out that the economy was basically in good shape with strong business investment, rising profits and strengthening employment growth. At that point, no-one could foresee just how bad things would get for Howard politically as 1997 unfolded. And certainly no-one suspected that, by their actions, conservative politicians were once again helping write the script for the political future of Cheryl Kernot.

In fact, it was not long after the Howard government was first elected that its political activities and underlying philosophical approach were beginning to disturb her. Initially, she acknowledged the electorate had spoken comprehensively in the Reps contest. The government obviously had a right to pursue its program. But, beginning with the 1996 budget, doubts began to mount in her mind. She was struck by the ruthlessness of the policy approach, built around a blind acceptance of the economic orthodoxy's slash-and-burn budgetary approach. She had been exasperated by some of the tactics used by Labor in trying to cling to power but she had expected so much more from the new government, even though Howard's strategy had been to play down expectations. Kernot was irritated by what she saw as tawdry government priorities. Labor may have got part of the economic approach wrong but at least it seemed to have a soul. Eventually, she would conclude the Howard government was mean-spirited and petty, incompetent in some areas, but, overwhelmingly, relying on an old-fashioned view of politics.

In the face of a national mood that was shifting with great speed against it, the government seemed to rely on a kind of outdated divisiveness, a 'them-and-us' approach in which some groups in the community were demonised and set off against others. It was dawning on Kernot that not only was this a political philosophy run out of ideas but it was one falling back, in a dangerous way, on outmoded strategies. In the 1990s, she figured, this approach would not cut with people. The electorate had had a gutful of posturing, manipulative politicians. In hard-nosed political terms, Kernot was mystified about what Coalition strategists thought they were achieving with such sclerotic thinking.

From what she could see of the political landscape after the 1996 election, there was simply no need for the Coalition to embrace such an approach. She couldn't see why the government's aim was not presenting a picture to the people of magnanimity in victory, high principle in decision-making, a touch of self-sacrifice in the bounty that comes with power and genuine concern with under-privilege. This was the idealistic political challenge she assumed the Howard administration would rise to on the ministerial benches. Some clever, sensitive symbolism, she felt, would only build on a large parliamentary majority to guarantee them two or more terms in power and finally vindicate Howard as an historic figure, not just a politician of the routine. Instead, within a terribly short period of time, she suspected that the people could see what she could see. Mediocrity.

After years talking big on the need for leadership integrity, between October, 1996, and September, 1997, John Howard found himself hemmed in by utter Cabinet incompetence. In that time, seven ministers or parliamentary secretaries would be sacked or resign, other ministers and prominent MPs would be under investigation or riding out political attacks over matters ranging from conflict of interest between their private business holdings and public duties to the misuse of the perks of office. The first minister to go, Assistant Treasurer Jim Short, had fallen foul of the Ministerial Code of Conduct that Howard had introduced in such fanfare within days of the parliament resuming after the election. This was the vanguard idea promoted as the mechanism to restore the public's faith in the political system. The Parliamentary Secretary to the Treasurer, Brian Gibson, suddenly resigned after it was revealed he had made a decision affecting a company in which he held a shareholding. Then, in 1997, the Parliamentary Secretary to the Health Minister, Bob Woods, resigned and the Minister for Small Business, Geoff Prosser, finally did the same over an alleged conflict of interest between his ministerial duties and his $50 million West Australian business empire. The sorry picture was not helped by the row in which the Minister for Education, Senator Amanda Vanstone, was forced to apologise to the parliament for using a bogus millionaire family to justify a controversial idea to means-test Austudy.

At his very first press conference as Prime Minister Howard had vowed to see ministerial standards lifted. Just months later, against the background of the unseemly Colston affair and Jim Short's resignation, his government seemed to be staggering. Much worse would come later in 1997 but in an effort to staunch hemorrhaging confidence, Howard announced his department would devise a new 'conflict of interest' ministerial code, hinting that he would come down hard on any careless ministers in the future. Responding to his move, Kernot sent him a proposal for an expansion of the government's ministerial code, based around her ideas for a new Joint House Ethics Committee and a Commissioner for Standards. The Ethics Committee would contain a member from each party and four members of the community appointed by the parliament to monitor the effectiveness of the code. The Commissioner for Standards would be an independent officer charged with investigating complaints against MPs and senators. Thus, the actual investigation of whether an MP has a prima facie case to answer would be taken out of the hands of the politicians. But, as had so often been the case in the past, the Kernot ideas were ignored.

She well understood that in its early years, the Hawke government too had had a difficult patch with inexperienced ministers. Perhaps the Howard team was just facing a period of adjustment, as government spin-doctors suggested. But it was not so much that various ministers were stumbling. Kernot became troubled by the mentality of some in the government, a certain arrogance. She saw an even greater obsession with orthodox economics, a slavish acceptance that all the nation's economic woes would be eased if government programs, public expenditure and public service jobs were cut to the bone. By the end of 1996 there was also disturbing evidence that some in the government brought a particularly blinkered world view—the one from the corporate boardroom—as if the world of stockbroking, international market machinations and shares options was all that counted as a philosophical starting point for running a nation. Kernot was horrified to hear one minister strike out at his critics during a rowdy exchange in the parliament, accusing Labor MPs of being 'public sector bludgers' for not investing in the private sector.

John Howard and Peter Costello struggled to emphasise the strong points in Australia's economic performance. Of course, experts differed on the relative merits of different gauges of well-being but by the middle of 1997 there was palpable evidence that unemployment, stuck at 8–9%, was undermining national confidence. Leading figures in the business community were rueing a lack of national vision. Howard hit back, saying Australians should start being optimistic about the future. He declared that the country had the 'best conjunction of economic fundamentals for twenty years' and that it should be looking forwards positively, rather than awkwardly backwards. As commentator Gerard Henderson observed, it all sounded rather familiar. Keatingesque in fact.[4]

But then, at around the halfway point in the first term, the Coalition was hit with the release of the second 1997 edition of Hugh Mackay's highly regarded market research study called *Mind and Mood of the Nation*. It made devastating reading. So bleak was Australians' outlook in mid-1997 that they were becoming 'somewhat embarrassed' about themselves, Mackay found. The jobs crisis had worn people down to the point that no leader was seen to have any solutions. But the stand-out finding was that since the previous such report in 1996 there had been a 'dramatic decline in respect' for Howard. The word most often used to describe him by interviewees for the survey was 'weak'.[5] Mackay wrote:

He strikes the voters as a man out of his depth; a man who is being overwhelmed by the job, rather than taking it by the throat. He reminds us too vividly of ourselves; we are uncertain and that's the very thing we don't want him to be; and yet, on issues ranging from media ownership to minimum wages, voters claim that's exactly what he seems to be. The three characteristics Australians seek in their political leaders are strength, integrity and inspiration. One of their great disappointments is that, on all three counts, Howard appears to be falling short.[6]

Halfway through Howard's first term, the nation was engulfed by a serious loss of confidence. It is possible to see this period as one in which, frustrated at the direction of things, Coalition politicians and their economic advisers looked desperately for answers. Or was it scapegoats? According to the economic orthodoxy, no budget ever seemed to cut hard, or deep, enough. When it refused to accept a departmental decision to slash hundreds of millions of dollars from a particular community program because it was socially intolerable, the Senate was to blame for the failure of the economy. When small business was not taking people on, the new right said unfair dismissal laws had to be changed. When the Democrats helped deliver that, it proved not to be the answer, either. More broadly, the whole area of industrial relations was never deregulated sufficiently. It was always the unions, with their strike record, their restrictive work practices, or their cosiness with the Labor Party which were to blame. Never mind the analyses of unemployment rates around the world that showed there was no unequivocal evidence that deregulated labour markets performed better than regulated ones. When the sort of policies the radical right had been pursuing for a decade or more were in place, and things still did not turn around, 'consumer confidence' was the problem. The consumer had to get out there and feel good.

For her part, Kernot kept plugging away with her key theme—suggesting that perhaps some changes to the conventional way of managing the economy could help. In particular, she resented the pressure on governments to dismantle programs without the slightest concern for the resulting social impact. In this, Kernot was informed by her own experience, as a member of the Uniting Church and of the work done by groups like the Blue Nurses.

This was an agency which, with a mixture of government assistance and voluntary help, took nursing services to those in desperate need in the community, visiting them in their own homes. In the frenzy to dismantle the State, Kernot saw services like this inevitably being starved of funds. In the

350

early days with the Democrats and as a member of the Blue Nurses Board, Kernot made time to actually go out on the road with the nurses to learn what their work entailed. It was a harrowing experience.

She recalls: 'The run I went on was around West End in Brisbane and the first person we went to was a psychiatric patient of around sixty. You had to go down into this boarding house where he lived in a couple of rooms that were basically empty and dirty. Here was me, with practically no experience of hospital in my whole life—except for having my tonsils out and then having Sian. I had my heart in my mouth. The nurse said to the old man she had come to check his colostomy bag. And he just dropped his dacks there and then with this great big full colostomy bag and she begins dealing with the opening. I thought to myself: "This is a test! You know, people live like this, you can't walk away or look away, you have to learn to deal with this." So I'm watching it. And I'm thinking, if this is the first one what is the rest of the day going to be like? But the nurse talked to him and he was really cheerful and she asked him about his housework and he said he hadn't been doing any and she talked about getting someone to come in and help him. She did a really good job and then later wrote a report that basically recommended other agencies try to get some domiciliary care in for him. And then we did the rest of the rounds and there were cancer patients in between chemo or other treatment. Some of them lived in some of the most depressing rented rooms ... an Italian woman who couldn't speak much English, an old woman of ninety-six who was spritely and kept her place as neat as possible. She was resisting the need for the nurse to even be there, saying her knee was all right and there was no need to bother ... this kind of stuff. Boy, that day was an eye-opener for me!'

Kernot saw in this the kind of essential service needed for a community with isolated, lonely or ill people. It was community helping itself. 'But the government pulled the plug on the funding for it. And they did it because I don't think they know how it works, what happens, how it helps people. When I went and discovered it for myself it was an awful eye-opener. But I bet Peter Costello has never done it. I bet he doesn't know the number of people who rely on this. I don't reckon the people making the decisions in Canberra have the faintest clue about stuff like this. They have no sense at all about this face of Australia.'

At the outset, Kernot bore no particular ill-feeling towards John Howard.

In her first contacts with him, she felt he was a decent person. But she came to see that he was as willing as anyone to use rhetoric for short-term gain, to manoeuvre politically, always with an eye to the vote. She saw as ill-conceived one key ingredient of the Coalition political strategy—basing policy-making on holding onto that segment of the old blue-collar, Labor-supporting working-class base, the 'Howard battlers' as the Liberal Party Federal Director, Andrew Robb, called them, the 600,000-odd voters whom ALP National Secretary, Gary Gray, identifed as having defected to the Coal-ition in 1996. Kernot was becoming quite uncomfortable with the kind of Australia she saw beginning to emerge as a response to this strategy: 'After a while it began to make sense of Howard's disappointing claim that he was about making Australians comfortable and relaxed. The political strategy seemed to be simply about how they could keep denying the blue-collar vote to Labor. It meant the government would be devoid of passion, bland, not rocking the boat. Where was the great vision? There was none. Instead there was a low risk, cautious plan to get there by other means. But I began to see that the other means were about pandering to insecurities and prejudices.'

Kernot began to complain of a narrowness in the government's thinking. 'When I saw some of Howard's ministers stand up in parliament and say to the Labor party "What would you know, you've never run a business", I thought, what would they know, they've never been unemployed! They wouldn't know an Aboriginal person. They've never been in public housing. Who says the sole criterion for running this country is that you've run a business? We need that, but we need more than that. We need all of it. Their view of what is successful is so very narrow. I look at some of the kids that turn up at schools around Australia. And teachers tell me about the violence and the dysfunctional families and the poverty and what they have to deal with as teachers. And how what they need to deal with some situations in schools now is not teacher aides but social workers. They need health workers and family counsellors. School students don't exist in isolation. They don't just present at a classroom to be taught anymore. They bring everything with them. No breakfasts, no lunch, no money. I just don't think John Howard's government has ever experienced this. Their kids don't go to these schools, they don't know this part of Australia.

'This is a hugely important thing, this not having had experience of something. They don't know that in parts of Australia the classrooms are spartan and have shocking desks and ratshit textbooks and limited computers. Because they just drive on and go through to another suburb where they are able to pay for their choice of schools. They don't use public hospitals. Life is OK for the elite and therefore governments don't have to do much to change anything else. Because if it is not in their experience, then change isn't necessary. The Howard government is eroding that egalitarian compassion we used to have in this country. That's what I get angry about.'

Out mixing with the wider community, Kernot reckons she detected the deep-seated apprehension about unemployment before it showed up in the work of people like Hugh Mackay. She saw that not only were unemployed people despairing, but there was an insidious insecurity spreading among people *in* jobs. Workers were apprehensive about their futures, the instability of their wages, the insecurity of their families. Those shifted to contract work with no long-term guarantees felt vulnerable, yet were afraid to speak up for fear of losing what little they had. No-one in government seemed to be articulating a cohesive, optimistic view of the future.

When BHP announced the closure of the steelworks in Newcastle, Kernot could see that the people understood this was a failure of government to ensure that industry policy worked properly. When international companies decided to lay off thousands of workers without doing the government the courtesy of informing it properly, where was the Prime Minister speaking up for Australia? There was no sense that government could work *with* business to mitigate the hurt that came with change, or to work out alternatives to the next plant closure. No suggestion that national government could step in and gather together affected agencies out in the community like local government, State departments, welfare, employment, industry services and the voluntary sector to try to work out some constructive options. Australia seemed leaderless.

Kernot saw multiple weaknesses in economic management. Like the gap between the attitudes of the elite—top bureaucrats, the bosses of right wing think-tanks, business journalists, academic economists and the mouthpieces for various industry bodies—and the attitudes of the actual business people out in the real world, working to make a crust. She believed that far more people actually working in business could see the need for a pro-active industry policy than the economists, who claimed to represent them, would concede. But there was also a gap between what many of the people inside the political/economic system—many of them businessmen pursuing a particular vested interest line—really thought and what they were prepared to say publicly.

Travelling the country, meeting and talking to people, Kernot began to detect a gap between the public face and the private view. 'People get out there in public and talk their specialised language and mouth their predictable jargon, depending on where they're coming from, and then they take their job hat off, their business suit off, and they'll tell you how their kids are really changing their views on things. I've sat alongside so many people at official lunches and dinners and these people are bureaucrats, they're industry leaders. But fundamentally they're having their views challenged by their own children. And when they are being people and not highly sectionalised leaders, they'll say things like the unemployment rate and its social impact, and long-term, intergenerational unemployment are all really worrying and governments have got to have answers. They will acknowledge the social damage of these policies.

'But then, stick a microphone under their noses when they're being a spokesperson for some body and it all changes. That's what's wrong with this country. I don't know how you can change it. Even when you get people together for a summit, they all come as the representatives of some competing, vested interests. You can't blame them, I suppose. They have to keep their jobs and they're not going to walk out on their work just because they have a few doubts about some things in the backs of their minds. But it is a problem. I just wish we weren't all so divided up as a society into so many competing, vested interests. Competing for airwave time, competing for funding, competing for influence.'

In short, Kernot saw the Howard government relying on a dated politics which actually served to foster, and then exploit, adversarial demands between vested interests. To the extent that the business community—or at least its perceived interests—were served by this approach, she believed there had to be a big change in thinking. Business had to see division could only damage it, too. 'I have this dream that political leaders should be able to talk directly and honestly to a country. And to sit down and tell its business community that it is part of that country, part of our whole, and that it is counter-productive for it to be thinking only of itself. I long for someone to be trying to find solutions that are fair and who can say to business that they are all part of it, but that they can't run the show alone. And someone who can say to business that it's not in their interests to have a yawning inequality gap. Maybe the reason this hasn't happened is that among the politicians playing the games it's assumed there is more political mileage, more votes, in prolonging the system of confrontation and vested interest where you pander to your own constituency.'

Kernot became convinced the strategic approach of the Howard government was contributing to an erosion of tolerance. This would be most clearly spelt out in the handling of the race issue but it was much more than just the emergence from under a rock of neanderthal racist sentiment. She believed she saw, in the broad, a cynical and deliberate manipulation of social division by one side of national politics to claw electoral benefit for itself. There was arrogance within the economic elite. It was blindingly obvious that the market forces dogma was not enough, yet the orthodoxy would never admit it. The coming of the Coalition government seemed to coincide with the appearance of a particular breed of opinionated corporate powerbroker. It was a climate in which, it seemed to Kernot, there was less patience with alternative views than at any other time since she was in parliament. All this was driven home by two incidents shortly after the Telstra vote was taken.

Having narrowly missed a connecting flight to Brisbane one evening, Kernot settled down in the Ansett VIP lounge at Sydney airport for a bout of paperwork. When she went to get a glass of water at the refreshments bar, she was confronted by a businessman, a retailer from National Party territory near Tamworth.

'Aha, took a big gamble and blew it, eh girlie?' the businessman sneered.

'I beg your pardon?' Kernot said.

'You weren't smart enough this time, were you, eh? You have to be smarter than that if you want to get something better for the country, like you're always claiming,' he said. The businessman then went into an agitated defence of the Telstra sale, saying her obstruction was a 'disgrace'. He expressed delight that the government had outsmarted her. 'You sit there in the Senate blocking everything and you don't understand, but you're basically destroying this country,' he said.

Battling to stay polite, Kernot said she was sorry if he didn't like the fact that she supported public ownership but that she had a responsibility to make sure decisions were made in Canberra in the interests of all Australians and not just for select groups. When he interrupted that she was just obstructing everything, she demanded to know what evidence backed that assertion. She pointed out that the government had got its IR package through. And its budget.

'Tell me, sir,' she said, her anger rising, 'what has John Howard got left on his list that we are obstructing? Tell me precisely all the things we're blocking that amounts to destroying the country.'

He accused her of stopping employers being able to implement junior pay rates. She said her contribution to the IR package made it possible for the IRC to look at what was a very vexed issue, to take evidence and try to pick its way through complex claims to discern the right course for the nation. As the temperature of the discussion climbed, the businessman stopped interrupting when Kernot repeatedly demanded the evidence. Where did he get these ideas? He mentioned two members of the National Party in the parliament but she suggested he should test things he was being told with wider opinion. The discussion petered out and a slightly flustered Kernot made her way back to her reading. She still had over an hour to wait. Sometime later she walked over to the lounge front desk to get an update on timing. Incredibly, when she was walking back past the refreshment bar she was accosted by yet another businessman.

'You're Cheryl Kernot, aren't you?' he asked.

'Yes, I am,' she said.

'Well, you're a damned disgrace. You're wrecking Australia and you don't deserve to be in the parliament.'

Kernot's jaw dropped. 'I don't believe it,' she thought. 'Here we go again!'

Much the same sort of abusive exchange then ensued but this businessman spoke in a much louder voice and constantly interrupted Kernot when she tried to explain herself. The battle began to catch the attention of other people around the VIP lounge, some of whom seemed to be moving within ear-shot. By now she was getting very angry indeed, demanding he produce evidence as well. She told him she made no apology for her actions and that she was sick and tired of male businessmen thinking that their interests had to be served, and never mind the ordinary people of Australia.

'And if I get up your nose, and people like you, then that's just fine by me because you, and people like you, don't give a stuff for the people. All you are about is feathering your own nests. I hate what people like you are doing to Australia. There's no sense of the interests of the community, no compassion. This is just the politics of division.'

By now both were lost in fury. The businessman said the best thing that could happen would be for the government to pull on a double dissolution election and then Kernot would lose. That, he said loudly, would be the best thing that could happen for all Australia. Kernot said that athough the government had prevailed on Telstra, the majority of Australians felt as strongly as she did about a huge public asset being sold off.

At the height of the argument, the man gestured and yelled: 'You're just a stupid woman! Your brain is about this size!'

'Oh, and you're so smart,' she replied. 'Look, my friend, why don't you get into parliament and do something about it then?'

'Yeah, well, I saw you in the back row of a restaurant in North Sydney with Kerry O'Brien, plotting to change all the questions he'd ask you on the 7.30 Report ... making sure you only get the questions you want to answer!'

Kernot was at melt-down. 'Excuse me, sir, but who the hell do you think you are? How dare you intrude into my life and insinuate things like that about my motives? That's an outrage and you're the disgrace, not me!' Amid a lull in the exchange, Kernot turned to the refreshments bar to get a drink and then the man, incredibly, offered her his business card. 'Keep it,' she snapped. 'I couldn't give a stuff who you are. Your views are of absolutely no interest to me whatsoever.' With that, she walked away.

Later, when she had cooled down, Kernot kept mulling over the exchanges. She was amazed at the ferocity of the attacks, particularly from the second man. She was accustomed to strong criticism and fiery debate, but these two had come at her not to exchange views, simply to abuse. In six-and-a-half years in public life, nothing like it had ever happened before. And certainly not twice in the space of an hour. Kernot realised she was thoroughly sick and tired of a pinstripe-dominated, ideological agenda which, in its purest form, seemed fanatical. It made her begin to think quite hard about the state of Australian politics under the Coalition government. About the future of the country. And about her own.

20
NARCISSUS

The tensions that developed between Kernot and the Howard administration had one little-noticed side effect—the decline of her relationship with the Democrats' founder, Don Chipp. Glossed over publicly at the time, animosity that bubbled to the surface between the pair in 1996 ran quite deep. Before she even became involved in politics, as an ordinary voter Kernot had always been a bit unsure of this lined and jaunty figure, Don Chipp. She thought of him first and foremost as a Liberal. He seemed to her to be a bit of a show-pony and she sometimes thought she detected feigned indignation. But when she became active in the Australian Democrats as an official in Queensland, she began to have contact with him up close and developed an appreciation of his unique political skills. She would learn a good deal about the art of big-time politics watching Chipp in action.

At Brisbane airport where she had driven to pick him up for an electioneering visit to Queensland, she was struck by the friendly, 'Good on ya', Chippy' welcomes he got as they walked through the terminal. Here was a person who had clearly managed to create an idosyncratic presence in Australian politics, and one that people reacted to, in the main, with warmth. While giving an interview in a Brisbane radio station, Chipp produced, with typical passion, an appealing line of argument. He reckoned that if there was enough good will demonstrated between people, if they were able to sit down around a table and talk amicably, and if they were willing to devote as much time to the exercise as necessary, then there was no political impasse that couldn't be resolved, no problem that was unfixable. This apparently heartfelt, defiantly optimistic view of the capacity of people to find answers made a big impact on Kernot as she sat in a studio ante-room listening to the interview going to air. A simple idea, full of idealism, it struck her as a valuable starting point for an operational credo in politics. It was an idea that fostered hope, one that unlocked the possible in human relations. Kernot also respected Chipp for the way he realised the time had come to leave politics and for having the foresight to back a woman as his successor.

When he took up writing a newspaper column, however, she could see Chipp reverting to his old Liberal Party instincts. The potential for a major blow-up slotted into place when, after she became leader, he appeared to have no compunction about criticising his old party, and by inference its leader, for its approach on specific policy issues and also on strategy. But the decline in the relationship probably really dates from the moment Paul Keating named the date for the 1996 election. Kernot was incensed with the response she got when she rang Chipp to ask him to appear with her at the launch of the party's slogan, his old refrain about 'those bastards'. According to Kernot, Chipp said that he had given the issue a lot of thought and concluded he could not do it. He said he could not afford to be associated with any political party because he was on the short list to be appointed Governor of Victoria.[1] Kernot was flabbergasted. And furious.

'But this is your party, Don. You started it. You can't just walk away from it like that. You're part of our history and continuity. I need you to be part of our presentation in this campaign!'

'Cheryl, I can't do it,' Chipp said. 'It's your party now.'

Then, not long after the election when much public focus was shifting to the upcoming conflict between the government and the Senate over Telstra, Chipp went public on the vexed issue of the definition of mandate. He argued in his newspaper column that Kernot had led the party with 'flair, imagination, care and commonsense' and had achieved a rare accolade—respect. But then he added: 'It's sad that this and all the achievements of the past twenty years are now being put at risk over a misconception about what constitutes a mandate.'[2]

Chipp argued that the electors rarely vote for a party on one issue—the rare exception being Vietnam back in 1966—and that neither Howard nor Kernot could claim a mandate for their actions on Telstra. Sniffing a good story, once the media had leapt on his article, Chipp was quoted as saying that it was counter-productive for Kernot to keep chasing the Telstra windmill. 'I'm suggesting to her that for the good of the nation, the

Don Chipp, rallying for support for his new party,
the Australian Democrats, in 1977. *Fairfax Photo Library*

Janet Powell and John Coulter, both former leaders
of the Australian Democrats. *Fairfax Photo Library*

Democrat fundraising dinner with Kernot, former leader Janine Haines and
Michael Macklin, himself party leader for six months in 1990 after Haines' defeat.

Cheryl Kernot and Senators Meg Lees, Karin Sowada, Sid Spindler and
Vicky Bourne (*standing*), Robert Bell and John Coulter (*seated*) 1993. *David Foote*

A gathering of all the female senators in 1990. *Right to left*: Sue West, Cheryl Kernot, Jean Jenkins, Margaret Reynolds, Olive Zakharov, Florence Bjelke-Petersen, Margaret Reid, Shirley Walters, Jocelyn Newman, Amanda Vanstone, Susan Knowles, Janet Powell, Meg Lees. *Sitting*: Vicky Bourne, Kay Patterson, Bronwyn Bishop, Jo Vallentine, Pat Giles, Rosemary Crowley.

Cheryl with the World Cup winning Australian Women's Cricket team in January, 1998. *Fairfax Photo Library*

Grabbing some rest during the marathon debate over
the political broadcasting bill in 1991. *Fairfax Photo Library*

Kernot doing a media interview in Canberra, 1995. *George Fetting.*

Kernot launches a book on disability, Canberra, 1994.
The Photographers/Heide Smith Photography.

Cheryl at a Telstra rally, 1995.
Fairfax Photo Library

Cheryl and Peter Reith swap the agreement they reached over the
workplace relations bill in 1996. *Fairfax Photo Library*

Cheryl walking to the Reps' side of the House with David Epstein,
Kim Beazley's Chief of Staff, just after the announcement of her defection.
Fairfax Photo Library

Gareth Evans, Kim Beazley and Cheryl Kernot at the joint press conference announcing
Kernot's defection to the ALP. *Fairfax Photo Library*

Cheryl meeting Labor Party members in the federal seat
of Dickson shortly after her defection. *Fairfax Photo Library*

Kernot on Capital Hill after the defection. *Fairfax Photo Library*

Democrats should accept the will of the people. Telstra should not be barricades time for the Democrats.' Elaborating on ABC radio, Chipp said only 11% of the people voted for the Democrats and 'of that 11%, there wouldn't be many of them who would desperately and passionately want Telstra to be blocked'. It was pointed out to him that Kernot had disagreed, saying that people *were* stopping her in the street urging her to keep Telstra public.

'Well, I'm very much in the Menzies mould,' Chipp said. 'If private enterprise can do it, let private enterprise do it. Only when private enterprise can't do something, then let the government do it.' The die was cast for a clash between two powerful egos.

Later, Chipp became concerned with the direction Kernot was charting in the negotiations with the government over IR. He believed that as the party committed to helping small business and free enterprise grow, the Democrats had no role in trying to affect things like right to strike and unfair dismissal legislation. 'I always come back to one of the guiding principles at the start of the Democrats, our passionate affection for small business. You tie small business up by enshrining the right to strike, by keeping the unfair dismissal laws intact and all you are doing is putting a rope round the necks of small business. That, to me, is totally opposed to the whole reason the Democrats exist. This country depends on private enterprise and small business to survive. If you are going to strangle it with this kind of thing, it amounts to national self-mutilation.'[3]

In the wake of the early IR talks, Chipp and his wife Idun were talking one afternoon when she began to express concern over the direction of their old party. 'This is not the party I joined, Don,' she said. 'I'm wondering whether I should resign from it.'

Chipp said that was a decision for her to make but then she asked what it would mean for him. Chipp said he could not do the same as he was the Democrats' only life member. So they resolved that she would do it quietly in a private letter to Kernot in late July, 1996. Sent off soon after, the letter read:

It is with deep sorrow that I resign my membership of the Australian Democrats. The party has become unrecognisable from the Australian Democrats we formed and though I realise that the party can move in different directions, I feel that I can no longer travel with it. I wish you well.

Idun Chipp.[4]

A number of factors informed the Chipps' thinking. They had been privately developing concerns about Kernot for some time. At a dinner in mid-1996 to mark the retirement from the Senate of Sid Spindler, Chipp had become worried at suggestions there that instead of just 'keeping the bastards honest', the party was now actively seeking to impose its own policies on the nation.[5] Chipp had long had deep apprehension about the question of the power of minor parties to affect the will of governments in the Senate. For him, the party's raison d'etre should be restricted to refining the elected government's policies—not blocking them, and certainly not seeking to impose in their place the Democrats' own platform.

The problem with this interpretation is that previous leaders, including Chipp himself, had sought to reject budget measures. Kernot and her supporters argued Chipp and Janine Haines had set ample precedents for the approach of the late 1990s. In the mid-1980s he had explicitly rejected the notion that the Senate should be limited to dealing with all legislation, except money bills. Back in the early 1980s, his party room was split over the decision to oppose the Fraser government's sales tax on the necessities of life. That was the moment when he suffered his heart attack and when his colleagues prevailed upon him to give his support from a hospital bed to the move to block the government measures. Today, Chipp looks back with some regret that in giving way, he 'let the genie out of the bottle'. But, in doing so, he gives hint of his own confusion on this issue, even now. While he argues he is not sure he did the right thing on the necessities of life tax, he says he was at least responding to what he perceived as the community will: 'I think I do regret not fighting against it a bit harder. It leaves the way open for every Johnny-come-lately to pursue their own agenda in the Senate. The only thing that I say in my defence there is that at that time when we were split, between the time when the vote was taken there was overwhelming feedback from the community to reject ... massive input of feeling from the constituency ... overwhelmingly in favour of rejecting the sales tax on necessities ... so I suppose I felt we had to listen. That was what turned my mind. What the hell are we here for if we don't listen to the voters?'[6]

But this is precisely the rationale used in her own defence by Kernot—that is, that she detected the people *wanted* her to intervene. At its core then, the philosophical argument between Kernot and Chipp on mandate comes down to their differing interpretations of the relative merits of what they argue was compelling feedback from the electorate about individual budget measures.

But Chipp also long argued it was dangerous for the Democrats to think about trying to establish a big presence in the Reps. To do that, he said, they would have to kowtow to vested interests, and take positions that never offended anyone so they could garner votes. The beauty of the Democrats, he always said, was that in the upper house their senators could remain above sordid deal-doing and be one voice of reason speaking the truth untrammelled by anxiety that in so doing, their electoral position would be undermined. Chipp believed that by concentrating on the Senate the party ultimately might grow to have two senators elected from each State.[7]

But on both counts—the Democrat mandate and lower house expansion—Kernot was out there arguing lines distinctly at odds with the founder. She acknowledged there had long been a tension inside the party over whether it should be just a watchdog or pursue its own policies from the Senate. 'Time alone will lessen this tension, and I believe it has lessened considerably since 1990,' she said.

> We are increasingly accepted as acting legitimately in both roles. Roles which are not mutually exclusive, but the management of which does sometimes require astute and balanced political judgement. Over time, I am confident that this tension will cease to exist altogether and that our voters will be happy to support us for being more than a watchdog. Indeed, anecdotal evidence suggests that this is already happening. More and more we are attracting support for our ideas.[8]

At this point in time—late 1995—Kernot was guardedly optimistic that eventually the Democrats might conquer the Reps. By early 1997, however, her view on that had shifted appreciably to the extent that she came to share Chipp's doubts. But aside from their different views of strategy at times, there were niggling personal tensions between Chipp and Kernot.

On one occasion, for example, he was in Canberra having a quiet chat with Paul Keating in his office when a call was put through from that of Kernot requesting the PM participate in a joint 'photo-opportunity' for the media. Chipp was irritated by this presumption that the Democrat Leader could interrupt the PM with such a minor request. At the end of 1996 Chipp was irritated that he was not invited formally to the celebration of the party's twentieth anniversary. That was an executive decision taken by the party officials. Kernot says she was not consulted about it. Against the background of the general rising animosity, it then fell to Sam Hudson to ring Chipp with a suggestion that he send a message to the gathering. No-one seriously thought he would attend and, in fact, he had no intention of doing so, but he was offended at the off-hand way it was all handled. Idun Chipp's concern seemed to be that from the Janet Powell leadership onwards the party had been pushed too far left. But she made it absolutely clear that the Kernot position on Telstra and mandate was the 'final straw'.[9]

No-one is sure how the news first got out, but with the leaking of the Chipp letter and some cutting commentary by a couple of journalists about Don Chipp's concerns, Kernot found her patience at an end. She didn't like having to go public to attack her party's founder but she believed she had no alternative. She faced a barrage of media inquiries, all seeking her response to what seemed significant criticism of her. She responded in typically up-front manner. Kernot had been accumulating beefs of her own about Chipp. Apart from his refusal to help with the slogan launch, she had told him in no uncertain terms on the telephone in mid-1996 that she resented his attempt to intervene on behalf of Treasurer Peter Costello.

When Chipp and Costello had bumped into each other at a funeral in Melbourne, the Treasurer had complained that Kernot was inaccessible, reflecting his concern at the time about speculation that she was refusing to deal with him because she had a direct line into John Howard's office. Kernot had gone out of her way to discount this suggestion, but Costello complained to Chipp that he had heard she had actually said she 'didn't talk to Treasurers, just to Prime Ministers'. Costello basically asked Chipp if he could help build a dialogue so his budget wasn't 'savaged'.

Kernot was at home in Brisbane when Chipp rang. He pointed out he had talked to Costello and suggested he be mediator in a meeting between the two. Having listened to Sid Spindler's farewell speech and having talked to other people, Chipp said he was becoming really concerned about the 'block this, block that' mentality slipping into the party.

Kernot interrupted. 'Look, Don. I'm in charge of budget strategy in this party and I'm not out to wreck the budget. I've made that clear over and over again. I don't need any trumped up meeting with Peter Costello and I don't need you as mediator. I'm surprised you're doing their bidding.' Not-withstanding her prickliness, Chipp satisfied himself that he had Kernot's word that her intent was not to destroy the budget.

The conversation and other hints about Chipp's contacts behind the scenes with the Liberal Party in Victoria suggested to Kernot once again that the founder of her party was now, more than ever, reverting to his conservative roots. Kernot saw him simply as a Liberal whose political genius had been to create another political entity by embroidering onto his conservative economic ideology some leftist environmental and peace movement thinking, as well as embracing the imported radical ideas of others, like the Australia Party's John Siddons with his passion for industrial democracy. Kernot divined that in Chipp's period as leader the focus had not been so much on economic issues. Once she herself had put the party into the big picture debates, Chipp had a hide to be sniping from the sidelines. She was unrepentant that while he had to earn a living as a writer, he should have the good grace to do as Janine Haines had done—avoid meddling in party matters that could cause trouble for a leader trying to give the party a contemporary role.

Publicly, Kernot went for the jugular. Based on advice from Democrat officials, she challenged Idun Chipp's claim to have been a co-founder of the party, pointed out that 83% of the Democrat membership had joined the party since Chipp had left and suggested the leaking of the letter had been part of a Liberal strategy to intimidate the Democrats in the lead-up to the budget. This attack infuriated the Chipps. He had talked for years about the contribution of his wife, his loyal backstop, all the way back to the early years when they travelled the nation, exhausted, setting up the party structure. Ms Chipp said publicly she had been there 'every step of the way' with Don back in 1977, adding contemptuously of Kernot: 'She wasn't there!'[10]

But then, in asserting that the resignation may have been part of an organised campaign, Kernot dropped the bombshell: 'I think it's interesting to note that Mr Chipp is on the short-list of Liberal nominations for Governor of Victoria.' It was a huge political play, infuriating Chipp further. When approached about it by the media, he refused to make any more comment. When the office of the Premier of Victoria was approached about her claim, a spokesman confirmed Chipp's name had been suggested 'before' as a possible Governor. But the spokesman said it was inappropriate to discuss a successor to the incumbent Richard McGarvie who was not due to complete his five-year term until April, 1997.[11]

After Kernot's counter-attack, privately Chipp became even more scathing about her. To confidants he wondered that she would take aim at him so hard simply because he had criticised her on policy. Basically she had probably killed whatever chance he may have had of becoming Victorian Governor. He told friends he believed her to be suffering what he called 'a massive lack of humility' and evincing 'the worst manifestation of narcissism'. He said it was a troubling signal that, when put under sustained criticism, Kernot would strike out. He put her in a category with Gough Whitlam and Bob Hawke, arguing that when a politician loses humility, they begin to decline.

The postscript to the soured relations with Chipp came in Canberra towards the end of 1996 at a big party thrown to farewell a stalwart of the parliamentary press gallery, the Nine television network's Peter Harvey who was moving to Sydney. Along with many other major politicians, Kernot was invited. And so were Don and Idun Chipp. The MC for the night was radio man Mike Carlton and, typically, he made humorous mischief at the expense of many of the pollies present. One of his targets, of course, was the fact that Kernot and the Chipps were seated at different tables. During the early part of the night they had no contact, not even acknowledging one another across the room. As the evening wound down, the Chipps wondered if Kernot would have the 'hide' to come and speak to them. For her part, Kernot thought very carefully about the appropriate thing to do and resolved that she should show some maturity and at least acknowledge the founder of her party, instead of being seen to keep the feud going. She opted to walk over and at least say hello.

Chipp told his wife to stand up when the function came to an end so they didn't get caught talking to her. 'Otherwise she'll be all over us like a rash,' he said. When she approached their table, the Chipps were on their feet.

'Hello, Don,' she said. 'Did you laugh at Mike Carlton's joke? I did.' Idun Chipp had turned her back.

'Look, you just have a good night, Cheryl,' Chipp said abruptly through gritted teeth, before walking away through the crowd with his wife. Chipp would later confide to friends that the mere fact that Kernot had come over after all the 'bagging' she had done of them 'indicates the narcissistic nature of the woman'. Kernot returned to the company of a couple of people at her table, some of whom had seen the snub. Their view, as put to her, was that it was childish.

21
RACE AND RANCOUR

The suspicion that the Howard government was narrow, even mean-spirited, seemed borne out by the bad press it attracted during the visit to Australia of US President, Bill Clinton, and his wife Hillary at the end of 1996. A key part of the criticism emanated from a snub meted out to a small group of prominent female figures in Australian public life, including the Democrat Leader. At a lunch for the Clintons, attended by some 650 guests in the Great Hall of Parliament House, the keynote speech by Prime Minister Howard attracted flak for being pedestrian, overly serious and grey, particularly in comparison to a more vibrant one delivered by Kim Beazley. But the lunch was held amid rumours that public figures including Kernot, ACTU President Jennie George and Australia's most senior indigenous woman, the Aboriginal and Torres Strait Islander Commission Chairperson, Lois O'Donoghue, had not been included in the group to meet with Hillary Clinton at a function the following day at the Sydney Opera House. There, Mrs Clinton was due to deliver a speech, to be followed by the private meeting over coffee with some thirty women leaders.

The First Lady had made it clear she wanted to meet senior Australian women with an interest in the policy areas that intrigued her—health, child welfare, the law and anti-discrimination policy. The meeting was to be hosted by John Howard's wife, Janette, and the Minister for the Status of Women, Jocelyn Newman, but there was speculation that there had been a difference of opinion between Howard's office and the Clinton party over the invitation list. One rumour suggested a list from the Office for the Status of Women had been vetoed by Mrs Howard herself. Kernot knew the event was on, had half-expected an invitation and was surprised when none was forthcoming.

During the day of the Canberra lunch, walking from the Senate chamber, Kernot bumped into the government leader, Robert Hill, and mentioned the rumours. She said that if it was true that certain people had been black-banned, it was unnecessarily petulant. As a new administration, the government could afford to be magnanimous. At the Great Hall lunch, Kernot was seated with an influential US State Department official travelling with the Clintons, and Gough and Margaret Whitlam. In passing, Margaret Whitlam told Kernot she had been following her work closely and had a lot of time for the sort of things she was trying to achieve. The State Department woman was obviously well briefed about Australian politics, knew a great deal about the Democrats, and of Kernot herself. The American asked why Kernot was not going to the function the following day.

'I'm only the leader of a minor party,' was the reply.

With that, Margaret Whitlam suddenly interrupted, saying that Kernot was, in her view, the most sensible politician in Australia. In fact, she wished she could be in the Labor Party. Mrs Whitlam went on to say she thought it disgraceful that women like Kernot were being excluded from the Opera House function and that it would leave an unfortunate impression about Australia. The next morning—the day of the Sydney function—newspapers were full of stories about the snub, revealing those excluded also included Kim Beazley's wife, Susie, the former Office of the Status of Women boss and feminist guru, Anne Summers, and female ministers from the NSW Labor government. The invitees, however, had included the Howards' daughter Melanie, one of her friends from university, as well as a bevy of conservative female politicians and political spouses.

In light of the criticism, however, there was an eleventh hour rethink. At 9.20 on that Thursday morning, Kernot got a call from Robert Hill who apologised on behalf of the government, and invited her to fly to Sydney for the afternoon function. A few minutes later, Peter Reith rang, saying he now hoped the 'outrageous' oversight had been sorted out. At 1 pm Kernot dashed from parliament to pack at home, en route to the airport for Sydney. At the Opera House she sat in an audience of some 300 people, including Margaret Whitlam, Hazel Hawke, Kathryn Greiner, Ita Buttrose, Susan Ryan, Hilary McPhee, Anne Summers, Ruth Cracknell, Rachel Ward and Jana Wendt for Mrs Clinton's main speech of the visit. And then, with a small group of other last minute invitees, including O'Donoghue and Justice

Mary Gaudron, it was in to the closed coffee and champagne session in a specially cordoned-off section of the Opera House main foyer.

Kernot was very taken by the core messages of Mrs Clinton's speech, in which she argued that an historic, recent change in American politics had brought 'kitchen table issues', previously dismissed as marginal, to the centre of the national debate. Mrs Clinton said the issues included the question of leave taken from work to care for sick children, mothers spending sufficient time in hospital with their newborn and health care for the aged and poor. More and more, she said, women were voting to have the issues they cared about at the forefront of national debate but this was perplexing US commentators, accustomed to the 'big issues' of defence, diplomacy, economics and trade. This shift, often derided as the 'feminisation' of politics, Mrs Clinton preferred to call the 'humanisation' of politics.

> After all, don't fathers worry about how long their wives and babies can stay in hospital when they need care? Don't men want to be able to take time off when a family member is gravely ill? Don't sons want to ensure that their elderly parents have health care coverage in the later stages of their life?

Mrs Clinton said true democracy was about how people's personal concerns could be translated into politics.

> What women are saying today—loudly and clearly—is that national politics is not just about realpolitik. It is about real-life politik. Will democracies on every continent come to understand that issues affecting women are not soft or marginal but central to the progress and prosperity of every nation?

That would involve education being made accessible for all women, business introducing family-friendly reforms such as child care, flexible hours and parental leave and equal pay for equal work.

> Will we admit that there is no formula for being a successful or fulfilled woman in today's society? That one can choose full time motherhood and homemaking or be committed to work outside the home

without marriage or children or, like most of us today, balance work and family responsibilities?[1]

Mrs Clinton's remarks stirred Kernot. Later, over coffee, she quickly saw that the function that had created all the fuss was being dominated, as one would expect, by the women attached to Coalition politics. Not wanting to push in, she and O'Donoghue resisted overtures from an official from the American Consulate to ease them into the circle of Liberal women gathered around the First Lady. After a while, though, Mrs Clinton was moving around the room and for a short period she and Kernot discussed the ideas underpinning the speech. The American seemed interested to hear about the carers case Kernot had taken to the IRC. Then she remarked on the colourful Aboriginal print dress being worn by Lois O'Donoghue. She obviously knew of, and admired, Aboriginal art. Alluding to the 2000 Olympics and the boost that would give all things Australian, she wondered if enough thought had been put into the issue of protecting the intellectual property rights of Aboriginal artists so they financially benefit from their culture. Soon the function was drawing to a close, with Kernot impressed with a very contemporary female leader who came over as canny, tough but warm.

When fronted by the media about the snub brouhaha, Kernot said she had been grateful to be included, even if it was at the last minute. Mrs Clinton's remarks had reinspired her thinking about women. 'I needed a boost of inspiration like that. But I must say I felt a little bit guilty because I think there are some prominent Labor women who would have enjoyed it just as much as I did. Mrs Clinton confirmed for me, in a very powerful way, the importance of some of the things I believe in. She said that she welcomed the debate ... it's a contentious debate ... but women will help to shape the answers we seek.'[2]

While Kernot would not belabour the question of the snub, others were more forthright. Commentator Alan Ramsey pointed out in the *Sydney Morning Herald* that the government had tried to impose petty restrictions on the media coverage of Bill Clinton's short meeting with Kim Beazley. Ramsey argued that getting to the end of his first year in office with some big wins under his belt, John Howard could afford to act with magnanimity. The landscape of Australian politics lay before Howard to sculpt:

Instead, he is quickly falling back into small-minded and mean habits, with sour behaviour that makes him appear for all the world like a Captain Mainwaring figure out of a *Dad's Army* script, who still thinks he has to prove himself to himself.[3]

Privately, Kernot was amazed, finding the small-mindedness of the snub a bit incomprehensible. But by the end of 1996 there were other, far less ephemeral, issues over which her regard for John Howard was being corroded. The key one was the manner in which the government was managing the Aboriginal Affairs portfolio, for Kernot saw the destructive winds of racism being fanned.

Bolstered by the traditional, conservative perception that, for decades, governments had been throwing money away in wasteful programs, Cabinet had moved quickly after the election to signal some big changes in Aboriginal affairs. Pointing out that something like $12 billion had been spent on Aboriginal affairs under Hawke and Keating, ministers were asking what there was to show for it. In the wake of new accusations of financial mismanagement, controversial measures were signalled, including the setting up of an audit of ATSIC, legislation to impose an administrator on the body and the installation of a chairperson appointed by the government, rather than elected by Aborigines. Early on, Kernot asked how such decisive measures could be taken when the new Minister, John Herron, had only been in the job a matter of weeks. But by the time it was clear Peter Costello's first budget would slice $400 million out of the portfolio, indigenous Australia was in uproar. Kernot was horrified at what she saw as a cynical effort by the government to play to the prejudices of that hard-core constituency that always believed Aborigines had 'privileged status'. To her this was a double-edged appeal—to racism, but more importantly, also to the 'blue collar' old Labor vote that Howard had attracted to underwrite his big 1996 win. But she would be further exasperated by the unfolding attitude of the government to native title.

Howard himself made it clear his government would move to amend the native title legislation to make it more 'workable' and to eliminate problems it might cause for major resource development projects. And in December, 1996, in an historic ruling in the Wik case, the High Court found, by a 4 to 3 majority, that the granting of pastoral leases, which cover something like

40% of Australia's land, did not automatically extinguish native title rights. This highly contentious ruling took the Mabo decision a step forward by refuting the 1992 judgement that native title was extinguished on pastoral leases. In response, in September, 1997, Howard introduced in the Reps a 264-page legislative package built around his so-called 'ten-point plan'. These proposed changes to the original native title law denied Aborigines the power to force negotiations over the terms of resource developments on pastoral leases, introduced a native title six-year sunset clause (a time limit on its applicability), sought to protect farmers by declaring a wide range of farm activities exempt from claim, and imposed a new, tougher test on whether claims would be accepted in the first place. In arguing this was a complex package simply concealing the intent of the government to wind back native title, critics of the move argued that the new law would allow the States to extinguish native title on pastoral leases so that pastoralists could be given upgraded freehold title. Thus, the scene was set for another showdown with the Senate, amid speculation that Wik could ultimately prove the trigger for a double dissolution election.

Kernot always believed that the work of the Council for Aboriginal Reconciliation, on which she served, was seriously underestimated. Set up inside the Department of Prime Minister and Cabinet, the Council set up programs in the community to try to achieve reconciliation between black and white by the new millennium. But with budget cuts affecting so many areas of its work, a meeting of the Reconciliation Council in mid-1996 had decided to scrap its scheduled agenda and spend the whole day discussing whether it should disband, with its members announcing their resignations in protest.

Reluctantly, a dispirited Kernot was talked into staying on the Council, but the body resolved to demand talks with Howard and his senior ministers to convey its displeasure. The result of these discussions left Council members including Kernot and the former National Farmers' Federation boss, Rick Farley, firmly of the view that Howard and Herron were fixated with outdated stereotypes about Aborigines. Kernot argued that where there had been examples of financial wrong-doing, ATSIC had taken correct action like referring specific cases to investigative bodies like the Federal Police and the Australian Securities Commission, but there had been no follow-up by them. Why then was ATSIC being castigated? On balance, there was actually minimal serious financial impropriety yet the government's approach created the impression that all blacks were crooks, so perpetuating the stereotypes. But Kernot battled to get across one critical underlying message, an idea that validated a more generous view of Aboriginal Australia. It was that the behaviour of contemporary Aboriginal people was a function of their historic mistreatment. To begin the task of healing the tensions between the two, whites had simply to acknowledge the heinous wrongs of the past. This was an idea with which John Howard, for one, fundamentally disagreed.

Howard was passionately opposed to what he called the 'black armband' version of Australian history. He claimed Australian children were being wrongly taught that their country had a racist and bigoted past. He argued that the balance sheet of Australian history was basically a positive and optimistic one, and that it was disturbing how so many people were inclined to self-flagellation about the past. Asked to respond, Kernot defended school-teachers from the accusation that they were incapable of presenting the past in an historically accurate way.

'I do not believe that we dwell on racism or bigotry in our teaching of Australian history and the Prime Minister is captive of a bleak and blinkered view if he believes this,' she said.[4] She insisted that Australia could not, however, ignore the reality of what white Australia had done to indigenous people. Kernot would find herself firmly at loggerheads with Howard over the implications of the past, particularly with the release of the riveting report by the Human Rights and Equal Opportunities Commission into the so-called 'stolen children'.

In advance of that, though, the debate about Aboriginal affairs found a new, troubling dimension when, at 5.15pm on September 10, 1996, Pauline Hanson, the forty-two-year-old, independent MP who had won Bill Hayden's old seat of Oxley in Queensland, made her maiden speech in the Reps. Bringing to the parliament political views hewn from a background as a small-business fish-and-chips shop proprietor, Pauline Hanson would not simply fade into backbench anonymity, like so many other new MPs. Her maiden speech, with her voice fluttering with nerves, sent shock waves around the nation, signalling the arrival of not just some new political phenomenon, but the advent of a singularly dangerous one, using rhetoric that threatened to cut through the social fabric of the nation.

In this first, and other speeches, Hanson demanded an end to Asian immigration, the dismantling of Australia's post-war multicultural social compact and new restrictions on aid to developing nations. She urged the abolition of ATSIC and the elimination of specialist funding to Aboriginal programs, reflecting an underlying paranoia that blacks, like migrants, had been long bleeding the system dry of the sort of special privileges denied 'ordinary' Australians. Hanson argued Australia was being 'swamped' by Asians who formed ghettoes and refused to assimilate. She said Australia had to stop immigration and halt the multicultural experiment to avoid the morass of ethnic clashes that haunted nations like Bosnia, Ireland, Somalia and Rwanda.

Originally endorsed as the Liberal Party candidate, Hanson had been disowned during the 1996 election campaign by Howard and the Liberals because of nervousness that her views could blow up in his face. As her notoriety and seeming support in the electorate began to grow, this controversial new figure on the scene, her jaw set under tight lips and red hair, spoke long and often about these blights on Australia, and began travelling the nation promoting her new 'One Nation' Party. Wrapping her ideas in the flag, Hanson basically argued the time had come for patriots to challenge Aborigines and Asians, fat-cat bureaucrats, big-business, economic rationalist policy-makers and even international bankers. Basically, her pitch was that of a person who had never held her hand out in her life, but had made a success of it by hard work, and had a right to ask questions of the bludgers exploiting her country, exploiting her.

But Hanson's views sparked outrage among the liberal-minded and saw 'flying squads' of volunteers formed to protest at her meetings, bringing about scuffles, abuse and a sense of violence that no-one had ever dreamed of seeing in Australia. Critically, those views also exposed Australia's hard-won reputation as a tolerant nation to international ridicule. By the middle of 1997—nearly a year after she first surfaced, clear evidence was emerging that Hanson's presence was damaging Australia diplomatically and as a trading nation in Asia. Asian tourism was dropping off. The numbers of Asian students coming to Australia for education were tapering. Asian business leaders were predicting that if she remained in the parliament or her party grew into a viable entity, Australia's reputation would be irrevocably damaged. Businessmen like mining industry chief, Sir Roderick Carnegie, were calling for the two major parties to join forces to 'crush' Hanson at the next election. In August 1997, the Foreign Affairs Minister Alexander Downer launched a scorching attack on her during a visit to Singapore, charging that her policies were 'ethically reprehensible' and suicidal for Australia's economic prosperity. The Howard government was also forced to take the extraordinary step of setting up a special diplomatic/PR unit to provide information to offset the impact of Hanson's remarks in Asia. By the end of 1997, this woman had sparked an extraordinary, official damage-limitation exercise. But it was a long time coming—a year earlier the picture had been so different.

Back in late 1996, with Hanson first emerging from the shadows, the reaction from Prime Minister Howard had been much more muted. Working from the outset on the basis that it was best not to draw attention to Hanson and thus fan her media-status, Howard initially said he did not make a practice of responding to everything that every new MP said in his or her maiden speech. In remarks that exposed Howard dangerously to allegations of a lack of vision and leadership weakness, he said: 'She is entitled to express her view—I defend her right to say what her views are,' before going on to insist his government would continue its non-discriminatory immigration policy. But, prominent as the first major politician with no hesitation in taking Hanson on, was Cheryl Kernot.

When first fronted by the media over the Hanson view, Kernot let fly: 'I don't believe she's a true representative of the majority of Oxley voters but every bigoted, ill-informed, neurotic, conspiracy-motivated Australian has found a voice in her,' Kernot said. How the hell did she get through the initial preselection process of the Liberal party? she asked. But more than just attacking Hanson, Kernot responded immediately to Howard's refusal to step in. 'I think it's important to remember that evil flourishes where good men and women sit and do nothing,' she said. She urged Howard to say categorically that Hanson had used her maiden speech to say things about Asians and Aborigines that were 'blatantly untrue'.[5]

When Hanson went as far as to suggest multiculturalism could trigger civil strife in Australia, Howard did speak up, describing her as silly and uninformed but as she began to generate intense media coverage, the government began to come under growing pressure to take more meaning-ful action. With Kernot warning the debate was getting out of hand, some government MPs began suggesting there might need to be a joint resolution by both sides of the parliament reinforcing the message that Australia promoted a non-discriminatory immigration policy. When Kim Beazley moved in, inviting Howard to join him in a joint motion deploring racism, Kernot agreed to be a signatory. She was already seeing evidence in her private life of the damage that the Hanson campaign of hate was engendering.

As the race debate gripped the headlines with an unusual ferocity, sporadic incidents began to surface involving threats, intimidation and occasional violence to Asians. Sian Kernot was walking in the street in Brisbane with some of her Asian friends, when they were set upon and abused by a small number of youths. While Howard appeared to be back-pedalling and cautious on the escalating row, Kernot went onto the front foot once again. She accused him of being weak in not speaking up early and forcefully against Hanson's arguments. Kernot's concern was that by remaining so restrained, Howard ran the risk of giving the impression he was sending a covert message to those Australians attracted to the Hanson line that he, too, supported it.

'He's been a wimp,' Kernot told Sydney radio. 'I've been appalled. You don't get to be Prime Minister of this country just to sit back and say nothing. He has a greater moral responsibility to stand up and challenge those views.'[6] Kernot said the Liberal Party had been trying to have 'two bob each way' by sending out party officials to denounce Hanson instead of Howard himself. Then turning on the Member for Oxley again, the Democrat Leader said she manipulated statistics about Asian immigration and misused the facts about Aboriginal welfare money to suit her arguments. 'I find her a very shrill, harsh woman. When she says she cares, I find it very hard to see a chink of warmth in her. I'm sure she cares about her beliefs but I am not yet persuaded by her manner and the tiny bit I've seen of her that she actually has a depth of understanding and human compassion for the universal condition—whether it's in Ipswich, whether it's in Doomadgee or whether it's in Bosnia. I just don't detect that in her.'

Kernot acknowledges that as the first Australian politician to speak out against Hanson, she was particularly strident. 'Yep, I went for her. Because, unlike John Howard, I believe she had to be challenged. I understand that people have a right to their views. But it's not the right of a parliamentarian, in my view, to inflame bigotry. Politicians are there to lead. And to lead people to understanding and tolerance. It's a fine line when you start talking about democracy. I don't believe that parliament is a place to peddle lies. She was misinformed, so while she has a right to stand up and speak I think everybody listening has a right to stand up and say "you are wrong". She didn't go to the election campaign on any of those things. Because I'm passionate about indigenous people, I knew that the things she was saying were absolutely wrong. Pauline Hanson clearly didn't even know anything about the immigration history of this country. When she was cross-examined by the media, like on *60 Minutes*, she was really found wanting … she knew nothing. Her big contribution was to ask why Aboriginal people can't pick up their litter. You know, it's the superficial way at looking at the symptoms all the time, not the cause of the problems. And the lack of compassion! Pauline Hanson and John Howard, by his inaction, made it possible for bigotry to be acceptable in this country. I've seen the scape-goating before. I spent half my life trying to rebut the myths and knowing how hard it is. But I was just disgusted with how other politicians had hung back, waiting to sniff the wind. I felt quite strongly that, given something like 53% of people didn't vote for John Howard, somebody should be speaking up for them.'[7]

For weeks, Howard earned the scorn of some of the nation's leading political and social commentators for the cautiousness of his responses. By the end of April, 1997, Geoff Kitney, writing in the *Sydney Morning Herald*, said he had been wrong about the 'Hanson factor' in late 1996 and was still wrong. Kitney wrote:

> [Howard] justified his refusal last year to use his prime ministerial authority to condemn her because he said she was a one-day wonder who would quickly disappear. Yesterday, he repeated his view that she is an empty populist who won't last. But Mr Howard is burying his head in the sand. It was a serious failure of judgement last year not to take a strong stand against Ms Hanson and her brand of politics. It will be an even greater failure not to confront her and the threat she poses now.[8]

In an equally impassioned condemnation of the Hanson phenomenon, commentator and author, Paul Kelly, pointed out that Hanson was not essentially important in her own right. It was what she represented that was the key. Critically, Kelly said:

> Hanson symbolises an alienation within part of the community caused by a conjunction of forces—globalisation, economic restructuring and social changes—where people need scapegoats to explain their frustration.[9]

Here was perhaps the most important observation that had been made about the Pauline Hanson roadshow. Here was the core of the problem. In his book *The End of Certainty*, Kelly described the processes of revolutionary global economic change that were irresistible, that a country like Australia could not hope to deny. Now he was linking Hanson to that economic awakening. The implication was that globalisation had caused such social unease that the preconditions for the arrival of such a politician were in place. But it was left to others, including Cheryl Kernot, to take the next step—to ask some tough questions about the nexus, to not simply let it rest there. She noted the views of Ross Fitzgerald, the Associate Professor of History and Politics at Griffith University who tellingly probed this nexus. Fitzgerald argued that those attracted to the Hanson message were not all bigots, racists and anti-social conspiracy theorists. They were also ordinary people battered by the economic gale of the 1980s and 1990s:

> The underlying reason Hanson's perceived attacks on Aborigines and Asians are having such resonance is the devastating impact that economic upheaval, orchestrated by recent governments on both sides, is having on so many ordinary Australians. This especially applies to those who historically have been blue-collar workers and the small-scale self-employed, especially outside, or, on the margins of, the big metropolitan areas.[10]

Fitzgerald argued that it was no surprise that Hanson hailed from Ipswich, a once-proud provincial city, now hit by structural unemployment. This was because two region-sustaining industries—coal mining and the railways—had been destroyed through a combination of technological change and 'inept' government policy. Hanson was simply articulating the 'unease, fears and the sense of disenfranchisement' held by many people in the area.

> Unlike most members of the bourgeoisie and the intelligentsia, they are not insulated against the effects of random violence and vandalism, and the increasing emergence in some country towns of actual 'no-go' areas. Those who live on the margins of subsistence often object to the ways in which their tax money is too often wasted. Moreover, their tolerance limits have been tested in ways that many middle-class urban dwellers have largely avoided. More importantly, the effects of economic rationalism and of so-called 'free trade' policies have been disastrous. To many of Hanson's wider constituency, unskilled migrants are as much a threat as economic reforms and widespread technological change. The erosion of our manufacturing base following the lowering of tariff barriers has resulted in huge job losses. It is not surprising that many of the long-term unemployed—and those in work who fear both retrenchment and their inability to handle rapid economic change—seek scapegoats.[11]

Thanks to the absurd conspiracy between the major parties in Canberra, discussion about the impact of free trade was off the agenda. This 'virtual silence' was 'baffling'. The street kids of Ipswich were a potent symbol of the rage and alienation that a lot of Australians were feeling. 'However crude and ignorant her methods, Pauline Hanson is their messenger,' Fitzgerald concluded.[12]

Amid speculation that Hanson would ditch her seat and set up Senate tickets to run in each State, thus taking her into direct competition with the Democrats, the Howard government finally acknowledged the seriousness of the situation by agreeing to join the Opposition to pass a bipartisan parliamentary motion denouncing racial intolerance and reaffirming the right of all Australians to be treated with equal respect irrespective of their race, colour, creed or origin. There was some criticism that the government had insisted on taking the word 'multiculturalism' out of the the proposed wording. Moving the motion, Howard said it was designed simply to send a signal, particularly to the Asian region, about what kind of society Australia was. 'It is put forward to this parliament by the government, and I trust by the Opposition, not in any sense of apology ... but as a simple, direct and unambiguous statement of certain common values and principles.'[13]

Speaking in the Senate, Kernot said the motion was necessary because the debate had been 'absolutely spiralling out of control' and because of the immense damage being done to the nation. Kernot pointed out that in the other chamber Howard was asserting his own core personal belief that Australia was too apologetic about its past and far too self-conscious about its achievements.

'How ironic that many other countries in the world consider our success in multiculturalism to be one of our achievements? But we're not allowed to talk about our past,' she said. Leadership, she added, was incredibly import-ant. It created understanding. But lack of it allowed people's fears to be exploited. The core failure of leadership, she asserted, lay in the mismanage-ment of the pace of economic change and in the absence of an articulate explanation of the reasons for that change. And that was a result of the economic rationalist policies of the previous decade. This was why people felt so insecure about the future, she said. 'But it doesn't mean that they are excused in taking refuge in ignorance and racism.'[14]

In early 1997, Kernot recalled how disturbed she was at the time when Sian and her friends had been told to 'get back where you come from' in a city street in open daylight. A Vietnamese couple buying petrol in a Gold Coast service station were also attacked at around that time. 'Now, in all her life, my daughter had never seen that. All these latent, tribal fears were stirred and when times are tough, it's easy to blame others. There is massive anxiety out there and all this is a manifestation of that. It's a cry from the heart. Now, some people have said that Pauline Hanson has been worth it because it has been a cry from the heart about the anxiety, drawing attention to the fact of our fears. But you should never validate racism. There have been too many Aboriginal and migrant people hurt by this. The cry from the heart has been very long. And very vicious as well.'

The arrival of the Hanson phenomenon coincided with the release of the report of the Human Rights and Equal Opportunities Commission inquiry into the government policy of forced removal of thousands of Aboriginal children from their natural parents and their 'assimilation' into white homes in the 1950s and 1960s. Called *Bringing Them Home*, the report would expose both the insensitivity and the strategic judgement shortcomings of the Howard government. In early and mid-1996, both Howard and his minister, John Herron, expressed either reservations about the need for such an inquiry or were equivocal about the true meaning of its findings. For a long time, it was argued that there was no way that a government could contemplate any kind of formal apology because it could be seen as an admission of liability and expose the taxpayer to the prospect of compensation claims. By mid-1997 Howard was still telling the Liberal party room in Canberra that the electorate did not believe in 'intergenerational guilt'.

'Some of the past practices, although they might be condemned now, were done with the best motives and intentions and many people were in fact cared for in warm and loving homes,' he said.[15] Others, including Kernot, were far less conditional about their responses to the report.

In reading the often gut-wrenching accounts by some 600 witnesses of the forced removal of children from their families by government agencies, she was reduced to tears. It was estimated that tens of thousands of children were involved. But, most importantly, Kernot saw the myth perpetuated by Howard and Herron that what had been done in the past was not necessarily the responsibility of the present—that what's done can't be undone. For this report graphically breathed life into Kernot's core claim about contemporary indigenous Australians: that their suffering and failings were products of the past and that there was cause and effect that mitigated the inadequacies that some in white society saw in them. Basically, the report argued that Aboriginal people today were living out, in so many ways, the tragic impact of what was done to them as children. It was estimated that every Aboriginal family had been affected in some way by a process in which social workers had taken some children, screaming, from the arms of their mothers. Forty-three of the ninety-three deaths investigated by the 1991 Royal Commission into Aboriginal Deaths in Custody were found to have involved people separated from their families as children.

John Howard's core claim was that apologies about the past could achieve little—that the important thing was to get the nuts and bolts of policy right today, to ease the plight of black Australia. The argument just did not wash, however, when he thumped the podium in asserting it at the three-day-long Reconciliation Convention convened under the auspices of the Council for Reconciliation on May 27, 1997. Reconciliation would not work, Howard said, if it was premised solely on a sense of national guilt and shame.

Our purpose in acknowledging history should not be to apportion blame and guilt for past wrongs but to commit to a practical program of action that will remove the enduring legacies of disadvantage,

he said. Australians of this generation should not be expected to cop the blame for policies over which they had no control. This was the gathering at which Aboriginal members of the audience rose in their chairs and turned their back on the PM as he spoke. It was also the one at which Cheryl Kernot chose to take the big step, and publicly apologise to Aboriginal Australia for the wrongs of the past.

In her speech to the 1800-strong audience, Kernot said Australia was at the crossroads in indigenous policy-making.

Recent events have shown us how easy it is to derail the path of reconciliation with fear and racism; how easy it is to resort to scape-goating behind the rhetoric of accountability. But we're here today in hope—hope that we can prevent fears and lies and bigotry from holding us back from a mature and responsible future.

Reconciliation, she said, was undermined when rights were taken away. It was devalued by assertions that pastoralists' rights were sacrosanct but indigenous rights were not. Reconciliation was about understanding the causes of disadvantage, the reasons for the high Aboriginal imprisonment rates and juvenile crime rates, the alcoholism, the unemployment, the dys-functional families. It was about having the maturity to own our history, the honesty to deal with the past.

You don't have to wallow in guilt or black armbands to accept that past wrongs were committed against Australia's indigenous people and to acknowledge that the plight of indigenous people today is a consequence of that history.

From acknowledgement, comes learning, the wisdom not to repeat the mistakes. 'It's not hard to say you're sorry,' Kernot told the massive audience.

Isn't that what we teach our children? The ability to apologise is a sign of emotional maturity. And we need that maturity in Australia today. There are a lot of things we should apologise for. But on behalf of many Australians, in a spirit of reconciliation and owning and learning from our real history, I take this opportunity to apologise for the past policy of stealing Aboriginal children from their parents. I apologise for the pain and trauma inflicted on an entire generation of indigenous Australians and their families. I apologise for the way in which this injustice has been ignored in the past, and I apologise for the way in which some are sliding around it at the present. And apology is not about money. It's about healing. I hope indigenous Australians can find it in their hearts to forgive us for the mistakes so that we can move forward from this point.

Thirty years after the historic referendum of 1967 [Aboriginal enfranchisement], it is important to recognise what's at stake for our nation. We have an important choice to make, a clear, stark and nation-defining choice: either we take a real shot at a harmonious, inclusive and fair society, or we become a totally divided one with inherent racial tension and protracted court actions. That will not be a comfortable and relaxed Australia.

22
THE DILEMMA

For a long time it was clear to a lot of good judges of Australian politics that Cheryl Kernot was wasted as leader of a minor party. From all sorts of vantage points in the system, people could see she was a natural. Sam Hudson, who did so much to assist her rise and was devastated by her defection, always believed that one of the secrets to Kernot's appeal was that while she undoubtedly had charisma, she also looked as if she was one of the people. Hudson would often say privately that unlike other politicians, Kernot somehow conveyed the impression that she would never lord it over ordinary folk. When they worked together, Hudson's view was that Kernot never evinced a longing for power for its own sake, but did genuinely seem to want to make the world a better place. Perhaps Hudson's view would be altered as time put the defection, and the question of Kernot's motives, into a wider perspective. But given her unique vantage point, the Democrats' National Secretary was never particularly surprised by the speed of Kernot's rise.

'There was always something there, that indefinable "it",' she once told a friend. 'You know, in whatever area some people have got it … whether it's fashion sense or whatever. In politics Cheryl had "it", although I don't know exactly what "it" is and I don't know anybody who does know. I wasn't surprised when she did as well as she did; when she started in the Democrats, she was always the one to come through. It just happened because it was so natural.'

Politics being politics, of course, Cheryl Kernot made her enemies. Don Chipp, John Coulter and Janet Powell were antagonistic. With the defection, disgruntled Democrats would forever see her as a traitor. Her detractors in the corporate community and some influential writers in the business media were contemptuous. In the main, the Coalition had always violently opposed her on policy but some Liberals became incandescent with anger after the defection. And whatever the post-defection chumminess, back in the early 1990s there were those on the Labor side, too, who resented her success. Before she shifted, MPs on both sides would often complain that it was fine for Kernot to waltz around the place, all precious and sanctimonious when, from her exotic perch in the upper house, she would never have to face the tough decisions of government or mainstream Opposition. That criticism, at least, hit the rocks in October 1997.

Out in the electorate, however, Kernot had a dazzling impact as Democrat Leader. And a great many political players who had contact with her recognised the chemistry at work. Few were not intrigued by her political style. Rod Cameron, the boss of Australian National Opinion Polls (ANOP) and former ALP pollster, developed an extraordinary view of Kernot's political potency even while she was still a Democrat. He believed she was one of a tiny band of genuinely charismatic politicians, the kind of leader that came along very, very rarely. Cameron said that in his twenty-five years in politics he had never seen a leader able to sustain credibility as long as Kernot had managed with the Democrats. His description of her got enormous airplay in the immediate wake of the defection, but he made these same points in an interview back in early 1997: 'If you gather all of the characteristics that a political leader needs in this country in terms of credibility, how well they sound, perceptions of their strength, their basic goodness and worth as human beings and consistency ... and put them all in the computer and tell it to produce the identikit of *the* perfect, contemporary politician—out would pop Cheryl Kernot.'[1]

But what precisely was it about Kernot that explained her appeal? Cameron was expansive: 'The people want strength, not macho strength, strength of conviction and consistency: inner strength. She gives the impression she has got that. She looks and sounds good. They don't want a film star but she has just the right combination of good looks without being glamorous. She is the right gender. She looks and sounds good on television. She is good at handling the media in whatever context she finds herself— either a longer, more verbose interview with print where she can expand an argument or the TV thirty-second grab. She is the right balance between arrogance and passivity. She is just where the electorate likes to see politicians—strong enough to be seen to be dominating her party but not perceived as arrogant. This thing called charisma is a bit overplayed, but she has enough of it. But perhaps most importantly, she is seen as not just a political animal. She has other well-publicised outside interests. She is not dominated by Canberra. She gives the impression of understanding ordinary Australians. And she has been there long enough to be recognised and not be a flash in the pan. Her other attribute is her intelligence, [she's] a genuinely bright person and the electorate sees that. She is nice, but not so nice as to be weak and lily-livered. A nice person but strong. She is absolutely one out of the box. She is a real political leader and is perceived as such. Now, that just doesn't happen that often.'[2]

Another who saw her as wasted with the Democrats, social scientist Hugh Mackay, developed the view a long time before the defection that in the light of the ALP's activities in the 1980s, some people came to see Kernot as 'more legitimately Labor than Labor': 'It's as though her heart was really with the Labor Party but it was a pragmatic decision to go into the Democrats. After the 1996 election there was this quite widespread belief that she was the de facto Opposition Leader in that Kim Beazley had not yet fulfilled the brightest expectations of him. There was this sense that Kernot was the feisty one, focused, with a position, in genuine opposition to the government, and yet, at the same time, was more reasonable, open to negotiation, as the talks with Peter Reith over IR showed.'[3]

Here, said Mackay, was a politician mature enough to pull no punches when the occasion demanded, yet willing to sit down and negotiate through to a solution. His research in the early and mid-1990s suggested the Kernot 'look', her physical image, the way she presented was a huge positive with voters. As Democrat Leader there had begun to be a suggestion that while she sounded 'sort of "mother Kernot", mother knows best, all confident and reasonable', some people could tire of the judgemental voice. But the key to Kernot's appeal, says Mackay, was never the way she looked, but in what she said: 'A lot of people do like the look of her in a motherly way. There is something really comforting about her. She is blessed with the eyes and mouth and figure that add up to making her an appealing figure. But, underneath it, she talks in the way that people say they wish politicians would talk. That is, she sounds as if she is trying to express things in ways that everybody can understand. She tries to avoid economic jargon and expresses great impatience when it is used by the major parties. She wants to explain things and understand things the way the rest of us might want it. She asks questions that seem reasonable. She tends to remain unruffled. She doesn't go red in the face or do her block and shout. And she does seem quite gently to expose hypocrisy and say what many people think about the system and its players.'[4]

In the lead-up to the 1996 election, Mackay interviewed the leaders of the four parties as part of an in-depth series for the *Australian* newspaper. The one with Kernot was by far the longest and most comprehensive of any of the leaders and Mackay was impressed by her 'clarity of views' as well as her 'absolute openness'. She was organised, set aside plenty of time, and seemed completely at ease that he would represent her views accurately: 'At various points in that conversation it was quite hard to believe that she was a senior political figure. Because senior political figures tend to be too care-ful, defensive. You can almost see them thinking that this is how what they are saying is going to appear in print. And if they are going to relax they will want to turn off the tape. None of that with her. Open. And personally warm, prepared to talk about personal life, her own tragedies.'[5]

All sorts of people who have worked closely with Kernot reflect glowingly on her powers. But Rick Farley, the former Farmers' Federation boss who helped craft the strategies in Aboriginal affairs—Mabo and reconciliation—is particularly incisive. Farley says that because the cameras 'love' her, it is easy to underestimate Kernot. 'She seems reasonable—she can see both sides of the argument and so on, but underneath she is steel. On one hand, she is a really nice person yet she has this very tough political mind. She is reasonable but then, when the situation demands, she won't take a backward step. That's the dichotomy. She stays calm. She's like everyone's Mum yet she has this steely political core. I think primarily she is motivated by trying to make the country a better place but, equally, she knows you can't do that without exercising political power. As she goes along, she becomes more adept at exercising power. She will never make the same mistake twice.'[6]

One of the strategic difficulties for the Howard government in tackling the defection was the fact that over the years members of the Coalition, too, had tried to talk Kernot into making the shift to them. There were all sorts of whispers in her ear about how wasted she was and how great it would be if she came over. In 1994, at a lunch with Malcolm Turnbull, the prominent merchant banker and chairman of the Keating government's Republican Advisory Committee, Kernot did discuss the possibility of the Democrats evolving into a broader, socially progressive, pro-business political party, in response to the crisis of confidence then splitting the Liberals. But earlier that year she sent some Coalition people into a rage when she mentioned in a magazine article that three Liberal moderates had suggested privately they might actually join *her* party out of frustration with all the infighting behind John Hewson's back. Although she took the remarks of the MPs to be 'the smallest sign of interest', Kernot suffered the wrath of senior Liberals, with some leaping in to say the suggestion was 'utter crap', and others saying she was either a liar, 'prone to exaggeration' or having a joke. But she lost count of the number of times political figures, their spouses, staff or friends mentioned how they wished she was part of their operations. Liberals had talked in these terms but knowing how damaging it would be for them to be named, Kernot steadfastly refused to do so. The real action lay, however, in the overtures quietly made from Labor, the moves to court Kernot that culminated on 15 October, 1997.

The genesis of this extraordinary decision lay in the intriguing coincidence of three separate conversations with three powerful players in the Labor constellation, beginning in late 1994. The first arose after a clash between Kernot and John Coulter in the Democrat party room over strategic direction. She was still steamed up about it as she walked through one of the big internal courtyards of Parliament House late that evening. She was heading to the Great Hall, where the government was hosting a diplomatic reception. On her way, Kernot bumped into the influential ALP right wing factional boss and senior minister Robert Ray, who was heading to the dinner too. A huge man of swarthy complexion and dark hair with, for years, a tobacco connoisseur's love of the pipe, Ray was one of the genuine heavy-hitters of modern Labor, running the right wing faction's numbers in Victoria and heavily influencing much else in the management of the party nationally.

'God, I hate these functions,' he said as he and Kernot walked along together.

'I do, too. We must be anti-social,' Kernot joked. She began to reflect on her tough day, lamenting how hard it can be as a leader dealing with diverse personalities. Ray observed that one of the hardest things in politics was actually dealing with people in your own party, adding that it must be particularly difficult in a small party room like the Democrats.

'Yeah, sometimes it makes me feel like asking somebody like you whether you've got a spare safe seat,' Kernot joked. Ray laughed and, just then, Prime Minister Keating and Foreign Minister Gareth Evans came into view walking towards the reception hall with a group of foreign dignitaries. To avoid being dragged into the formalities, the two tired politicians darted sideways down the corridor to find another entrance to the function room.

The next day, Kernot was walking across the red carpet of the Senate chamber, heading for one of the many exits, when her path crossed that of Ray. As he strolled past, he whispered out of the corner of his mouth, with that typical Robert Ray poker-face: 'I've found the seat', before continuing on, and out. For a moment Kernot was nonplussed, having forgotten her throwaway remark of the previous day, but when she mused on it, she felt flattered that a Labor man of Ray's seniority would have reacted in that way. Little did Cheryl Kernot know that in that moment, her journey into the Labor Party had begun.

Quite independent of this innocent incident, a few days later, Gareth Evans, government leader in the chamber, rang Kernot with a list of important Senate agenda matters that needed tending. They agreed to get out of the parliament building and work through the list over dinner elsewhere in Canberra. They chose the famous Lobby Restaurant near old Parliament House.

Recent opinion polls had suggested Kernot and her Democrats were going very well. At one point Evans changed tack from the Senate agenda discussion. 'Cheryl, you're really very good at what you do. You stand out from the others. That's clear to everyone. Do you ever wonder whether you'd rather be sitting on the front benches?'

'What do you mean by that?' she asked.

'Does it never occur to you that maybe you could have a ministry in a Labor government, actually implementing the things you believe in? Running a department, having the satisfaction of actually doing things?' Snapping his fingers, Evans said: 'I'm certain that if you were at all interested in joining the Labor Party, we would give you a ministry like that.'

Kernot said no-one had ever suggested that to her before and that it was a bit unbelievable. How could anyone, even in his position, talk about delivering something like that? 'I must say, though, sometimes I do wonder what it would be like to be in a position to get more done,' she said.

'Well, you should think about it,' Evans urged. Quite independent of the first, and born in an equally casual thought, the second point of contact had been made. The third involved the key left wing powerbroker, Senator John Faulkner from NSW, who had developed a very high regard for Kernot watching her work in the Senate.

Kernot was in the habit of pulling a pair of jogging shoes on and going for long walks around Capital Hill to clear her head from the pressures of the day, as well as get some exercise. Sometimes she walked with Democrat colleagues and staff, Labor and Liberal MPs for business or just social chats, and occasionally with journalists. One of her regular companions became Faulkner. In September, 1994, the pair went out on a particularly long walk, tracking down off Capital Hill towards the nearby suburb of Manuka. It was around 8.30 pm, a cool Canberra evening, and the walk would last an hour-and-a-half. They had not long left the Hill and were tramping over the grass near the Department of Foreign Affairs building when Faulkner said there was something special he wanted to mention to her. He said private ALP research showed she was the most respected national political figure, far and away. He said that from what he could see, she was a mainstream leftist thinker and could slot easily into the ALP. Had she ever thought seriously about coming over, to be an ALP senator? Once again, Kernot was somewhat stunned that yet another such senior Labor person had raised this with her. Again she evinced scepticism, arguing that even if there were no ideological obstacles, there would certainly be problems moving from one political culture to another.

Robert Ray, Gareth Evans and John Faulkner were smart enough to know that here was a relatively green politician but one with enormous potential. While the matter would not, at that time, be pushed hard, the question of Kernot's future would periodically be raised with her in a light-hearted way or in jest by the Labor people, particularly Evans. This was a period when Kernot was having a lot of contact with them, by dint of her balance of power work. She told them clearly, however, that while she was flattered, she had a job to do getting the Democrats back on the rails at the 1996 election. She believed she effectively had a contract with her party to try to get as many senators elected as possible and preserve that balance of power role. It was her commitment and she would not alter course. The matter then lapsed, pushed on to the backburner—that is, until everything was changed by Kernot's views on the raw, at times erratic, politics of the Howard administration.

By the middle of 1997, the concerns which began to develop soon after the government came in led Kernot to despair of her ability to continue as Democrat Leader. And as Evans and Faulkner sensed this deepening frustration and reported it back, the Labor heavyweights were talking among themselves, in high secrecy but quite seriously now, about the possibility of a party switch. Carefully, the 'loop' which included ALP National Secretary Gary Gray, was gently widened to test more opinion. Gray took discreet soundings about Kernot's appeal, trying to factor her into party research without alerting anyone. Amid tight security, attention began to turn to the factional lay-out of various Reps seats in NSW, Victoria and Queensland. When the idea was thought to be sufficiently advanced, the powerbrokers took it to Kim Beazley. He and his Chief of Staff, David Epstein, realised that with Wayne Goss, a Kernot candidacy held out the prospect of important wins in seats in Queensland.

The fact is, that by sometime in the middle of 1997, a seismic change in the political life of Cheryl Kernot became inevitable. Earlier that year there was a period when she seriously contemplated the other option—leaving politics altogether. She had reluctantly concluded one thing—she could not see herself leading the Democrats to another election as the party 'in the middle'. She had run out of steam for that task, so angry was she about Coalition politics. Various Labor players began saying a move to Labor would be potentially a huge circuit-breaker, but she still had her doubts. She knew how rough it would be, how big a target she would become. Was it worth it? she asked herself. Perhaps the best option was to get out altogether? But then, the politician's ambitious streak reasserted itself. She began to wonder if a move to Labor *would* provide a way to help put things right. She began to sense that if she did do it, and had a chance to fully explain her reasons to people, they would accept her in good faith. For she became passionately sure that the horror she felt in the direction of national policy-making was felt just as deeply out in the electorate. She figured people would really relate to the reason why she was pushed to the move.

She concluded that if she was to achieve more in politics, this was the way to do it, despite the risks.

By September, 1997, Kernot realised she had to make a decision one way or another. To Labor or out. The die was cast when she attended a meeting convened in John Faulkner's Parliament House office with Kim Beazley, Gareth Evans and Faulkner on Wednesday, October 1. Over what was to become a famous plunger of coffee, the deal was sealed. But the scene was set for that meeting at another one, two days before on September 29, in Beazley's office. In attendance were Beazley, Robert Ray, Gareth Evans, John Faulkner and David Epstein. There Faulkner spoke first, pointing out there was a threshold question for all of them to finally resolve: was it in Labor's interests to take Kernot into the fold? Basically, they all agreed it was; some of them saying they had never swayed from the idea that it would be a dynamic development. They talked of how she would have to be found a spot on the front bench, and how consideration would have to be given to the role she would play if she was out of the parliament until the election. Then on the Wednesday night, the Labor consensus was explained to Kernot. They had thought it all through and concluded that a switch was 'do-able'. Kernot's chief concern was how the government would attack the Democrats. While no-one stood up and made any bold statements, by around 7.30 that night it was clear to everyone in the room it was really on. No-one was jubilant. They all knew a traumatic time lay ahead for the woman who, from that moment, essentially ceased being Democrat Leader.

While it should not be overstated, it is possible to argue that Cheryl Kernot did not go to the Labor Party—the Labor Party came to her. Or at least the position in public policy that she had sketched out. She became terribly disillusioned with the Coalition but she was also heartened by Labor's gradual change in policy direction. Some of the private letters Kernot received as Democrat Leader bear out Hugh Mackay's thesis that for a long time before she joined the ALP, she had effectively represented Labor views to a lot of people. There was one dignified message from a Queensland pensioner who had, ironically enough, somehow gained the impression Kernot could be leaving politics. He spoke of how devastated so many people would be if she did leave.

Please be assured that many Australians are impressed by your integrity, your sense of fairness, your refusal to be bullied, your clarity when expressing an opinion, when debating or during a media interview and they are touched by your sincerity. How you manage to do all that and still keep smiling is quite beyond me but I do know that Australia's political life would be impoverished without you. I should say that I have been a Labor voter all my life, so you have had to earn respect, as it were, and this you have achieved handsomely. Incredibly, this must be unique in this country—I have never heard anyone say a word against you. However, I am sure you have, so next time it starts getting tough, please remember this letter. Finally, no, I'm not a starry-eyed teenager. I'm sixty-two, and I simply want you to know that you are doing a fine job.[7]

Then, there was a letter from another old fellow who would not consider himself a starry-eyed youngster either—the former Whitlam government minister and Labor traditionalist, Clyde Cameron. He was prompted to write in 1993 by an impressive television interview Kernot had with Laurie Oakes. It saddened him to meet so many lifelong supporters of the ALP who saw the Democrats as closer to the party to which they once gave their unquestioned loyalty. Cameron wrote:

What hurts me most is to find ordinary working people saying that what has passed for a 'Labor' government over the past ten years went further to the right than the Liberal governments of Menzies, Gorton or even Fraser.[8]

When he challenged them, Cameron said, they pointed out that 'old-time Tories' would never have sold Qantas, Australian Airlines or the 'people's bank', the Commonwealth. Labor people resented the way a Labor government deregulated the financial system and 'handed control of the exchange rate of the dollar to the manipulators of the international money markets'. They were angry about tax breaks for the corporate sector and the antics of tax-dodging high income groups, while their wages were driven down and only offset by minor tax relief. The poor had not benefited from dividend imputation or negative gearing but had lost ground as the tax-free threshold was not indexed. He said it was odd that senior members of the ALP had been showering Kernot with praise for her stances.

> I'm too old and too biased to ever vote against the Labor Party but it does sadden me to find so many of my lifelong Labor friends now saying that Cheryl Kernot and the Democrats are nearer to the principles preached and practiced by Ben Chifley and the Labor party of yesteryear than what passes for Labor now. I hope your pleasure in receiving this matches my sadness in feeling obliged to write it.[9]

If she was more Labor than Labor in the early 1990s, it would still take a great deal to convince Cheryl Kernot of the need to walk away from seventeen years of work. The trigger was the chasmic apprehension she developed about the Howard government, evolving against a background of growing frustration. Those frustrations gathered strength through late 1996 and into 1997. As Kernot said in her defection statement, she was never a politician intent on time-serving. If she perceived she was not making the kind of contribution she valued, then her mind would turn to other things. The fact is, she was becoming bored, restless for a new challenge. After something like seven years in parliament, she was struggling to resolve in her own mind some tough questions about the Democrats and her position as Leader. In some ways she was a prisoner of her own success.

A vibrant figurehead, everything turned on her activities. When the party needed a lift, it was for her to provide. One of the contradictions of Kernot was that she coveted success yet, in some ways, the spotlight made her uneasy. She was irritated that so much rested on her shoulders and she tried to provide other Democrat MPs with resources to help lift their profiles. Her success had, in a sense, made the job more demanding. Media interview requests were unceasing. She found it hard to maintain the balance between her private and public lives. Having dealt with governments of both persuasions, she began to struggle with the constrictions of the role as arbiter, conscience, paragon of fairness and propriety. She had never set out to cultivate this 'St Cheryl' image—she reckoned she had just reacted to political circumstances as they arose. Apart from anything else, Kernot was always uncomfortable with the image of her as 'goody-two-shoes', and the moral sanctimony it suggested.

During the 1996 election campaign, a shop in the Queensland town of Maryborough refused to hang a Democrat sign in the window because the 'Keep The Bastards Honest' slogan would give offence. Later, Kernot was canvassing in a Cairns shopping centre, when a local woman was introduced, and snapped: 'Hello, pleased to meet you. But I don't like you using that slogan about bastards on television! It sets a bad example for my son.' Kernot was momentarily set back, till the woman's eighty-year-old mother piped up:

'Oh, it doesn't worry me. I like you. Good on you. Keep doing a great job.'

Kernot remembers: 'I thought "Hallelujah!" when the older woman interrupted. But it was also interesting that I got a bit of criticism on radio during the campaign about the slogan. A couple of women rang in and it started a debate about whether Cheryl Kernot should say "bastards". People were suggesting I sounded uncomfortable saying it. I was a bit annoyed because it was this kind of reverse sexism that a woman shouldn't be able to say things like that. But I hate being seen as on a pedestal. I loathe it because I'm not a goody-two-shoes and I never want to be. I have the same drives, flaws and failings as anyone. I don't like a political system that puts women on pedestals. I've had to fight this, saying it in interviews all around the country for years.

'When the Carmen Lawrence thing was on, and she said women get judged more harshly, my reaction was that she was wrong, that we are politicians, and we are judged by our actions. I've never identified with the women-as-victims school. Some people *have* been discriminated against and victimised. But to frame a whole response to policy based on the premise that someone is a victim, is incredibly limiting. I'm very uncomfortable with it. I hate judgemental people. I hate judgemental Christianity. I hate clap-trap and hypocrisy. So I'm the worst candidate to be placed on a pedestal and called goody-two-shoes. I understand human failure ... I mean, look at my brother. You have to understand human fallibility. Most of the people I've ever come across who are incredibly sanctimonious with the poker up their bum are deeply repressed, I reckon.'

Kernot was also increasingly irritated that the Democrats were seen as the 'goody-two-shoes' party. She felt it wasn't enough for a party to be positioned thus. She wanted to have a go more often, but felt held back by her advisers. She wanted more than the 'Keep The Bastards Honest' raison d'etre, urging the party on to inject ideas into the national debate. While she was seen as a powerful figure, she was often frustrated that her power was, in fact, quite limited. She wanted to do more. Against this backdrop, she reached something of a watershed at the Australian Democrats' twentieth anniversary conference, staged at the Australian National University in early 1997. There she found the words of Ken Carty, the Canadian expert on third parties, compelling. For many of the participants the two days of talk in the end were condensed into a key conclusion—the critical one, long held by Chipp—that it was pointless for the Democrats to mount a major campaign to try to break into the Reps. In celebrating its own longevity, the party too seemed to have become a prisoner of its success.

Ken Carty argued Australia had long underestimated the Democrat achievement. The party had contributed to the creation of this unique 'twin-layered' election system which people well understood. It should be happy with that. It did not need to be a big player in the Reps to have an ongoing and significant role. While the Democrats had clearly shown it was possible to challenge the established patterns of political organisation, they would probably never attract mass support. The 'closed' systems of the major parties would only ever be changed when those parties decided to do so themselves. But Carty said it was inappropriate to judge all parties by the same standards:

> The Australian Democrats have their own distinctive niche in electoral politics and they ought to be judged in terms of how well they fill it, not some generalised notion of what is expected of parties in a Westminster system. The failure of pundits—but not voters—to appreciate this surely accounts for why so many predictions of the Democrats' imminent demise have been foiled. At the same time, this is also a cautionary lesson for those in the party who think they ought to ape the forms and activities of the larger parties. The British Social Democrat Party provides an example of the dangers of that path and a reminder of just how much the Democrats owe to the political life of the Senate.[10]

Answering questions from delegates, Carty said explicitly it was unlikely the Democrats could ever become a force in the Reps.

It is difficult to break into, and break up, the kind of House system where it is a winner-take-all system. In fact, there really are no such cases, I think you can say, where that has happened. Some would argue that the Labour Party in Britain was a case, but in fact that was a kind of generational replacement thing where Labour came to replace the Liberal Party. In fact, there is probably no comparative case in a plurality or majority electoral system where a new party has come along and simply replaced one of the two major parties and become a kind of alternative. It hasn't happened yet. The system seems so brutal and loaded against it.[11]

Unless a way could be found to change the voting system, the Democrats just had to accept life as a Senate-bound party. For Cheryl Kernot, the message was clear. Despite the urgings of some in the party for her to think about an assault on the Reps, Carty reinforced her suspicions. Perhaps, she thought, in the long term the Democrats may become a viable lower house player, smashing the two-party nexus. But that would probably not happen in her time in politics. If she ran for a Reps seat as a Democrat, the major parties would surely gang up and use dirty tricks or the preference system to stop her, as they did with Haines. And even if she got into the Reps, how would the dynamic of the party room then work, with the leader of a balance of power group not even in the chamber where the balance of power equation is fought out?

As the months of 1997 wore on, other factors were bearing on Kernot's thinking. Labor was beginning its historic policy shift to the left, away from the Keating doctrine. A major analysis was underway under the leadership of Gareth Evans, looking at the mistakes of the Hawke/Keating period, focusing on the elements from that period to be taken forward and developed and looking to contemporary developments elsewhere around the world. In talking to the Labor people she could see this shift in thinking. She was taking her own soundings, trying to determine if it was real, or just propaganda for a dispirited tribe. But even in the face of all this, the defection— a decision of such moment—still required a catalyst. And, by his actions, words and approach, John Howard finally provided it. He produced the critical mass of disquiet in Kernot's mind.

An interview she gave in Canberra in mid-1997 gives hint of the depth of her feelings. She was asked if she believed in God and she said that while it might seem a funny thing to say, the change in government had presented her with something of a test of faith. 1997 was the first year in which she did not attend the church service for the opening of parliament. And she had stopped going to Parliamentary Christian Fellowship meetings. She said she couldn't stand the hypocrisy of people who put in place policies that hit the vulnerable and then turned up in church, as if they could be divorced from the consequences of their decisions.

While she had always believed in the teachings of Christ, she feared Canberra had made her into a bit of an agnostic. She was finding it hard to reconcile her belief in the Christian doctrine with what was being done 'in the name of economics'. Her concern about the Coalition government's approach was that it was 'economics over community, no matter what'.

'Isn't there a fundamental contradiction between saying family values are so important while having no compunction about destroying the bonds that hold communities together? It's hypocrisy. Now, Labor did start this, but at least they had social policy areas that saved them—like in Aboriginal affairs and welfare safety nets—and they're more socially progressive and less judgemental. But these people seem to just be into scapegoating. If it's not the blacks, it's public servants or unions or the ABC or the unemployed or migrants ... and this, after a campaign where John Howard said he was going to govern for all of us.' The arrogance in the worldview of some in the Coalition was troubling.

'The Liberals never seem to talk about the dignity of people's labour. It's all about wealth and the pursuit of individual ends. We need people to start saying that we are grateful for people's work effort. We need to say we are all making a contribution. If I see a migrant woman cleaning the toilets at the airport I go and thank her and tell her I appreciate her doing that work. People are just looked down on but government should be finding a way to speak to these people, to everyone, to make them feel that everybody's contribution counts. You don't have to pass laws—just say to people 'thank you' for everything they do. There is not enough leadership, not enough contact. Government doesn't use novel ways to talk to the people because of these silly rules ... like, if government says something on television, then the Opposition should automatically have equal time. The rules are stopping us doing what needs to be done.'[12]

23

AFTER THE DEFECTION

The most compelling image of the first hours after Kernot's defection to Labor on October 15, 1997, was the poignant newspaper photograph of her walking away from the press conference along a Parliament House corridor alone, but for David Epstein, the Labor apparatchik, at her side. This was a political event of electrifying drama. Comparable in its impact to Paul Keating's coup against Bob Hawke in 1991, it had 'changed the map of Australian politics', according to the *Age* newspaper.[1] Kernot walked down that corridor, not back to her old Democrat office but into the arms of the Labor Party leadership on the Reps side of the building. Cruelly, her fax communications to her ex-party colleagues would bear the inscriptions of Labor offices.

It would fall to Epstein, Beazley's Chief of Staff, to organise the removal of her personal effects from her old office. Resigned as a member of parliament, entitlements like transport, phone and support staff ceased. Thereafter, she would be Ms Cheryl Kernot, citizen, in the building as a guest of Labor. It was a traumatic time, and never more so than when she returned to the telephone in an office made available to her inside the Labor suite to talk more widely to Democrats—enduring their venom, riding through their incredulity and fears. At one point, Kernot just had to get out of the building, walking quietly in the private courtyard adjacent to Beazley's office to compose herself.

Labor was jubilant. This was an extraordinary coup. Until that point, it was only a remote possibility that after only one term, the electorate would tip out the incumbent government, an unprecedented event. But, in the extravagant response to the defection, it became clear it would lift Kim Beazley up out of a trough and carry him appreciably closer to overturning

403

the Coalition's thumping forty-five-seat parliamentary majority. In the months before her announcement when she agonised over the right course, Kernot had drawn considerable comfort from evidence of the significant policy rethink underway inside the ALP under the guidance of Gareth Evans, the Shadow Treasurer. Without this, the switch would never have happened. In essence, the Labor Party was moving back to the left—on some policy fronts, to much the same position Kernot herself had occupied for seven years.

Labor's repositioning, first signalled in early 1997, culminated in the release of a brace of new policy ideas and a rewritten draft party platform at the end of the year, in advance of the 1998 ALP National Conference. In March, 1997, an incisive article in *Business Review Weekly* first proclaimed that Labor was 'burying' Keating's economic framework.[2] This was a seminal shift. Despite his association with the Hawke/Keating project as a senior economic minister, Beazley was encouraging Evans, Simon Crean and others in the construction of a new policy rationale, one far more aligned to traditional Labor precepts. Under Beazley's Labor, government would be 'intervening'—here, finally, they were not afraid to use the word—to help develop the nation's health services, education programs and regional areas of the country. Emerging in significant detail were Crean's long-time, firmly-held views about how government could be used to work with industry to help Australian companies grow. Some ten industries would be identified for 'strategic action plans' and incentives would be offered to attract foreign investors. Crean, one minister who, years before, had the guts to stand up to Keating on this, showed just how close his thinking was to Kernot's: 'We're embracing the notion that the community is more than just the marketplace—it's a society,' he said.[3]

With his background as Foreign Minister, Evans was tough-minded enough to know that Labor could not completely junk its past—it was locked into international deregulatory and free trade obligations. Yet there would be new conditions attached. In an automotive plant in Adelaide, Beazley and Crean unveiled plans for a freeze in the rate of tariff reduction in the car industry. Future Labor support for further cuts in protection would be conditional on Australia's trading partners doing the same. There would be specific free trade agreements with individual countries. Evans was also asserting that while the new Labor economic program would be produced within a tightly disciplined fiscal framework, the party was not going to be 'spooked' by financial markets.[4]

On IR, Labor began voicing reservations about the slide towards enterprise bargaining and promised a comprehensive rethink in office, including greater emphasis restored on the IRC and awards. Labor leaders began talking about the need to start building up depleted social infrastructure, particularly in the regions. There was a plan to use the $750 billion in superannuation funds to help sustain rural and regional businesses. The Howard government's 'gutting' of the public service would be reversed. There would be no further privatisation of Telstra and none of Australia Post. All this represented a clear break with Keating's intoxication with the market. A Beazley government would not be some throwback to drawbridge protectionism but the days were clearly gone when the market was seen as the sole arbiter of economic reason.[5] In all this, Labor was plugging into cutting-edge thinking elsewhere around the world. By the middle of 1997, for example, the World Bank, long one of the citadels of orthodox thinking, had produced a report which startlingly abandoned its long-running support for minimal government in favour of a new model—based on a strong and vigorous State. Suddenly, instead of an obsession with cutting essential services, the world was realising that an effective State—'clever government'—was the cornerstone of successful economies.[6] So much of this sat easily with the Kernot view. She was not just relaxed about the new Labor vision—she was positively excited by it.

Against the background of this repositioning, and developing her theme about the coming of a new politics, Beazley said the defection was a symbol that Labor was about renewal and new ideas—the things Australia would need for a new millennium. With opinion polls showing the defection was a turning point which pitchforked Labor ahead of the Coalition, ALP people shrugged off whatever discomfort they may have felt over the 'ratting' element. The Liberals attacked by pointing out that only months before, Labor itself had gone after Mal Colston. Labor retorted that it was rich for people like Peter Reith to be invoking Billy Hughes and Joe Lyons—both Labor figures whose defections had helped lay the groundwork for the modern Liberal-National Party Coalition. In the 1930s Joseph Aloysius Lyons, a former Labor Premier of Tasmania and Acting Federal Treasurer, resigned from the ALP and brought together anti-Labor forces to form the

United Australia Party (UAP), became UAP Prime Minister in 1932, and died in 1939, so heralding the arrival of Menzies. Hughes, a Labor Prime Minister, split with his party over conscription and his own fervently British views. He went on to govern as Nationalist Party leader, becoming a UAP minister in the 1930s and contesting the UAP leadership against Menzies on Lyons' death. Later Frank McManus, Jack Kane and others left the ALP to form the ultra-conservative Democratic Labor Party and keep Labor from power for a generation. Even Don Chipp, who defected from the Liberal Party to form the Democrats, started out a Labor supporter.

From the start, behind the scenes Beazley, Evans and other Labor figures were acutely sensitive to the pressures on Kernot. Labor hard-heads were astounded at the courage she had demonstrated. Within an hour of the defection she took a phone call from Bob Hawke who said she should not underestimate the importance for Australia of the step she had taken. She took a call from the General Secretary of the New Zealand Labour Party inviting her across the Tasman to attend its upcoming national conference. In the light of the extraordinary community reaction to the switch, media critics became muted. Soon Laurie Oakes was acknowledging Kernot had had to strike pre-emptively if she was to get her complex rationale across at the outset. She had handled the affair with 'extraordinary strength and calm' in what was essentially her 'coming out as a politician'.[7] Sitting with Kernot, Evans and others in his office over a cup of coffee just hours after the announcement, Beazley said he would ensure she got all the support she needed.

'Look, the fact is you may have helped us win the next election today, Cheryl,' he said. 'I understand what this required of you.'

Soon it would become conventional wisdom that the defection put Beazley on the map. And that was the case because from the start, and particularly behind the scenes when things got tough for her, he was supportive, generous, open-spirited. Beazley had a very relaxed view of the leadership question. He saw the Kernot magic as reinforcing, not as any kind of threat. It gave him the opportunity to restart things, to be remade. Kernot was not even going to be in the parliament until after the election. But, in arguing discordantly that Beazley lived in fear of his job because of her arrival, Howard and his ministers completely misunderstood the nature of the Labor man. ALP National Secretary, Gary Gray, was also a key player in helping Kernot settle into her new twin-roles, helping the policy review process and campaigning in marginal seats. The post-defection reaction was dramatic confirmation of his hope that this could be the circuit-breaker that put Labor back into the contest. He still knew how remote was the likelihood of coming back far enough to win in 1998. But when Kernot came over, party morale all around the country went sky-high. People were walking in off the streets to join up.

Amid the turmoil, Kernot herself was concerned at the hype. She genuinely had not expected the reaction. People were deaf to her protests that she was not some kind of messiah or miracle worker. With the Democrats she had long battled to temper the personality-cult stuff, often saying in interviews that she was a human being, with faults, just like everyone else. Now, she was reinforcing that at every turn. She didn't want to be on any pedestal. Her political opponents, however, did see her being feted. The community had given her a special place and, for the Liberals, that was very dangerous indeed. Somehow she had to be pulled down.

And so, like moths to a flame, figures in the Liberal Party were drawn to her so-called 'past'—her twenty-one-year-old relationship with Tony Sinclair. Even as the initial wave of hostility over the defection was being overtaken by the outpouring of support—one thousand letters and faxes and literally hundreds of phone calls—a subterranean campaign intent on destroying Cheryl Kernot was already underway. This knee-jerk reversion to the tactic of tawdry denigration was symptomatic of the panic inside conservative politics that the defection could become the catalyst that turned the Coalition dream of a long-running period back in power into a one-term puff of smoke. High stakes were involved here. Despite their massive parliamentary majority, conservative strategists saw as no longer remote the possibility that Howard could be a one-term PM. The defection had come towards the end of an appalling political year for him.

Just weeks before, a second wave of casualties had engulfed the ministry, triggering questions about the inherent capacity of this government. And of Howard's suitability as leader. The PM was forced to dispense with the services of Administrative Services Minister David Jull, Transport Minister John Sharp and Science Minister Peter McGauran in the 'travel rorts affair'. As well, he lost two of his own staffers, including his closest personal friend and all-important strategist, Graham Morris. The affair moved commentator

Paul Kelly to note in a front page article in the *Australian* that there had never been a 'bloodletting' like it:

> Not under Whitlam or Fraser or Hawke or Keating. It is Shakespearean more in its farce than its tragedy. But John Howard's resort to the sword guarantees that his own future performance has no margin for mistake ... Mr Howard leads a government that is staggering under its own incompetence ... This suggests a depth of political and administrative ineptitude that is generic rather than specific. It brings to a climax much of the private complaint from those who deal with this government—that it lacks either the process or the talent to master the issues.[8]

Labor's policy reposition posed an electoral threat. Its softer, nationalistic, more inclusive pitch contrasted to the harshness of Coalition decisions like cutting protection for the sugar industry. The Howard Cabinet was itself split over industry policy, basically because of seemingly intractable unemployment. Under pressure from the motor manufacturing industry, Howard had buckled in June, 1997, and accepted a four-year freeze on car tariff reductions from the year 2000 to 2004. The slowdown was a slap in the face for the Treasury line and a huge win for the pragmatic, electorally savvy Industry Minister, John Moore, who knew the government could not sustain further job losses. But the decision infuriated the economic orthodoxy. Writing in the *Australian*, Alan Wood talked of 'the very worst sort of mindless mercantilism' that put Australia's standing at risk in world free trade forums.[9]

Then, in September, Moore won Howard's support to override the orthodoxy once again and do the same for textiles, clothing and footwear. While the PM talked about how the decision was for 'job security', the orthodoxy frothed about his capitulation to opinion polls and the inability of his adviser Graham Morris and even the head of the Prime Minister's Department, Max Moore-Wilton, to 'really understand' the economic issues involved. But the sense of confusion in economic policy was not just reflected in the predictable flak from right wing economic opinion. What about the bush? The rationalists had prevailed on the National Party to accept lower protection for rural industries yet all farmers could see was despair for the sugar industry while politically-powerful metropolitan-based industries were being looked after. All sorts of special interest groups on the left were up in arms over budget cuts, like the extraordinary decisions over nursing home accommodation policy, which ultimately produced a Howard back-down. So the government was getting it from everywhere—the left, the right and the bush. And then there was the disturbing national row over native title.

Defiantly insisting his ten-point legislative plan was the appropriate response to the Wik High Court decision, John Howard entered election year 1998 apparently primed to use a race debate as the trigger for a double dissolution election. The Wik judgement galvanised a PM who basically believed the pendulum in black issues had 'swung too far' in favour of Aboriginal rights and had to be brought back. At the end of 1997, the government stood toe to toe, slugging it out with Aboriginal Australia, the ALP, the Senate, the churches, the liberal intelligentsia and even protesting arts and film industries over its central claim that without the ten-point plan, Wik meant large sections of Australia were vulnerable to takeover by blacks. Howard stood by while conservative politicians, rural groups and mining and pastoral bodies claimed even domestic backyards were not safe. This was despite the insistence of lawyers that the High Court had specifically ruled that grants of exclusive possession, such as freehold title, extinguished native title.

No less a figure than the Governor-General, Sir William Deane, said he would 'weep for our country' if the process of reconciliation between black and white was allowed to collapse. While he said he did not agree with the suggestion, Howard said he sympathised with the feelings of one MP who called for a boycott of the churches when they vehemently criticised the government over Wik. The Aboriginal leader Noel Pearson called the architects of the late-1997 Wik legislation 'racist scum'. And government ministers failed to distance themselves from claims that pastoralists were arming to defend themselves against black takeover of their land.

This was the climate in which the Kernot defection settled into place. Pitched into an opinion poll free-fall, amid questioning of Howard's future as PM, some Liberals decided her shift demanded a tough response. Within twenty-four hours of October 15, Kernot took a phone call from a friend who reported that a Liberal Party operative—whose name she was given—

was on the ground in South Australia and Queensland talking openly of a 'sex scandal' in her life before she entered politics.

It did not surprise Kernot that her five years with Tony Sinclair in the 1970s should resurface. She and Tony and his wife, Cathy, had often remarked on its inevitability. Kernot was ready for the day when she would be required to talk publicly about it. It was an episode for which she felt absolutely no need to apologise. The only rawness for her would be the prospect that it could rekindle hurt for other people. The fact that she and Sinclair had lived together in Brisbane was well known among the St Leo's fraternity and circles on the north side of Sydney in the late 1970s. It had become part of the school folklore. But over the years it had also become the subject of all sorts of exaggeration, innuendo and rumour. School-yard fantasy, retrospectively embroidered with the fact that after they met up in Queensland, Kernot and Sinclair lived together for five years, was a potent combination for the Sydney rumour-mill.

Within days of the defection, an infamous whispering campaign was underway, with intelligence feeding back to Labor officials, as well as Kernot and her friends. Liberal Party figures were briefing journalists about the 'scandal' that would 'finish' her. One prominent Sydney MP toured the parliamentary press gallery in Canberra inciting journalists to make inquiries. Sydney journalists were provided with the names of people to be fronted for information. Business people were reporting Liberals as saying the opinion polls didn't matter because they 'had the dirt' on Kernot. Many long-time Kernot friends or people associated with St Leo's such as ex-teachers, students or their families were contacted. There were reports of cheque-book journalism discussions involving figures of $10,000 demanded for accounts of what individuals knew of Kernot's early life. Even while she was still coping with an avalanche of media demands, the Labor Party welcome and the emotionally wrenching talks with Democrat colleagues, Kernot was receiving disturbing details of the frenzy of muck-raking under-way behind the scenes. Some of the rumours were absurd.

In one account, for example, she was said to have been sacked by the school amid lurid scandal, a suggestion stridently denied by former officials who insisted she had been a respected and outstanding teacher. A suggestion that she had left the school in disgrace with end-of-year exam preparations in chaos was dismissed with equal passion. She was said to have had sexual relationships with a number of boys while at the school, a claim which brought some of her former colleagues to fury. It was suggested she had 'run off' with Sinclair, when in fact there were other reasons for her departure from Sydney. The problem for those doing the dirt-digging was that the rumours did not stand up.

Kernot's position about her past life was straightforward—like everyone else, if she had her time over, there were probably things in her life she would have done differently. But her relationship with Tony Sinclair did not fall into that category. She had nothing to be ashamed of in a friendship she had valued for most of her adult life. She thought what mattered was her work as a public figure, not her emotional life of twenty years past. If she was to be smeared, then she believed the consequences would fall most heavily on those who smeared her.

Clearly, Kernot's move to Labor handed the Howard government a dilemma. After the initial public attacks were swamped by community support for her, the administration fell back to keep its powder dry. Ministers resolved to attack her on one big weak front—the apparent policy differences between her old party and new one that could not be papered over by the Labor policy repositioning. For example, as Democrat Leader she had instituted a review of tax reform, including a GST, which Beazley had ruled out. And what of all her criticisms of Labor over the years? She had even attacked Minister Beazley over privatisation.

Essentially, she and Beazley argued that after the 1996 election, the page had been ruled off on all that. With her out of the parliament for a year or so, it would be very hard for the Coalition to attack her directly on policy inconsistency. That would really look desperate. There was a suggestion that Howard might call a by-election in Dickson to get her into the bull ring ahead of the election so he could attack her record and exploit the perception of leadership pressures on Beazley. But that plan was discounted. All the time, the danger for the Coalition lay in Gary Gray happily sending her around the nation, campaigning in marginal seats.

And so came the smear.

On December 13, 1997, the *Sydney Morning Herald* saw fit to publish a major feature article entitled 'The other side of Saint Cheryl'. Charging that there were 'two faces' to Kernot, it alluded to her life at St Leo's. It pointed out that after teaching there, in 1976 she was living in Brisbane with a 'teenager' who had been school captain in 1975. Beyond that, the article was a patchwork of disparate assertions that sought to sculpt a picture of a tough, autocratic operator who bullied the Democrat team to get her way and was to some of them 'Machiavelli incarnate'. As directly related by some bitter Democrats, Kernot was presented as having used the relationship with Spindler to help kill off Janet Powell, as having worried that John Coulter was plotting against her and been unsettled by the rise of the senator who replaced Coulter, Natasha Stott-Despoja. In plodding detail, the article cited as her other 'crimes' matters of apparent high importance including refusing to allow her staff to use her Canberra office toilet, leaving her make-up behind when she defected and once refusing to have coffee with Green Senator Dee Margetts. The point of the article, of course, was to finally get on the public record the relationship with Tony Sinclair. It certainly prepared the ground for what some argued was a new low point in the descent of Australian journalism into the tabloid gutter the next day. The *Sun-Herald* followed up, running a front page story about Kernot's 'Secret Past', naming Tony Sinclair, insinuating there had been a cover-up, confirming Kernot's 'political opponents' had embarked on a campaign to get her and quoting Queensland Liberals as saying she should not be above scrutiny.

In the windstorm of controversy the stories sparked, Kernot would suffer hurtful abuse. But there was also widespread public outrage at the precedent established, particularly by the Sunday paper. Liberal-minded people everywhere, including many of her friends, came to Kernot's defence. Leaving aside the issue of the distinction between private and public lives, a huge question was posed by this episode. A telling new precedent may have been created. Was it now open season in Australia on the private lives of public figures going back twenty or thirty years, decades before they even entered the spotlight? Many people in the public eye all around the country winced at the implications. Some openly admitted their own lives of decades ago would not stand up to scrutiny.

One or two commentators went for Kernot's throat, demanding more detail of the Sinclair relationship, asserting that parents would fear for the safety of adolescent boys against 'manipulative' women. But the campaign of denigration faltered as the hostility to it mounted.

The respected commentator Gerard Henderson wrote a hard-hitting article, published in the *Sydney Morning Herald* and *Age* newspapers, which talked about the collapse of the admirable Australian convention of leaving politicians' private lives—where they did not impinge on their public duties—private. Moving in on the self-righteousness inherent in some attacks on Kernot, Henderson held up to examination the private lives of some of the individual journalists who had castigated her in the most caustic terms. Here was ripped open the big question about the 'private lives' of *everybody* in the political system—including journalists who had previously had affairs with married politicians and politicians who had previously had them with staff members. Henderson revealed that one commentator who had hit out at Kernot in vicious terms had, in fact, admitted publicly to having had a homosexual relationship with a lawyer who later became a Chief Justice. At the time the columnist was twenty-one, the lawyer sixty-one. This particular columnist had also written a defence of a Liberal MP who had fathered a child out of wedlock as a young man. The columnist had earlier argued any attempt to raise this would be 'vengeful' and he decried the absence of a 'generosity of spirit in politics'. So what was so different about the journalist as a young man and Tony Sinclair, Gerard Henderson asked? Nothing much, he concluded, except the columnist's double standards. Here were high sentiments being applied in the most notoriously discriminatory fashion.[10]

While she had half-expected an attack, Kernot was saddened at the raw, jaundiced exposure of her life. She was really learning about the big time. She was also greatly dismayed that it would reinforce the notion that this kind of thing only deterred competent people from seeking public office. This had long been a concern for many women. But the campaign contained big risks for those who targeted her. The danger was that support for her could, in fact, solidify. She knew the old truism that mud always sticks. She was realistic enough to know the fact that she had had a romantic relationship with one of her former students—in whatever context—would come as a shock to people. Many would disapprove. Her political reputation would be dented. On the other hand, perhaps the strength of people's regard for her would merely shift to another, more realistic, level. Off the pedestal maybe, but potentially as an even more 'ordinary' person to whom others, with their own tragedies and 'secrets', could relate.

In fact, the really interesting thing about Cheryl Kernot was never her private life—it was the way she had been invested with this special mantle

413

in politics. They called Bob Hawke 'the messiah' in the early days, full of hope, after 1983. She may have hated the thought, but Kernot *was* seen as some kind of saviour. Her October 15 defection, and the words she spoke, basically picked the mood and reflected the temper of the times. Nothing more clearly illustrates this than Hugh Mackay's July, 1997, *Mind and Mood of the Nation* survey. This was the one that demonstrated the startling decline in Howard's high standing from his 1996 guns debate, the 'palpable sense of let down'.[11] The surprising thing about this survey was the way so much of its sentiment coincided with Kernot's rhetoric. The exasperation of the people with the ills of globalisation and economic rationalism—the heartless 'downsizing', the way employees were seen as expendable, the backlash against leaving everything to the market, the growing feeling that government needed to step in to soften the ruthless rules of the economic game—it was all there in the sixty-odd pages of quotes from Mackay's interviews with the citizenry. There was the concern that globalisation was simply a means of producing riches for the already rich, and less for the battler. People sensed a rise in inequality and knew it to be a danger. The research showed that the people wanted the core dilemma of the Aboriginal issue resolved. Although racism existed, Mackay's work suggested that even the most hardline bigot understood the views of Aborigines would not just go away and that the world was watching Australia's response. On tax, for example, the people did not see that the GST was a dirty word anymore but understood that it had to be dealt with squarely as part of a full rethink.

Fundamentally though, the people saw a 'vision vacuum', with no politician talking about the things that troubled them. That, of course, was where Pauline Hanson had come in. Mackay talked of how she had plugged into the unease, presenting, at least, an interesting, purposeful and seemingly strong presence on a stage littered with bland leaders. But Mackay's analysis also strayed into the area of moral purpose. He talked of the conflict between people's pursuit of material well-being and their feeling of 'moral discomfort'. For example, parents actually felt a moral dilemma, wrestling with the issue of whether both should be out working to maintain their living standards when no-one was at home when the kids got home from school. People were uneasy that in the wake of the recession and globalisation, they had become tougher, more heartless. Against the background of so many institutions being tarnished by scandal or mistrust, all this conspired to make people long even more for the emergence of a leader with the three key Mackay attributes—strength, integrity and inspiration.[12]

In the end, some truly intriguing questions are begged about the Cheryl Kernot phenomenon. For example, what are the ingredients that comprise her special 'chemistry'? And, arising from that, what is *the* element in her that inspires so many people? What does the future hold for her? Would she be able, as a senior minister, or even as Prime Minister, to achieve the sorts of changes she advocates, to make big breakthroughs, to shift the ortho-doxies and entrenched power blocs that have thwarted other competent politicians? But, critically, could she ever possibly live up to the noble sentiments, the idealism, the dreams that she herself stirred?

Much has been written and spoken about her 'surface' appeal—the intellectual gifts, the genius for communication and a physical presence that is at once so calm and ordinary yet projects so dynamically with an infectious smile, distinctive posture and voice. But beyond all that, the key to the individual components of her appeal really lies in her journey from the sun-baked backstreets of provincial Maitland to the hub of national power. Rolled into that journey were probably just enough lessons about life to equip her for greatness: lessons she never expediently filed away in the dusty past as her life moved on, places she never turned her back on, people she never disdained, mistakes she would never try to disown. These are the lessons that formed her, informed her. They are the lessons she has wilfully refused to forget. And more than that, the lessons she tried to inject into her work, her ideas, her politics.

Kernot's friend Beth Gilligan drew a portrait of her as a person always in transition through life, being made and unmade, reinventing herself, growing. The country girl who went urban. The naif whose acute senses soaked up the meaning of things at such a frantic rate, even for a while outpacing her emotional development. The unsettled young woman who became wife and mother. A politically unaware person whose sudden realisation one Queensland night about how power really worked brought a Damascusian determination to go home, pick up the phone and change the nature of politics itself. A person who began with some traditional left wing ideas but became a pragmatist, realising fundamentalist positions only led to marginalisation. And a person who wanted to see society hang onto many of its traditions whilst developing a new progressive consensus that actually

415

did something about inequality and community, instead of just mouthing platitudes.

But during that journey, and through the processes of learning, key contradictions of character and psychology were created that make Kernot such a complex figure. Here is a person of great compassion who understands instinctively the meaning of ruthlessness, a kind person who can be quite demanding, a generous and understanding woman who can be uncompromising when provoked. Highly principled yet refusing to bow to convention, Kernot is a voice of reassurance yet the ultimate risk-taker. Charismatic yet a loner, she is a born leader who wants to bring others along, sharing the load and the spotlight

Some of Kernot's closest friends talk of how there is a core dichotomy— a warm person who still has a reserve about her. Someone who reaches out to embrace, yet still manages to keep a distance between herself and others. Friends like Tony Walters saw this 'barrier' become more substantial after she began to make her way in politics. Says Walters: 'She has this reserve. She is very warm and engaging, very charming. If she meets a distressed person, or an Aboriginal person, she can be very compassionate and very engaging. But there is always still a reserve about her. I think that has been very important for her to be able to survive in politics, to get to where she is. To be able to survive that life you need that kind of natural reserve. [She's a] private person … and she can compartmentalise different parts of her life.'[13]

In no way is Cheryl Kernot a snob in the coarse sense. She never looks down on people. But this trait of reserve carries a hint of intellectual superiority. She is driven, very able, and impatient. That combination gives rise to irritability when things are not moving the way she thinks they should. Then the cutting Cheryl emerges, the one who can ride staff, make demands of friends, even get a bit rattled and overreact. Some, but not all, of those around her are able to ride with it, understanding that she is always pressing for quality work, that all natural leaders are magnets for pressure and that the causes they serve are what count and outweigh the day-to-day foibles of personality. The reserve does create animosity, and enemies among those who are offended, can't cope or aren't allowed in close. But fundamentally, the trait is a wellspring of leadership, a thing that sets apart those who lead and those who follow. How else does a person, particularly one who needs privacy, deal with the hands endlessly reaching out to touch her? This sometimes vague sense of distance, and the strength of purpose it implies, also makes such a person more personally intriguing. People are drawn to those with self-belief, willpower, a sense of destiny. In her heart, Cheryl Kernot does have a sense of destiny. She feels what happens to her is all part of something, going somewhere, for a reason. But she does not know what, nor does she have any great masterplan—that is old politics. She walked into the October 15 press conference on her own, not with any gang, faction or conspiracy behind her. She is driven by a very personal sense that there is something she has to achieve. But she will only know it when she finally sees it.

In pursuing her ideas Kernot became entranced by the precepts developed by an Australian management consultant guru called Alistair Mant who has lived for many years in a late-Victorian villa-house in the suburbs of Brighton on the southern English coast. Kernot was asked to launch Mant's new book in 1997, *Intelligent Leadership*. When she read an advance copy, she was inspired.[14] In meeting her, Mant recognised the kind of intellect his book urges nations to nurture. He built a career travelling the world, advising business, government and voluntary sector clients how their operations were badly structured or run wrongly. And how, by developing and harnessing people instead of exploiting them, they could succeed. Mant argues that in politics, as well as business, nations should look to the special people, the risk-takers who hold the key to progress even though their gifts may be concealed by our preoccupation with the short-term or fear of the unconventional.

In *Intelligent Leadership* Mant charges that often the main reason we fail is that our leaders are not up to the job. He homes in on the ability of leaders to think and provides a definition of intellectual powers. He explains a theory of intelligence first postulated by Harvard University's Professor Howard Gardner in his 1983 book *Frames of Mind*. Gardner talked of various kinds of 'intelligence'—including 'linguistic', like the gift of the poet, and the logical, mathematical know-how of the scientist or engineer. There is a musical intelligence but also a 'spatial' ability in which people can hold in their heads a model of the organisation of the world around them. There is 'bodily/kinaesthetic' intelligence, the use of the body to create fashion, art or dance. Then there is 'interpersonal' intelligence, the

417

awareness to be able to get along with other people; and, finally, self-knowledge—itself a form of intelligence. Basically, Mant asserts, too few leaders are multi-gifted with these intelligences. In fact, he argues that 'multi-giftedness' is actually a normal condition, so long as children are brought up and educated in a visionary way. But, in a climate in which society is not developing people as well as it should, every once in a while along comes a leader who is what Mant calls a 'broad-bander'—a person of acute versatility in his/her work and social relations who can easily bring into play 'the entire repertoire of the intelligences'. When he met Cheryl Kernot, Alistair Mant was delighted to realise she was a broad-bander. Instantly, she was elevated in his mind to a place of some importance—the sort of human asset which, in times of great unease, should be utilised properly.

Mant's further big idea is that people are divided into two types—what he calls 'binary' and 'ternary' mindsets, habits of thinking. The binary basically see the world in terms of what it means for them. Their preoccupation is with interpersonal influence ... 'If I win, you lose' ... 'What's in it for me?' ... At its core, this is the Darwinian survival instinct and the fulcrum of orthodox economics and conventional adversarial politics. But then, Mant says, there are 'ternary' people—those who do what they do for reasons other than the personal. For them, basically the relationship of everybody to a higher-order ideal takes precedence over win/lose relationships between individuals or sectional interests. Some people always remain binaries, others remain ternaries. Broad-banders tend to be ternary people with the capacity to understand systems, the complex way the world is interwoven. And the ability, if circumstances require, to act in an occasionally binary fashion. Cheryl Kernot, he sees, as a ternary broad-bander.

After meeting her, Mant concluded that if she could navigate her way through the minefields to real power, Kernot could be a very important historical figure for Australia. Apart from her obvious 'intellectual firepower' she had 'precious intuitive gifts'. At this time in history, it was so interesting that this all be found in a woman. Her strength, he saw, was that she came across as a 'dependable object' to a whole range of different people. 'Factor X' was her capacity to appeal, almost in a subconscious way, to people who were yearning for reassurance. Mant had long argued that Australia's political cycle was a nonsense. Elections every three years, called at the whim of government, meant the nation never had time to deal with policy ideas properly. As Australia headed into 1998 amid speculation of the latest imminent poll, he hoped Labor would realise Kernot was not just an electioneering totem but had ideas and had to be supported in developing them. As a Democrat she had relied on her intuition but now the challenges were more complex. To get the best out of Cheryl Kernot, he believed, there had to be a system to help her function.

If there is one basic ingredient that explains the Kernot appeal it is not simply that she specifically enunciates a lot of the criticism people have about politics and government. It is the set of beliefs, the basic values reflected in her words. Particularly after the smears, those on the right of Australian society would never be comfortable with her worldview. The moral right assailed her for hypocrisy. But Kernot is part of the 'baby-boomer' generation, that huge wave of people born in the immediate aftermath of the war. Many 'boomers' exalted in the social liberation that came in the 1960s and '70s but, approaching middle age, having been influenced by 'post-materialism' and having suffered Thatcherism, they began to enter a mid-life crisis of significant proportions about the direction of things. Kernot's demands for answers resonated with them. But, more particularly, they identify with the underlying precepts that motivate her. They may feel unsteady at times, but the idealism of the 'boomers' remains largely intact. And Kernot speaks to it.

Her values do not only reflect just those of some of her generation, though. Hugh Mackay has shown disturbingly how youth today is grown so cynical, suspending their sense of commitment to anything until they are sure they can find something worth believing in. And the babyboomers' parents have been through enough to bridle at cant and hypocrisy too, to believe they have known a better world than the present one, and to yearn for something better for their grandchildren. The most conservative of them and the ones who have drifted with the times to a more liberal view, share an unease about the world. Many older people, too, think they detect in Kernot a person fighting for principles.

After the defection, many people hoped she had taken the first step to one day leading the nation. Rod Cameron reckoned she had a very good chance of, indeed, becoming Australia's first female Prime Minister. He felt the people were just waiting for the right woman to emerge. Hugh Mackay wondered if one day Kernot would finish up President of Australia. At the end of 1997 one thing was certain—the road would get no less rocky for her. She would continue to be tested.

In early 1998 it was starkly apparent that no-one in the ALP, and certainly not Kernot herself, had anticipated the scale of her new celebrity. She was under huge pressure, walking through a new political minefield, one with which she was simply unfamiliar. The media focus was unrelenting, and every party function she attended drew huge crowds. Soon she would be cruelly made aware of how little room she had to manoeuvre.

As a Democrat, it had all been easy. She had been free to have personal views. But now every utterance would be scrutinised for hidden meanings, inconsistencies, naivety or political error. Her critics argued *she* had made the decision to play in the big league. The terrain around her had altered and perhaps at first she did not understand just how drastically. In the foreground there were her friends, members of the public or crowds of Labor supporters pressing forward, hugging and congratulating her, wishing her well. But beyond the television lights, in the shadows lurked a newly formed coalition of enemies.

The Liberal and National parties would use any apparent policy inconsistency to destabilise her; the reactionary right would continue decrying her, both as a turncoat and over her private life; a few people in the ALP who resented her meteoric rise watched and waited for any stumble; the economic orthodoxy would argue she was a throwback to failed Keynesianism; and some of her former Democrat colleagues who felt they had suffered her moods or worked tirelessly for her were driven by a new loathing. And then there was the media.

Given she herself had upped the ante, journalists pointed out, Kernot had no right to be above scrutiny. For four years a combination of her personal affability, her empathy with the profession and the somewhat insulated status of the Democrats had made her a media darling. But journalists were much tougher on the main parties. As well though, some in the media decided they basically didn't like what they saw as her egotism. Some were influenced by an old-fashioned Laborite view of ratting. A few were still smarting that they had missed the defection story. Maybe there was also an element of pulling down the tallest poppy of them all. It took Kernot some time to grasp that her approach to the media had to change as well. She was in a precarious position and had to watch what she said. But of all places, she did not need her first serious glitch to come during the ALP National Conference in Hobart in January, 1998.

When news reached her in Hobart that a removal truck had smashed into the front of the house in Brisbane into which her family was moving, injuring her husband, memories came rushing back of the fire and the charred West End wreckage in which the Kernots lost everything in 1991. The truck accident rattled Kernot and completely threw her preparations for conference, where she was to give a keynote speech. Clearly distressed when fronted by journalists early in the morning after a flight to Brisbane, she hit out at the media intrusion but then uttered words that resonated around the conference venue in Hobart. She suggested she would have to talk to her family about whether politics was worth it all. Later she referred to her policy role as representing 'babyboomers', and was accused of claiming too much credit for the turnaround in Labor's fortunes in the first draft of her speech. All this was gratefully leapt on by a government keen to show she couldn't handle pressure and could actually be a liability for Labor in an election campaign.

Kernot had made clear in her original defection speech that if it did not work, she would leave politics. Whatever the pressures bearing in on her since October and her exhaustion, however, it was a major blunder to speak in such an undisciplined way. For a brief moment public perceptions of her were shifted damagingly. The Kernot phenomenon had taken on a life of its own—if nothing else, the ALP had invested a great deal in her and did not need her wearing her heart on her sleeve. But the effect of the incident and the resulting bad press was to galvanise her. It made her begin to really understand how monumental a challenge she faced. She saw she had to roll with the pressures more, but far more importantly, she actually emerged reinforced by a fuller realisation of just how many people were depending on her. She could see more clearly that her defection had had great meaning for many ordinary people. She concluded that to give in to the pressures would be tantamount to surrendering to the people who would destroy her—and whose values, ideas and aims she basically found repugnant.

Among the criticisms she endured was that she had a massive ego and was not basically a team player. Both accusations missed the mark. Kernot's ego was no bigger than any other top-line politician. She had grasped from the start that her new role in the ALP would mean living with its collective decisions. She actually looked forward to being a team player. But there still was significance in her slip-up during the conference—the hint it provided about her fundamentally unorthodox political approach. In the end, she could see that she had made a political error but there was still that defiant streak. She privately insisted that, despite what the predictable, adversarial political system made of it, ordinary people would not mark her down for having expressed concern for her family, for having been, for a moment, vulnerable.

The real long-term question mark hanging over Cheryl Kernot's future is not smear campaigns or media pressure. It has to do with this vexed problem of how an unconventional thinker adjusts in the transition into an orthodox, rigid political culture. Perhaps she will come to find the harsher demands of a very male-dominated party too much. Even though she is essentially motivated to be part of the team making the big decisions, maybe she will find it hard to make some of the compromises required behind closed doors in a ministry or shadow cabinet. Some of her greatest achievements with the Democrats were based on political compromise, but the key thing about Kernot is that she can be quite adventurous in her political judgements—her instincts are often to have a go. Those who have worked closely with her and admire her have, on occasion, been amazed at how her gambles so often pay off. Indeed, she has specifically argued that Canberra needs less caution. Handed real power though, does her journey ultimately end with her banging her head against brick walls? Perhaps she will learn that the dreams were easier to dream, after all.

This brings into perspective one of Alistair Mant's important arguments about her future. He says the challenge for Kernot in the Labor Party is to preserve what she is, not to be changed by the defection. It is vital for her to be part of a mainstream party, while still maintaining herself slightly removed from the game-playing, preserving that independence of outlook and determination of spirit. She must play a central role but still not be subsumed by party political pressures that would smother her distinctive qualities. If she can manage that, it will surely stand as her abiding contradiction.

The bottom-line answer to the questions about Kernot's future is that, because she is one of Alistair Mant's 'ternary' people, she could indeed just walk away from it all. In fact, Mant says that while politics-hardened, binary

ALP powerbrokers may have been amazed at her guts in the defection, it all looked tougher than it really was for her. This is because her mind is such that it was not the be-all and end-all:

> If you are in ternary mode, you know you can just walk away, it doesn't matter. She just knew life with Labor would be less boring than it was before—that she would have new challenges. But if that fell through, she would just go off and find other challenges elsewhere. She *is* a brave woman but binary people misunderstand the nature of that bravery.[15]

Perhaps a combination of in-built resistance to 'new politics' in the system of government, the bureaucracy and the ALP itself and the pressures on family might one day convince Kernot to give up her challenging journey. Perhaps the best the nation can hope for is to have had what Kernot represents, rather than what she could develop. In other words, perhaps just to have had someone up there for a while, providing a modicum of inspiration will be enough to engender confidence again. And faith. But would her departure from politics leave Australia a lesser place? Whatever she finally does, for a lot of people Cheryl Kernot will continue to be a figure of inspiration.

If she is vulnerable, even de-sanctified, if she is ruthless and tough at times, if she is a mass of contradictions, then so are the rest of us. Here is the final contradiction. Cheryl Kernot is at once something special, but also just one of us—gloriously ordinary.

She not only inspires people to keep believing in the potential for something better. The defection was an extraordinary feat of guts and self-belief. She fended off the smears with dignity and calm, just as she stood up for her brother. In times of trial, she demonstrates an indomitable spirit. And that spirit is what infects people. But it is, in the end, a spirit built on optimism.

In mid-1997 she said: 'You have to be an optimist, no matter what. Because there are wonderful, positive things about most human beings. If you look at the evolution of mankind's efforts some of it is awful but a great deal is not—the human spirit, generosity, brilliance of the mind, the music, the art. These are wonderful things. It's awe-inspiring what human beings are capable of doing. I just think the fact that some people are born with talent and choose to make a contribution to society and further the lot of others is important—and good. We have had wars and we're stuffing up the environment but there are a lot of people who know it and are taking steps to fix it. The big challenge is whether it can be done in time. But I couldn't live in doom and gloom. I think this hardline economic view of the world will eventually kill itself because of the brutalism and the illogic of it. People see through it and I take comfort from their common sense. I'm optimistic enough to hope for something better. And I just have faith that with our innate talents and resources, we *should* be able to make things better.'[16]

It's fitting to end back where the journey of the politician Cheryl Kernot began—as a schoolteacher with a passion for learning; an instinct for innovative ways to open minds to the wonders of history and literature; and with an optimism that ideas and credos like fairness can advance us. The attempt to destroy her politically by the moral right harked back to the time with her students. They were the first people she inspired. In 1996, years after he had gone on to a career as a leading classical musician, former Churchie student, Chris Latham, sent her a copy of his just-published book of poetry. It contained a personal note, inscribed on the inside cover:

I send this to you because you are responsible for it in a way, for protecting a boy's sense of wonder and encouraging his expression of those things he found beautiful in a school where that often didn't happen. I look at you, think of the people you have to work with/against and the serious demands on your time and energy and the real costs you must have to bear on the quality of your family life, and I think of that great Longfellow quote: 'The bravest are the tenderest, the loving are the daring'. How that exemplifies you. I imagine a day will come when you count the cost and withdraw but I hope at that time you aren't left wondering whether it was worth it. Because I think the thing you will change that is more important than any policy is how the business of government works. You shame them all with your dignity and it will be just as it was, say, with Pasteur's vaccination for small-pox. It becomes immoral for a seemingly insoluble problem to continue once a viable solution is found. I hope that you continue to stand up in a field where cynicism and resignation and survival's most primitive instincts are the order of the day. Because offering possibility in the face of despair is essentially not about politics but about the most fundamental human struggle. You inspire so many with your courage in that fight, in ways you will never know and will not be able to count on the day that fight overwhelms you. I have no strong religious feelings but what I do have are contained in Rilke's poem *To Fly*:

'If I don't manage to fly, someone will,

The spirit wants only that there be flying

As for who happens to do it

In that, he has only a passing interest.'

Anyway, all the best with your soaring. I know the work it takes.[17]

REFERENCES

PREFACE

1 Ramsey, Alan, 'Could this be her worst decision?', *Sydney Morning Herald*, October 16, 1997, p. 1.
2. Kelly, Paul, 'Big stakes in play for power', *Australian*, October 16, 1997, p. 1.
3. Rintoul, Stuart, 'St Cheryl: the image versus the reality', *Australian*, October 18–19, 1997, p. 1.
4. Howard, John, 'The cosiest deal of all', *Daily Telegraph*, October 17, 1997, p. 19.
5. Quadrant Research Services, Press Release: 'Big jump in ALP support since Kernot defection', October 19, 1997.

1

THE NEW STAR

1. Brown, Wallace, 'Budget left in limbo. Senate flexes its muscles', *Courier-Mail*, August 19, 1993, p. 1.
2. Newspoll, conducted August 20–22, 1993, *Australian*, August 24, 1993, p. 1.
3. Garran, Robert, 'Changes possible: Willis', *Australian*, August 25, 1993, p. 2.
4. Burton, Tom, 'Deliberate campaign to spook Senate', *Australian Financial Review*, August 25, 1993, p. 4.

427

2

ROOTS

1. Interview with Merv Paton, Fingal Bay, February, 1997.
2. Summers, Anne, *Damned Whores and God's Police*, Penguin Books, 1994.
3. Cogan, Brian (ed), *Newcastle and the Hunter: The Revolution of a Region*, Focus Books, 1991, p. 42.
4. Ibid., p. 43.
5. Interviews with Zena Paton and Margaret Manion, Fingal Bay and the Gold Coast, February, 1997.
6. Interview with Merv Paton, loc. cit.
7. Merv Paton, ibid.
8. Interview with Zena Paton, Fingal Bay, February, 1997.
9. Merv Paton, loc. cit.
10. Merv Paton, ibid.
11. Interview with Margaret Manion, the Gold Coast, February, 1997.
12. Zena Paton, loc. cit.
13. Margaret Manion, loc. cit.
14. Merv Paton, loc. cit.
15. Merv Paton, ibid.
16. Interview with Rita Dunn, Maitland, February, 1997.
17. Merv Paton, loc. cit.
18. Merv Paton, ibid.
19. Merv Paton, ibid.
20. Merv Paton, ibid.
21. Merv Paton, ibid.
22. Merv Paton, ibid.

3

ZENA AND MERV

1. Interview with Zena Paton, Fingal Bay, February, 1997.
2. Interview with Merv Paton, Fingal Bay, February, 1997.
3. Zena Paton, loc. cit.
4. Interview with Cheryl Kernot, Canberra, January, 1997.
5. Interview with Gail Martin, Maitland, February, 1997.
6. Gail Martin, ibid.
7. Gail Martin, ibid.
8. Zena Paton, loc. cit.
9. Merv Paton, loc. cit.

10. Merv Paton, ibid.
11. Zena Paton, loc. cit.
12. Zena Paton, ibid.
13. Zena Paton, ibid.

4

DRIFTWOOD

1. Interview with Zena Paton, Fingal Bay, February, 1997.
2. Interview with Joan Stephens, Maitland, February, 1997.
3. Joan Stephens, ibid.
4. Joan Stephens, ibid.
5. Interview with Clare O'Shea, Sydney, February, 1997.
6. Interview with Joan Palmer, Maitland, February, 1997.
7. Interview with Merv Paton, Fingal Bay, February, 1997.
8. Merv Paton, ibid.
9. Merv Paton, ibid.
10. Interview with Clem Ellis, Maitland, February, 1997.
11. Merv Paton, loc. cit.
12. Interview with Gail Martin, Fingal Bay, February, 1997.
13. Merv Paton, loc. cit.

5

A SAFE HARBOUR

1. Interview with Beth Gilligan, Sydney, February, 1997.
2. Beth Gilligan, ibid.
3. Interview with Margaret O'Shea, Sydney, February, 1997.
4. Margaret O'Shea, ibid.
5. Interview with Beth Gilligan.
6. Interview with Milton Morris, Maitland, February, 1997.
7. Interview with teaching colleague from Churchie, Sydney, February, 1997.
8. Interview with Stuart Page, Sydney, February, 1997.
9. Stuart Page, ibid.
10. Stuart Page, ibid.
11. Interview with Chris Latham, Sydney, February, 1997.
12. Chris Latham, ibid.
13. Interview with Tony Sinclair, Sydney, February, 1997.

6
THE POLITICS OF HOPE

1. Senate Brief, 'Electing Australia's Senators', Research section, Department of the Senate, Parliament House Canberra, No. 1, August, 1996.
2. Hewitt, Tim and Wilson, David, *Don Chipp*, Visa Books, 1978, p. 8.
3. Chipp, Don and Larkin, John, *Don Chipp: The Third Man*, Rigby Ltd, 1978, p. 20.
4. Chipp and Larkin, ibid., p. 19.
5. Ibid.
6. Hewitt, Tim, and Wilson, David, *Don Chipp*, Visa Books, 1978, p. 31.
7 Chipp, Don, *Parliamentary Debates*, House of Representatives, 24 March, 1977, p. 556.
8. Interview with Sid Spindler, Melbourne, February, 1997.
9. Sugita, Hiroya, *Challenging Two-partism: The continuing contribution of the Australian Democrats to the Australian party system*, PhD Thesis, Department of Politics, Faculty of Social Sciences, Flinders University, July, 1995, p. 47.
10. Siddons, John, *A Spanner in the Works*, Macmillan Australia, 1990, p. 160.
11. Hewitt and Wilson, op. cit., p. 55.
12. Chipp and Larkin, op. cit., p. 178.
13. Ibid.
14. Sugita, op. cit., p. 48.
15. Siddons, op. cit., p. 154.
16. Siddons, ibid., p. 161.
17. See Sugita's important evaluation included in PhD thesis, Flinders University, 1995.
18. Carty, Ken, Paper: 'The Australian Democrats in Comparative Perspective.' Paper to Twentieth Anniversary Conference of the Australian Democrats, Burton and Garran Hall, Australian National University, January 18–19, 1997.
19. Sugita, Hiroya, 'The Australian Democrats' Policy Formulation, Ideology, Policy and Practice.' Paper presented to Twentieth Anniversary Conference of the Australian Democrats, Burton and Garran Hall, Australian National University, January 18–19, 1997.
20. Chipp and Larkin, op. cit., p. 187.
21. *Australian Democrat Journal*, October, 1977.
22. Chipp, Don, Extract from policy speech, the *Age,* October 9, 1980.
23. Larkin, John, *Chipp,* Methuen Haynes, 1987, p. 100.
24. Siddons, op. cit., p. 221.

25. Sugita, Hiroya, *Challenging Two-partism: The continuing contribution of the Australian Democrats to the Australian party system*, PhD Thesis, Department of Politics, Faculty of Social Sciences, Flinders University, July, 1995, p. 96
26. Kelly, Paul, *Australian*, March 3, 1990.
27. *Sydney Morning Herald*, March 10, 1990.
28. Grigson, Paul, 'Democrats recycling Evita's policies, says Walsh', *Sydney Morning Herald*, March 10, 1990, p. 3.
29. *Australian*, March 10, 1990.
30. Barnett, David, 'Economy Versus Environment', *Bulletin*, April 10, 1990, p. 30.
31. Haines, Janine, 'Haines bows out after "dirty tricks" campaign', *Canberra Times*, March 25, 1990, p. 5.
32. Austin, Paul, *Australian*, May 26, 1990.

7

A NATURAL

1. Barker, Geoffrey, *Financial Review*, August 7, 1996, p. 16.
2. Ibid.
3. Interview with Democrat official, Sydney, January, 1997.
4. Interview with Cheryl Kernot, Maitland, February, 1997.
5. Interview with former Queensland Democrat official, Melbourne, January, 1997.
6. Interview with Queensland Democrat official, Brisbane, January, 1997.
7. Interview with member of Democrat national executive, January, 1997.
8. Interview with former member of Democrat national executive, January, 1997.
9. Interview with Cheryl Kernot, Melbourne, February, 1997.
10. Interview with Merv Paton, Fingal Bay, February, 1997.

8

FAIRIES AND GOBLINS

1. Hansard Debates, the Senate, August 22, 1990.
2. Ibid.
3. Siddons, John, *A Spanner in the Works*, Macmillan Australia, 1990, p. 209.
4. O'Reilly, David, 'Democrats bite the bullet', *Bulletin*, August 27, 1991.
5. Frith, David, 'Need for public accountability of foreign investment', *Australian*, February 15, 1994, p. 48.

6. Kernot, Cheryl, Foreign Investment Policy Launch speech, Cairns, March 10, 1993.
7. Seccombe, Mike, 'The High Priest of the Democrats', *Sydney Morning Herald*, October 17, 1992.
8. Sugita, Hiroya, *Challenging Two-partism: The continuing contribution of the Australian Democrats to the Australian party system*, PhD Thesis, Department of Politics, Faculty of Social Sciences, Flinders University, July, 1995, p. 339.
9. Ibid., p. 346.
10. Ibid., p. 347.
11. Seccombe, Mike, 'Campaign launch that blew up for Coulter', *Sydney Morning Herald*, March 1, 1993.
12. See interview with Hiroya Sugita, March 8, 1994, quoted in Flinders University PhD Thesis.

9

GLORIOUSLY ORDINARY

1. Kernot, Cheryl, 'Power, Passion and Balance' speech to National Press Club, Canberra, May 5, 1993.
2. Interview with Cheryl Kernot, Canberra, January, 1997.
3. Ibid.
4. Interview with Democrat senator, Canberra, January, 1997.
5. Burton, Tom, 'How Backbench protest turned to revolt over Keating budget', *Australian Financial Review*, September 1, 1993, p. 4.
6. Shanaghan, Dennis, 'Kernot's new order', *Australian*, August 28, 1993, p. 23.
7. *Sydney Morning Herald*, 'The Kernot Budget', editorial, September 1, 1993, p. 16.
8. Keneally, Tom, 'Keating warned over speech', *Telegraph-Mirror*, October 1, 1993, p. 7.
9. Kernot, Cheryl, letter to Paul Keating, November 1, 1993.
10. Hewett, Jennifer, 'Is this Australia's best politician?', *Australian Financial Review*, Weekend Magazine, February 25, 1994, p. 1.
11. Wild, Dorian, 'Running on normal', *Ita*, December, 1993, p. 37.
12. O'Brien, Kerry, 'New captain, new pitch', *Time*, December 20, 1993, p. 11.
13. Kernot, Cheryl, interview on *Lateline*, November 25, 1993.
14. Ramsey, Alan, 'Big pictures have sharp corners', *Sydney Morning Herald*, December 4, 1993, p. 29.

10

PREPARED TO OWN OUR HISTORY

1. Willmot, Eric, 'Future Pathways: Equity or Isolation', the Frank Archibald Lecture, National Library, September 16, 1986.
2. Interview with former Democrat official, Sydney, January, 1997.
3. Kelly, Paul, *The End of Certainty*, Allen and Unwin, 1994, p. xix.
4. Ibid., p. xx.
5. Brennan, J., 'Lead Judgement in Mabo versus Queensland No. 2', quoted in Department of Library paper, *The Mabo Debate—A Chronology*, Parliament of the Commonwealth, 1994, p. 1.
6. Kelly, Paul, op. cit.
7. Department of the Library, *The Mabo Debate—A Chronology*, Parliament of the Commonwealth, 1994, p. 2.
8. Gordon, Michael, *Paul Keating: A True Believer*, University of Queensland Press, 1996, p. 272.
9. Department of the Library, *The Mabo Debate—A Chronology,* Parliament of the Commonwealth, 1994, p. 10.
10. Ibid., p. 21.
11. Department of the Library, *The Mabo Debate—A Chronology*, Parliament of the Commonwealth, 1994, p. 37.
12. Whimp, Kathy, 'Mabo: The Inside Story', *Arena*, February/March, 1994, p. 19.
13. Ramsey, Alan, 'Even at Christmas there was mud', *Sydney Morning Herald*, December 18, 1993, p. 21.
14. Interview with Gareth Evans, Canberra, January, 1997.
15. Ibid.
16. Ibid.

11

THE MALE BASTION

1. Cameron, Rod, 'Feminisation: The major emerging trend underlying future mass audience response', an address to the eleventh National Convention of the Public Relations Institute of Australia, October 19, 1990.
2. Barker, Geoffrey, 'End of the road for the great whiteboard hope', *Financial Review*, January 17, 1995, p. 3.
3. Butcher, Andrew, 'Democrats call for Kelly to quit', *Herald Sun,* February 11, 1994, p. 2.

4. Dunlevy, Sue, 'Mixing sex and politics', *Telegraph-Mirror,* February 14, 1994, p. 11.
5. Dunlevy, Sue, 'Mixing sex and politics', *Telegraph-Mirror*, February 14, 1994, p. 11.
6. Harari, Fiona, 'Critics give Lawrence's Madonna role mixed reviews', *Weekend Australian*, August 12, 1995, p. 2.
7. Sawyer, Marian, 'Topsy-Turvy Land—Where Women, Children and the Environment Come First', paper to twentieth Anniversary Conference of the Australian Democrats, Burton and Garran Hall, Australian National University, January 18–19, 1997, p. 14.
8. Interview with Cheryl Kernot, Canberra, January, 1997.
9. Ibid.
10. Kernot, Cheryl, 'The environment movement—a gendered perspective', speech to conference at Murdoch University, 25 May, 1995.
11. Interview with Cheryl Kernot, loc. cit.

12

A TRAINED INCAPACITY TO LEARN

1. Kelly, Paul, *The End of Certainty*, Allen and Unwin, 1994, p. 52.
2. Keating, Paul, speech to annual dinner of Press Gallery, National Press Club, December 7, 1990.
3. Edwards, John, *Keating: The Inside Story*, Penguin Books, 1996, p. 179.
4. Ibid.
5. Mathews, Russell, 'Financial Markets and Failed Economic Policies' in Sheehan, P., Grewal, B. and Kumnick, M. (eds.), *Dialogues on Australia's Future,* Victoria University, 1996, p. 56.
6. Toohey, Brian, *Tumbling Dice*, William Heinemann, 1995, p. 4.
7. Emy, Hugh, *Remaking Australia*, Allen and Unwin, 1993, p. 14.
8. Pusey, Michael, *Economic Rationalism in Canberra*, Cambridge University Press, 1991, p. 74
9. Ibid., p. 107
10. Emy, op. cit., p. 13
11. Gruen, Fred, 'The quality of life and economic performance' in Sheehan, P., Grewal, B. and Kumnick, M. (eds.), *Dialogues on Australia's Future*, Victoria University, 1996, p. 363.
12. Mathews, op. cit., p. 55.
13. Harding, Anne, 'Recent trends in income inequality in Australia', *Dialogues on Australia's Future*, p. 283.

14. Gregory, B. and Hunter, Boyd, 'Increasing regional inequality and the decline of manufacturing', *Dialogues on Australia's Future*, p. 308.
15. Connolly, David, *Australians Speak: A Report on the Concerns, Hopes and Aspirations of the Australian People,* Australia 2000 Program, 1991.
16. Mackay, Hugh, *Reinventing Australia*, Angus and Robertson, 1993, p. 17.
17. Emy, op. cit., p. 168.
18. Stillwell, Frank, *Beyond the Market,* Pluto Press, 1993, p. 201.
19. Sheehan, Peter, 'Economics and the National Interest', in Sheehan, P., Grewal, B. and Kumnick, M. (eds.), *Dialogues on Australia's Future*, Victoria University, 1996, p. 401.

13

THE KISS OF LIFE

1. Ohmae, Kenichi, *The End of the Nation State*, Harper Collins, 1995, pp. 5, 12.
2. Ibid., p. 15.
3. Ibid., p. 39.
4. Ibid.
5. Ibid.
6. Kernot, Cheryl, 'The kiss of life: reviving Australian politics', speech to the Sydney Institute, September 25, 1996.
7. Kernot, Cheryl, 'Corporatising the community: community services in an era of privatisation', speech to Wesley Central Mission, Melbourne, November 2, 1995.
8. Hutton, Will, *The State We're In*, Vintage, 1996.
9. Parliamentary Library Information Service, 'Downsizing the workforce: the good, the bad and the ugly', news file on Stephen Roach, Department of the Parliamentary Library, September 18, 1996.
10. OECD Revenue Statistics, Member Countries, 1995.
11. Davies, Anne, 'Time to bite the tax rise bullet', *Sydney Morning Herald*, December 3, 1994, p. 42.
12. Kernot, Cheryl, 'The new reality: Australia's place in the global economy', speech to Australian Institute of Management, October 4, 1994.
13. Ibid.
14. Interview with Cheryl Kernot, Canberra, January, 1997.
15. Quoted in *Woman's Own* (Magazine), Britain, October 31, 1987.
16. Quoted in *Independent* newspaper, Britain, December 11, 1995.
17. Kernot, Cheryl, 'The leadership test: Australia in the next twenty years', speech to the Australian Democrats National Conference, Canberra, January 17–19, 1997.

14

CELEBRITY AND PRESSURES

1. Wild, Dorian, 'Running on normal' *Ita* magazine, December, 1993, p. 38.
2. Ibid., p. 40.
3. Wright, John, 'The Tragedy of Eric', *Courier-Mail*, January 21, 1992, p. 9.
4. Interview with Clare O'Shea, Sydney, February, 1997.

15

IN SEARCH OF TRUST

1. Kernot, Cheryl, *FIRB Needs to be Outed,* press release, April 21, 1993.
2. Davies, Anne, 'Inquiry likely into PM's talks with Black', *Sydney Morning Herald*, November 23, 1993, p. 3.
3. Taylor, Lenore, 'Black may be allowed to lift Fairfax stake', *Australian*, November 19, 1993.
4. Transcript of Prime Minister Keating's interview, Seattle, November 18, 1993.
5. Kernot, Cheryl, *Keating's Media Deals Raise Huge Questions,* press release, November 21, 1993.
6. Transcript of Prime Minister Keating's interview, Seattle, November 18, 1993.
7. *Sydney Morning Herald*, 'PM offered 35%, says Black', November 26, 1993, p. 1.
8. Markey, Randall, 'Keating snubs Senate probe', *West Australian*, November 25, 1993, p. 1.
9. Taylor, Lenore, 'Senate heads for legal showdown with Willis', *Weekend Australian*, February 12, 1994, p. 4.
10. Peake, Ross, 'Kernot's jail threat in power battle', *Canberra Times,* February 14, 1994, p. 1.
11. *Australian*, 'Lavarch lashes Constable Kernot', February 15, 1994, p. 1.
12. Editorial, 'Senator Kernot turns jailer', *Adelaide Advertiser*, February 15, 1994, p. 2.
13. *Mercury*, 'Kernot move dubious ploy', editorial, February 15, 1994, p. 19.
14. Stewart, Cameron, 'The ultimate division', *Weekend Australian*, February 12, 1994, p. 21.
15. Tingle, Laura, 'PM challenge on Senate', *Australian*, March 4, 1994, p. 1.
16. Kernot, Cheryl, Aide-Mémoire, November 25, 1993.
17. *Sydney Morning Herald*, 'PM's Senate sledgehammer', March 5, 1994, p. 30.
18. Davies, Anne, 'PM condemned over Fairfax bid', *Sydney Morning Herald*, June 10, 1994, p. 6.

19. Kernot, Cheryl, 'How democratic is Australia?', speech to Jewish Democratic Society, Melbourne, November 2, 1995.
20. *Bulletin* magazine poll of 531 electors, conducted on evening of August 31, 1995.
21. Kernot, Cheryl, launch of *Charter for Reform—The Australian Democrats' Thirty Point Plan for More Honest, Open and Accountable Government*, January 31, 1996.
22. Kernot, Cheryl, 'The Senate and Supply options: necessary reform', speech to the ANU Law School Conference on the Constitution, Canberra, November 9, 1995.

16
TRIUMPH AND PAIN
1. Steketee, Mike, 'Keating strategy misfired', *Australian*, 6 July, 1996.
2. Interview with Democrat staffer, Canberra, January, 1997.
3. Steketee, Mike, 'Kernot private battle with Green guru', *Australian*, January 30, 1996.
4. Kernot, Cheryl, transcript of interview with *Face to Face*, January 21, 1996.
5. Kernot, Cheryl, *Democrats Give Howard Funding Options for Environment Policy*, press release, February 5, 1996.
6. Kernot, Cheryl, *No Privatisation of Telstra*, press release, February 13, 1996.
7. Interview with Democrat staffer, Canberra, January, 1997.
8. Bean, Clive; Simms, Marian; Bennett, Scott; and Warhurst, John, *The Politics of Retribution: the 1996 Federal Election*, Allen and Unwin, 1997.
9. Bean, Clive, 'The Australian Democrats after twenty years: electoral performance and voting support', paper to twentieth Anniversary Conference, Burton and Garran Hall, Australian National University, Canberra, 18–19 January, 1997.
10. Ibid.
11. Moir, Anne and Jessel, David, *A Mind to Crime*, Michael Jones, 1995, p. 149.
12. Gladwell, Malcolm, 'The Criminal Brain', *Independent* newspaper magazine, London, 1996.

17
NEW ERA, SAME OLD FIGHT.
1. Kernot, Cheryl, 'Don't sell public ownership short', *Australian*, May 22, 1996.
2. Kernot, Cheryl, *Telstra Chief Nails His Colours to the Mast*, press release, June 20, 1996.

3. Stone, John, 'Kernot put in her place', *Australian Financial Review*, June 27, 1996.

4. Kitney, Geoff, 'Howard attack backfires', *Sydney Morning Herald*, July 6, 1996, p. 4.

5. Peake, Ross, 'Kernot faces rocky times', *Canberra Times*, July 13, 1996, p. 17.

6. Peake, Ross, 'Kernot faces testing time', *Canberra Times*, July 13, 1996, p. 17.

7. Ibid.

8. Peake, Ross, 'Libs threat to the Senate', *Canberra Times*, August 8, 1996, p. 1.

9. Scott, Keith, 'Downer suspicious of Senate voting change', *Canberra Times*, March 7, 1994, p. 4.

10. Grattan, Michelle, 'Kernot acts the spoiler', *Age*, March 30, 1996.

11. Short, John, 'Democrats may block key bills for Budget', *Australian*, June 3, 1996, p. 1.

12. Wood, Alan, 'Greater entitlement restraints show true compassion', *Australian*, June 4, 1996.

13. Walsh, Max, 'Kernot's high ground not necessarily moral', *Age,* September 27, 1996, p. 38.

14. Kernot, Cheryl, 'Reality check: Economic responsibility and the 1996 Budget', speech to National Press Club, August 7, 1996.

15. *Financial Review*, 'Kernot plots a wrong course', editorial, August 9, 1996, p. 26.

16. *Australian*, 'It is time for Kernot to retreat', editorial, August 14, 1996, p. 12.

17. AGB McNair Poll, 'Telstra Sale: Poll shows support rising', *Sydney Morning Herald*, June 4, 1996.

18. Wheeldon, John, 'In defence of the power of the Senate', *Sydney News*, September 5, 1993.

19. Ibid.

20. Carty, Ken, 'The Australian Democrats in comparative perspective', paper to twentieth Anniversary Conference of the Australian Democrats, Burton and Garran Hall, Australian National University, January 18–19, 1997.

21. Ibid.

22. Ibid.

18

A SHIFTING BALANCE

1. Contractor, Aban, 'Colston deals double blow for Labor', *Canberra Times*, August 21, 1996, p. 3.
2. Woods, James, 'PM welcomes Colston move', *Courier-Mail*, August 22, 1996, p. 2.
3. Gordon, Michael, 'Colston warns Labor attack may backfire', *Australian*, September 4, 1996, p. 3.
4. *Sydney Morning Herald*, 'Senate puts Telstra sell-off in jeopardy', editorial, September 11, 1996, p. 3.
5. Kitney, Geoff, 'Sting in the Treasurer's tail', *Sydney Morning Herald*, August 23, 1996, p. 3.
6. Shanaghan, Dennis, 'Violence will not sway us', *Australian*, August 20, 1996, p. 3.
7. *Financial Review*, 'Kernot gets a hard lesson', editorial, August 23, 1996, p. 26.
8. Interview with Peter Reith, Canberra, February, 1997.
9. Interview with Democrat staffer, Canberra, February, 1997.
10. Gordon, Michael, 'Architect of the industrial revolution', *Australian*, May 23, 1996, p. 9.
11. Interview with Peter Reith, op. cit.
12. Ibid.
13. Wood, Alan, 'It's better than expected', *Australian*, October 28, 1996 p. 14.

19

THE PROMISE DISSOLVES

1. Ramsey, Alan, 'Why the PM has Ross Free to thank', *Sydney Morning Herald*, October 21, 1995, p. 5.
2. Tingle, Laura, 'Coup for Howard on Telstra', *Age*, December 6, 1996, p. 1.
3. Interview with Democrat staffer, Canberra, February, 1997.
4. Henderson, Gerard, 'PM's temple of doom', *Sydney Morning Herald*, August 26, 1997, p. 15.
5. Mackay, Hugh, *The Mackay Report: Mind and mood of the nation*, July, 1997, Mackay Research, Report No. 88.
6. Mackay, Hugh, 'How Howard lost the plot', *Australian*, July 19–20, 1997, p. 23.

20

NARCISSUS

1. Interview with Cheryl Kernot, Fingal Bay, February, 1997.
2. Chipp, Don, 'Don't block Telstra', *Sunday Telegraph*, March 24, 1996.
3. Interview with Don Chipp, Melbourne, February, 1997.
4. Letter from Idun Chipp to Cheryl Kernot, 1996.
5. Milne, Glenn, 'Chipp quits the new bloc', *Australian*, August 12, 1996, p. 9.
6. Interview with Don Chipp, Melbourne, February, 1997.
7. Ibid.
8. Kernot, Cheryl, 'Facing the future: The Australian Democrats and Australian politics', the Findlay Crisp Lecture, Australian National University, October 9, 1995, p. 5.
9. Chipp, Idun, 'Why I dumped them', *Herald Sun*, August 13, 1996, p. 19.
10. Gordon, Michael, 'Chipp exit a Lib ploy', *Australian*, August 13, 1996, p. 4.
11. Savva, Niki, 'Kernot says Chipp is tip for governor', *Age*, August 13, 1996.

21

RACE AND RANCOUR

1. Steketee, Mike, 'Hillary talks up kitchen table', *Australian*, November 22, 1996, p. 1.
2. Contractor, Aban, 'Hot tickets to PM's girl and friend', *Canberra Times*, November 22, p. 1.
3. Ramsey, Alan, 'How Beazley stole the PM's lead', *Sydney Morning Herald*, November 23, 1996, p. 45.
4. Chan, Gabrielle, 'PM rejects black history doctoring charge', *Weekend Australian*, October 26, p. 4.
5. Speedy, Blair, 'Kernot hits PM over Hanson', *Canberra Times*, October 2, 1996, p. 5.
6. Dore, Christopher, 'Kernot lambasts "wimp" PM's response to immigration row', *Australian*, October 22, 1996, p. 4.
7. Interview with Cheryl Kernot, Sydney, February, 1997.
8. Kitney, Geoff, 'Howard just goes on getting it wrong', *Sydney Morning Herald*, April 30, 1997, p. 1.
9. Kelly, Paul, 'A test of our future', *Australian*, April 30, 1997.
10. Fitzgerald, Ross, 'The voice of the underclass', *Bulletin*, October 22, 1996, p. 20.
11. Ibid.

12. Ibid.
13. Millett, Michael, 'Hanson absent as MPs join to deplore racism', *Sydney Morning Herald*, October 31, 1996, p. 1.
14. Kernot, Cheryl, speech to Senate on Race Relations Bill, October 30, 1996.
15. Wright, Tony, 'Why we can't sleep soundly', *Sydney Morning Herald*, May 28, 1997, p. 17.

22

THE DILEMMA

1. Interview with Rod Cameron, Sydney, February, 1997.
2. Ibid.
3. Interview with Hugh Mackay, Sydney, February, 1997.
4. Ibid.
5. Ibid.
6. Interview with Rick Farley, Sydney, February, 1997.
7. Letter to Senator Kernot from Queensland elector, October, 1993.
8. Letter to Senator Kernot from Clyde Cameron, September, 1993.
9. Ibid.
10. Carty, Ken, 'The Australian Democrats in comparative perspective', paper to twentieth Anniversary Conference of the Australian Democrats, Burton and Garran Hall, Australian National University, January 18–19, 1997.
11. Ibid.
12. Interview with Cheryl Kernot, Sydney, February, 1997.

23

AFTER THE DEFECTION

1. The *Age*, 'Kernot changes the map of Australian politics', editorial, October 16, 1997, p. 18.
2. Forman, David, and Way, Nicholas, 'Labor buries Keating', *Business Review Weekly*, March 3, 1997, p. 41.
3. Ibid., p. 42.
4. Ibid.
5. Ibid., p. 45.
6. World Bank, 'The State in a changing world', Oxford University Press, 1997.
7. Oakes, Laurie, 'Democrat helps steer Labor ship back on course', *Bulletin*, October 28, 1997, p. 52.
8. Kelly, Paul, 'Howard fires his best mate', *Australian*, September 27–28, 1997, p. 1.

9. Wood, Alan, 'PM sells us a lemon', *Australian*, June 6, 1997, p. 1.
10. Henderson, Gerard, 'Case of humbug and hypocrisy', *Sydney Morning Herald*, December 16, 1997, p. 17.
11. Mackay, Hugh, *The Mackay Report: Mind and mood of the nation*, July 1997, Mackay Research, Report No. 88.
12. Ibid.
13. Interview with Tony Walters, Burnie, January, 1997.
14. Mant, Alistair, *Intelligent Leadership*, Allen and Unwin, 1997.
15. Interview with Alistair Mant, Brighton, UK, November, 1997.
16. Interview with Cheryl Kernot, Sydney, February, 1997.
17. Note to Cheryl Kernot from Chris Latham, June, 1996.

BIBLIOGRAPHY

Argy, Fred, *An Australia That Works: A Vision For The Future*, CEDA Research, 1993.

Bean, Clive; Simms, Marian; Bennett, Scott; and Warhurst, John, *The Politics of Retribution: The 1996 Federal Election*, Allen and Unwin, 1997.

Beilharz, Peter, *Transforming Labor: Labor Tradition and the Labor Decade in Australia*, Cambridge University Press, 1994.

Benn, Tony, *A Future For Socialism*, Fount, 1991.

Britton, Karl, *John Stuart Mill*, Penguin, 1953.

Bryant, Chris, (ed.), *Reclaiming the Ground*, Spire, 1993.

Bryant, Chris, (ed.), *John Smith: An Appreciation,* Hodder and Stoughton, 1994.

Carew, Edna, *Keating: A Biography*, Allen and Unwin, 1988.

Cogan, Brian, (ed.), *Newcastle and The Hunter: The Revolution of a Region*, Focus Books, 1991.

Chipp, Don and Larkin, John, *Don Chipp: The Third Man*, Rigby Ltd, 1978.

Coghill, Ken, (ed.), *The New Right's Australian Fantasy,* McPhee Gribble/Penguin Books, 1987.

Connolly, David, *Australians Speak: A Report on the Concerns, Hopes and Aspirations of the Australian People*, Australia 2000 Program, 1991.

Considine, Mark and Costar, Brian, *Trials In Power: Cain, Kirner and Victoria 1982–1992*, Melbourne University Press, 1992.

Cotton, Ian, *The Hallelujah Revolution,* Warner Books, 1995.

d'Alpuget, Blanche, *Robert Hawke: A Biography*, Schwartz Publishing, 1982.

Daly, Herman E., and Cobb, John B., *For the Common Good*, Green Print, 1990.

Dunant, Sarah and Porter, Roy, (eds.), *The Age of Anxiety*, Virago Press, 1996.

Edwards, John, *Keating: The Inside Story*, Penguin Books, 1996.

Emy, Hugh, *Remaking Australia: The State, the Market and Australia's Future*, Allen and Unwin, 1993.

Etzioni, Amitai, *An Immodest Agenda*, McGraw Hill, 1983.

Etzioni, Amitai, *The Spirit of Community*, Simon and Schuster, 1993.

Fergusson, David A.S., *John MacMurray in a Nutshell,* Handel Press, 1992.

Flannery, Tim, *The Future Eaters*, Secker and Warburg, 1996.

Franklin, Jane, (ed.), *Equality,* Institute For Public Policy Research, 1997.

Fraser, Antonia, *The Lives of the Kings and Queens of England*, Phoenix Illustrated, 1993.

Freudenberg, Graham, *A Certain Grandeur*, Macmillan, 1977.

Fukuyama, Francis, *The End of History and the Last Man*, Hamish Hamilton, 1992.

Fukuyama, Francis, *Trust,* Penguin, 1995.

Galbraith, J.K., *The Good Society: The Humane Agenda*, Sinclair-Stevenson, 1996.

Garner, Helen, *The First Stone*, Picador, 1995.

Gordon, Michael, *Paul Keating: A True Believer,* University of Queensland Press, 1996.

Gruen, Fred and Grattan, Michelle, *Managing Government: Labor's Achievements and Failures,* Longman Cheshire, 1993.

Haines, Janine, *Suffrage to Sufferance: 100 Years of Women in Politics*, Allen and Unwin, 1992.

Handy, Charles, *The Hungry Spirit*, Hutchinson, 1997.

Harris, Stewart, 'Nugget Coombs' in *The Greats: The Fifty Men and Women Who Shaped Australia*, Angus and Robertson, 1986.

Hewitt, Tim and Wilson, David, *Don Chipp*, Visa Books, 1978.

Hutton, Will, *The State We're In*, Vintage, 1996.

Hutton, Will, *The State To Come*, Vintage, 1997.

Jaensch, Dean, *The Hawke-Keating Hijack*, Allen and Unwin, 1989.

James, Chris; Jones, Chris; and Norton, Andrew, (eds.), *A Defence of Economic Rationalism*, Allen and Unwin, 1993.

Kelly, Paul, *The End of Certainty*, Allen and Unwin, 1994.

Kelly, Paul, *The Hawke Ascendancy*, Angus and Robertson, 1984.

Kelly, Paul, *The Unmaking of Gough,* Angus and Robertson, 1976.

Kerr, Duncan, (ed.), *Reinventing Socialism*, Pluto Press, 1992.

Kennedy, Paul, *The Rise and the Fall of the Great Powers*, Unwin Hyman, 1988.

Kennedy, Paul, *Preparing for the 21st Century*, Harper Collins, 1993.

Kung, Hans, (ed.), *Yes To A Global Ethic*, SCM Press Ltd, 1996.

Langmore, John and Quiggan, John, *Work For All*, Melbourne University Press, 1994.

Larkin, John, *Chipp*, Methuen Haynes, 1987.

Leach, Robert, (ed.), *The Alliance Alternative in Australia: Beyond Labor and Liberal*, Catalyst Press, 1995.

Mackay, Hugh, *Reinventing Australia: The Mind and Mood of Australia in the 1990s*, Angus and Robertson, 1993.

MacMurray, John, *Persons in Relation*, Faber and Faber, 1961.

McKinlay, Brian, *The ALP: A Short History*, Drummond/Heinemann, 1981.

Mandelson, Peter and Liddle, Roger, *The Blair Revolution*, Faber and Faber, 1996.

Mant, Alistair, *Intelligent Leadership*, Allen and Unwin, 1997.

Marquand, David, *The New Reckoning*, Polity Press, 1997.

Marsh, Ian, (ed.), *Governing in the 1990s*, Longman Cheshire, 1993.

Mill, John Stuart, *On Liberty*, Norton Critical Edition, 1974.

Mills, Stephen, *The Hawke Years*, Viking, Penguin Books, 1993.

Moir, Anne and Jessel, David, *A Mind To Crime*, Michael Joseph, 1995.

Mulgan, Geoff, (ed.), *Life After Politics*, Fontana Press, 1997.

Oakes, Laurie, *Crash Through Or Crash: The Unmaking of a Prime Minister*, Drummond, 1976.

Ohmae, Kenichi, *The End of the Nation State: The Rise of Regional Economies*, Harper Collins 1995.

Osborne, David and Gaebler, Ted, *Reinventing Government*, Plume Books, 1993.

Phillips, Melanie, *All Must Have Prizes*, Little Brown and Company, 1966.

Pusey, Michael, *Economic Rationalism in Canberra: A Nation Building State Changes Its Mind*, Cambridge University Press, 1991.

Rees, Stuart; Rodley, Gordon; and Stilwell, (eds.), *Beyond The Market: Alternatives to Economic Rationalism*, Pluto Press, 1993.

Rentoul, John, *Tony Blair*, Warner Books, 1995.

Reynolds, Margaret, *The Last Bastion: Labor Women Working Towards Equality in the Parliaments of Australia*, Business and Professional Publishing, 1995.

Reynolds, Margaret and Willoughby, Jean, (eds.), *HERstory: Australian Labor Women in Federal, State and Territory Parliaments, 1925–1994*, Margaret Reynolds, 1994.

Robinson, John A.T., *Honest To God*, SCM Press Ltd, 1963.

Rolls, Eric, *From Forest To Sea*, University of Queensland Press, 1993.

Schneider, Russel, *War Without Blood*, Angus and Robertson, 1980.

Scott, Andrew, *Fading Loyalties: The Australian Labor Party and the Working Class*, Pluto Press, 1991.

Scruton, Roger, *A Dictionary of Political Thought*, Macmillan Press, 1996.

Segal, Lynne, *Is The Future Female? Troubled Thoughts On Contemporary Feminism,* Virago Press, 1987.

Senate Economics Committee, *Report on Consideration of the Workplace Relations and other Legislation Amendment Bill, 1996.*

Sheehan, Peter; Grewal, Bhajan; and Kumnick, Margarita, (eds.), *Dialogues on Australia's Future*, Victoria University, 1996.

Siddons, John, *A Spanner in the Works*, Macmillan Australia, 1990.

Somerset, Anne, *Elizabeth I,* Phoenix Giant, 1997.

Sugita, Hiroya, *Challenging Two-partysim: The Continuing Contribution of the Australian Democrats to the Australian Party System,* PhD Thesis, Department of Politics, Faculty of Social Sciences, Flinders University, July 1995.

Summers, Anne, *Damned Whores and God's Police*, Penguin Books, 1994.

Thurow, Lester, *Dangerous Currents,* Random House, 1983.

Thurow, Lester, *Head to Head,* Nicholas Brearley Publishing, 1993.

Thurow, Lester, *The Future of Capitalism*, Nicholas Brearley Publishing, 1993.

Tingle, Laura, *Chasing the Future,* William Heinemann Australia, 1994.

Toohey, Brian, *Tumbling Dice: The Story of Modern Economic Policy,* William Heinemann, 1995.

Vintila, Peter; Phillimore, John; and Newman, Peter, *Markets, Morals and Manifestos,* Institute of Science and Technology Policy, 1992.

Walter, James, *Tunnel Vision*, Allen and Unwin, 1996.

Woodward, Dennis; Parkin, Andrew; and Summers, John, (eds.), *Government, Politics and Power in Australia,* Longman Cheshire, 1985.

World Bank, *The State in a Changing World*, Oxford University Press, 1997.

INDEX

447